REVOLUTIONARY
THINGS

signed by the author

GEORGE WASHINGTON'S
MOUNT ★ VERNON

REVOLUTIONARY THINGS

MATERIAL CULTURE AND POLITICS

IN THE LATE EIGHTEENTH-CENTURY

ATLANTIC WORLD

ASHLI WHITE

Yale UNIVERSITY PRESS

New Haven and London

Published with assistance from the Annie Burr Lewis Fund.

Published with assistance from the foundation established in memory of James Wesley
Cooper of the Class of 1865, Yale College.

Yale University Press books may be purchased in quantity for educational, business,
or promotional use. For information, please e-mail sales.press@yale.edu (U.S. office) or
sales@yaleup.co.uk (U.K. office).

Set in Sabon type by Newgen North America, Inc.
Printed in the United States of America.

Library of Congress Control Number: 2022941452
ISBN 978-0-300-25901-8 (hardcover : alk. paper)

A catalogue record for this book is available from the British Library.

This paper meets the requirements of ANSI/NISO Z39.48-1992 (Permanence of Paper).

10 9 8 7 6 5 4 3 2 1

For EE & P

Contents

REVOLUTIONARY THINGS

Introduction

Object Lessons from the Revolutionary Atlantic

IN THE WINTER of 1790, authorities in northern Saint-Domingue were very interested in the contents of Vincent Ogé's luggage. That autumn, he and a group of like-minded free men of African descent had attempted to compel the Cap Français assembly to acknowledge the political rights granted to some *hommes de couleur* by the revolutionary legislature in Paris. After a standoff of several weeks, the colonial militia apprehended the dissidents, who were charged with insurrection. Guilty verdicts for the perpetrators were guaranteed: Ogé, as a ringleader, would be broken on the wheel, and his head severed and displayed on a pike in the public square.[1] Before the sentence was carried out, government officials sought to learn more about the scope of his designs. As part of their investigation, they searched Ogé's possessions and discovered things that, they suspected, had abetted his campaign. Authorities inventoried reformist pamphlets, books, and decrees gathered during a recent stay in Paris. They pressed him about weapons allegedly procured in Charleston, South Carolina, a stop on his return voyage to the Caribbean.[2]

Given Ogé's aim to extend rights by force to free men of African descent, the guns and revolutionary tracts were predictable. Yet investigators inquired about less expected objects as well. Early in the interview, they quizzed Ogé about a trip to the Sèvres porcelain manufactory and

Figure I.1. Portrait of *Vincent Ogé*, 1790. (Jean Fouquet, designer, Gilles-Louis Chrétien, engraver, Paris, France, Ink and watercolor on paper, 2017.0013.001, Museum purchase with funds provided by the Henry Francis du Pont Collectors Circle, Courtesy of Winterthur Museum, Photo funded by NEA.)

the thousands of livres' worth of coffee wares that he had acquired there and then sold. They wondered how he afforded such a hefty outlay, and if it was true that he had worn a National Guard uniform to the factory visit. At another session, they referenced his engraved portrait, copies of which were in his bag (figure I.1). They wanted to find out whether he had devised the motto—"He loves liberty and knows how to defend it"—that encircled the rim of his silhouette. On one of the last days of questioning, they brought in items from his trunk, including several military garments that the clerk described in detail, right down to the imported metal buttons stamped with the arms of Paris. They concluded their show-and-tell by unveiling some pieces of jewelry, among which were two "small ceramic medallions depicting a chained slave in bas-relief."

In his responses, Ogé downplayed the political significance of his things. He claimed that the jewelry was for his commercial work, that the Parisian printer had composed the slogan on his portrait, and that the uniforms were merely a requirement of his militia commission. None was intended, as he put it, "to excite revolt" on the island. The authorities remained unconvinced by these denials, as Ogé no doubt anticipated. Everyone in that interrogation room knew that these objects thrummed with meaning, but the officials' persistent questions and Ogé's resolute disclaimers suggest that their revolutionary implications were up for discussion. These contentious exchanges compel us to ask, How and why did these objects provoke strong reactions? What do they reveal not only about Ogé's quest for political rights but about the power of material culture in the age of Atlantic revolutions more broadly?

The objects in Ogé's collection were representative of much larger trends, as the American, French, and Haitian revolutions influenced the production, circulation, and consumption of millions of things. This book argues that in the late eighteenth and early nineteenth centuries, this material culture shaped in distinct ways how people understood vital keywords such as *equality* and *freedom,* and how they tried to promote and thwart the realization of these ideals on the ground. Crucially, these contests occurred at the level of everyday life: the clothes on individuals' backs, the plates from which they ate, the maps that guided their movements, the diversions that amused them. And these engagements involved enslaved and free, women and men, poor and elite, whose encounters with objects were not limited to local concerns. Rather, through things, actors across the social spectrum contributed to ideological disputes that transcended borders.

This emphasis on material culture yields a vantage on Atlantic revolutions that helps us to make sense of a central dilemma: the relationship between change and continuity. For all the remarkable transformations wrought by revolutions—ones that toppled long-standing orders and gave rise to new states—the American, French, and Haitian revolutions also perpetuated hierarchies that undercut avowals of liberty and equality for all. Self-interest, the desire for power, inertia, and hypocrisy were instrumental in fostering some continuities, yet *Revolutionary Things* reveals new dimensions to this fundamental tension. It does so by using the material world to recalibrate our understanding of the tempo of transformation and by reframing how we interpret material culture as a mechanism for revolutionary change.

On one level, the American, French, and Haitian revolutions moved at a blistering pace, as histories that focus on ideas and on the events and people inspired by those ideas have shown. The shared goal of creating political orders based on new principles generated an outpouring of words and a rapid sequence of deeds, especially in the face of resistance. It is not surprising, then, that scholars assess the achievements of this watershed by tracing the fast rate of declarations and decrees, of uprisings and battles, and evaluating each episode's or proclamation's effects on revolutionaries' ambitions.[3] Time and again, however, actors learned that it was easier to pledge to slough off the past than to actually do so. When they fell short of or reneged on their lofty ideals, historians attribute these setbacks to the intractability of anciens régimes.[4] Even as they admit the constant slippage between promise and practice, these readings assume a firm dividing line between what revolutionaries envisioned and what existed beforehand.[5] Continuity from one era to the next exposes the limitations of revolutions.

The material world, though, brings to light another dynamic, one in which equating the "new" with revolutionary change and the "old" with a stubborn status quo breaks down. In an age of revolutions, it was even harder to overhaul the material world than it was to win battles or persuade minds, and this circumstance stems in part from practical factors. To be sure, there was vibrant novelty in material culture. Production rates for some goods, like ceramics, metalwork, and textiles, increased impressively in the eighteenth century, as did stylistic variety within genres of items. All told, more things were available to more people than previously. And yet a swift pace—one that could keep up with evolving ideas, personalities, and events at substantial scales—was not technically viable with many media. Furthermore, most individuals could not afford precipitous turnover nor, as important, did they necessarily want it. Among those who did avidly pursue material change, new acquisitions persisted alongside older ones.

In light of these conditions, we might be tempted to regard objects as obstacles to revolutionary aspirations, and at times, exasperated rebels complained that they were. Nevertheless, things were indispensable to everyday life, and so they were imperative to revolutions, too—just not always as assorted actors then wanted, or as we subsequently have supposed. This state of material affairs calls on us to reappraise how things were and were not instruments for change by looking more carefully at how they operated in practice. In surveying an array of politicized objects, this book demonstrates how their contributions to revolutions varied by type: the impact of Ogé's portrait differed from his purchases at Sèvres. Even within a single genre, an object could promote or check change, depending on who acquired and used it, how, where, and to what ends. This tension across and within revolutionary things made them sites of contest, as people teased out political possibilities and encountered obdurate restrictions in the world of goods.

This view of the revolutions requires adjustments to our perceptions of things and their relationship to politics in this period. Although ideas and events dominate narratives of this moment, objects have been central to studies of political culture. In the United States, France, and Haiti, revolutionaries decried the trappings of their predecessors on symbolic grounds and encouraged the adoption of republican motifs on ordinary goods. Consumers purchased cockades designed to communicate political loyalties, bought ceramics decorated with catchphrases, and collected prints of famous episodes. These items were essential not only for broadcasting the messages of republican governments but also for transforming the cultures of the populations who were now the foundation of those governments. Revolutionaries agreed that lasting political change entailed the cultural rehabilitation of things both monumental and mundane. While these efforts were piecemeal, the aesthetic innovations with some objects, and the affective national ties those items cultivated, shaped the distinctiveness of each country's political culture for centuries.[6]

But this interpretation considers things only within a single national context. Ogé's transatlantic itinerary and those of many others signal that revolutionary objects were not confined to national borders and domestic politics. Huge quantities of goods associated with individual revolutions moved through the Atlantic world. Some originated at a revolutionary site and traveled beyond it, while others were fabricated outside of the United States, France, or Haiti but referred to those places (for instance, British- or American-made items about the French and Haitian revolutions). A national framework alone is insufficient to explain the significance of things in motion: of a Parisian military uniform worn by a man of African descent in Saint-Domingue, of a life-size figure of Toussaint Louverture on display in Baltimore, or of confiscated Louis XVI furniture in London parlors.

There is a tendency in studies of political culture to see things not only as geographically fixed but also as ideologically stable. Scholars gravitate toward objects emblazoned with slogans and iconography—the new ones promoted by revolutionaries—because they seem to echo the political ethos of the time. As early as the mid-nineteenth century, a ceramics collector maintained that one could chart the phases of the French Revolution by the various emblems found on plates from the period.[7] In his reading and in many since, an object is classified as pro- or anti-revolutionary, usually through its decoration (a liberty cap versus a fleur-de-lis) and, by extension, so are its maker and owner.

Objects, however, do not simply transmit fixed messages. Material culture theorists and practitioners emphasize that people affect things and that things affect lives in fundamental and sometimes unforeseen ways. While not an independent agent per se, an object "act[s] in the world" and inspires actions from people. Its effects depend on several factors—what is frequently called its materiality.[8] By way of illustrating this approach to material culture, take those plates with French revolutionary motifs. According to an active view of things, a plate's impact derived from its ornamentation as well as from the method and location of its production; its worth; who acquired it, where, and how; the modes of eating it encouraged; what it felt like to hold it; what it took to clean it; what other objects were collected around it; and so on. Each feature promotes assorted connections and practices among people and between people and things. We tend to categorize these qualities as social, economic, cultural, or haptic, yet they contributed to political resonance, too—the where, when, how, and for whom those plates had political meaning. In this way, an object cannot be "read" like a text because "reading" fails to capture people's multivalent experiences with things.

It also follows that not all objects reverberated in the same ways. Genre mattered, as the traits unique to a category figured in its specific political capacity. This book analyzes a range of things—ceramics, metalware, and furniture; military clothing and accessories; maps, prints, and life-size wax figures—to gauge the political prospects of objects from across the material realm. As we will see, Ogé's uniform and the millions of others from the era spoke to equality, whereas his and others' printed portraits influenced debates about popular sovereignty. Not only did different kinds of objects engage with different issues, but each type had limits that were distinct to its form as well. These bounds were structural, in terms of where and of what things were made, and they were socially constructed, in that people had thresholds for tolerating alterations to facets of their material world and to those of others. An object's characteristics conditioned its political content and its parameters.

The dynamism of objects complements cutting-edge analyses of revolutionary politics. As numerous studies have made clear, late eighteenth-century actors in North America, Europe, and the Caribbean cannot be divided into tidy, consistent ideological camps. Within the course of a single revolution, individuals switched sides multiple times for numerous reasons, and some sectors, like Black loyalists and Indigenous people, joined anti-republican forces in bids for freedom and independence.[9] Moreover, all three revolutions drew inspiration from a mixture of intellectual sources. Participants were animated by the Enlightenment canon and by religious, royalist, and "non-Western" ideological currents.[10]

In sum, decades of scholarship have demonstrated that late eighteenth-century republicanism was a moving target in substance and in application. For all these permutations, though, leaders professed their commitment to what at the time were identified as republican principles. Tenets like liberty and equality constituted one set of connective threads that supposedly linked the revolutions. But the exact content of these principles and the forms they took varied from one revolution to another and even during a single revolution. The implementation of equality in, for instance, revolutionary Saint-Domingue diverged from that in the United States, and within the French colony itself, it evolved from 1790 (Ogé's rebellion) to 1794 (the formal abolition of slavery and the granting of citizenship) to 1804 (independence). Gens de couleur had a conception of equality distinct from that of the enslaved or of poorer whites. As a result of these fluctuations, Atlantic observers constantly evaluated and took stands on those professed republican aims, and material culture proved a powerful way to navigate conflict and to generate meaning about revolutions as they occurred.

All this instability with things and politics seems to lead us down a slippery slope toward an interpretation that is thick with messy complications and thin on definitive arguments. But this unsettled situation underscores that Atlantic revolutions were processes instead of foregone conclusions, and that objects joined in and affected, rather than merely depicted, those processes.[11] To show the full spectrum of their engagement, I concentrate on three components of objects' materiality: fabrication, use, and context. These facets are frequently taken for granted, but on closer inspection they reveal with greater precision how things became politically operational in the Atlantic world. The first aspect of materiality reminds us that things are made, and their construction reflects a society's technical abilities with certain materials at a particular moment. In the late eighteenth century, the capacity of clay—its possible forms, speed of manufacture, and so forth—differed from that of metal or silk, wax or paper. Distinctions among materials and among their methods of production are central to comprehending the scale of things—how many goods of a specific type could be manufactured, distributed, and thus possibly politicized.

Although these physical and structural factors impacted the fabrication of revolutionary objects, so, too, did the sensibilities, aims, and choices of makers. They decided what they wanted to create and for which markets. Sometimes they were motivated by personal political allegiances; more often they were concerned with profit. They calculated which items appealed to the largest swath of consumers, and their judgments determined what was available, where, and for whom. Production lays bare the supply side of revolutionary things; that is, which objects were accessible for politicization among the greatest numbers of people.

Second, things have functions. A vase, a map, and a coat do different work, and the purpose of an object shapes people's expectations about its application in their lives. During the revolutions, function had political salience, too. The now classic example comes from the American Revolution, when teapots featured in patriots' critiques because of their association with tea, an imported commodity subject to a controversial British tax. Things also became politicized when they malfunctioned.

An object does not always operate in predictable ways; it wears, breaks, goes awry. For things whose performance was necessary to revolutionary wars—such as uniforms, maps, or guns—object failures affected participants severely and on numerous occasions stirred protest.

The utility of things also informed and was informed by people's behavior, which brings us to a final, deceptively obvious point on materiality: things are social.[12] The contexts in which an object functioned— the who, where, and when—influenced its politicization. In the case of eighteenth-century objects, this aspect of their nature is regularly examined in spheres of sociability (how they were instrumental to rituals like coffee and tea drinking) and of status (how things did or did not sustain hierarchies of class, race, and gender). Idealized standards for objects mirrored a culture's notions about propriety: how best to use an item and who was the most appropriate user. There were expectations about who could wear a cockade and how, or about the proper ways to sit on a chair or to hold a cup. Things, however, were not always employed in the stipulated manner by the prescribed people. Consumers adopted and adapted items to suit their needs and desires, and in so doing, they challenged the status quo. Revolutions expanded opportunities to upend the social, racial, and gendered hierarchies of objects, and these confrontations became politically charged when groups resisted losing privileges that things reinforced.[13]

But objects are not social in just these respects. They participated in a wide array of relationships because of the diverse practices around things.[14] From selling and buying to moving and using to repairing and destroying and beyond, each activity facilitated interactions among people and between people and objects. Our varied vocabulary for material culture hints at the breadth they supported: *goods* evokes a constellation of actions distinct from that of *artifacts* or *stuff*.[15] I employ assorted terms for material culture to mark these relationships, and in their diversity, they provide opportunities to detect instances when and circumstances in which objects became politicized by gathering people in the name of revolutions, of the status quo, or of some point in between.[16]

Appraising the political impact of the fabrication, use, and context of objects is demanding enough in one locale, but our task is to assess them in motion. After all, Ogé brought to Saint-Domingue items acquired in France, England, and North America, and to situate these

things, we need an Atlantic perspective. The revolutions were a sweeping phenomenon that rippled across four continents for over fifty years.
This book addresses the North Atlantic during the first phase of this
era, from roughly 1770 to 1810, when the American, French, and Haitian revolutions dominated. Of course, the reverberations of each revolution were felt for decades. Each site experienced the aftershocks of
these conflicts, and in the 1810s and 1820s, Latin America witnessed
independence campaigns that were influenced in some measure by endeavors in the United States, France, and Haiti. These developments in
the early nineteenth century were fundamental to the age. But the focus
on this group of three allows us to consider how things contributed
to people's understanding of revolutions in the thick of the moment,
when participants and observers had to make sense of events, agents,
and ideas as they surfaced. The quick succession of the revolutions,
and in the case of France and Haiti their contemporaneity, facilitate
our inquiry into the effects of objects on the revolutionary present,
instead of their role in nationalism and commemorations of the revolutionary past.

   With this ambition in mind, I work with objects that, although affiliated with a revolution, moved through the Atlantic world rather than
remained in one place. Not all things traveled to the same degree or
crossed borders with the same ease. Some politicized objects—North
American homespun, artifacts seized from French religious institutions,
and drums used by Haitian revolutionaries, to name just a few—were
primarily national in scope because they did not circulate in sizable
numbers outside of local contexts. What's more, certain places that
are crucial for histories of eighteenth-century consumption—Africa,
China, and India—do not feature prominently in this story. These regions helped to create and foster the wider consumer world, yet they
did not participate centrally in the making, distributing, or procuring
of the revolutionary things examined here.[17]

   Among these Atlantic-oriented revolutionary objects, I highlight
those that reached substantial numbers of people, as evidenced by their
sheer quantity or by the publicness of their display. One-of-a-kind items
mattered in this era, but so, too, did pervasive goods of a more ordinary
sort. Instead of rare English-made ceramics with political slogans or
fanciful designs for outfits for the republican *bon ton,* we pay attention
to the tons of plain Queen's ware, military garments, and cockades that

crisscrossed the ocean. This parameter brings in not just more people but a broader assortment of people into the narrative.

In evaluating individuals' encounters with these objects, this book follows populations active in all three revolutions. While Indigenous people shaped the American Revolution profoundly, including through material culture, their presence and sway were not nearly as pronounced in the French and Haitian revolutions. The experiences and views of people of African descent do come to the fore, however. Through objects, eighteenth-century Black actors expressed their personhood, preserved aspects of West African cultures, and cultivated community. This persistence, in spite of slavery and racism, was in and of itself a political statement, and during the age of revolutions, these currents remained essential to enslaved people's battles for freedom and rights. This moment also shows that people of African descent were acquainted with and appropriated, when it suited their needs, European material culture. By obtaining and demonstrating their knowledge of the uses and values of these things, Black men and women advocated for radical goals on terms grasped by Black and white audiences and pushed objects to their fullest political capacity.

The Atlantic world serves as an organizing feature for this analysis of material life, and at the same time, this book contributes to our view of that changing Atlantic world. Over the years, scholars have disputed notions that key aspects of the revolutions—transformative ideas, cultural trends, imperial policies—originated in and radiated out from European metropoles. They accentuate the homegrown elements of anti-colonial movements in important correctives to center-periphery models and the assumptions about European supremacy that sometimes undergird them. For all the political ingenuity of the colonies, though, Atlantic things reveal how Europe dominated the production and circulation of goods that revolutionaries needed. Ironically, European-made things afforded openings for people to join in rebellious movements, to shape their courses and goals, and to fight imperial orders. British goods, for instance, had extensive Atlantic trajectories and were employed in ways not in keeping with that government's antagonism to all three revolutions. French-made items had some traction in certain niche markets, although their range was not as great as policymakers hoped.[18] By contrast, mercantilist imprints on North American and Caribbean economies meant that their capacity to fabricate manufactured objects for Atlantic markets was limited, even if commodities like sugar, coffee, grains, and timber traveled far and wide. In sum, "Old World" material culture adapted nimbly to political upheaval, and this agility suggests a new take on how anti-colonial movements such as the American and Haitian revolutions could be opposed to empires and still very much embedded in them. Elements of imperial systems were central to perpetuating revolutionary things— and hence revolutions.

Material culture holds enormous interpretive promise for comprehending major issues of this period, yet it presents methodological challenges. As any curator will confirm, typical objects survive far less frequently than extraordinary ones. Extant collections have more pieces of Louis XVI Sèvres porcelain than they do common soldiers' garments because individuals and institutions tend to save rare, expensive, or sentimental objects. Archaeological evidence fills in some gaps, but only for things that do not decompose readily, those of metal and ceramic. Cloth, paper, and wood, among other materials, remain out of archaeological reach. Whenever possible, surviving objects anchor my interpretations, and the insights gleaned from extant things inform readings of those that no longer endure, items that appear only in written records. Despite the very real problems with representation in the archives, textual sources provide invaluable evidence for everyday objects. Traces of their presence emerge from diverse records: advertisements; newspaper and magazine articles; diaries; travel accounts; personal and business correspondence; customhouse and auction records; and the papers of artists, merchants, manufacturers, and government agencies.

The combination of material and written sources yields a set of things that cuts across media, function, and value, and this broad range works on two levels. On the one hand, it establishes the prolific politicization of material culture in the late eighteenth century. The phenomenon animated objects found everywhere, from bodies and bedchambers to battlefields and taverns. On the other hand, their variety elucidates meaningful distinctions among objects. Accessories, because of unique attributes of their materiality, engaged with issues different from those of maps or tableware. To these ends, each chapter discusses the specific characteristics of a genre, underscoring its material traits as well as its Atlantic (versus domestic) context. The goal is to make revolutionary objects less familiar.[19] The ostensible similarities between our material world and theirs—recognizable forms and uses, the rise of novelty, greater manufacturing capacity, wider distribution of goods— obscure vital divergences.[20] We need to restore these objects to their eighteenth-century moment to grasp how exactly they influenced the age of revolutions.

The sequencing of genres matters, too, in this double move of de- familiarization and recontextualization. The book begins with things normally not considered political—ceramics, metalware, and furniture without explicit revolutionary or royal emblems on their surface deco- ration. It then moves through forms that become, for us, increasingly legible as having political affiliations: military uniforms, accessories with allusions to groups or issues, maps of contested spaces, prints of individuals and collectives, and wax figures of revolutionaries. This order recalibrates our assumptions about the political consequences of things in the eighteenth century. We start by identifying less overt, but no less powerful, paths of politicization for things, and then apply those sensibilities to locate new meanings from objects whose impact we thought we already knew.

The chapters are further organized into three sections, each of which reframes the usual ways of approaching material culture and revolu- tions. The first part takes on the question of politicization. Typically, scholars deem a thing political if it becomes a source of debate or if it reflects—in its physical composition, its aesthetics, or its adoption— the interests of a particular party.[21] But these two chapters on ceram- ics, metalware, and furniture argue for additional routes to politiciza- tion. Recall the inquisitors' fascination with Vincent Ogé's purchase at Sèvres of hundreds of cups, dozens of sugar bowls, and seventeen milk pitchers, which he sold to Parisian retailers to finance his return trip to Saint-Domingue.[22] Sèvres was not yet producing porcelain with republican iconography, and so the wares might appear passé for a city in the throes of revolution. Yet as their prompt sale implies, consumers desired them and, more surprisingly, the profits went toward the launch of a campaign for equality an ocean away.

This episode was just one of many instances in which status quo items became politically charged because of who procured them, where, how, and for what ends. In the case of housewares, they moved through two mechanisms: manufacturers who tried to capitalize on revolutionary upheaval to access new markets for their products in extant styles, and armies and governments that seized goods from enemies and sold them on the secondhand market. These circuits of distribution demonstrate that access and purpose were key to the politicization of objects in the Atlantic, and in so doing expand the scope of people who agitated for change through things.

The next part builds on these insights in its examination of clothing, a genre of material culture whose proximity to the body is understood as shedding light on individuals' senses of self. As a vehicle for personal expression, clothing is both intimate and public, and during the age of revolutions, it is often interpreted as a material declaration of one's political sentiments. Ogé's choice of garments and accessories signals support for revolutionary causes. The National Guard uniform allied him with republicans in Paris—those who had stormed the Bastille in 1789 and looked to implement reforms that reined in aristocratic privilege and broadened political participation among "the people." The ensemble became so emblematic of their platform that in the spring of 1790, not long after Ogé's trip to Sèvres, the legislature approved a measure granting voting rights to any man who bought his own uniform.[23] Combine Ogé's uniforms with the anti–slave trade medallions, and his vanguard views seem transparent.

The interrogators' reactions indicate, though, that his ownership and wearing of these items reverberated differently in Saint-Domingue than in France. Explaining these distinctions entails not only a reconsideration of these objects' assumed allegiances but also a close look at how eighteenth-century actors acquired, valued, used, and thought about clothing and accessories. The chapters in this second part analyze military garments, cockades, and medallions—items that circulated in vast quantities among people from various backgrounds. These articles were more than badges of endorsement for a cause; rather, they challenged the ideological content of those causes. With uniforms, men pressed for equality, and through accessories, disenfranchised sectors lobbied for their right to take part in politics and to determine the forms of that involvement, including through violence. Here, we track the shifting resonances of the material culture of political affiliation as it dispersed through the Atlantic to individuals of diverse circumstances and goals.

The third part explores the visualization of revolutionary news. We tend to interpret maps, prints, and other imagery as depictions of the period's transformative events and figures. Ogé's printed portrait exemplifies the trend. As he maintained in his testimony, many men, especially the new legislative deputies, were having their portraits engraved in Paris. Through these inexpensive and reproduceable images, they hoped to broadcast their faces as representative of the new government. Printed portraits were one of several popular items—maps, wax figures, miniatures—that helped Atlantic observers envisage the people, places, and incidents about which they read and heard so much.

But translations from words into things were not straightforward. Instead of faithful illustrations of written and verbal accounts, these objects were powerful interpretations that affected how people comprehended their present. Renditions were shaped by their makers' intentions and by a given genre's materials, conventions, uses, and contexts. Maps legitimized and denied the spatial alterations wrought by revolutions, while prints of individuals and collectives raised questions about the parameters of popular sovereignty. Wax figures and miniatures presented selective takes on revolutionary-era violence and its legitimacy. This part demonstrates how material culture contributed to understandings of revolutions as they happened and how the materialization of people, places, and events sometimes conflicted with contemporary texts.

This book is positioned at the intersection between the study of history and material culture, and with such interdisciplinarity, there is risk—for authors and for audiences. Material culture scholars may find that I do not give enough attention to the extraordinary attributes of individual objects and to vernacular variations of material life. Meanwhile, historians, particularly those of a single revolution, may want more coverage of "their" revolution. But the goal of this book is to occupy a middle ground between these disciplines and among the three revolutions. In so doing, it advocates for the interpretive and methodological benefits of that in-betweenness through innovative arguments about the meanings of things to this age. These interventions unveil a dynamic relationship between material culture and politics in which things emerge as a central mode through which individuals from across geographies and across the social spectrum disputed, capitalized on, and tried to steer the routes of revolutions.

At its core, this book addresses a classic question that has sparked curiosity about the revolutions since they transpired: what changed because of the revolutions? Thomas Paine made it sound easy when he proclaimed in 1776, "We have it in our power to begin the world over again."[24] However, starting the world anew was hard, not only because people had conflicting ideas about what that newness should involve but also because they had to work within the material conditions of their times. Not everything could be, literally, made new. In some cases, novelty was not necessary to achieve change, and in others, material continuity served as a check on realizing political transformation. Recognizing this important force is imperative for comprehending what revolutions did and did not accomplish, and why. Moreover, these material legacies are still with us—in our museums, historic sites, libraries—and to understand what these things could mean for us now, we must gain a better sense of what they meant to revolutions then.

I
WHAT'S OLD IS NEW

IN 1793, JUST a few years after Vincent Ogé visited the Sèvres porcelain factory, Antoine Régnier, its longtime director, received a letter from the minister of the interior ordering him to destroy Sèvres's pre-revolutionary molds, models, and stock. Régnier hesitated. Sèvres, which produced some of the finest porcelain in the world, had been the king's manufactory, so much so that its mark was the royal cipher. The loss of its generous patron and those affiliated with him had brought hard times. Régnier had toed the revolutionary line at the manufactory by planting liberty trees around the grounds, changing the name of the main courtyard from "cour royale" to "cour de l'Égalité," and dating pieces according to the republican calendar. Sèvres had also begun work on wares that featured liberty caps, the tricolor, and other symbols. But this latest mandate gave Régnier pause. It required the annihilation of articles that had taken months, in some cases years, to fabricate, and at significant cost. Having received no confirmation that the director had carried out the initial order, the minister sent a sternly worded reminder. This time Régnier acted, and workers demolished the questionable items. Régnier's reluctance, though, had tarnished his revolutionary credentials, and he fell out of favor with the government.[1]

This episode points to a central dilemma of the era: what to do with material culture that revolutionaries defined as "old regime." Across the Atlantic world, they took several approaches, all of which informed Régnier's exchange with the administration, and which bring to light, for us, the political stakes of these old things. One prominent line of attack, as the minister's injunction indicates, was to raze it. Assaults on property pervaded all three revolutions, with actors singling out things owned by or associated with the governments they contested. In the case of Sèvres specifically, some republican officials felt that the obliteration of its products was not enough, and they proposed closing the manufactory, seeing it as an accomplice to aristocratic extravagance. The goal in this instance, and many others like it, was to undercut the material culture of the former rulers' power and to ensure that it could not be redeployed in the future.

For all their propensities to eradication, revolutionaries recognized the value of some of this stuff, so they pursued another tack: its rehabilitation. Authorities admitted that Sèvres's wares commanded international prestige that they were loath to squander.[2] And so there and elsewhere, revolutionaries called on manufacturers and artisans to introduce styles that complemented the ideological sea change that republican movements inaugurated. Administrations promoted new modes of dress, designed new buildings, and put forward new motifs that appeared on everything from wallpaper to teacups to snuffboxes. These were didactic projects, meant to inculcate among inhabitants the virtues deemed necessary for republican societies. This aesthetic overhaul signals the grandeur of revolutionaries' ambitions—their desire to make the world anew in a literal sense.[3]

These two solutions—destruction and rehabilitation—have garnered the most scholarly attention because they seem to reflect, materially, what's old and what's new about revolutions. And yet, even working in tandem, these two tactics were not enough to deal with the problem of "old regime" things because of one important condition: many consumers still wanted them just as they were. People from across the political spectrum—radicals, moderates, and royalists—found it hard to give up these items, and what's more, the disruptions of revolutions offered additional opportunities to acquire them. During the 1790s, everyone from the Prince of Wales (the future George IV) to the American patriot James Swan bought old-style Sèvres and other "aristocratic" wares. Régnier's hesitation, then, may have had less to do with his personal politics than with his understanding of the marketplace. He knew that consumers desired the very goods the minister had ordered him to destroy. And here lies a seeming contradiction—or, more accurately, a stubborn consistency—of the revolutionary period: the aesthetic status quo persisted, and alleged ancien régime items remained popular. The most ardent revolutionary and the most avowed royalist sometimes coveted and purchased the same goods.

The two chapters in this part focus on this sector of persistent "old" things and appraise their political impact. In the case of later revolutionary movements, like the Russian Revolution, scholars have argued that the shared aesthetic ground between previous and new regimes demonstrates the limits of leveling impulses. No matter how hard revolutionaries tried to upend hierarchies, bourgeois elements lingered, even among their own ranks. But other historians have contended that this was not necessarily how contemporaries viewed the constancy of material culture. From their perspective, access to formerly out-of-reach goods represented one of the successes of revolutionary projects: their ability to extend material bounty to more people.[4] While insightful, both interpretations often associate these things with social position; they were a way either to assert superiority or to emulate one's betters.

A closer look at the late eighteenth-century moment reveals that class is just one component of the relationship between this category of material culture and revolution. As purportedly old-style goods circulated throughout the Atlantic world, they became a significant means through which revolutions were evaluated, and the diversity of buyers shows that assessments did not fall into neat pro- and anti-revolutionary camps.

Rather, so-called ancien régime goods became useful instruments for assorted political goals, including radical ones. Locating this dynamic requires paying attention to the material contexts surrounding these "old" goods—how they were attained, by whom, where, and when. To this end, these chapters spotlight domestic decorative wares—ceramics, metalware, furniture—that were some of the biggest investments for buyers and therefore were slower to change in households. Over their lifetimes, most eighteenth-century actors bought fewer clocks and platters than shirts and books. The tendency toward longevity in this category of goods, combined with the continued appeal of what revolutionaries classified as old-style aesthetics among them, push us to look beyond surface decoration for political salience.

The first chapter considers how manufacturers of ceramics and metalware navigated the revolutionary era. With their production geared to the export market, these industries had generated by midcentury enough variety in their stock to target niche consumers across the Atlantic. Revolutions became another factor to weigh as they decided what types of items to sell where. They had to gauge whether to incorporate republican iconography into their stylistic lexicons, a calculation based, in no small part, on what they thought consumers preferred. For these makers, consistency was economically safer and smarter, and yet some actors in certain moments and in certain places leveraged this consistency for revolutionary aims. These approaches to weathering the aesthetic challenges of revolutions expose what makers and buyers were and were not willing to overturn at their dining tables and in their parlors in the face of political change.

While the first chapter examines new wares, the next focuses on the active market for secondhand goods that revolutions intensified. All sides of each contest plundered from their foes. They kept some seized items, but they also sold many to further their causes. Sometimes pillaged goods were the very sort of "old regime" wares republicans derided, and yet they relied on the continued desirability of these items—among constituents and enemies—to hawk them. Pillaged wares bring to the fore novel dimensions of the radical political potential of "old" things and of material culture knowledge that cut across class, race, gender, and geography. Finally, the mechanism for distributing plunder—auctions—became politically charged as sides jockeyed for military and moral superiority.

Together, these chapters challenge our expectations about what "ancien régime" meant. Our impressions of these supposedly old goods and of what they represented have been shaped by republican voices which, while condemning old regime wares in public, still appreciated, bought, and sold them. But hypocrisy and greed explain only so much. The persistence of the aesthetic status quo reveals how ostensibly ancien régime things were a crucial part of, not standing outside of, discussions about the impact of Atlantic revolutions on everyday life. In the process they show how in the material world continuity could be an accelerant rather than a drag on perpetuating revolutionary transformations.

1   Makers and Markets in Revolutionary Times

CONSIDER ONE ICONIC object from the age of revolutions: the teapot. In its fabrication and function, this particular example signals key developments in eighteenth-century politics, economy, and society that would in subsequent decades become hallmarks of modernity (figure 1.1). First, its prominent motto protests a tax levied by Parliament on stamped paper imported by the North American colonies. Opposition to the Stamp Act would be seen in hindsight as among the earliest in a series of events that led to the American Revolution. Next, the teapot is a product of a manufactory that began to exhibit characteristics of what would emerge as modern industry. Crafted in Staffordshire, England, for North American buyers and their supporters, it signals pottery manufacturers' sophisticated understanding of and ability to cater to diverse, far-flung markets. Finally, the teapot belongs to the category of decorative wares: small-sized household objects made of ceramic, metal, and other materials. Eighteenth-century consumers found these goods convenient and stylish, and for scholars they are compelling evidence of the economic and social impact of consumption on everyday life. In the case of this teapot, it indicates an investment in the polite sociability of tea drinking, and its material (affordable earthenware instead of expensive porcelain) speaks to the practice of this genteel activity among assorted ranks.[1]

Figure 1.1. Teapot, ca. 1766–70. (Division of Cultural and Community Life, National Museum of American History, Smithsonian Institution.)

Historians debate whether these changes in politics, industry, and consumption were truly revolutions and whether they originated in the eighteenth century. But if we accept certain trends for this period—that some manufacturers became more adept at offering greater variety and volume of items, that more individuals had the capacity and yearning to purchase and use such products, and that changes in governments mattered, then the teapot works as an expedient encapsulation of several of the most notable transformations of the era.

Yet this interpretation is only part of the story of the politicization of material culture. For all their explanatory appeal today, revolutionary-themed decorative wares were extremely unusual in the eighteenth-century Atlantic marketplace. Many manufacturers decided against rolling out politically themed wares in significant quantities. Extant examples show that makers chose only a few shapes—teapots, mugs, pitchers, punchbowls—for politicized embellishment; the teapot, for instance, stands alone rather than as part of a set of slogan-bearing cups, saucers, and so on. In other words, potters did not invest intensively in political motifs within certain genres (such as entire tea sets) or across forms (from dinner plates to celery bowls to vases). In the millions of pieces exported by the Staffordshire potteries, intentionally political goods comprised a tiny fraction of the total.

The structure of the eighteenth-century Atlantic economy accounts in part for their singularity. Europe was home to the main manufacturing centers for pottery and for other goods like metalware and textiles that scholars have identified with the industrial vanguard. Two main sites of revolutionary protest—North America and the Caribbean—did not fabricate these items in abundance and so did not control their appearance and distribution. As for France, although it was renowned for its luxury goods (in porcelain, ormolu, and silk), the production time for these articles was slow, their prices high, and their clientele select. Those French makers who targeted the middling and the masses, such as numerous faïence manufactories, concentrated on domestic and French colonial rather than Atlantic markets. (Faïence is a tin-glazed, thick-bodied earthenware with hand-painted decoration.) Many faïence plates bearing French revolutionary symbols and mottos survive, but few circulated among customers outside the so-called Hexagon.

In general, British manufacturers had the greatest Atlantic reach in the eighteenth century, and it might be tempting to conclude that this provenance accounts for the scarcity of revolutionary-themed wares. After all, Britain opposed the revolutions in the United States, France, and Haiti, and went to war with each to assert its interests. This position constrained expressions of support among Britons sympathetic to republican causes. While homegrown political pressure was real, Europe, North America, and the West Indies were the top three markets for English decorative wares, and so makers had powerful economic motivations to meet those consumers' demands, including for political wares. Moreover, manufacturers had the capacity to do so, possessing both technical know-how and the awareness of different preferences among buyers in various locales. They were constantly appraising prospective sites for their products, timing their entrées into those areas, and assessing what distant consumers favored.

Still, manufacturers resisted producing explicitly political wares at large scales because they did not think Atlantic consumers wanted them. A final look at the teapot suggests why. The rhetoric of revolutionary leaders implies that political and aesthetic transformation went hand in hand, yet the teapot's style does not introduce anything new, let alone revolutionary. With painted flowers and scrollwork, a handle and spout molded with naturalistic motifs, and a delicate knop, the teapot adheres to rococo trends. The slogan looks like an addition to an existing model. Admittedly, the teapot reflects a moment of resistance rather than revolution, but U.S. iconography did not proliferate on English pottery until the nineteenth century.

What people desired, even in revolutionary regions, were decorative wares already in production, and we have overlooked how *access* to extant goods had tremendous political implications for some populations—far more so than overtly republican items.[2] As a genre, decorative wares became politicized in the Atlantic world more often through the context of their consumption than through their ornamentation. The place and moment of acquisition as well as the social and racial profiles of consumers imparted political significance to mainstream housewares. To take the most radical example, the procurement and use of ceramic tableware by enslaved people in the Caribbean and North America tested racial hierarchies that buttressed the status quo.

Locating this form of politicized consumption requires first taking a fresh look at fabrication—at how exactly manufacturers understood and tried to take full advantage of markets. Two of the most prolific and internationally oriented products in late eighteenth-century Britain—pottery and metalware—shed light on this process. These manufacturers' perceptions of the Atlantic world and their management of its revolutionary disruptions determined, to a large degree, what decorative goods were available to which consumers, when and, to a certain extent, why. Their perspective lays the groundwork for analyzing the implications of purchases in revolutionary North America, France, and the Caribbean. If boycotting specific goods, like stamped paper and tea, was one form of protest, acquiring certain manufactured items—even those without republican emblems—could be another.[3] These instances of "buying into the world of goods" represented a spectrum of political views, revealing how the intersection between the political, industrial, and consumer revolutions was much less straightforward, but also much more dynamic, widespread, and powerful, than the No Stamp Act teapot suggests.[4]

THE MANUFACTURERS' ATLANTIC

From exploitative labor practices and environmental degradation to innovations in technology, marketing, and distribution, manufacturing in this period portended changes that would become central features of modern industry. Despite its foreshadowing of future developments, eighteenth-century manufacturing reflected its times, and the activities of manufacturers are useful for recapturing this context. Manufacturers were not just managers of factories, overseeing laborers and setting policies about production. Rather, they were makers in their own right, trained in the traditions of their crafts, and they transformed those practices by applying the era's scientific insights. Eighteenth-century manufacturers were also merchants, employing diverse strategies to place their wares in markets at home and abroad. Their pursuits in these three realms reveal what from their perspective was logistically possible and economically profitable in the production and dissemination of decorative goods during the age of revolutions. Their vision of the Atlantic world had concrete repercussions for consumers and for the political potential of the items purchased.

Nowhere are these dynamics seen better than in England's West Midlands—the region that encompasses the city of Birmingham and the county of Staffordshire and an area whose manufactories experienced meteoric growth in this period. Their ascent is associated with two giants in the region's primary industries of pottery and metalworks: Josiah Wedgwood and Matthew Boulton, respectively. The two men were friends, collaborators, and sometimes rivals. Although their success and renown were extraordinary, the trajectories of their careers, especially their orientation toward export markets, illustrate approaches and features that were standard among their peers and for their moment.

Before the eighteenth century, the West Midlands was not easy to reach. No major roads connected it to Atlantic ports like Liverpool and Bristol, and while several navigable rivers—the Severn, Trent, and Mersey—serviced the area, they were neither deep enough nor straight enough to handle heavy traffic. More frustratingly for shippers, the rivers failed to link up north and south, east and west. Notwithstanding these drawbacks in transportation, the area had natural assets that encouraged industry. It had excellent access to coal, which fueled the furnaces and kilns necessary to metal and pottery making. Staffordshire possessed considerable clay deposits that were essential to ceramic production.

These advantages had supported smithies and potteries in the region for centuries, but in the eighteenth century, these industries thrived thanks to emerging consumer societies and expanding empires. Across the Atlantic world, more individuals had greater wherewithal to buy manufactured goods. Often they invested not just in necessities but also in items that made daily life more comfortable, pretty, and sociable. The manufactories of the West Midlands were poised to capitalize on these trends. Birmingham's main industry had been utilitarian ironmongery—tools, nails, and so forth, but at midcentury its manufactories concentrated production in two arenas: guns and "toys," the period term for assorted small items, worked mostly in metal.[5]

To a certain extent, then, the markets of metal and pottery makers intersected, as both created dizzying ranges of decorative wares. The diversity in the toy trade seemed so infinite that one chronicler noted in the 1780s, "It would be difficult to enumerate the great variety . . . practised in Birmingham, neither would it give pleasure to the reader."[6] Bearing this caution in mind, a modest inventory includes things like buckles, buttons, snuffboxes, candlesticks, watch chains, silver-plated tableware, japanned goods, and pins, among others. For its part, Staffordshire emerged as the pottery capital of England, churning out tea- and tableware as well as ornamental articles like vases, busts, and plaques—all destined for the dining rooms, parlors, and libraries of the upper and middle classes. Its factories specialized in a type of earthenware called creamware, which mimicked the whiteness and delicacy of porcelain but at a fraction of the cost.[7]

By the time of the North American crisis, the number of factories in the West Midlands had grown significantly. Over one hundred potteries were active in Staffordshire, ranging from small-scale operations like Thomas Whieldon's pottery which, as of 1750, employed only sixteen people, to Josiah Wedgwood's Etruria, a bustling compound of at least three hundred workers.[8] Birmingham supported even grander endeavors. John Taylor's enameled snuffbox manufactory had a workforce of five hundred people at its height, and Matthew Boulton's Soho accommodated up to a thousand laborers.[9] An American Quaker merchant who visited Soho in the mid-1770s celebrated its "hundreds of little apartments" in which "the whole Scene is a Theatre of Business, all conducted like one piece of Mechanism, Men, Women and Children full of employment according to their Strength and Docility."[10]

Although these "Bee hives" of the "Sons of Industry" featured, in some cases, sizable numbers of laborers, these were not the stereotypical factories of the nineteenth century.[11] For starters, owners like Boulton and Wedgwood remained makers in a very practical sense. Their fathers had been in the trades and they had trained their sons.[12] Boulton and Wedgwood knew the ins and outs of their crafts intimately, and this knowledge remained indispensable to their businesses, as they applied the latest scientific advances to their manufactories. Science fascinated both men, and they participated in the Lunar Society, an informal group centered in Birmingham that sought to merge technical and philosophical knowledge for new ends. Although the society's membership fluctuated, its devoted contributors included not only Wedgwood and Boulton but also the English scientist and dissenter Joseph Priestley; the Scottish engineer and inventor James Watt; and the poet, medical doctor, and polymath Erasmus Darwin. The men, along with visitors from across Britain and beyond, met once a month to discuss recent discoveries in the natural and physical sciences, engineering, and medicine, and shared findings from their own investigations. Boulton read voraciously the works of contemporary scientists and filled notebooks with designs. Equally informed, Wedgwood grasped chemistry so well that he made bespoke instruments for Priestley's laboratory and that of the French chemist Antoine Lavoisier, and published works in *Philosophical Transactions,* the journal of the Royal Society.[13]

These efforts brought Boulton and Wedgwood recognition throughout the Atlantic world. One editorial in the *New-England Palladium* celebrated their achievements alongside those of Bacon, Kepler, Newton, Locke, and, of course, Benjamin Franklin, noting that "the important discoveries and inventions of such men contribute to the necessities, the conveniences, and the happiness of mankind."[14] As the author's references to "necessities" and "conveniences" emphasize, Boulton and Wedgwood were interested in the creation and acquisition of what was called useful knowledge—expertise that had application to everyday life, including their trades.[15] They looked for ways to introduce novelty and to improve the pace, efficiency, and cost of fabrication. Over thirty-five years, Wedgwood conducted nearly five thousand trials, testing new clay compositions and glazes and experimenting with methods to measure kiln temperatures more accurately. Boulton perfected techniques for creating silver plate, devised machines for stamping coins, and, most famously, collaborated with James Watt on creating a steam engine that powered some of these tasks.[16] While these innovations are often celebrated (and rightly so) under the rubric of science and technology, these disciplines did not supplant the intellectual, practical, and physical know-how that Boulton and Wedgwood gained as metalsmith and potter. Rather, the two branches of knowledge worked together.[17] In order to expand their manufactories, Boulton and Wedgwood still needed to be eighteenth-century artisans. They had to understand that their workers could carry out, repeatedly, the new processes and recipes devised. Otherwise, their experiments would fail to effect the broader transformations in manufacturing to which each man aspired.

As part of this vision for improvement, both men built manufactories, ones that reflected their bold and, as they would have seen it, enlightened enterprises. Boulton, for instance, was determined to erect "the largest Hardware manufactory in the World," and it was, for the time, massive.[18] Soho began in the mid-1760s with a main three-story building measuring 180 feet by 55 feet, flanked by other, smaller structures that formed an orderly courtyard at the rear. It cost an astonishing £10,000 (£8,000 over budget). Over the years, Boulton added other structures to support emerging ventures: a forging workshop, a two-story engine shop, a mint, slag furnaces for melting scrap metal, a spring-latchet (a type of locking device) works, a buckle-shop extension, a replacement mint building, and a gallery and tearoom for visitors. Boulton cared not just about the size of his factory but also about its appearance. He hired an architect for the main building—an unusual move for an industrial project—and the result was a Palladian façade complete with an arched doorway, numerous expensive windows, and a cupola. One visitor described it as more "like the stately Palace of some Duke" than a factory.[19] Within a few years of the main building's completion, print shops sold views of it on the British, French, and German markets.[20]

At the same time as they invested in their individual manufactories, Wedgwood, Boulton, and their counterparts in Staffordshire and Birmingham worked to create institutions and infrastructure that would integrate the West Midlands more easily and more competitively into the Atlantic economy. After a long and heated campaign, Boulton

persuaded Parliament and then the Crown to authorize the establish-
ment of an assay office in Birmingham in 1773. The office allowed
manufacturers interested in the production of silver goods to have
their wares authenticated as sterling in Birmingham rather than sending them to London. As a result, Birmingham silversmiths could give
London ones a better run for their money.[21]

Crucial to both industries were improvements in transportation.
By midcentury Birmingham was connected to London by two turn-
pikes, although these roads were soon snarled in traffic as the volume
of carriages hauling cargo increased. Road travel was pricey, too, and
in the case of Wedgwood, the ceaseless jolting on bumpy roads put his
wares at risk. Not surprisingly, then, Wedgwood and Boulton, along
with other like-minded manufacturers in the area, lobbied for canal
construction, and by the early 1780s, Birmingham had water routes
to Bristol, Hull, and Liverpool, and Staffordshire to Liverpool. Thanks
to these investments, manufacturers brought raw materials to the factories and transported finished goods to chief cities more swiftly and
more cheaply.[22]

These developments—with factory sites and the infrastructure sup-
porting them—underscore that manufacturers were oriented toward
the export market. West Midlands makers expanded production capacity and pursued better integration within Britain in order to get their
wares to ports and from there into the Atlantic and beyond. As early
as 1765, Josiah Wedgwood acknowledged to William Meredith (a bar-
onet, member of Parliament for Liverpool, and, at that time, a Lord of
the Admiralty), "The bulk of our particular Manufactures [pottery] you
know are exported to foreign markets, for our home consumption is
very trifleing in comparison to what are sent abroad, and the principal
of these markets are the Continent and Islands of N. America."[23] While
domestic buyers sustained Birmingham's industries in the first half of
the eighteenth century, firms increasingly looked abroad for outlets.[24]

Manufacturers took an active role in locating export markets, and
their efforts on this front resemble those of eighteenth-century merchants, so much so that historian Peter Jones refers to men like Boulton
and Wedgwood as "merchant-manufacturers."[25] One contemporary
noted the change in approach from previous eras: "The practice of the
Birmingham manufacturer, for, perhaps, a hundred generations, was
to keep within the warmth of his own forge. The foreign customer,

therefore, applied to him for the execution of orders, and regularly made his appearance twice a year; and though this mode of business is not totally extinguished, yet a very different one is adopted."[26] Soho and Etruria maintained showrooms to welcome both domestic and foreign visitors; on one occasion in 1781, Boulton remarked on the international constellation of tourists to his factory: "Our house has been like that of Babel, by bad English, French, Italian, German and bad translations."[27] Over the span of fifty years, Soho entertained guests from across Europe, including Russia, Poland, and Scandinavia, as well as Canada, America, and the Ottoman Empire.[28]

The scope of their ambitions spurred manufacturers to employ other, more proactive ways to drum up business abroad. In 1786 Matthew Boulton, his son, and James Watt went with John Wedgwood (Josiah's son) and Tom Byerley (Josiah's nephew) to France. They visited Versailles, shopped at the Palais Royal, met up with Lavoisier, Claude-Louis Berthollet, and other leading lights of science, and toured factories, including Sèvres porcelain and the metalworks at Berry, south of Paris.[29] John Wedgwood and Tom Byerley made the acquaintance of two dealers (Dominique Daguerre and Mr. Sykes), with the hopes of coming to an arrangement for selling Wedgwood in France.[30] For their part, Watt and Boulton pursued the possibilities of transferring their technological innovations to French manufactories.[31]

When manufacturers could not visit personally, they looked to establish footholds in foreign markets through agents, who came in various guises. Some were merchants. Wedgwood contracted with different firms in Manchester to gain footholds in Mexico (via Cádiz), Italy, and Turkey.[32] In these joint ventures, the merchants carried some of Wedgwood's stock and took a percentage of the profits from whatever sold. For one endeavor in 1773 Wedgwood wrote to his London partner, Thomas Bentley, "We shall want some hundreds of small dishes to send abroad as patterns the next spring. We shall pack a 10 inch dish of a pattern, about 8 patterns in oval boxes, and these the Merchants will put into their packages without any trouble to them."[33] Wedgwood felt more comfortable with arrangements in which the merchants agreed to "return any of the first specimens sent which were not approved of. They would return them *safe*, and in a *given time*, or pay for them." As he explained to Bentley, "There seems something reasonable in the proposal, all circumstances consider'd."[34] The manufacturer shared some financial risk with these speculative ventures, but for a specific period only. That said, Wedgwood was willing to take the occasional gamble, shipping, for example, items to North America, where they would be transferred into "meal tubs, and so run into the Spanish territories in S. America."[35]

Working through merchants who specialized in certain regions provided outlets for trade and important information about those markets. In 1773 Wedgwood met with a Manchester merchant, Edmund Radcliffe, and concluded that "he seems quite dispos'd to assist in the most friendly way to disperse and circulate our Manufacture . . . as far as his connections reach, and they are very extensive; and for this purpose he sent for his address book into the Parlour—A large Folio Fill'd with the names of the Capital Houses all over Europe with proper remarks, of their connections, to what amount it may be prudent to credit them."[36] As scholars have detailed for merchant networks, manufacturers, too, sought out reliable information about markets and about trustworthy contacts in those locales in order to appraise the risk of enterprises abroad. Manufacturers pursued other foreign intelligence unique to their trades. In the 1760s and 1770s, Boulton looked to his agents in London and Paris—Moses Oppenheim and then Solomon Hyman—for the latest technical know-how. Hyman arranged for Boulton to meet with a Parisian artisan to learn how to "boyl brass work in color." A few years later, Boulton wrote to Hyman asking for the latest French recipes for gilding.[37] The roles of merchant and manufacturer were mutually reinforcing.

Sometimes the process of finding an agent was not straightforward, and manufacturers turned to contacts in politics, society, and elsewhere to gain entrée into distant markets. Incensed with his inability to crack into the East India trade in 1771, Wedgwood implored Bentley to wield whatever influence he could among his connections: "Many of our Ships I see by the Papers are sailing for the East Indies, and never a Vase or Bass relief on board! This is wrong and should be remedied—Pray speak to your friend Mr Knot, and Mr Shonnen."[38] Wedgwood also used British diplomats—and their wives—to get his ceramics into new markets. They carried his wares personally or found him representatives at their postings.[39]

Contacts could take a while to cultivate, and the process of cultivation could become elaborate, as was the case with Boulton's dealings with the Russian court. At the outset of the American Revolution, Boulton looked to Russia—an untapped market for him—as one way to ride out the disruption to trade caused by the war with the colonies. He began to draw the attention of court members by "having paid the Empress many compliments, both in Sculpture and Painting" until he was eventually "noticed by her." Connection made, Boulton and his partner, John Fothergill, "were now going to send over a Genteel young Man, of a very pleasing address and polite Education, constantly to attend the Court and introduce their fine things, take orders &c." Fothergill suggested to Wedgwood that their agent "might be usefull to [Wedgwood and Bentley], and made [them] an offer of the services of their young Man, as he would have time enough to act for . . . both."[40]

Boulton's dealings with the Russian court were soft politics, using flattery and favors to gain access and orders. Wedgwood tried the same when in 1770 he shipped a crate of assorted creamware vases and urns to the French finance minister, duc de Choiseul, with the aim of persuading him to reduce French tariffs on British goods.[41] Manufacturers engaged in politics more directly, however, by lobbying key members of the British government to create conditions favorable to international trade. During the American Revolution, Wedgwood had private meetings with leading men to air his views. In 1777 he called on Lord Gower, whose seat was in Staffordshire and who was also lord president in Lord North's administration, responsible for overseeing Privy Council meetings and presenting business for the monarch's approval. Wedgwood avoided direct discussion of the American Revolution (which he supported, and Gower emphatically did not), but he managed to work into the conversation a plea for freer exchange: "I told his Lordship that the sale of our manufacture had been greatly extended of late in Germany, Russia etc. and our business continued good notwithstanding so many prohibitions and high duties had been laid upon it abroad, and I believed the demand for it at foreign markets, under all these disadvantages, was owing to its being the best and cheapest pottery ware in Europe, and that we had no objection, as potters, to a free trade with all the world, except the East Indies."[42] With better trade agreements (especially ones with lower tariffs) with more places, Wedgwood intimated to Gower that English pottery (because it was the "best") had unlimited potential on world markets. This argument was a common one among British manufacturers, as steep tariffs on certain items, particularly on textiles, ceramics, and metalware, were a steady source of frustration. After the American Revolution, Wedgwood and Boulton led the charge in urging Parliament to broker a more advantageous trade deal with France, which finally came to fruition in 1786.[43]

In a manner similar to merchants, manufacturers deployed networks of influence in their attempts to place wares abroad under auspicious circumstances. Also like their merchant counterparts, manufacturers saw an opportunity to reach individuals outside their circles through print culture. Beginning in 1773 Wedgwood issued catalogues for his wares, having some translated into French and Italian.[44] At one level, the catalogues were akin to retailers' newspaper advertisements, but manufacturers—at least those of certain wherewithal and ambition— used print more shrewdly. Whereas advertisements listed sundry goods, with occasional qualifying adjectives, ceramics and metalware cata- logues incorporated images of shapes and designs. Sometimes these pictures were only outlines of forms; others were more detailed, such as Boulton's 1790 catalogue of silver-plated wares, which featured beautiful full- or half-page etchings of teapots, lamps, and even egg caddies (figure 1.2).[45] Whether the depictions were elaborate or simple, catalogues allowed readers to visualize more precisely manufacturers' products.

These tactics for finding new markets were not just about growth. They were also, as Boulton's Russian endeavors show, about managing interruption. Manufacturers of decorative wares experienced periodic disturbances and slumps because of the revolutionary wars. Associates abroad became enemies, and the status of neutral powers was tenu- ous and prone to encroachment from rivals. Shipping became more hazardous and hence more costly. There were fewer vessels available as navies scrambled to bolster their fleets, and navies, pirates, and priva- teers preyed on military and civilian vessels of enemy—and sometimes neutral—nations. While these attacks did not target vessels filled with decorative wares (if only!), the seizures had detrimental knock-on ef- fects for these industries. In 1776, when North American privateers captured 250 ships in the British West Indies, merchants and planters there sustained financial losses that diminished their spending power for goods.[46] Between 1778 and 1781, Boulton reduced Soho's work- force by half as sales flagged.[47] In 1778, as the American war deepened, Wedgwood was saddled with "an enormous old stock" that, "gorgon

Figure 1.2. Illustrations of creamer and teapot made by Matthew Boulton, from the manufacturer's catalogue of silver-plated ware. Notice the numbers below each, intended to streamline the ordering process. (Image copyright © The Metropolitan Museum of Art. Image source: Art Resource, NY.)

like," weighed down his business.[48] Even after the conclusion of a war, some manufacturers remained cautious. Wedgwood described how he and his Staffordshire colleagues were reticent to extend credit and wares to merchants trading in North America since so many had run up substantial debts and had ceased paying them.[49]

But revolutions also provided opportunities. In the early days of the French Revolution, Boulton's Parisian contacts placed orders for buttons for National Guard uniforms and for over 6 million *médailles de confiance,* or medallions that could be exchanged (like currency) for their face value of 2 or 5 sols.[50] When sundry French Caribbean colonies surrendered to invading British forces, British manufacturers looked to send their decorative wares to these islands. Some prospects proved fleeting, and doubtless manufacturers and their laborers experienced hardship and contraction because of revolutions. That said, statistics from the period testify to manufacturers' overall success in international markets. During the last half of the eighteenth century, British exports and reexports experienced staggering growth, rising in value from about £12.7 million at midcentury to £68.4 million by the end of the Napoleonic wars. Between 1750 and 1815, the total value of metal exports alone rose from £489,000 to £871,000. Most of these items flowed into the Atlantic rather than the Asian trade.[51] For all the disruptions caused by the revolutions, the numbers indicate there were opportunities, at least for the savvy, the versatile, and the lucky.

Thanks to their skills as makers, merchants, and manufacturers, Boulton, Wedgwood, and their West Midlands counterparts succeeded in channeling their wares into the eighteenth-century Atlantic world of goods. They worked to expand and improve processes of production at home and to cultivate markets for their merchandise. These endeavors required constant attention, as manufacturers adapted to the ever-shifting Atlantic landscape of openings and closures. But their success raises the question: What *exactly* did they make and send in this period? This determination was crucial to efforts to sustain vibrant export markets. After all, it was not a given that consumers would want what Wedgwood, Boulton, and their peers were selling, and they knew it. In calculating what to ship, manufacturers took into account the social status of the buyers and their locales. In an age of revolutions, politics came into play, too, and makers like Boulton and Wedgwood had to decide if and how their products would engage with these movements. Meanwhile, consumers had their own ideas about the political potential of decorative wares, some of which manufacturers could not anticipate but which added to the salability of their goods.

REVOLUTIONARY EXPORTS

According to some scholars, the dramatic development of manufactured export goods abetted political revolutions well before they got under way. The more varied material world that manufacturers perpetuated encouraged a "corrosive logic of choice" among populations. In the decades leading up to revolution, the story goes, individuals became accustomed to making decisions in their everyday material lives, selecting from many options which platter or shoe buckle best suited their needs and preferences. Eventually, they brought that same sensibility to the political arena, contributing to the move toward revolution.[52]

But this interpretation tells us little about why people bought what they did *during* revolutions. Decorative wares of English provenance remained popular, even in regions and among individuals who challenged the standing orders and were sometimes at war with the British. Understanding this persistent appeal requires an appraisal of how manufacturers conceived of the dynamics of fashion and what allowances they made for differences according to class and region—essentially, how much leeway they gave to consumer choice. For consumers, it entails not just considering selection as an act but examining who made that selection and what was selected as well. Their decisions politicized these objects in ways that manufacturers, for all their market research, did not control, and that suggest the revolutionary potential of status quo things.

Josiah Wedgwood's manufactory first made its mark thanks to its creamware. This white-glazed earthenware had been made in Staffordshire since the 1730s or 1740s, but Wedgwood refined it, so much so that he inspired imitators throughout England, if not the world.[53] After years of experimentation, he managed to perfect a creamware whiter and smoother than previous incarnations—qualities that consumers prized in dinner-, dessert-, and tearwares. In 1767 he dubbed his version "Queen's ware" after Queen Charlotte ordered a set of dinnerware and designated him "Potter to the Queen." In subsequent years Wedgwood introduced other ceramic bodies: pearlware in 1779–80 (a white ceramic with a more luminous glaze) and jasper (a colored biscuit-like body for vases, plaques, and so on), among others. But Queen's ware remained a mainstay of his business and of his brand.

Similar to Wedgwood's trajectory in Staffordshire, Boulton got his start by following the already established toy industry in Birmingham and then improving it. Birmingham's "toys" had a shoddy reputation, and Boulton (first with his partner John Fothergill and then, after his death, with John Scale) honed his line of buckles, buttons, sword hilts, and the like to please the most discerning customers. Boulton, however, was restless, more so than Wedgwood, and throughout the 1770s and 1780s, he diversified. He manufactured larger decorative items—teapots, candlesticks, lamps, ornaments—in silver, silver plate (sometimes called Sheffield plate), and ormolu (gilt brass or gilt bronze). In the 1790s, Boulton established a mint at Soho and went on to strike currency and medallions for Britain, the United States, France, Sierra Leone, and the East India Company, among others. Most ingeniously, Boulton and Watt designed and constructed steam engines to facilitate fabrication, and they sold this machinery to other industrialists.[54] And if all that were not enough, Boulton dabbled in "mechanical paintings," a period term for machine-based attempts to copy oil paintings onto canvases.[55]

In their business ventures, Boulton and Wedgwood saw elite clients as essential because they provided valuable endorsements. King George and Queen Charlotte bought items from both makers, as did other European royals and aristocrats. Often these purchases were unique commissions, and Boulton and Wedgwood used them to every possible advantage. For elite patrons, Wedgwood made lavish, one-of-a-kind items that showcased his pottery's virtuosity with forms, glazes, and patterns. Perhaps the most spectacular was a dinner and dessert service commissioned in 1773 for Catherine II, empress of Russia. It became known as the "Green Frog Service" because each piece included a diminutive green frog, an allusion to the nickname for the Chesme Palace, for which the set was intended. (The palace was located near a frog marsh.) Frogs aside, the service was audacious, with over nine hundred pieces that featured more than twelve hundred hand-painted distinct scenes of places in England, Scotland, and Wales. The set required over two dozen artists just to execute the pictures and borders, and it cost about £1,500 to produce (figure 1.3).[56]

Empress Catherine paid Wedgwood well for his efforts, but he was an astute entrepreneur and sought to increase his revenue beyond a single commission. Before shipping the service to Russia, Wedgwood displayed it in his London showroom for several weeks. People who flooded in to see it were tempted to take home one of Wedgwood's simpler and less expensive articles for themselves. The metropolitan showroom was an inspired and profitable innovation. He and his partner Thomas Bentley, who oversaw the London side of the operation, created eye-catching arrangements to entice customers.[57] No exertion was too much to please, as Wedgwood put it, "my Ladys," but quite a few men wanted Wedgwood's ceramics as well.[58] In 1771 he designed a series with hunting animals, explaining, "All Country Gentlemen are sportsmen; there is scarcely anything that gives them so much pleasure to look upon as Dead Game."[59]

Boulton, too, exploited royal approbation to attract more customers. In 1770 Queen Charlotte ordered several ormolu vases from Boulton, and for the next three years he tried to leverage her patronage by staging

Figure 1.3. Wedgwood platter from Empress Catherine's "Frog" dinner service. This platter shows Wedgwood's extraordinary artistry, and, in comparison to the example unearthed at Mulberry Row at Monticello (figure 1.4), it testifies to his versatility as well. He could offer the same form with different levels of decoration and finish, thus catering to consumers of various means. (© Victoria and Albert Museum, London.)

splashy sales at James Christie's auction house in Pall Mall. Advertisements in London newspapers celebrated the "exquisite workmanship" of Boulton's wares, which were "replete with elegance and true taste," and he invited members of the nobility and gentry to exclusive pre-sale viewings.[60] His efforts drew in the elite, and buyers at the 1771 auction included earls, lords, ladies, and sirs, while at the 1772 sale, the Prince of Wales as well as a few dukes made significant purchases. Although only the highest echelon could afford to buy (Horace Walpole grumbled about exorbitant prices), the auction as an event drew in many others who came to browse, and Boulton hoped that because of his firm's glamorous associations, they would buy something from one of his more affordable lines.[61]

For both Boulton and Wedgwood, elite approval helped the visibility of their products. As Wedgwood mused, "If a Royal or Noble introduction be as necessary to the sale of an Article *of Luxury,* as real Elegance and beauty, then the Manufacturer, if he consults his own interest will bestow as much pains, and expence too if necessary, in gaining the former of these advantages, as he would in bestowing the latter."[62] But high-end commissions could be sources of exasperation—in terms of time spent and income earned. Boulton's ormolu production trailed off in the 1770s because it was too steep to sustain; the labor and materials were costly, and he never managed to sell enough stock to recoup his outlay. Adding insult to injury, some vaunted clients shirked payment, with Boulton absorbing the loss.[63]

Although Wedgwood, it seems, had a better head for finances than Boulton, he groused about the fickleness of well-heeled "sponcers." In 1779 he was irritated by the lukewarm reception that architects (key liaisons with the wealthy clients) gave to his jasper, lamenting that "it must have a hard struggle to support it self, and rise from under their maledictions."[64] He griped about the caprice of elite requests. Of a recently received order from a noble patron, he complained, "Must we make pebble Tea ware? . . . I can *make* a little time to attend to the forms, [and] we will see what can be done, but I could sooner make £100 worth of any ware in the common course that is going, than this one sett. It is this sort of *time loseing* with *Uniques* which keeps ingenious Artists who are connected with Great Men of taste poor, and would make us so too if we did too much in that way."[65] Pebbleware, which mixed several clays together for a marbled look, had been fashionable in earlier decades. For Wedgwood, the commission diverted time and resources from sounder ventures and, he hinted, cost him more than he would see in return.

Manufacturers balanced the need to satisfy patrons' bespoke demands with the more lucrative and more efficient fabrication of their standard lines of goods. While at times at odds, the two modes of production were inextricably linked. As Wedgwood pointed out to Bentley, "The Great People have had their Vases in their Palaces long enough for them to be seen & admir'd by the *Middling Class* of People, which class we know are vastly, I had almost said infinitely, superior in numbers to the Great, & though a *great price* was I believe at first necessary to make the Vases esteemed *Ornaments* for *Palaces* that reason no longer exists. Their character is established, & the middling People would probably buy quantitys of them at a reduced price."[66] In this case, Wedgwood wanted to revamp the fabrication of his vases to produce versions "at one half the expense we have hitherto done."[67] Sometimes this transformation was not materially possible. Boulton could not make ormolu or silver wares for the masses; the laborious techniques of manufacture and dear materials prohibited it. That said, his toy and plated lines could mimic aspects of the style of his higher-end items, giving middling consumers a taste of those more expensive goods.

The windfall from commissions, then, came from the ability to translate their cachet—if not in full, then at least in essence—into wares that were affordable for the public. As all the West Midlands manufacturers understood, the middle classes were the largest and most reliable sector of buyers. Boulton summed up the sentiment: "It is better to work for the gross mass of the people of the world than for the lords and princes of it."[68] For Boulton, "better" meant financially more secure, and this held true for many manufacturers. However, even Boulton felt that he could not forsake one clientele for the other. The continued straddling of high and middling markets reflects an eighteenth-century grasp of what impulses drove consumption. It was a model based on emulation, in which lower orders imitated as much as possible the material worlds of their social betters. Middling men and women saw vases or candlesticks in palaces and country seats, and they wanted them, too.

But emulation was only one component of consumption. The middling classes had their own aesthetic preferences, and manufacturers had to appeal to these inclinations as well. Take the case of Wedgwood's Queen's ware. Despite the sensation surrounding his ornamental lines, what most people bought most often were plainer wares—white dishes with some decoration along the edges and perhaps at the center. These were what Wedgwood called his "Usefull" wares, and their ubiquity was a source of pride and anxiety.[69] As early as 1774, he protested to Bentley, "I apprehend our customers will not much longer be content with Queens ware, it being now rendered vulgar and common every where."[70] His innovations with pearlware and jasper were in anticipation of the end of Queen's ware's reign. Notwithstanding his apprehensions, it continued to sell for decades at a brisk pace, and this constancy was essential to Wedgwood's business. Boulton's manufactory suggests a similar trend. Although production for Boulton's luxury goods in silver and ormolu came and went, he continued with toys for over three decades.

The steadiness of certain goods was a boon to manufacturers, but even here they looked to manage choice whenever possible. To be sure, there was considerable variety among "useful" wares, and yet Wedgwood tried to control the range in order to streamline manufacturing and boost profit. Although he came out with novelty shapes from time to time, four basic patterns—royal, queen's, feather, and shell edge—formed the core of his tableware, and customers chose assorted borders—feather, basket, vine, flowers—in various colors.[71] When ordering hollowware (teapots, coffeepots, tureens, mugs, and so forth), buyers specified the type of spout, handle, and knop. But these options were not a free-for-all, as can best be seen in Wedgwood's (and Boulton's) catalogues. While a smart marketing technique for disseminating wares abroad, the catalogue also presented a structured method for consumers to choose goods. The manufacturers decided what to include, based on what they thought customers wanted and on their needs as manufacturers. In his first catalogue, Wedgwood highlighted his round terrines because he thought the form would show well in print and because they were "in *Dead stock*" and he wanted to shift them.[72]

This concern about directing choice influenced the pace at which manufacturers rolled out new wares. In elite circles, the introduction of the latest fashions coincided with the "season," the months when the *bon ton* arrived in London, Bath, or other eighteenth-century hotspots of seeing and being seen. Producers brought out their novelties at these moments for maximum impact—and hopefully, maximum sales. But strategy was involved. For the fall season in London in 1770, Wedgwood and Bentley presented a selection of tried-and-true wares "*sprinkled over*" with a few new articles to give them an air of novelty."[73] This mixing was economically sensible; if the latest items did not appeal to customers, then there were still plenty of the proven patterns and forms available. Boulton learned this lesson the hard way. His 1771 and 1772 ormolu auctions were triumphs for his reputation, but not for his ledgers. He staked so much on new wares that when a large number of lots failed to sell, Boulton was stuck with the stock as well as the costs of their production.[74]

These practices indicate how manufacturers sought not only to appease consumer desires but also to channel them—a tactic that provides an interesting vantage on fashion. Although novelty was vital for the industry, it was seen as something that had to be controlled to turn a profit. In a letter to his brother Thomas written around 1790, Josiah Jr. described the relationship between fashion and consumers that guided the factory:

> I think you are right with respect to the impropriety of adopting the whims of customers and bringing them into use; but in this matter I believe you must not be too rigid. There are many cases in which it is necessary to humour them, especially in a business which depends almost entirely upon fashion. However it is right I think to let all whims but good ones stop with the owner and not to bring them into the warehouse as common articles of manufacture. You must consider that it has been a great measure owing to the taking up hints given by customers and bringing them to perfection that this manufactory has established its character for *Universality*.[75]

The term *universality* stands out in an age of revolutions. Josiah Jr.'s description of ceramic manufacturing reads like political philosophy: the people (the customers) will have many bad ideas and a few good ones; the governing body (the factory) takes up the good ideas, perfecting and applying them. Wedgwood's perspective indicates the limits of choice and the ways that novelty could be disruptive rather than productive and lucrative. After decades of frustration, Boulton reached a similar conclusion, advising his son "never to engage in any manufactory that depend on Fasion, tast, Caprice & Fancy of lords and ladies but to confine his persuits to things usefull rather than ornamental."[76] The type of good shaped how well a manufacturer could weather the vagaries of fashion. Ceramic manufacturers could not recycle their items once fired, whereas occasionally metalworks could recoup some outlay by melting down unsold stock and reusing the metal. As the eighteenth-century historian William Hutton pointed out about the sudden unpopularity of buckles, "This offspring of fancy, like the clouds, is ever changing. The fashion of today is thrown into the casting pot tomorrow."[77] Wedgwood might point out that at least metalsmiths had casting pots.

From the manufacturers' perspective, then, not all fashions resulted in profit. Elite trends did not always translate easily—in terms of material and desire—to middling consumers, and although the middle classes formed the bedrock of businesses, manufacturers sought to direct their inclinations. This project was complicated enough when navigating the dynamics of class, but regional and national preferences made fashion more fraught. Both Wedgwood and Boulton, along with their counterparts, allowed for what they perceived as differences in national tastes, and were willing to some extent to accommodate these idiosyncrasies. But they were wary of going too far in this regard, fearful of the costs and risks, and of squandering their status as British goods.

In designing wares, British manufacturers tapped a wellspring of sources shared by elites across the Atlantic world. They turned to antiquity (Greeks, Romans, Egyptians), the Renaissance, the French, and other traditions. As Boulton explained in a letter to one of his clients, "As [the fashion] of the present age distinguishes itself by adopting the most elegant ornaments of the most refined Grecian artists, I am satisfied in conforming thereto, and humbly copying their style, and makeing new combinations of old ornaments without presuming to invent new ones."[78] Boulton followed the craze among the well-heeled for dining in the French mode, producing silver and plated services with individual place settings and serving dishes intended for symmetrical arrangement on the table.[79]

Although drawing from pervasive aesthetic trends, British manufacturers thought that certain types of items, colors, and decoration appealed to particular nationalities. Wedgwood strategized on this front as he looked to diversify markets. He wondered whether his Queen's ware could make a "*complete conquest of France*," given its consumers' penchant for "*Frippery*" and things "*covered over with ornament*."[80] In 1772 he moaned that the Russians were so behind the times that they would not be ready for his vases until the nineteenth century, but he proposed that he might be able to create a "bright . . . *Straw colour*" ware that would please them—and the Germans.[81] He deliberated over which goods might best suit the Italian market and was disappointed to learn that in the opinion of the British envoy, only the "cheap and gawdy" would do.[82]

Since exports were crucial to their livelihoods, British manufacturers incorporated national and regional predilections into some of their products. They did so with discretion, unwilling to develop distinct lines for each export market. It was simply too much of an investment of time, labor, and risk, and so they worked largely within extant fabrication frameworks. For manufacturers, the American, French, and Haitian revolutions presented interesting challenges in this respect. All three regions—North America, France, and the Caribbean—were important markets, and manufacturers were already sensitive to the stylistic proclivities of each place. Yet late eighteenth-century political movements attempted to redefine these sites in various ways, one of which was aesthetic, as revolutionary regimes experimented with lexicons of symbols, iconography, and color. Manufacturers had to decide whether to integrate allusions to these trends into their wares.

To a degree, the political views of individual manufacturers informed their choices. (Or at least revolutionary regimes made that a litmus test for domestic makers.) But it was also a collective project between consumers and manufacturers, and the goods produced during these years demonstrate in what ways both constituencies were and were not willing to embrace revolution in this sector of their material worlds. Wedgwood's Queen's ware provides an excellent case study to see these dynamics in action. Despite its unapologetically British and royal associations, Wedgwood's Queen's ware maintained its popularity and entered new markets; between 1785 and 1800, exports of English creamware doubled.[83] These wares took on new political—even revolutionary—meanings in new settings. In so doing, they reveal the ways that extant things became politicized because of context—who bought them, where, and for what ends. In the hands of people of African descent or of disaffected Frenchmen, these "old" goods could be as politically powerful as wares with republican slogans.

Wedgwood was active in politics for the sake of his pottery and that of the British manufactories more generally, but his involvement went beyond business. Whereas Boulton was ambivalent about Atlantic revolutionary movements, Wedgwood was more candid. Throughout the 1760s and 1770s, Wedgwood criticized the British administration's treatment of the North American colonists; as early as 1767, he predicted that its policies would lead them to break from the empire—in his view, justifiably.[84] Sympathetic to their complaints, Wedgwood had considered decorating his Queen's ware with a portrait of William Pitt to "take advantage of the American prejudice in favour of that great man."[85] This early scheme did not come to fruition—an outcome that proved the norm even as the pace of revolution quickened.

Wedgwood's decision on this score was influenced less by his personal political views and more by economic considerations, as was the case with his deliberations about distinctive wares for other markets. Thanks to technological innovations, engravings, like one of Pitt, could be transferred onto creamware vessels through a method called bat printing.[86] This process, although it was becoming more common, was costly in the last quarter of the eighteenth century: printed decoration required an extra firing, which drove up the price, making it, along with enamel-decorated wares, the most expensive type of earthenware.[87] Potters concluded that investing heavily in a niche market was dicey, especially in wartime, and most American consumers found the price too high. As such, transfer-printed ceramics in this period represent a sporadic speculation or a bespoke commission.[88] An 1802 inventory of a New York merchant in Liverpool shows that of two hundred crates containing almost 110,000 ceramic items, only 3 percent had on-glaze printed decoration.[89] In Josiah Jr.'s formulation, they represented a "whim" that did not become "common articles."

Equally significant, there was not much of a demand for revolutionary-themed useful wares, including in the United States. A shopkeeper in Maryland had purchased four teapots, two coffeepots, and six pitchers (called "jugs")—all enameled with the "No Stamp Act" slogan. In 1771, five years after the repeal of the Stamp Act, two jugs still stood on his shelves, gathering dust. Even this modest venture in political customization fell short of the retailer's expectations.[90] Or take the ceramics purchases of George Washington. Just before a colonial boycott went into effect in 1769, Washington ordered a table service of 250 pieces of "ye most fashionable kind of Queen's Ware" for Mount Vernon. While in New York during the war, he picked up additional pieces from loyalist merchant Philip Rhinelander, and in 1779, when in New Jersey, Washington asked his deputy quartermaster general to locate yet another set of Queen's ware. Other purchases followed in 1781 and 1783.[91] Clearly, Washington liked his Queen's ware—and these pieces didn't feature dead game. As he led the military campaign for independence from the British, he still bought their ceramics, and his compatriots followed suit. By the end of the eighteenth century, U.S. newspapers advertised Queen's ware more extensively than any other British good.[92]

For both Atlantic consumers and manufacturers, tableware was not usually the site for overt political gestures. The faïence industry in France is an exception that proves the rule. No doubt responding to pressure from government officials, faïence manufacturers in Nevers and elsewhere produced items that celebrated the iconography of every stage of the revolution: from king as defender of liberty to king as traitor.[93] The symbols changed so quickly, though, that faïence manufacturers could not, at moments, sell their stock, fearful that its suddenly out-of-date symbolism would invite censure. In fact, so much revolutionary-themed faïence survives today that one wonders whether it was ever used at all.

In general, tableware avoided politics because of its function. Dining was a site for social display and exchange in the eighteenth century, and the table was invested with some of the best articles that a family could afford.[94] As historian Amanda Vickery has emphasized, "The cheapness and disposability of objects today . . . make it easy to forget just how long the life of a household object could be, and the extent to which Georgian artefacts were serviced, repaired and carefully husbanded."[95] Except among the very wealthy, most individuals did not overhaul their tableware often, nor did they have multiple complete sets. Although individual pieces might be had for a few shillings, a medium-sized service of creamware cost between £3 and £5, a significant investment for many families (as much as a cow).[96] Given the expense, most people sought to use tableware for as long as possible, and a prudent buyer looked for a style that would honor his or her table for years. Politically themed wares did not fit the bill.

Despite the importance of the North American market (it was second only to Europe), the revolution there did not lead to a noticeable change of styles in tableware at Wedgwood or the other potteries. Wedgwood's location in the heart of the empire that had just lost thirteen colonies may have made such an endeavor foolhardy. But as important, North Americans did not demand otherwise. At the end of the revolution, U.S. merchants wanted what was selling in England: a 1784 order from the Boston firm of French and Simpson pleaded, "We beg your particular attention that they be of the most Fashionable and Newest Paterns, and sorted in due Proportion."[97] While Americans may have rejected monarchy, they continued to desire wares from the queen's potter. Not until the nineteenth century did Staffordshire potteries create lines specifically for the U.S. market.[98]

Americans' stubborn yearning for British tableware could be explained in terms of cultural legitimacy: now independent, the residents of the new nation wanted to assert that their society was on par with that of the former mother country. Scholars have defined this behavior as indicative of a decades-old "creole" anxiety ("creole" in its eighteenth-century context meaning simply born in the Americas).[99] Determined to counter European arguments about the innate inferiority of everything American, creoles sought to demonstrate their worthiness partly through consumption. While a factor, this reading reduces the significance of all types of things down to a single purpose: refinement. But the presence of Queen's ware in other revolutionary places presents different interpretive possibilities.

Wedgwood's ventures in France and the Caribbean are cases in point. The trade agreement of 1786 opened the door for British goods in France, and Staffordshire potters saw great potential for their ceramics. French pottery production covered the extremes: there was rarefied porcelain that only the aristocracy and royalty could afford, and then there was faïence for everyone else.[100] English pottery fit nicely in between—more polished than faïence but cheaper than porcelain—and Wedgwood and his peers wagered that the bourgeoisie, and even some aristocrats and royals, would fall for their goods. In addition, toward the end of the century, some Frenchmen had developed a taste for all things British, a fad rooted, in some circles, in an appreciation of British society and its political system, which was seen as more enlightened and less corrupt than the French. Wedgwood's Queen's ware encapsulated the British penchant for what was called "neatness"—pretty but given its lower price, sensible.[101] In this vein, one could interpret the consumption of English creamware in pre-revolutionary France as a political statement. In the heady summer of 1789, one American observer was shocked to find "Every Thing is à l'Anglois and a Desire to imitate the English prevails alike in the Cut of a coat and the Form of a Constitution."[102] While the purchase of a creamware plate might be seen as the lingering of empire in the United States, it could be associated with soft critiques of absolute monarchy in France.

Wedgwood launched into the French trade with gusto, sending over his first shipment of goods in 1787. There were glitches, as he struggled to discern which of his styles and forms appealed to French consumers. After the arrival of one shipment, Wedgwood's French associate Mr. Sykes noted bluntly, "We don't want Soup plates," and he advised Wedgwood to send plates only in the "Royal" pattern (which had an undulating outline rather than clear "royalist" ornamentation).[103] One thorny issue was sizing. Sykes and Company observed that in general the plates were too big for the French taste and recommended that Wedgwood stick to dishes between ten and sixteen inches.[104]

Despite these frustrations, Wedgwood witnessed success with his foray into the French market, as did the English potteries generally. The numbers of English earthenware exported to France rose almost twelve-fold in just four years, from 256,575 pieces in 1785 to 3,167,854 in 1789.[105] In Wedgwood's case, he captured some prominent clients: duc d'Orléans, the king's cousin, who during the revolution would become "Philippe Égalité," commissioned a dairy service, and Marie-Antoinette requested a "tea and table service for Children."[106] For all their quibbles, Sykes and Company kept dealing with Wedgwood at a considerable volume. Between June and December 1787, Sykes sent at least six orders to Wedgwood for goods totaling almost £3,000.[107] Events of the summer of 1789 failed to slow the pace, but as political volatility mounted, the window for the market was closing. In October 1789 Sykes admitted, "Trade is quite at a stand here, Peoples Minds being Engaged with Public Matters."[108]

The situation in France not only hampered trade to the region, it also began to reverberate negatively in Britain. Although sectors of the British public supported the revolution in its early days, opponents became adamant about stamping out sympathy for the cause. Edmund Burke's diatribe *Reflections on the Revolution in France* hit the streets in November 1790, provoking a firestorm of debate. As the tempo of revolution accelerated on the Continent, it became more difficult, if not dangerous, for Britons to back French endeavors. In July 1791, Birmingham mobs ransacked the house and laboratory of Wedgwood's friend Joseph Priestley, an outspoken advocate of the French Revolution. (Boulton's Soho was spared, and in gratitude, he held a large party for his workers, accounts of which circulated as far as Kingston, Jamaica.)[109] Numerous "associations" formed to pressure citizens to declare fidelity to the British Constitution. Wedgwood told his nephew that he would refuse to take an oath, not for lack of loyalty but because he saw the groups as "worse than useless" as they intended to "set one part of the nation against the other."[110] After a contentious build-up, France and Britain went to war in 1793, and legal trade between the two countries ground to a halt.

If the French Revolution polarized politics in Britain, then the Haitian Revolution galvanized them—mostly in strong opposition. Wedgwood was a staunch supporter of the British anti–slave trade movement, designing its famous emblem of a kneeling slave, weighed down with chains, asking, "Am I not a Man and a Brother?" (see figure 4.3). (Incidentally, this motif did not appear on Queen's ware in the 1790s.)[111] But Wedgwood's voluminous correspondence and his wares fail to register the Haitian Revolution as an event. Given his propensity to comment on just about everything, his silence is conspicuous—but common. The British anti–slave trade movement persisted with its limited version of abolitionism, despite, if not because of, the Haitian Revolution. In fact, some argued that the end of the slave trade was the only way to avoid similar rebellions in the British Caribbean.[112] Moreover, with the French emancipation decree in 1794, the battle in the Caribbean between Britain and France became one, in large part, over slavery—an issue that Wedgwood and other anti–slave trade proponents were not ready to contemplate fully.[113] Finally, since Wedgwood Sr. died in 1795, he did not witness Haitian independence.

Although Wedgwood turned a blind eye to the political impact of the Haitian Revolution, the Caribbean was very much in the pottery's sights as an economic theater in 1790s, thanks to British military campaigns there. In 1793 the British invaded Saint-Domingue, and from 1794 to 1802 they occupied Martinique. They held Guadeloupe briefly in 1793–94 and fought to maintain inroads in St. Lucia and Grenada. These conquests, if temporary, resulted in access to new clientele. For decades, Staffordshire potters had exported earthenware to the West Indies by the millions.[114] As early as 1766, Wedgwood had entered Caribbean markets, noting, "Green desert ware is often wanted, in *reality* for the West India Islands—I have a few crate[s] on hand, some gilt, some plain, Ergo should be glad to part with them on very moderate terms." He suggested that this style might also go over well in "Pensacola [and] the new discover'd Islands."[115] Newspapers from the British West Indies feature advertisements for ceramics, sometimes mentioning Wedgwood and his famous Queen's ware by name.[116]

In light of this success in the British Caribbean and in other colonies, some British merchants gambled on the prospect of selling ceramics in the occupied French West Indies, and for Wedgwood, one of the biggest requests came from Thellusson Brothers and Company, a London firm with long-standing ties to the Caribbean. They were slave traders and plantation owners as well as merchants.[117] Looking to tap into new markets, Thellusson Brothers sent Wedgwood no fewer than five orders in the summer and early fall of 1794. Each list is multiple pages, enumerating a wide range of dinner, tea, and ornamental wares—the quantity, style, and size all noted with specificity. In sum, there were 111 hogsheads and 40 crates of ceramics worth over £3,500. By the 1790s, this mixed-crate approach was a standard strategy for merchants trading ceramics in the Caribbean. The idea was that there was something for everyone, and metropolitan merchants and potters did not have to wait for cues from Caribbean customers.[118]

The volume and value of the orders are striking, but so, too, are the styles, which are in keeping with the British home market. Clearly, the Thellussons thought that French Caribbean consumers craved similar goods. The possible roots of that desire for British wares, though, were multiple and varied. In several Caribbean colonies, leaders had advocated for more open trade for decades, and the arrival of such wares could have been read as evidence of that achievement. Feeling betrayed by the radicalism of the revolutionary regime in the early and mid-1790s, some white French colonists welcomed all things British as a way to repudiate the metropole. Items, like Queen's ware, that had been progressive in France just a few years before were now conservative. Still other individuals, whatever their personal political beliefs, looked to ingratiate themselves with occupying forces. And of course, there were those who found it useful, novel, and pretty.

Whatever the motivations of buyers, Wedgwood's trade in the Caribbean could be seen as a sign of his imperfect devotion to abolition. After all, many of his ceramics ended up in the homes of slave masters, positing an interpretation of Wedgwood as a canny capitalist who, when push came to shove, was willing to sell whatever to whomever.[119] But as archaeologists have shown, some people of African descent also acquired goods made in Europe and imbued them with meaning, and ceramics form an important evidential basis for this assertion.[120] Black men and women may not have been in the purview of manufacturers

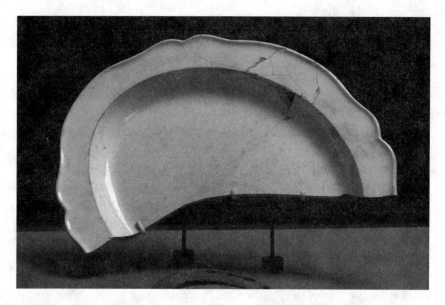

Figure 1.4. Queen's ware platter, royal pattern, late eighteenth century. This frag-
ment was found during the excavation of "building s," located at the eastern end
of the slave quarters called Mulberry Row at Monticello. Construction on these
quarters began in the early 1790s. (Thomas Jefferson Foundation, Monticello;
Photograph by Walter Larrimore/Smithsonian.)

as potential consumers of decorative wares, yet they engaged with this
domain of goods.

Enslavement circumscribed Black people's ability to acquire decorative wares to the same extent as free people, and when they managed
it, they often had the cheapest and plainest wares. Despite these constraints, there was more variety than one might expect. At Mulberry
Row, a line of slave quarters at Monticello, archaeological digs have
turned up mid- and late eighteenth-century creamware sherds of tea-
and tableware, including a platter in Wedgwood's royal pattern—the
same shape preferred by French consumers (figure 1.4). Work at Mount
Vernon's House for Families, occupied from 1759 to 1793, has yielded
diverse ceramic finds. Scholars have proposed that on large plantations
some enslaved people, especially those working in closer proximity to
the main house, were able to tap into broader material realms—either
by receiving goods secondhand from owners or through their own purchasing power.[121]

Examples from the Caribbean shed more light on questions of access and use among people of African descent. Wade Stubbs, a white American loyalist refugee, established a plantation in North Caicos in the Bahamas, where he and the enslaved had similar ceramic consumption, as far as the range of styles and forms. This surprising parity reflects the isolation of North Caicos: over four hundred miles from the nearest large port of Nassau, Stubbs did not have the luxury of reinforcing social and racial hierarchies through careful consideration of pottery purchases. It was much easier for Stubbs to order a mixed crate at a set price and distribute whatever ceramics arrived among his household and those of the enslaved.[122] Because of difficult supply lines, African-descended people on Stubbs's plantation had an array of European pottery at their disposal.

The enslaved tried to exercise what choice they could over ceramics and their use. At the Brimstone Hill Fortress in St. Kitts in the 1790s, slaves scratched patterns into the glaze of creamware plates, bowls, and other items to claim ownership and to express their aesthetic sensibilities.[123] On the western end of New Providence Island, an enslaved family purchased European wares that differed from the master's, preferring another color palette and edge decoration. Several mismatched teacups at the site indicate West African foodways, as they could be used as vessels for sundry condiments central to West African cooking and for the consumption of stews, soups, and teas (thin broths) still prominent today in Afro-Bahamian cuisine.[124] Like others in the early modern Atlantic world, enslaved people obtained European-made pottery, whenever possible, to create meaningful material worlds for themselves.[125]

It is doubtful that Wedgwood and merchants like the Thellussons were aware of the pottery preferences of enslaved inhabitants in the Caribbean, or of the creative applications to which they put their choices. But they provide further insight into why the Thellussons' endeavor had such potential for a payoff—more than they realized. Although it is unclear how well this specific venture fared, the example emphasizes how revolutions could open new markets for seemingly old goods. With some variation, inhabitants in North America, France, and the Caribbean consumed the same types of ceramic wares, which accommodated customers whose sympathies ran from royalist to revolutionary, pro-slavery to abolitionist. Manufacturers like Wedgwood desired this kind of consistency, a "universality" of fashion within a range, to ensure that the goods they produced would sell. As Wedgwood put it, the aim was to offer "variety enough for our reasonable customers."[126] This parameter was crucial, given the distance that wares had to travel and the time it took to get them to markets, both of which became erratic during war and revolution.

Individual manufacturers sought to channel choice, but restriction was generated from below as well. Revolutionaries were unwilling to challenge or reject outright standards of taste, even when they had an opening to do so. With decorative wares, what many buyers wanted was greater access to existing goods. In some instances, the very process of acquisition—for example, with enslaved people and Queen's ware—was an act that challenged the status quo, defying the social and racial hierarchies that sought to curb their abilities as consumers. And for individuals across the spectrum—from disgruntled Frenchmen to Caribbean planters to North American patriots—they all discovered in manufactured decorative wares an outlet for their various views on revolutions. The very flexibility of these wares made them a boon to consumers and manufacturers in a tumultuous age.

The case of British manufacturers and their goods widens our perception of the points of intersection between material culture and politics. On the one hand, developments in industry, politics, and consumption had progressed to such a degree that the production of a distinctive item like a No Stamp Act teapot was possible—those new, rehabilitated wares that revolutionaries promoted. On the other hand, they do not represent the most common way that decorative wares became politicized in this era because they were not really desired in the Atlantic marketplace—by manufacturers or by most consumers. The making, distribution, and uses of these items discouraged political ornamentation.

Continuity, rather than novelty, was the source of political possibility in decorative wares, as people found greater versatility by procuring goods already in production. The exact content of the challenge depended on who obtained what, where, and when, but whatever the context, eighteenth-century actors argued through these items that they were entitled to join in wider social, economic, and political trends. The power of their calls was compelling because of the common wellspring of material culture on which they drew. Shared understandings of decorative wares made clear the competing visions of different sectors—those of enslaved versus free, of commoners versus elites, and so on—about who could participate in this revolutionary world in process, and on what terms. These assertions, and the debates surrounding them, became more emphatic when individuals did not just buy into a world of goods but seized it from others as part of realizing their political agendas.

2   Seizing the Status Quo

PERIOD DESCRIPTIONS OF revolutions, particularly those penned by their opponents, frequently highlight damage to property. Saint-Domingue is the prime example. As planter Bryan Edwards bemoaned in his 1797 history of the island, the insurrection of 1791 transformed in "a few dismal hours the most fertile and beautiful plains in the world . . . into one vast field of carnage;—a wilderness of desolation!"[1] While the wreckage was real, it was not, as Edwards implied, indiscriminate. As Black people fought for freedom, they struck out at plantations and other places that had perpetuated their oppression. Admittedly, in eighteenth-century Saint-Domingue there were a lot of these sites, and pro-slavery and racist observers like Edwards claimed that this scale was evidence of the rebels' abandon. But as with Parisians who stormed the Bastille or New Yorkers who dismantled the statue of George III, revolutionaries in the French colony destroyed strategically whenever possible. Their violence against specific categories of things and spaces was a form of iconoclasm that Atlantic revolutionaries saw as necessary to overturning standing orders and establishing better ones.[2]

In all three revolutions, a calculated approach to devastation was essential to an important war tactic: the confiscation of property. For centuries, seizure was a common means through which material culture circulated in times of unrest. Governments and militaries encouraged the practice, within certain parameters, because it debilitated and humiliated foes and enriched victors.[3] Various mechanisms facilitated the appropriation of goods during wartime. Governments granted commissions to civilian vessels, called privateers, that allowed them to attack the enemy's commercial ships in return for a sizable portion of the spoils.[4] Their actions complemented those of navies and armies, for which every victory was not only a strategic triumph but also a potential financial boon, as the vanquished forfeited possessions in defeat. Throughout the revolutions, governments authorized the seizure of property from civilian traitors to neutralize their influence and to punish their treachery.

While each mode had unique features, the windfall for captors, regardless of the specific manner of confiscation, came in two guises: they could keep appropriated wares for their own use, or they could sell them. In the eighteenth century, provisions and military and naval stores fell most often into the first category, as did discrete items that individuals pilfered during raids. But the lion's share of profit from confiscations came from hawking articles on the secondhand market. As one deputy vendue master explained, "A British military invasion proclaims a kind of fair, which is welcome in the West Indies. The variety of things arriving for sale, and the wider markets opened to produce, increase circulation."[5]

The American, French, and Haitian revolutions separated possessions from their owners on an unprecedented scale, and the secondhand market united those objects with eager consumers throughout the Atlantic world. Arguably, when considering issues of social and economic change, land and real estate were the most substantial property that changed hands. But moveable property is revealing because of its mobility. Many secondhand objects crossed borders and oceans, and in so doing, they demonstrate Atlantic circuits of property transfer in very concrete ways. Not all confiscated objects attracted foreign buyers: religious items impounded during the French Revolution and goods taken from North American loyalists, for instance, stayed closer to home. And individuals kept items as trophies of their exploits. But objects with transnational ambits help us analyze why and how some confiscated things had Atlantic resonance, and they also draw attention to the broad range of actors who participated in their dispersal. Land-based plunder, which involved greater numbers of people than that at sea, reveals the scope of this engagement. Pillaging and the market for ransacked objects drew in everyone from enslaved people in Saint-Domingue to aspiring elites in the United States to aristocrats in Great Britain. All took part in property seizures as captors, sellers, or consumers, and sometimes all three. These populations are usually not considered in the same material culture rubric, and yet with plunder we see how they shared understandings of its value and of its economic prospects for resale.

In an era of revolutions, this bonanza had political repercussions in two respects. By laying claim to widely appreciated goods, some actors, especially people of African descent, rising republican rulers, and commoners, asserted that they were worthy owners. In so doing, they challenged social and racial hierarchies surrounding these items, as some individuals did with new decorative wares. But seizure, as a means of acquisition, added a political dimension different from that of purchasing. While an accepted practice, plunder provoked controversy because every stage of a pillaged item's movement—from appropriation to sale to use—was associated not just with war but with revolution. Property confiscations raised thorny questions about the motivations of participants. Did justice or greed guide militaries, governments, and others who profited from plunder? The answer to this oft-repeated question mattered to all sides of these conflicts because they jockeyed for military supremacy, economic advantage, *and* the moral high ground. Since revolutions opposed the status quo because of its alleged lack of virtue (among other crimes), instances of plunder became flashpoints for sectors looking to prove or disprove republicans' contentions.

The heated discussions over procurement informed the consumption of confiscated items, as the case of revolutionary France shows vividly. There, republican governments launched an ambitious campaign to sell internationally millions of luxury goods—furniture, porcelain, pier glasses—commandeered from aristocrats, royals, and their sympathizers. Compared to the more ordinary, albeit valuable, things that soldiers filched, these wares represent a rarefied clientele, which is one of the reasons we can trace them: they were prized among collectors then and ever since.[6] Nevertheless, thanks to the French Revolution, these luxury goods became accessible to a wider swath of buyers; the new owners were still elites, but not necessarily of the highest cadre, and some were avowed republicans.

Moreover, the mode of selling of these items, usually at auctions, attracted the attention of the public, which, even if its members could not afford the goods on offer, had opinions about what they meant. In preparation for these public sales, French revolutionaries tried to disassociate these articles from their ancién regime origins; yet they struggled to impose on this material culture their sense of what was politically suspect. The motivations of consumers underscore the difficulties in reframing these items according to revolutionaries' categories. Many buyers were attracted to French luxury goods for the sheer pleasure of indulgence, the frisson sparked by owning something so coveted and of such pedigree. This desire intersected with assorted political outlooks: from those who revered the royals to those who supported the revolution (in varying degrees) to those who simply relished the enemy's spoils. In other words, these ancien régime wares remained obstinately present as actors wrestled to determine to what extent and on what terms they were willing to renounce the past in their material worlds.

THE POLITICS OF PILLAGING

In the spring of 1781, the London publisher Edward Hedges advertised a new satirical print, *The Late Auction at St. Eustatia* (figure 2.1). The British capture of the Dutch Caribbean colony of St. Eustatius in February had been a cause for celebration—a bright spot in a frustrating war. But the two commanders in charge of the campaign, Admiral Sir George Rodney and General John Vaughan, soon elicited criticism when they spent over three months ransacking the island and auctioning the spoils, purportedly to the detriment of their military mission. The print lampoons the commanders' dogged involvement in the secondhand market. Rodney stands at the rostrum, asking for any advance on the 22 shillings already bid for a pair of shoe buckles. An international cast of buyers—a Spaniard, a Frenchman, and a Dutchman—mill about the room, and one asks Vaughan, who is busy tallying the profits from the previous day's sales, whether he might purchase naval stores and provisions "that were formerly mine" and ship them to a "neutral island." Vaughan replies that the man can do anything he likes—for a "good price."

The Late Auction at St. Eustatia lays bare Rodney and Vaughan's avarice to comic effect. Rodney works the room to drive up bids on

Figure 2.1. *The Late Auction at St. Eustatia* (London: E. Hedges, June 11, 1781). (Courtesy of the John Carter Brown Library.)

the smallest of items, and both men are willing to sell to enemies, as long as the price is right. With humorous exaggeration, the satire of the situation on St. Eustatius taps into important controversies over plunder in this period. Militaries and governments walked a fine line between pillaging for strategic ends and doing so for personal gain, and the print draws attention to three crucial aspects of this balancing act: what was seized and sold, from whom it was taken, and who bought it. While these concerns had animated debates over military plundering in other eras, they took on heightened significance in the late eighteenth century, when revolutionaries attributed the necessity of their political movements in part to the corruption of ruling regimes.

Plunder turned a profit because there was an active Atlantic marketplace for secondhand goods. In the early modern period, the trade in previously owned items was as substantial, in volume and worth, as the retail market, and some scholars speculate that the sale of old wares surpassed that of new.[7] Not all this activity resulted from plunder, but the lively secondhand market supplied a ready and familiar mechanism through which to dispense with and profit from seized goods. Several outlets offered secondhand commodities, sometimes alongside new ones. Newspapers included almost daily advertisements for auctions of the property of debtors, of the deceased, and of people leaving town to try their luck elsewhere. These sales were community events that enticed a cross section of buyers, and anything and everything was sold. Auctions were a major channel for distributing new items, too. If a merchant needed to unload cargo quickly, he flogged it to a crowd of storekeepers and other merchants who bought goods to fill out their stock. At times individuals attended these cargo sales, seeking items in bulk for personal use. When Sarah Kemble Knight, an Englishwoman traveling through North America, wanted reams of a specific type of Dutch writing paper, she found it at a vendue sale (a type of wholesale auction). In cities, pawnshops provided another means through which used items circulated, and some retailers, like jewelers and dry goods merchants, offered previously owned articles and recently manufactured wares. This practice was prevalent in rural areas, where stores were fewer.[8]

Authorities throughout the Atlantic world were aware of the significant traffic in secondhand goods, and they sought to regulate it. In France, auctioneers purchased their positions from the king, a system that theoretically guaranteed the integrity and controlled the number of auctioneers, while in colonial North America, appointed vendue masters kept order and ensured fair pricing, or at least they were supposed to.[9] Worried about the trade in stolen items, lawmakers in several early U.S. cities prohibited secondhand dealers and pawnbrokers, especially those in the furniture, metal, and clothing trades, from accepting articles from minors, apprentices, servants, and slaves.[10] Given the extensiveness of the secondhand market and the limits of early modern bureaucracy, though, these directives were impossible to enforce completely.

In this way, secondhand wares were essential to experiencing the world of goods. As the range of venues and attempts at regulation suggest, eighteenth-century consumers were as accustomed to buying goods at auctions, pawnshops, and dealers as they were at shops and stores. Part of the appeal of the secondhand market was the possibility of a bargain, and this prospect drew patrons from across the social spectrum.[11] There was something for every budget and every yearning.

Formerly owned goods of all sorts—from refined mahogany furniture to lowly tinware—turned up in the secondhand market.

That said, buying a used object did not necessarily mean that its value was less than that of a new thing. Some secondhand items suffered from wear and tear, and so their worth (in economic terms) declined. However, certain articles were as good as money because they held value, were in demand, and could be readily sold no matter where one went. When exiles from revolutionary Saint-Domingue, for example, fled the island to various places in North America and the Caribbean, they took with them as much silver and as many textiles as they could carry. Slaves, servants, and soldiers on the lam traveled with bundles of clothing—to disguise themselves by switching prominent garments but also to hawk them (despite prohibitory laws) to bankroll their flight.[12]

The dynamism of the secondhand marketplace accounts for the lucrative potential of plunder. Government authorities, high-ranking officers, common soldiers, and revolutionary rioters: all understood the possible financial boon to be realized by selling secondhand goods. There was, though, a protocol to plunder during war. Militaries first seized items of immediate benefit to their forces. Soon after taking over St. Eustatius, Rodney and Vaughan followed standard practice and shipped military supplies—ammunition, cordage, linen, lumber—to commissaries throughout the British Caribbean. In Saint-Domingue, commentators noted how Black armies favored horses, farm animals, weapons, ammunition, and tools when raiding plantations and ports.[13] At one moment in the French Revolution, administrators ordered the collection of fifty thousand mattresses from émigré homes for soldiers at the front.[14] This prioritization makes sense. To fight effectively, armies and navies had to keep their ranks constantly fed, clothed, and armed, and in North American and Caribbean theaters, production and supply lines were difficult to sustain. Pillaging filled in the gaps and in the process weakened enemies.

Too many plundered goods were as problematic as too few, however. Shortly after the capture of St. Eustatius, Mr. Laforey, the commissioner of the yard in Antigua, complained that his warehouses were bursting with naval stores from the Dutch colony—so much so that Laforey proposed flogging the surplus.[15] His recommendation underscores that the option to sell was crucial to pillaging. In this case, sale relieved the burden of overstock, but its role was even more central. When ransacking any site, plunderers gathered materials with an eye as much to their salability as to their instant utility. British military officials in St. Eustatius hoarded diverse commodities. From the storehouses of merchants, they seized valuable produce: casks of sugar, coffee, and tobacco.[16] But they also collected women's French heels, silk gloves, girls' morocco pumps, petticoats, shoe buckles, parcels of lace and ribbons, napkins and tablecloths, and "25 Shirts trimmed with stitched Cambrick Rufles."[17] Edward Hedges's print was nearer to the truth than he imagined: it mocked the commanding officers for selling not only shoe buckles but also, according to the notice tacked on the wall, "Sundry Hats Buttons Gloves Umbrellas Wigs Sleeve Buttons &c taken from the Inhabitants of this Island"—a list too close to the mark for Rodney and Vaughan's comfort.

Although we typically do not think of soldiers and sailors snapping up girls' pumps and ruffled shirts as spoils of war, it is not surprising that Rodney and Vaughan, as elites, had a sense of their market value and ordered their confiscation and sale. Moreover, in the Dutch colony, most of the loot came from its famous warehouses, which stretched across the lower town for over a mile. For decades, St. Eustatius had operated as a free port where vessels from various empires weighed anchor to trade. As a result, its mercantile population was cosmopolitan, and its goods originated from across the globe.[18] The unique situation in St. Eustatius meant that Rodney and Vaughan were collecting many new commodities that merchants had already deemed profitable on the Atlantic market.

The tactics of plunder in St. Eustatius represent the extreme (in amount and worth) of a typical trend. Other armies and navies looked for this low-hanging fruit, taking and selling merchant stock whenever possible. During the battle of Le Cap in 1793, men of African descent, "under the cover of the darkness, the disorder, and the paralysis of their masters," systematically emptied the richest storehouses on Place Clugny and Place d'Armes.[19] A Boston merchant who witnessed the event described its coordination:

> The seaboard was now lined with black troops on horseback, with long lines of mules tied to each other by their tails, and accompanied by black drivers. These mules . . . were at once loaded with the dry-goods and other articles easily transported from our stores. When one set was charged and led off, another line was brought up and loaded,

until all the articles from the stores and houses that could be thus carried away were sent off to the country. The whole bay for nearly three
quarters of a mile was stripped of its merchandise; and other parts of
town were doubtless plundered in the same manner.[20]

Rather than unbridled looting, Black armies selected and gathered what
they wanted in an orderly fashion—and to good effect, as estimates of
this haul's value ranged from 3,000 to 10,000 livres.[21]

The same approach—namely, the appraisal of goods for their potential gain in the secondhand market—informed seizures of property
from private estates. As we shall see, this practice had distinctive features in the French case, but it was prevalent throughout the Atlantic
world. White Saint-Dominguans griped about losing clothing, silver,
and books to Black revolutionaries.[22] In North America, Black loyalist soldiers took "everything valuable" from patriot homes, in one instance "bedding, wearing apparel, liquors, a watch, a stock of poultry,
and . . . two Negro girls."[23] Patriots retaliated in kind, appropriating
and selling the household goods of suspected loyalists. Martha Phillips
of Boston attested in her memorial to the Loyalist Claims Commission that "her Effects and household Furniture . . . were unlawfully
seized upon and the profit of them appropriated" for the rebels' use.
She submitted a list of over £500 worth of property that, in her words,
had been "plundered": large and small looking glasses, pictures "Gilt
framed & Glazed," "China & Glass," two dozen walnut chairs, and
so on.[24] Another petitioner, Benjamin Marston, Esq., presented an account from the auction of his seized moveable property, enumerating
items from a spinet that went for £30 to "4 Stone Dishes" that sold for
15 shillings.[25]

While descriptions and prints of wanton crowds ransacking private
homes proliferated, plundering was, as these episodes indicate, often organized, with authorities supervising the proceedings. In North
America, patriot committees oversaw the confiscation, valuation, and
auctioning of loyalist property, and during each phase of the French
Revolution, administrators did the same with enemies of the state. In
military seizures soldiers in all armies acted on the orders of superior
officers.[26] In these scenarios, the identification of items came at the
behest of men of some standing—individuals familiar with the ins and
outs of the consumers' world.

But in the process of appropriating property for authorities, people invariably lifted items for themselves. These thefts played into victims' cries of injustice and accusations of the moral waywardness of plunderers, which had political currency in the age of revolutions, yet they also reveal that members of the lower sort knew the resale potential of material culture. Joseph Donaldson of the firm Wallace, Donaldson, and Smith recounted that when a group of sailors and artillerymen came to seize naval and military stores from his warehouse in St. Eustatius, they "did take out of the said Store several Pieces of Checks, Irish Linens, Fine Holland Linen, Chintzes, and other Goods for their own use."[27] This last phrase could have been literal: the men took the textiles for their clothing. However, chintz, an imported cotton fabric decorated with lively floral motifs, was used more typically for bed coverings and women's clothing than for military men's attire. As such, the men probably intended to sell it, and perhaps some of the other fabrics, too. Sailors frequently traveled with small trunks of goods that they hawked when docked in ports in order to supplement their meager incomes, and they knew that textiles were desirable.[28]

The cognizance of the market value of items is most striking among people of African descent, demonstrating how well they understood aspects of material culture associated almost exclusively with the master class. Throughout the Haitian Revolution, white observers tried to deny that Black people had such knowledge, and yet various episodes belie these denials. In the fall of 1791, a planter on the northern plain returned to his plantation to find that rebels had destroyed everything except one building, which was inhabited by a local leader of the insurrection. The enslaved had stocked it with the planter's best furniture, all of which was "carefully maintained"—a sign that they appreciated its worth.[29] Often white commentators attempted to undercut the radical overtones of these appropriations through mockery. In representations of Black insurgents in "white" or "European" clothing, accounts played up the incongruity of their appearance as they incorporated garments from ex-masters and mistresses. The result, in the eyes of white observers, verged on the carnivalesque. In the 1795 engraving *Pillage du Cap Français en 1793*, people of African descent fill the foreground, looting and sporting recently acquired garments (figure 2.2). The odd combinations indicate the newness of possession and the failure to wear the articles in ways that white viewers considered proper: fancy coats

Figure 2.2. Detail from *Pillage du Cap Français en 1793* (Paris, 1795). The wagon is filled with goods, including furniture and household wares, and Black soldiers appropriate hats, coats, and other military honorifics. (Courtesy of the John Carter Brown Library.)

paired with ragged trousers and bare feet; a metal gorget with a toga; short skirts and elaborate hats; and towering wigs worn with shifts.

In this derogatory depiction, clothing reveals the remarkable extent to which the planters' world has been turned upside down. Suddenly, people who purportedly cannot respect these items, let alone use them correctly, have them in their possession. A few impeccably dressed white figures in the print make this dissonance evident. White observers exaggerated the absurdity of ensembles for racist and political ends, but the outlandish representations deserve deeper scrutiny. During the revolution, commentators drew attention to the large number of military coats and honorifics (epaulets, elaborate hats, and so forth) that Black men adopted. Several figure in *Pillage du Cap*, and it is a common remark in written sources. One white creole soldier recalled meeting a man of African descent who was "dressed in a jacket of ticking [a material used for covering mattresses or furniture], upon which showed the two epaulets of a General."[30]

The fixation on coats, epaulets, and the like suggests that Black people were familiar with the hierarchy of garments, especially their monetary value and cultural prestige. These items were expensive and signaled rank, regiment, and other trappings of distinction. They had practical applications, too, as men of African descent organized into armies, helping to demarcate units, differentiate officers from foot soldiers, and so forth. In other words, the formerly enslaved in Saint-Domingue went consistently for the garments of greatest worth (in all senses of the word—economic, cultural, and military). In so doing, they exhibited an awareness of so-called European mores and markets. This display of knowledge—in the cases of clothing and of furniture—had political import, as it challenged racist notions that denigrated the capacity of people of African descent to comprehend the "finer" points of "civilization."

These examples of pillaging by nonelites indicate another important aspect of plundering that shaped the phenomenon and its political ramifications: whose property was seized. Only official enemies were legitimate targets for pillaging, but war made this difficult to discern in practice. Allegiances shifted, and neutrality was precarious; as a result, identifying a foe could be a slippery endeavor. For instance, some residents in port towns occupied by the British during the American Revolution supported the imperial regime at first but became disaffected by strict policies and occasional abuse (including pillaging) and switched sides.[31]

Determining who was loyal and who was treacherous was even trickier in revolutionary Saint-Domingue. Planters and merchants protested that the seizure of their property by Black armies was unjust on two grounds: Black troops were not legitimate soldiers (they were rebel slaves), and they, as white colonists, were not enemies of the French nation but members of it. This interpretation failed to sway the metropole after 1794, when Black men were declared free and citizens, and many fought on the island in the name of the French republic. But during the Leclerc expedition of 1801, white colonists' arguments gained traction. As part of the attempted reconquest of the island, French soldiers looted the homes of Black leaders in retaliation: Toussaint Louverture's estate, Ennery, was ransacked; officers and troops lifted clothing, furniture, art, and jewelry. Jean-Jacques Dessalines decided to burn his property near Saint-Marc to the ground rather than see it fall into the hands of the enemy.[32] After Haitian independence, former white owners continued to claim victimization, and in the 1820s, the Haitian government was compelled to pay indemnities to them for property destroyed or appropriated during the revolution. In exchange, France officially recognized the nation's independence.[33]

While the controversies over legitimate targets of seizures in Saint-Domingue took decades to resolve, British petitioners in St. Eustatius had quicker success with their appeals. They based their protest on their rights as Englishmen, for, with the capture of the Dutch colony, King George III had ordered that "such effects as shall be proved to be the Property of British subjects, lawfully exported thither" were exempt from seizure.[34] But Rodney contended that British merchants in St. Eustatius were not good subjects. According to Dutch law, merchants from foreign countries could obtain the privileges of "burghers" after living in the colony for eighteen months. Rodney found it galling that "Men, who once had the Honour of being Englishmen . . . debased and forfeited that Name when they made themselves Dutch Burghers.—As such they are and shall be treated, and their whole Property confiscated." In letter after letter, he blamed "those calling themselves British Merchants" for perpetuating the war in North America by supplying the rebels, forsaking their country with their "iniquitous Practices" and "treasonable Correspondence and Assistance."[35]

They were, in short, enemies, and convinced by his own logic, Rodney commandeered their property and began to auction it. In formal complaints to administrators, petitioners emphasized that they were indeed Britons and therefore the seizures and sales violated their rights. Their arguments proved credible to some at the metropole and farther afield. Edmund Burke questioned what he saw as the specious treatment of Britons on St. Eustatius, proclaiming in the House of Commons that "there had been no distinction of country" with the confiscations.[36] An account from the *Amsterdam Gazette* (reprinted in London papers) declared that the "conduct of the English conquerers . . . [is] such, as all other civilized nations would be ashamed to be guilty of," and then noted that "even the English subjects who had connections with that island, have fallen victim to their rapacity."[37] Such interpretations drummed up sympathy for the Dutch and the British in St. Eustatius, and they validated claims of rebellious North Americans by delivering yet another instance of the British government trampling on the rights of Britons in the colonies.

In these theaters, the targets of seizure deployed the language of rights (as either subjects or citizens) to defend their property, and although this rhetorical move was not necessarily new, its resonance was all the more striking in an era when wars were fought to some degree over who possessed rights and which ones. The question of loyalty and the rights and privileges derived from that loyalty became even more contentious as observers debated how ransacked goods were sold and to whom. The quantity of items was so great in St. Eustatius that Rodney and Vaughan adopted an enterprising approach to attract bidders. Notices of the auctions, set to begin on March 15, 1781, appeared in French, North American, and Caribbean newspapers along with the guarantee that "All persons coming to this Island for the purpose of purchasing goods at the Sales will be permitted to pass freely to and from the Islands, without . . . molestation."[38] As critics pointed out, these generous conditions meant that the commanders could sell prizes to foes. Later that year, the *Whitehall Evening Post* published an account of a parliamentary debate, in which a member alleged: "Our Admiral and General who took the island, had ten times better have burnt the stores they found there, than have done what they did with them. They had sold them to go in neutral vessels, so that they fell into the hands of the very people from whom it was pretended they were kept." The repercussions of the sales were greater than provisioning the enemy; they had led to a major military defeat. Another member of Parliament concluded, "The capture of Lord Cornwallis [at Yorktown in the fall of 1781] was owing to the capture of St. Eustatius."[39] The practical and ideological fallout was significant.

During the Haitian Revolution, the sale of seized goods took on racial politics. In the early days of the rebellion, Spanish officials in Santo Domingo abetted the military aims of the newly forming Black armies. They reasoned that Black soldiers would so disrupt the French colony that the Spanish empire could capitalize on the disarray, supersede Black forces, and claim the other side of the island. For their part, Black armies acquired from the Spanish some items necessary for their campaigns by bringing plunder to Santo Domingo. These dealings across the border were one of the benefits of their clandestine partnership. But the relationship was uneasy, as Spanish officials struggled to contain the Black auxiliaries, whose fidelity to Spain was in constant doubt. Ties strained further when Spanish colonial officials could not keep pace with Black troops' insistent demands for supplies. Making the politics of plunder more fraught, authorities discovered that soldiers in Cuban regiments stationed in Santo Domingo bought from Black auxiliaries thousands of pesos' worth of furniture, jewels, plate, and sugar-processing equipment—all pillaged from estates and warehouses in Saint-Domingue.[40]

Authorities in Santo Domingo decided that the lure of plundered goods was eroding their chance to control Black forces. After the summer of 1793, when the recently arrived French colonial commissioners, Léger-Félicité Sonthonax and Étienne Polverel, offered emancipation to any slave willing to fight on their side, the provisionally Spanish Black auxiliaries opened contact with French republicans.[41] Rather than carrying out Spanish orders, then, Black armies had their own agendas when it came to leveraging plunder. On the one hand, their maneuvers speak to their savviness about what was salable in the secondhand market and how to take advantage of that venue to support a political and military cause determined to overturn the planters' world in Saint-Domingue. On the other hand, this subversive potential was circumscribed in that buyers used these items (like sugar equipment shipped from Hispaniola to Cuba) to bolster slavery elsewhere.

For all its financial promise, the acquisition and sale of plunder raised a series of politically contested issues during the revolutionary era. Pillaging, in its various phases, sparked discussions over rights and over political loyalties, and in the case of Saint-Domingue, it challenged racist hierarchies. At the heart of these battles over who seized what property and sold it to whom lay a fundamental moral issue: greed. Atlantic observers were not naïve. They knew that the quest for personal wealth motivated men to go forth and conquer. For soldiers and sailors, their fortunes could literally rise with that of the nation for which they fought. Some defended the practice of pillaging as just desserts: men risked their lives for their country, and they deserved some reward for it. When Louverture's troops retook Port-Républicain and Saint-Marc from the British, for example, he promised his army one-quarter of the profits from the sale of seized goods as recompense for their sacrifice.[42] This was a standard practice in wartime, and governments welcomed

such arrangements since the sale of plunder generated funds that allevi-
ated the financial pressure on governments to remunerate their forces.

Yet in an age of republican revolutions, when virtue was bandied
about prominently, confiscated goods brought out the contradictions
surrounding the profit motive of plundering. Officially, the government
was the chief beneficiary of confiscated items, but opportunities for individual gain were built into the system. This accommodation is most
transparent with privateers, who received a large proportion of the
cargo of any captured vessel, although they were required to hand over
a percentage to the government. With military and government confiscations, the seized property was, technically, the possession of the state.
From the outset in St. Eustatius, Rodney and Vaughan professed that
they acted under the assumption that "the whole was the Property of
the Crown," and they "had no Views whatever but doing our Duty."[43]
Rodney and Vaughan's experiences in the military—and those of every
other soldier and sailor in the Atlantic world—contradict this assertion. They knew the likelihood that they (as well as other members of
their forces) would receive a substantial portion of the loot.[44] When
Rodney first arrived in the Dutch colony, he breathlessly reported to
his wife, "The riches of St. Eustatius are beyond all comprehension . . .
the capture is prodigious; and I speak within bounds when I say, more
than two millions sterling."[45]

Sure enough, Rodney and Vaughan learned that the king, in recognition of their conquest, awarded all enemy property (with the exceptions of that of legitimate British merchants and military stores) to the
army and navy, divided according to rank. Given the amount of goods
on St. Eustatius, the commanders' individual takeaway promised to be
impressive, and disparaging remarks soon surfaced about their bald
desire for personal gain. Having secured the island, the commanders stayed on to oversee the seizures and sales rather than, as was the
norm, delegating the job to subordinates. Admiral Samuel Hood, Rodney's second in command, groused, "Notwithstanding they [Rodney
and Vaughan] talk aloud of their disregard of money, they will find it
very difficult to convince the world that they have not proved themselves wickedly rapacious."[46]

The question of plunder at St. Eustatius and elsewhere was not simply about the grasping nature of the men involved. Some contended
that it reflected poorly on the nation, and a series of articles in the

London Courant pointed out the pitfalls. Although acknowledging the "riches" gained at St. Eustatius, one writer observed, "It has at the same time completely irritated all other nations against [the British], as it furnishes fresh proof of their rapacity, which always makes them precede their declarations of war by secret orders to attack the enemy, and to seize their property before they are in the least aware of any hostile intentions."[47] (The British had held off proclaiming war against the Dutch until Rodney's ships were well on their way to the colony.) The deception behind the capture promoted further conflicts among the European powers—at a price so high that the spoils could not offset it. The cost was actual *and* figurative. According to another observer, "Not only the laws of nations, but the rights of humanity, have been most scandalously violated."[48] Because of the underhanded nature of the seizure, all the island's inhabitants—not only the British merchants—were victims of theft.

These articles suggest that everything about the affair was sordid—from the acquisition of the goods to the treatment of unsuspecting inhabitants to its role in the perpetuation of war. While the scale of plunder in St. Eustatius made it unique, its ideological sticking points were representative of the moment. George Washington wrestled with the political damage of pillaging as he laid down rules for the Continental Army. In the fall of 1776, he heard "many complaints that are hourly made of plundering both public and private property."[49] In one case, a group of men ransacked a house of its valuables, including "four large Peer looking Glasses—Womens Cloaths, and other Articles which one would think, could be of no Earthly use to [them]." When ordered to return the goods, the ringleader "not only peremptorily refused to do, but drew up his Party and swore he would defend them at the hazard of his Life."[50] Faced with repeated insubordination on this score, Washington demanded that officers search soldiers' bags and tents for pillaged goods, whip any transgressors on the spot, and report all instances to the chain of command.[51] Washington's concerns were twofold: first, that plundering might drive residents over to the enemy camp, and second, that if virtue was one of the fundamental qualities necessary for the formation of republican citizens, then the military had to practice what the new United States preached.[52]

For Black armies the debate around pillaging was even more charged because of racism. In revolutionary Saint-Domingue, white critics of emancipation maintained that Black people "were not made for freedom," and part of their alleged proof for this specious conclusion came from Black soldiers' supposed penchant for "pillage and plunder." It was trotted out as dubious evidence that Black people were "only capable of violence and criminality, which runs in their blood."[53] Sensitive to the political harm of these accusations, Black generals prohibited plundering, except on express command, and meted out the death penalty to any soldier or officer found guilty of pillaging without permission. Troops were encouraged to report any unauthorized instance of plundering they witnessed, however small. In one extraordinary episode after a battle near Mirabelais, Louverture stopped a caravan of white colonists who were leaving the area with two hundred horses carrying their possessions, including people they claimed as slaves. He interviewed the white Saint-Dominguans to find out if his soldiers had taken any belongings; after discovering they had not, Louverture let the white colonists pass with their property—except the Black people, whom he released.[54]

When it came to pillaging, leaders of both the patriot and Saint-Dominguan armies tried to instill restraint among their troops so that they could claim the virtue associated with republican men and their rights. But this discipline was difficult to maintain because of the deprivation militaries faced; armies and navies needed pillaged goods to sustain men and by extension the causes for which they fought. Beyond necessity, plunder was a long-standing component of the profits of war, and Atlantic revolutions instigated opportunities for it. People of all sorts got into the act—from established militaries to those that were just developing, comprised of former slaves in Saint-Domingue and former colonists in North America. Their experiences demonstrate the centrality of the secondhand market for facilitating the movement of goods and for disseminating knowledge about their value. This broad participation introduced new conversations about an old practice and about "old" goods themselves, raising their political and ideological stakes. These debates had important repercussions, not only on the supply side of pillaging but for the consumers of confiscated goods as well.

SELLING THE OLD REGIME

On an early summer afternoon in 1795, Elizabeth Drinker, a member of the Quaker elite in Philadelphia, went with her friend Nancy Morgan to a clock shop. Clocks, although expensive, had become somewhat standard items in the parlors of the upper and middle classes across the Atlantic world. They were not necessarily popular for their function of keeping time, since many inhabitants judged the day's progress by the sun and moon. Rather, a clock reflected the intellectual interests of its owner, demonstrating his or her access to the knowledge behind the object—the mechanics of crafting and maintaining it, and the currents of Enlightenment thought that embraced clock time for its efficiency. As a complicated and dear object, a clock signaled an owner's genteel ambitions.[55]

The women were not interested in making a purchase. Instead, they wanted to see a specific clock that had arrived from Europe and had caused a sensation in town. Drinker described it in her diary: "a very curious Clock and Organ . . . [that] plays twenty different tunes, stands on two large fluited mahogany pillars guilt." Rumor had it that when first completed, the clock had cost 1,000 guineas (£1,050) and had belonged to Marie-Antoinette. While in Paris as the U.S. minister to France, Gouverneur Morris had bought the clock for his longtime friend the financier Robert Morris for the reported bargain price of £500, and had it shipped to Philadelphia.[56] The clock was for Robert Morris's home, a grand, block-long and French-inspired structure under construction on Chestnut Street; there it joined other elegant furnishings: a mahogany sideboard, dining table, two card tables, china flowerpots, and several pictures and mirrors. According to a 1797 inventory, the clock was worth more than the rest of the front parlor furniture combined and was one of the most valuable pieces in Morris's estate, second only to four French carpets.[57]

Although the Morris/Marie-Antoinette musical clock was, as an object, extraordinary in many ways, it was emblematic of a broader trend of luxury secondhand goods moving out of revolutionary France and into the Atlantic world. Other revolutions distributed items across borders, but the French revolutionary confiscations afford the best opportunity to explore the consumption of pillaged goods. This is for two reasons: the quantity of goods seized by the government, and their irresistible appeal among a certain subset of consumers in Europe and the Americas. Beginning in late 1789, the French revolutionary regime confiscated the real and moveable property of the Catholic Church and, as the revolution radicalized, the net expanded to include émigrés and political criminals (*condamnés*), some of whom were the wealthi-est men and women in France. The most high-profile example was the royal family: the magnificent contents of their chateaux—Versailles, Fontainebleau, and Saint-Cloud, among others—became the property of the nation (*biens nationaux*), whose representatives decided to put it up for sale in order to defray debts and to fund the revolution.[58]

Elites and aspiring elites coveted these items. France was a mecca for sumptuous goods of the finest quality, and never had so many su-perb items arrived on the market at the same time. While these wares remained out of reach for many, they were purchased by—or, as with Drinker and her friend, seen by—a larger swath of people than be-fore the revolution. In fact, the revolutionary government counted on a wide dissemination as it sought to channel this veritable flood of opulence for the nation's benefit. Managing the bonanza, though, was a logistical and political challenge because the goods on offer, like the musical clock, were associated with what revolutionaries attempted to define, contemptuously, as the "ancien régime." They were the ma-terial embodiment of the very social and political world that repub-licans sought to eradicate.[59] Yet they needed these goods to remain valuable and desirable to consumers to buoy financially and ideologi-cally the republican project. As a result, the regime was caught in an ambivalent position, straddling the "old" and "new"—or, more accu-rately, that which they tried to make passé and that which they tried to establish as au courant. These ambivalent origins shaped consum-ers' experiences with these objects in France and beyond, as they saw these wares in terms that did not necessarily match the government's prescriptions.

French revolutionaries' decision to sell items affiliated with the so-called ancien régime was based on the supposition that there were ready consumers at home and abroad, and this assumption was at odds with the revolutionary project. In the early 1790s, French republican rhetoric emphasized sloughing off vestiges of the old order, including its extravagant material trappings. Angry crowds raided and destroyed property tied to the Catholic Church, aristocrats, and royals. In July and August 1792, for example, gleeful mobs sacked the Tuileries, the monarch's Paris residence, shredding tapestries, running bayonets through furniture, smashing porcelain and mirrors, and emptying the contents of the wine cellar into their stomachs.[60]

With their dissolute associations, old regime accoutrements threatened the rehabilitation of the nation; yet as objects, they were very valuable, and the revolutionary project was desperate for money.[61] One solution was to sell this royalist detritus to buyers outside of France, but for all the regime's aspirations to regeneration, it had a strong desire to conserve its cultural patrimony. In this vein, French representatives argued for a new way of understanding luxury goods. They contended that one must distinguish between the object and its owner: an owner might be corrupt, but the object itself was not. In fact, they maintained that these goods were the products of a glorious French civilization that had been, for decades, co-opted by the enemies of the people. In much the same way that citizens had reclaimed their nation from tyranny, their representatives had rescued France's cultural patrimony from despots and restored it to the people.[62]

From the start, administrators attempted to ensure that objects deemed significant—manuscripts, books, artifacts, artwork, and so on—were not destroyed or sold. They were transferred to a central depot in Paris with the intention that they would be preserved and displayed for the people's edification. Once a private palace, the Louvre was transformed into a public museum for this purpose. Some items were used in the offices and residences of revolutionary officials. In Years 4 and 5 (1795–97), the minister of the interior outfitted his family's apartment with over two hundred pieces of requisitioned furniture: "an ebony desk, the top covered with green leather with a frame of golden bronze," "a mahogany table à la francklin," and Sèvres dinnerware.[63] From the perspective of the government, this was material culture reclamation in action, as so-called ancien régime objects were serving the people. Yet it also shows how the material culture of the elite past folded easily into the republican present.

But the appropriation and repurposing of ancien régime luxury was harder to control as it was sold. Authorities touted the sale of *biens nationaux* as egalitarian in that the people acquired things previously unattainable, and in the process lent their financial support to the cause. Prior to the revolution, some commentators protested that auctions were a venue through which the middle and even lower classes had access to luxury goods, which blurred lines of social distinction. Female courtiers petitioned the French king to curb the "brazen usurpation and the temerarious enterprises of the Parisian bourgeoisie," who bought up so many elegant dresses at auction that they made it "impossible for the Ladies . . . to distinguish themselves . . . in clothes sufficiently more sumptuous as those worn by the common bourgeoisie."[64] What's interesting here is the circularity of the courtiers' argument: the woman relied on auctions to sell their older dresses (in order to afford new ones), yet they resented buyers for procuring and wearing them. Secondhand markets simultaneously buttressed and subverted social hierarchies.

French revolutionary officials tried to use the leveling possibilities of auctions to advantage. But the very act of selling *biens nationaux* drew on old regime practices and allusions that remained intractably front and center, no matter how hard the regime worked to change them. Given the staggering amount of goods, the government had to dispatch them quickly, and this meant that it had no choice but to auction them. The forum of the auction was itself problematic. Auctioneers had become suspect because of their ties to the Crown; they had been venal officers, a practice that came under fire as the number of these positions had grown markedly in the eighteenth century. Some critics saw auctioneers as prone to corruption; they were accused of manipulating bidding, price fixing, and taking bribes.[65]

Authorities attempted to mitigate these negative associations through new procedures. When assessing confiscated items, one set of administrators drafted an inventory, while another group ran the actual auction.[66] Before the sale, they were required to place notices in local newspapers as well as post broadsides in public (figure 2.3). The barrage of advertising was supposed to attract the largest pool of potential buyers, and this could have a democratizing impulse, inviting all into the circle of owners. It put forward an image of transparency, too: for a regime obsessed with uncloaking conspiracies, paperwork and publicity ensured the integrity of the auction.

In other ways as well the government sought to transform auctions into evidence of the republic in action. Broadsides listed not only important information about individual sales—time, date, location, and types of goods under the hammer—but also the names of previous owners, in bold capital letters, and the reason for the property seizure. The posters for "la femme Marbeuf" noted she was an émigré, Mr. Annisson-Duperron had been "condemned to death," and the king's cousin was listed simply, but correctively, as "Orléans (called

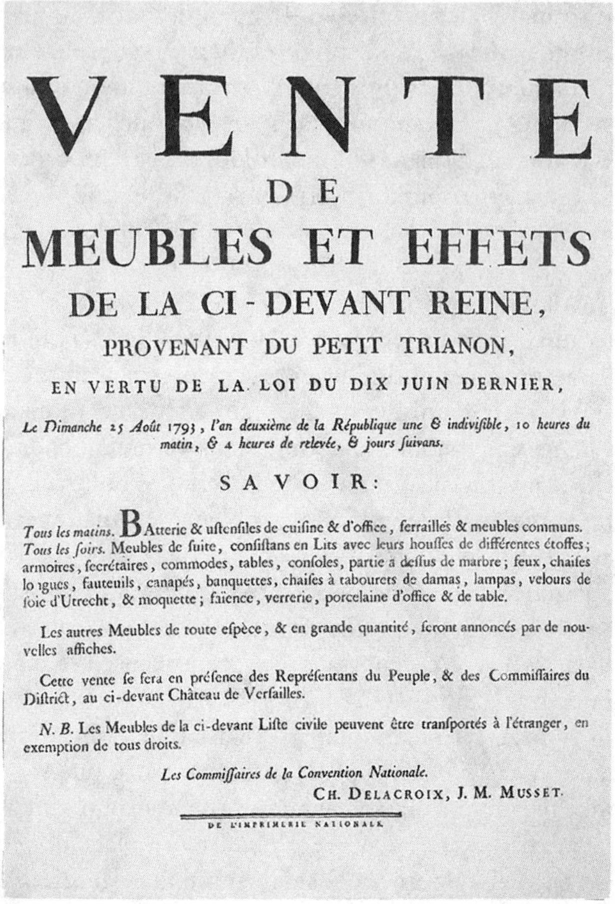
VENTE

DE

MEUBLES ET EFFETS

DE LA CI-DEVANT REINE,

PROVENANT DU PETIT TRIANON,

EN VERTU DE LA LOI DU DIX JUIN DERNIER,

Le Dimanche 25 Août 1793, l'an deuxième de la République une & indiviſible, 10 heures du matin, & 4 heures de relevée, & jours ſuivans.

SAVOIR:

Tous les matins. BAtterie & uſtenſiles de cuiſine & d'office, ferrailles & meubles communs.
Tous les ſoirs. Meubles de ſuite, conſiſtans en Lits avec leurs houſſes de différentes étoffes; armoires, ſecrétaires, commodes, tables, conſoles, partie à deſſus de marbre; feux, chaiſes longues, fauteuils, canapés, banquettes, chaiſes à tabourets de damas, lampas, velours de ſoie d'Utrecht, & moquette; faïence, verrerie, porcelaine d'office & de table.

Les autres Meubles de toute eſpèce, & en grande quantité, ſeront annoncés par de nouvelles affiches.

Cette vente ſe fera en préſence des Repréſentans du Peuple, & des Commiſſaires du Diſtrict, au ci-devant Château de Verſailles.

N. B. Les Meubles de la ci-devant Liſte civile peuvent être tranſportés à l'étranger, en exemption de tous droits.

Les Commiſſaires de la Convention Nationale.
CH. DELACROIX, J. M. MUSSET.

DE L'IMPRIMERIE NATIONALE.

Figure 2.3. Broadside: Sale of Goods and Effects from Petit Trianon, Paris, 1793. (Wallace Collection, London, UK © Wallace Collection, London, UK/Bridgeman Images.)

Égalité)."[67] The emphasis on the person and his or her crime made it clear that the auction was an exercise in revolutionary justice rather than a mundane estate sale.

That said, by advertising the names of former owners, the government deployed old regime ties to advantage. Certain people, like duc d'Orléans and Marie-Antoinette, were known for their excellent taste and impressive collections, and this cachet enhanced their goods' appeal.[68] Playing up the trappings of aristocracy was essential for realizing the best prices, a pressing concern for the regime, which needed substantial profits. Almost as soon as the auctions began, word circulated about exquisite goods being sold for far less than they were worth. The National Convention confronted these problems with a slew of laws in 1792 and 1793, but their application met with limited success.[69] There was too much property, and too many sales, to oversee.

In the meantime, officials continued to highlight the quality and provenance of goods in attempts to persuade bidders to dig deeply into their pocketbooks. A lengthy notice from an April 1793 auction shows how evocative these descriptions could be:

> Sale of furniture from a chateau in Chantilly, confiscated from the émigré Condé, consisting of a great number of beds—à la Turque, à la Polonaise, en niche, etc.; bed bases, mattresses of all sizes, Gobelins tapestries, drapes in silk, wool, toile; tables, secretaries, chests of drawers in marble, pier glasses, pictures and mirrors of various dimensions, clocks, sconces, chandeliers, fireplace equipment; curtains, ottomans, sofas, tiles, armchairs, stoves, cooking utensils; crystal, porcelain, and earthenware vases; linens and clothing of all sorts; wines from Balsac, Champagne, Cyprus, Spain, the Rhine, Malaga, etc.; games (billiards, bague, trictac), musical and scientific instruments; saddles, harnesses, theater decorations and costumes; orange trees and exotic shrubs; guns, feed, fodder, and a huge quantity of other precious and infinitely diverse objects.[70]

From the textiles and pier glasses to tropical plants and theater scenery, the advertisement conjures a world of affluence and leisure. It underscores the quality of goods: the prized origin of some items (Gobelins and the wines), the precious materials (marble, silk, toile, crystal), and up-to-date styles (particularly with the beds). To entice auction attendees, some officials staged the wares. One report noted that "after having waited for the number of shopkeepers and bidders to gather considerably, so there was strong competition, . . . [the administrators] introduced the public to the rooms and showed the shopkeepers and bidders the furniture [which had been] prepared and arranged in a way best suited for the ease and advantage of the sale."[71]

With their artful design and language of opulence, these auctions sold aristocratic living. On the one hand, they suggest that such luxury was open to anyone. On the other hand, the regime wanted—for the benefit of the republic, of course—to drive up bids on these goods, which made them unattainable for most of the population, who, at times, found it hard enough to buy bread. Officials knew that there were too many items for even the most patriotic and well-heeled *citoyens* or *citoyennes* to consume on the spot, and so they relied on second-hand dealers to relieve the spatial and financial pressures on national depositories. Auction authorities referenced the presence of "bric-a-brac traders," "buyers," and "shopkeepers, second-hand clothes dealers, second-hand dealers, [and] other people."[72] And these *revendeurs* (secondhand dealers) were instrumental to the circulation of goods beyond the initial auctions. One nineteenth-century scholar wrote that "Paris overflowed" with Versailles objects that turned up in the shops of *revendeurs*. Newspapers carried advertisements from storekeepers who offered "goods from Versailles and Trianon at a fixed price."[73] *Revendeurs* lured foreign buyers who, officials reasoned, would introduce stable currency into an economy suffering from ever-increasing levels of inflation.[74] Some merchants appealed directly to consumers abroad: Citoyen Eberts, a Paris *decorateur,* placed advertisements in German newspapers, noting that the goods available were not only "of the greatest richness and finest taste" but also "of very low prices."[75]

Some protested the exodus of items out of France. In a long report written in 1794, abbé Grégoire exclaimed, "What a triumph for the English, if it would be able to crush our commerce by the annihilation of our [industrial and decorative] arts, from which the culture enriches itself. . . . Citizens, conserve the arts and honor and protect those who cultivate them. That would be also to fight the English."[76] Atlantic buyers were stripping France of its wealth (both literally and culturally), and Grégoire called on French citizens to mobilize to stop the traffic. But many members of the regime saw seized movable property as a resource that could be easily traded to obtain provisions, war materiel, and other supplies—the very means necessary to defeat archenemies like the British. An advertisement for the auctions of goods from Petit Trianon included the note, "The furnishings listed can be transported abroad, exempt from all duties" (see figure 2.3).[77] No wonder Grégoire was furious: the government was losing the objects as well as the taxes on exporting them.

Although it is impossible to quantify how many *biens nationaux* left France, anecdotal evidence indicates the various channels through which these goods circulated. In some cases, the government brokered deals with individual merchants, but most often Atlantic consumers depended on buyers in France who purchased items on speculation or on commission. It is worth examining these routes in order to appreciate the dynamics of dispersal, especially the challenges of gauging the taste of potential Atlantic buyers and of shifting these goods out of France to other destinations. Such matters demonstrate the lengths to which people were willing to go—their investments in time and money—to acquire these items.

The French regime established a network of agents in Scandinavia, Germany, and Italy, but the best evidence (and it is wanting) for an Atlantic trade deal based on *biens nationaux* comes from the merchant James Swan. A Scotsman who had migrated to Massachusetts during the North American colonial crisis, Swan threw himself into economic and political ventures in almost equal measure. He joined the Sons of Liberty and sat in the Massachusetts legislature and on the war board, all the while speculating in land and real estate. The postwar depression hit Swan hard, and in 1788 he relocated to France in the hopes of improving his prospects. Getting his start in Le Havre and Rouen, Swan styled himself as an expert on trade between France and the United States, writing a treatise that caught the notice of sympathetic authorities on both sides of the Atlantic. By 1791 he had joined a French mercantile firm and moved to Paris, poised to capitalize on revolution. Swan parlayed his political past into concrete commercial gains, ingratiating himself with liberal aristocrats, then Girondins, next Jacobins, and finally Thermidoreans—no small feat. In 1793, through contacts on the *commission des subsistances* (the board in charge of food supply for civilian and military populations), Swan proposed that his firm could facilitate the importation of provisions to France from the United States and other neutral countries. Since the regime was strapped for cash and its credit uncertain, he suggested that France export its stockpile of luxury goods abroad. Swan's offer was accepted and continued for at least a few years, even when the commission was disbanded in the spring of 1794.[78]

The exact details of the exchange are murky. One account suggests that Swan and his contacts in France had their pick of confiscated items as long as the total value stayed below an agreed threshold. Swan had ideas about what Americans might want, specifying taffetas in "brown, *ramoneur* [literally, "chimney sweep"], Quaker, white, black, pink, gray, blue and chocolate" and cautioning against sending too many silk stockings of "de luxe quality."[79] American merchants—everywhere from Boston to Norfolk—acted as Swan's subagents, shipping cargoes of provisions and arranging for the sale of French items in the United States. But the phenomenon was bigger than Swan. As advertisements in U.S. newspapers attest, merchants with no clear connection to him sold various French housewares. In 1794 the duo of Odier and Bousquet in Philadelphia offered European "House furniture, as Tables, beaureau chifonieres, dressing tables &c &c all in mahogany, covered with marble, of the last taste, A large quantity of super-fine looking glasses from Paris, with gilt frames."[80] A February 1795 notice in the *Boston Gazette* listed French goods for auction by the caseload: cloth, looking glasses, "China," fans, walking sticks, lace, perfume, slippers, "House Furniture," feathers, leather gloves.[81] American merchants were finding ways to get their hands on sought-after French goods—and in significant quantities.

Although Swan advised stylistic restraint in articles sent to the United States, he had no problem indulging in the best revolutionary Paris had to offer for himself. He shipped a cache of spectacular items to his wife in Dorchester, Massachusetts: a marble-topped console table by the renowned cabinetmaker Adam Weisweiler; a pair of gilt bronze andirons by Pierre-Philippe Thomire, featuring hairy goats, cupids, grapevines, and pinecones; a marble and gilt bronze mantel clock with Egyptian figures; and a mahogany *secrétaire à abbatant* (fall-front desk) and commode (chest of drawers). Several of the pieces were not only made by premiere artisans but also had prestigious provenance. Swan acquired a pair of large Sèvres vases that had graced the mantelpiece in Louis XVI's council room at Versailles (figure 2.4). He bought an entire suite of bedroom furniture: an alcove bed, a *bergère* (an upholstered armchair with closed armrests and exposed framing), a kneeling chair (used for praying or to watch the action at the gaming table), a fire screen, two armchairs, and four side chairs, all of which were made by Jean-Baptiste-Claude Sené, the royal *menuisier* (a specialist in furniture that was not veneered) (figure 2.5). The suite came from the rooms of Thierry de Ville d'Avray, the former head of the Garde-Meuble de la Couronne. The Garde-Meuble had its headquarters in Paris, near what is now the Place de la Concorde, and it served as a warehouse for the Crown's most precious objects. Thierry, as *commissaire-général*, oversaw the furnishings of thirteen royal residences, and he brought the benefits of his appointment to bear in 1787, when he updated his own apartments at the Hôtel de Garde-Meuble, hiring the best craftsmen and using the king's funds to do so. During the revolution, the Hôtel de Garde-Meuble became the property of the nation. Thierry was imprisoned and died in 1792, his property seized, sealed, and eventually made available to Swan.[82]

Swan had discriminating taste, and he had access to quality goods. Despite its promise, the arrangement did not run as smoothly as Swan, his agents, or the French government would have liked, and it ended by 1798. The deal was complicated by the 1795 Jay Treaty, a trade agreement between the United States and Great Britain that the French

Figure 2.4. French vase, 1779, Sèvres Manufactory. (Photograph © 2023 Museum of Fine Arts, Boston.)

Figure 2.5. Alcove bed (Lit d'alcove), 1787, Paris. (Photograph © 2023 Museum of Fine Arts, Boston.)

government took as an insult, seeking to reply with injury by interfering with American shipping. Several U.S. merchants grumbled about Swan's secrecy and cliquishness, which limited the scope of the endeavor. One in New York informed his American partner in Dieppe that "the Conduct of Mr Swan [is] *passing strange.* Mr. Swan, I am told, has just arriv'd at Philada, whatever Ideas of speculation he may have, will no doubt be confined soley to his friend [John] Vaughan."[83] Elizabeth Meredith, the mother of Philadelphia merchant David Meredith, reported to her son that Swan was "artful" and "very unfit."[84] Everyone knew he was up to something profitable, and they wanted in on the action. That said, the proceeds of Swan's endeavors were not prompt in coming to him. Not until 1803, as part of negotiations for the Louisiana Purchase, did he receive his due.

Swan's agreement with the French regime was ambitious, grandiose, and unusual. Most *biens nationaux,* even those bought as business ventures, were purchased at government sales by agents. Some British firms employed professionals in France to buy on their behalf. Take the case of James Christie, the founder of the illustrious auction house of the same name. In the 1790s Christie saw an opportunity to acquire French luxury items for the British market. Although sworn enemies of the French for centuries, Britons still admired their high style, and this admiration did not wane during the revolution. Some observers critiqued the British elite for their Francophilia, but the lure was irresistible—to some extent because of falling prices for high-end French goods. Moreover, the aristocracy could justify their purchases as signs of solidarity with the ever-dwindling pool of French royals. None other than the Prince of Wales got swept up in the frenzy, buying numerous Sèvres pieces and piles of furniture that he eventually installed at Windsor Castle.

In response to the strong British market for French luxury wares, Christie obtained choice *objets d'art,* furnishings, artwork, and wine, and he did so through several means. In 1790 Christie hired Philip J. Tassaert, a Flemish art dealer, to travel to Paris to assess duc d'Orléans's famed art collection, a portion of which was up for sale. A few months before, Christie had auctioned the duke's London residence—the house and everything in it—and perhaps he hoped to follow up on that success.[85] Tassaert reported to Christie on the contents of the collection as well as what he thought the better paintings were worth. In the end, the price was too dear for Christie to earn much of a profit, but while there, Tassaert did purchase a few Old Master paintings, some at auctions and others privately. He explained that "those pictures I buy in the public sales must be paid for immediately[,] what I buy out of hand I can get time for—if I agree for it, but I assure you the ready money is the way to do Business here."[86] In the heat of revolution, sellers had little patience for credit—they wanted cash.

In addition to employing agents, Christie benefited from his connections with dealers who placed items with him for sale. One of the most well known was Dominique Daguerre, a celebrated Parisian *marchand-mercier,* a purveyor of luxury goods and interior decorator. Daguerre specialized in high-end furniture, both new and secondhand, as well as tableware, and in 1778 he emigrated to London, where he set up shop on Sloane Street in Chelsea. Daguerre had contacts with leading French retailers and with members of the French aristocracy on which he probably drew to procure goods during the revolution.[87] Despite having his own business, Daguerre collaborated with Christie on occasion because the auctioneer could move stock quickly. Since Daguerre often had to pay cash for items, he wanted a fast turnaround. Moreover, auctions could be bigger draws than shops, thanks to Christie's extensive advertising. For each sale Christie produced a catalogue, available at his showroom and at several London coffeehouses.[88] The title page announced the day and time of the auction and emphasized the quality and variety of goods under the hammer—much like the *biens nationaux* sales. A typical front page ran, "A Catalogue of an Assemblage of most Superb Articles in Or-Moulu and Bronze, in Girandoles, Vases of the Fine Verd Antique, &c. Tripods, Chandeliers, Enriched with a Profusion of Ornaments, designed with infinite Taste, and finished, in a most superlative Stile. Also, A Table Service of Silver, Valuable Jewels, and a Variety of Capital Articles, the Property of A French Lady of High Rank, Brought from her Mansion in France."[89] This infrastructure meant swift and significant profits for Daguerre, even taking into account Christie's fees. From a May 1792 sale Daguerre walked away with £346, while Christie's cut from those items alone was over £145.[90]

Although dealers and auctioneers turned to professionals to further their businesses, individuals acted as buyers for friends, relatives, and associates. For all the people fleeing France during the revolution, there were many going there as well—officials, tourists, adventurers, merchants. All of them, it seems, went shopping. A case in point is Gouverneur Morris. Morris arrived in Paris sometime in 1789, and after a short interlude in London, he was back in the revolutionary city in 1792, this time as the U.S. minister. Born into a wealthy New York family, Morris had been instrumental during the Constitutional Convention, shaping the document's form and pushing for its ratification. Life in Paris suited Morris: he spoke French well, carried on a liaison with the mistress of the famous diplomat Charles-Maurice de Talleyrand-Périgord, and spent copiously—for himself and for other Americans. Morris bought porcelain tableware, figures, and a mirrored plateau for George Washington; court clothes, mirrors, and wine for Thomas Pinckney (then in London); the musical clock, wallpaper, looking glasses, a sewing table, card tables, sofa, chairs, andirons, and carpets for Robert Morris; and furniture, paintings, porcelain, silverware, wine, and other items for himself.[91] His diary includes sundry entries of trips to the cabinetmaker, *tapissier* (upholsterer), *upholsterer* (a kind of interior decorator), Réveillon (the illustrious wallpaper manufacturer), Angoulême (a porcelain factory), and glass and lamp shops.[92]

He bought some of these things with an eye to outfitting his Paris residence, knowing that at the end of his term he could ship them to the United States. This was a common practice among the diplomatic corps. A few years later, when James Monroe was minister to France, Mary Stead Pinckney visited him, noting, "Mr. Monroe's furniture is handsome, but as he order'd it with a view to take it to America the chairs are not gilt, & do not suit the rooms" of his Paris house.[93] Her appraisal points to how Monroe considered which French articles would make the most sense in an American context, even if they looked somewhat out of place in his Paris quarters.

Like Monroe's, some of Morris's purchases were new items, but he also obtained *biens nationaux* from Versailles. The auctions at Versailles were comprised of nearly twenty thousand lots and took almost a year, beginning on August 25, 1793, and lasting until August 11, 1794.[94] During this period the French government demanded Morris's recall; fearing for his safety, he stopped keeping a diary. Under these circumstances, it is doubtful that Morris appeared in person at the auctions, but it was not necessary. Given his familiarity with the Paris shopping scene, Morris could have bought items from a local retailer or *revendeur.* According to family lore, he acquired a large stash of Imperial Tokay (which Louis XV had dubbed "Wine of Kings, King of Wines") from the royal wine cellars at a "cheap grocery shop" for only 25 cents a bottle.[95]

Morris left France with several pieces from the palace. The musical clock and a sewing table sent to Robert and Mary Morris had belonged to Marie-Antoinette.[96] For himself, Gouverneur Morris purchased a suite of furniture—at least two sofas, several armchairs, a *bergère,* and a screen—that had stood in the *cabinets* in Marie-Antoinette's private apartments. Most of the items dated to the late 1770s, but when the queen redecorated the rooms, she moved the set to her "morning room" and commissioned two new sofas to fill out the ensemble. The sofas were made by Georges Jacob, a prominent *menuisier,* and their design was intended to match the extant pieces. Featuring gilt frames delicately carved with flowers, leaves, and other details, the sofas were upholstered in white silk with an exuberant floral and medallion pattern.[97] Monroe decided against gilt furniture for American parlors, but Morris found it more than suitable.

Morris, the U.S. revolutionary, was pleased with his aristocratic purchases. In 1792 he shipped to his friend Pinckney in London several cases of wine, warning, "If you let your English guests know the Price of your Wine they will be apt to despise it for they pay nearly double for very bad Liquor."[98] But not everything could be had cheaply. French administrators gloated that some objects from the Versailles auctions fetched prices well above their anticipated values.[99] A few years later, Mary Stead Pinckney complained that it was impossible to "bid people down" at the Palais Égalité and that "every article of furniture [was] dear" and "china excessively so."[100] By the time Gouverneur Morris departed France, he had spent an estimated $41,000: he practically went broke saving money on luxury goods.

As the experiences of Swan, Christie, and Morris show, the second-hand market was crucial for distributing moveable *biens nationaux* into the wider Atlantic. In the eyes of many, the items' desirability made the economic and personal risks, which were of no small consideration in revolutionary France, worth it. This ambitious acquisition is more remarkable given what it took to ship these goods. The mobility of furniture and porcelain was an advantage compared to other types of valuable French property up for sale. In his advertisements, the decorator Eberts celebrated the fact that these goods, unlike chateaux, "can be transported abroad."[101] That said, many items were fragile and just plain cumbersome. When Jefferson packed up his Paris household in 1789–90, he hired the master *layetier* Grevin to handle the job, and the invoice attests to the enormity and complexity of the task. The packing materials alone were downright intimidating:

> 356 ells of coarse cloth [a French ell was about 54 inches], 10 pounds of oil, 526 ells of strong packing cloth, 887 toises of rope [a toise was almost 2 meters], 79 ells of oil cloth, 624 bundles of rye straw, 385 quires of coarse paper [a quire equals 24–25 sheets], 36 bundles of hay, 37 quires of *"papier de soye,"* 39 quires of ordinary paper, 397 pounds of shredded paper, 32 ells of flannel, 122 balls of twine, 60 pounds of hair, 6 pounds of cotton, 52 covers of coarse paper for

the carriages, furniture, and busts, 21 pounds of fine and large nails . . . and various other sundries.[102]

Once packed, the crates required extensive documentation to leave the country and were inspected at several points along their route. At Le Havre a mob became suspicious of the heaviness of some of Jefferson's crates, thinking that an aristocrat was smuggling out specie. They demanded that the crates be opened—but were disappointed to find busts of Voltaire, Lafayette, Franklin, Washington, Jefferson, and other republicans.[103] As the crowd's tenacity indicates, though, the movement of goods through France was open to public scrutiny and possible peril.

The troubles continued outside of France. Although the speed and reliability of transoceanic voyages had improved over the course of the eighteenth century, transportation was plagued with difficulties during the revolutions. Robert Morris was beside himself with worry as he tried to find out more information about a shipment from Gouverneur Morris. Writing to contacts in France, he was alarmed to "find that the Brandy, which I ordered to be shipped on board the Brig could not be obtained & therefore Mr. [Gouverneur] Morris employed her to bring away his Goods, and also a Quantity of Looking Glasses and Furniture which he bought for me; but what astounds me is, that to this Hour she does not appear, neither do I hear any thing of her from any quarter except that she was at Havre de Grace last November."[104] The shipment reached New York a month or so later, and Morris faced the additional headache of getting it to Philadelphia, as each city's customshouse vied for import duties. But Robert Morris was more vexed to find "that three Bales or Cases Containing part of the Goods bot for me by Mr. G. Morris are left behind [in Europe,] having by Mistake of the man from whom they were bought been sent to Switzerland instead of Havre de Grace."[105] He asked his associate in Paris to track down the crates and have them sent to him as soon as possible—at further expense.

For all the hassles of shipping these goods, desire and potential profits outweighed the risks. Even as he moaned about delays and mishaps, Robert Morris authorized his Paris colleague to purchase "such an Assortment of Articles as you think will sell to good Profit here, whether in Furniture Manufactures Wine Brandy &c & have them shipped in American Bottoms for this Place to my Address."[106] Such behavior is not surprising from Morris, whose audacious schemes in land speculation landed him in debtor's prison a few years later. But Robert Morris's ambitions were in keeping with those of his Atlantic contemporaries. There was an awareness of and vocabulary for luxury goods that stretched well beyond the city limits of Paris, and the tumult of revolution offered an opportunity for a greater variety of people in a wider sweep of locations to consume, or at least to encounter, these goods. Many buyers were considered elite in their home contexts, but the participants in this group were broader than the original owners. Men like James Swan were not among Sené's typical clientele, nor would Elizabeth Drinker have gotten anywhere near Marie-Antoinette's apartments to see and listen to her clock. And, if lampooning caricatures are anything to go by, Christie's auction rooms hosted scores of social upstarts.[107]

As new owners brought these items into their homes, they stood as evidence of cultural refinement and economic wherewithal. In the U.S. case, the turn among the elite to high-end French goods in the late 1780s and 1790s has been interpreted as instrumental in Americans' attempt to establish a "republican court"—a culture of sociability and taste befitting a republic. This move had its detractors, who railed against the dangers of luxury regardless of its country of origin; however, proponents saw the consumption of French things as one way to distinguish the new country from Britain.[108] But Americans were not the only ones interested in these goods in the 1790s. Despite decades of war with France, British royals, gentry, and aspirant elites still looked to their nemesis for stylistic cues, and revolution afforded them with plenty of opportunities to indulge.[109]

Confiscated high-end French goods had Atlantic appeal, and yet because of their provenance and the circumstances of their dispersal, they had unavoidable political connotations, too. While Atlantic buyers concurred about their aesthetic value, consensus about their political resonances was elusive. Local contexts account for some differences, but only to a certain extent. Consider the case of Christie's auction catalogues. Whenever he thought it to his benefit, Christie identified the original French owners of specific items. Sales featured objects attributed to the households of Louis XVI, Madame du Barry, comte de Mirabeau, and marechal de Noailles, among others—the fame of the owner, as with the *biens nationaux* sales, testifying to the superiority of the goods for sale.[110] With some lots, Christie wrote descriptions that highlighted aspects of their previous owners' pasts. Of a bronze figure emblematic of "the chase," he averred, in italics for emphasis, *"The above was made by the express order of the late King of France, and cost 200 louis d'ors* [4,800 livres]*, was brought from his palace at the Thuilleries."*[111] Christie emphasizes not only Louis XVI's personal interest in the work and its whopping original price but also how it was saved from the ransacked palace. The sculpture had survived the violence of revolution—as its former owner had not. The king, the master of the chase, had fallen victim to the hunt.

The narrative around the sculpture is in keeping with British attitudes toward Louis XVI after his death. He became a martyr in the eyes of many Britons, or at least a rallying cry for Britons to defend their monarchy from pernicious French designs.[112] Other items resonated differently. The auction of Madame du Barry's jewels in 1795 warranted an extensive preamble from Christie: "It is presumed the contents of this catalogue are a display of the most peculiar selection, in the superlative stile, that was ever offered to the public; as it was not only a selection from the Royal Cabinet, but from every Cabinet, both public and private, in the kingdom of France: and which, by order of the Administrator, will be tendered to the public and sold without the least reserve whatever."[113] Du Barry's stormy and scandalous past as the consort of Louis XV was common knowledge in Britain, since she had spent some time in London in exile. Christie's description alludes to her notorious thirst for diamonds and how Louis XV stopped at nothing, purportedly, to get them for her, running up debts and compromising his kingdom in the process. The diamonds reflect the folly of a French monarch and the grasping social aspirations of his mistress, and while the catalogue entry condemns du Barry's ill-gotten spoils, it hints at the possibility that bidders might get them for a song. There was a kind of delectation in buying scandal, especially that of one's enemy.

The experiences of Gouverneur Morris reveal the variety of political associations of French confiscated goods in the United States. After knocking around Europe for four years when his post in France ended, Morris returned to his estate, Morrisania, located in what is now the South Bronx. There his French purchases appeared prominently: Marie-Antoinette's suite stood in the parlor, and the family and their guests dined on the Angoulême porcelain service decorated along the rim with the "Bourbon sprig" (cornflowers).[114] In some of the most public places in Morris's home, allusions to French royalty were central.

Although Morris experienced a material culture windfall thanks to the execution of the French king and queen, a less cynical reading posits that Morris saw his furnishings as an homage to the monarchs who had abetted American independence. Jefferson, for one, labeled Morris "a high flying Monarchy-man."[115] But Morris's reflections about the French Revolution are not easy to pin down. When in Paris, Morris had met Louis XVI and Marie-Antoinette several times and often expressed, privately, his disapproval. As early as the spring of 1789, Morris professed his disdain for the opulence of Versailles, questioning the royal family's lack of restraint: "Perhaps there is not one of them who thinks of what ought to strike them all, that this Expense and others like this have occasioned their [the Estates-General] Meeting."[116] As the revolution deepened, Morris wondered whether the king was up to the task of "secur[ing] the Liberty of France," and he voiced his reservations about Marie-Antoinette, too.[117] In July 1792 Morris visited the queen: "Her Majesty is in good Spirits and very affable. I am not pleas'd, however, with her Conduct."[118] A few months later, he pointed to the king's "weakness" and saw the queen as "still more imprudent."[119]

At the same time, Morris criticized the revolutionaries, detailing in his diary and in official correspondence the intrigues, rash decisions, and general chaos. As he remarked in a letter to Jefferson, "We stand on a vast Volcano, we feel it tremble and we hear it roar but how and when and where it will burst and who may be destroy'd by its Eruptions it is beyond the Ken of mortal Foresight to discover."[120] He kept track of insults to the king and queen, and disagreed with Lafayette over the French Constitution: "He [Lafayette] asks what I mean by a good Constitution, whether it is an aristocratic one. I tell him Yes, and that I presume he has lived long enough in the present Style to see that a popular Government is good for Nothing in France. He says he wishes the American Constitution, but an hereditary Executive. I tell him that in such Case the Monarch will be too strong and must be check'd by an hereditary Senate."[121] Finally, Morris was linked with one plan to sneak the royal family out of Paris, and rumors circulated in some quarters that he worked for the king.[122]

At the end of 1792, Morris penned an in-depth appraisal of the revolution in which almost all participants shared the blame: revolutionaries (of all stripes), the royal family, courtiers, and the "Populace," among others.[123] The problem, in Morris's estimation, was that the French were unprepared for the revolution they had inaugurated. In this context, Morris's Versailles suite takes on another set of possible meanings. It represented the recklessness of the former owner as well as the revolutionaries (from moderate to radical) who brought her down. It served as a reminder of how quickly one's political and personal fortunes could turn. Or perhaps Morris agreed with Jefferson who, as historian Philipp Ziesche has argued, thought that Americans should imbibe French culture only once their moral compasses were fully forged at home.[124] In this vein, Morris could have seen himself as preserving for Americans the most valuable aspect of eighteenth-century France, its culture—the one thing that Frenchmen, it seemed to Morris, could no longer appreciate.

The range of interpretive possibilities puts the consumption of seized objects affiliated with the ancien régime in a new light. Their Atlantic ambits break them out of well-worn tropes of luxury and refinement and show relationships between people and objects that were unfolding, just like the revolutions that set them into motion. They were revolutionary goods—not in spite of ancien régime associations but because of them. Revolution made them available, and they were so important to the viability of the French project, in material and ideological terms, that officials sought to rehabilitate their meanings to serve republican ends.

But as with other aspects of the French Revolution, the results of the *biens nationaux* sales were unstable. The material culture of the "old regime" prompted repudiation and destruction, and at the same time encouraged preservation, but for varied and sometimes contradictory reasons. It was exhibited for the edification of the people, employed to outfit the offices of new governments, and sold for profit. As these items crossed borders, these bundles of contradiction went with them, as auctioneers like Christie narrated their histories from the rostrum and as individuals like Swan and Morris went to such lengths to buy, ship, and display them in the United States.

The *biens nationaux* were distinctive for their magnificence, and even at reduced prices, only certain sectors of the population could afford them. Yet they were part of a common phenomenon as the practice of pillaging across the Atlantic world set millions of goods in motion during revolutionary wars. The sheer volume broadened the range of revolutionary things that inhabitants of all ranks encountered. Whether a mahogany chair confiscated from a Saint-Domingue planta- tion or a looking glass from a Boston home or a vase from Versailles, none of these items was explicitly "republican" in aesthetics. However, they elicited discussions about revolutions because of the contexts sur- rounding their seizures, sales, and uses, and in the hands of new own- ers, like people of African descent and the lower classes, they provided opportunities to contest racial and class hierarchies.

There is a temptation to dismiss these secondhand goods—and the "old-style" manufactured goods discussed in the previous chapter—as holdovers from another era, as evidence of the tendency of people's political principles to cave in the face of objects of desire. And perhaps for some this was true. But this explanation falls prey to the period's polarizing rhetoric, which attempted to cast individuals as either for or against the status quo. Political allegiances on the ground, including among self-avowed revolutionaries, were much less stable. In fact, the starkness of the rhetoric can in part be chalked up to the need to clarify alliances. If the iconography of liberty, equality, and fraternity adorning faïence, furniture, and other items represented the ideal—what revo- lutionaries wanted to achieve—then these "old" goods encapsulated the messiness of the revolutionary present and how much remained unresolved. They offer insight into the contingency of the moment as individuals struggled to make sense of the revolutions as they occurred and show us how actors leveraged diverse objects at their disposal to achieve assorted political aims. These things point to the ways that material continuity perpetuated and hindered revolutionary change and shaped how various people understood the content of that change. This dynamic of object politicization informed not only the decorative wares people used in their homes but also the very garments they wore in public.

II
POLITICAL APPEARANCES

WHEN IT CAME to clothing, Atlantic revolutionaries had strong opinions and grand plans. Like everyone else in the eighteenth century, they knew that appearances mattered in the world of politics. The ruling classes had long projected power through their dress, deploying the wealth, reach, and grandeur associated with garments to argue for those same acclaimed characteristics in their persons and states. Among the wider populace, clothing had been read as a barometer of individual virtue and, by extension, as an indicator of the general moral health of a nation.

By the age of revolutions, though, critics of standing orders pointed to monarchs' and elites' extravagant dress as signs of political corruption. Finery became frippery as the thirst for luxury compromised the integrity of leaders and governments. Not surprisingly, then, revolutionaries, as part of their agendas, proposed to reclothe the nation. Some, like the artist Jacques-Louis David, designed fantastic apparel modeled on Renaissance and classical precedents for the judges, legislators, and other functionaries of the new French republic.[1] Sartorial inspiration came from below, too, from men known as *sans culottes*.

With their baggy pants and short jackets, these workingmen became emblematic of an early moment in the French Revolution, so much so that the phrase *sans culottes* was used as a shorthand throughout the Atlantic world to celebrate—or deride—any firebrand.

These sartorial innovations have provided proof of the impact of revolutionary politics on everyday life—right down to the shirts and chemises on people's backs. In these readings, dress was a way through which ordinary women and men participated in politics and changed their societies. But very few people wore this self-consciously revolutionary clothing. David's patterns never made it off the page, and *sans culottes* were a brief fashion among a select few rather than a transformation in men's dress.[2] This pattern held true in the United States and in Saint-Domingue as well. Some notable Americans like George Washington wore homespun on distinct occasions; however, it did not become a lasting and widespread trend. Toussaint Louverture proposed new ensembles for public officials—everyone from mayors to the copyists in his entourage—yet his prescriptions were short-lived.[3] Most revolutionaries on the island, especially the formerly enslaved, did not reject the clothing of the master class. Instead, they appropriated it on their own terms whenever possible.

So, although some leading revolutionaries cried out for dress reform, most actors did not revamp their wardrobes in response. They could not afford to jettison garments as fashions, political or otherwise, shifted. Certainly, more individuals enjoyed more articles of clothing than they had in previous centuries, but textiles remained dear, so much so that items were mended and modified rather than discarded when styles or personal preferences dictated.[4] Revolutionaries' calls for sartorial overhaul were somewhat elitist; they were well out of reach for the lower and middle classes, let alone the previously enslaved.[5]

Dress *did* become politicized during this era—just not necessarily as revolutionaries envisioned. The following part explores two prevalent arenas where it took place. The first is military clothing. Hundreds of thousands of men fought in the three revolutionary wars, and troops were entitled to garments annually. But the process of getting so many articles to so many men was difficult, and all armies witnessed periodic clothing shortages because of production lapses and transport interruptions. These mishaps had practical consequences in that they compromised men's efficacy on the battlefield. And they had political ramifications as soldiers used military clothing as one means by which to measure the worthiness of regimes that they defended. Soldiers' acknowledged claim to garments informed how they understood their rights as individuals vis-à-vis governments, offering tangible evidence as to whether states delivered on their promises to outfit men within a given rank equally. Despite the hierarchal nature of militaries, clothing emerged as a way through which men, white and Black, demanded a kind of equality.

The second site, the realm of accessories, straddles civilian and military spheres. Affordable, diverse, and prolific, accessories like cockades and medallions became visible channels through which various populations engaged with political movements. Factions turned to accessories to mark out adherents and to promote ideological outlooks. Manufacturers sought to profit from this contest while attempting to avoid its negative repercussions. In the meantime, consumers had their own approaches to wearing, buying, and creating accessories, and they did not always fit neatly in the divisions that political camps tried to enforce. Women, men of African descent, and common white men employed the conventions around accessories to lobby for their ideas about who could take part in revolutionary politics and how. For all involved, accessories proved a mutable mode to weigh in on the potential and limits of popular sovereignty.

Military clothing and accessories redirect our gaze away from the splashy sartorial plans of the revolutionary vanguard and toward the more ubiquitous ways in which regimes, makers, and consumers joined in and made sense of revolutions through garments. As leaders anticipated, individuals participated in Atlantic revolutions through one of the most intimate, and yet most public, facets of their material lives.

But their involvement was not as straightforward or as transparent as governments hoped. Clothing in this era did not simply reflect political categories; rather, garments presented an opportunity for soldiers and civilians, elites and the enslaved, men and women, pro- and anti-revolutionaries, to shape the political content of those categories.

3 Clothing the Cause

IN THE WINTER of 1780 Nathanael Greene, the beleaguered quartermaster of the U.S. Continental Army, surveyed the troops under General Gates's command and found that they were "literally . . . naked." Observations of soldiers' deprivation have testified to the extraordinary sacrifices of average men for revolutionary causes—from Valley Forge to the mountains surrounding Cap Français to Valmy. But in his report to Thomas Jefferson, then governor of Virginia, Greene emphasized another set of concerns about clothing. He explained, "The Article of Clothing is but a small Part of the Expence in raising, equipping and subsisting an Army, and yet on this alone the whole Benefit of their Service depends. I wish the State [of Virginia] to view this matter in its true Point of Light: some may think it is urged for the Sake of military Parade, but be assured you raise men in vain unless you clothe, arm and equip them properly for the Field." In Greene's estimation, if soldiers were not appropriately clothed, then they were a detriment to the army—not only because they were physically unprepared to fight but also because they began to question the war's purpose: "No Man will think himself bound to fight the Battles of a State that leaves him to perish for want of Covering."[1] Clothing made the man *and* the cause.

From a modern perspective, a government's obligation to clothe soldiers is a seemingly self-evident requirement to conduct war effectively, yet Greene's adamant defense reminds us that the practice is relatively new. Prior to the eighteenth century, European armies did not issue garments to soldiers; most men wore whatever they had at hand. But from the late seventeenth century on, monarchs developed a keener interest in the appearance of their forces, both for its tactical advantages and as a means of inculcating hygiene, discipline, and national pride.[2] Administrators drafted many regulations about military clothing, and the numerous wars of the era gave states opportunities to test systems of production and distribution as well as sartorial designs.

Despite decades of trial and error, the standards and infrastructure for fabricating, transporting, and issuing military clothing were still evolving at the end of the eighteenth century as European wars expanded to a global scale. Governments mobilized to acquire, transport, and disseminate massive amounts of garments to their armies. As far as volume and reach, military clothing is perhaps the most prolific revolutionary good because of the numbers of men who needed it. While the U.S. patriots bore the burden of providing garments to tens of thousands of soldiers, the French and British states outfitted hundreds of thousands of men across all three revolutions.[3] As a result, governments measured and moved clothing by the tons, with the totals for single items—shirts, stockings, hats—tallying into the millions.

Although the mechanisms for clothing manufacture and dissemination faced constant setbacks, the expectation that governments would furnish soldiers with garments, or at the very least the fabric for them, had become an established norm. As Greene's letter underscores, the slippage between the ability to supply and the commitment to do so became politically charged in the age of revolutions. Officers, usually of higher social status, bought their ensembles out of pocket. The common soldier, however, lacked the wherewithal to equip himself from head to toe, and so at enlistment, he agreed to the garnishing of his wages to defray the cost of his attire.[4] This arrangement established an obligation: since the soldier paid for his garments, the government had a duty to deliver them in a timely manner. Each soldier anticipated receiving a certain number, range, and quality of items on an annual basis.

In this way, clothing formed a central component of the contract between soldiers and their governments.[5] Clothing figured in other types of agreements, too: indentured servants and apprentices obtained new suits at the end of their terms, and clothing was essential to women's dowries. But military garments took on ideological significance because lives were on the line in the name of causes that were attempting to re-define, or safeguard, the compacts between people and governments. For revolutionary movements, the capacity to provision soldiers was evidence of whether (or not) new states were better than derided pre-decessors, and for those regimes, like Great Britain, that were on the defensive, equipping soldiers was touted as proof of their reliability. For hundreds of thousands of men in the revolutionary wars, military clothing became a repeatable litmus test of governments going beyond cant and making good on their promises.

Clothing was also important because it was one of the few concerns that soldiers could press claims for with any hope of success. Whether fighting for or against revolution, common troops relinquished many rights, submitting to military law and to the orders of their superiors, whatever the circumstances. Soldiers frequently resented and tested these constraints, yet they had little leverage since with enlistment they had consented to military authority.[6] With clothing, though, the chains of command recognized men's prerogatives. This was true of other items for which soldiers paid, like provisions, but clothing differed from these military goods in two respects. First, unlike food or weapons, a soldier took his clothing with him when he returned to civilian life, and given the value of cloth and clothing in the early modern period, these garments could improve a man's assets.[7] The possible longevity of gar-ments meant that troops sought to ensure that they received their due, and when their due was not forthcoming, they voiced their discontent in ways that could derail the military and political aims of regimes.

Second, clothing was, and still is, a mode through which people ex-press individuality—a custom at odds with the army's incipient ideal of uniformity. Consequently, although higher-ups conceded that garments belonged to soldiers, commanders and bureaucrats attempted to police what that attire was and how it was worn and maintained. Sometimes the opinions of troops and authorities aligned, but at other moments clothing became a source of contention as men defended their rights over what they considered their property.

These practical and political challenges with clothing occurred ev-erywhere soldiers were deployed, but they had particular reverbera-tions in North American and Caribbean theaters because Black men became an increasingly prominent presence in armies there. Thousands of enslaved and free African-descended men served in European and North American militaries, and in the case of the Haitian Revolution, they created huge armies of their own.[8] Some Black men offered support services to military operations, while others joined the rank and file. This latter group qualified for clothing on the same terms as white soldiers, and, like them, Black troops appreciated the economic and personal value of clothing and saw it as theirs. This understanding derived from experiences with textiles in the civilian world, where some societies attached textile ownership to the person who wore it, including to married women and the enslaved, who lacked legal claims to other forms of property.[9] Well before donning uniforms, Black and white men accepted that textiles afforded wearers the ability to exercise certain rights.

In civilian life, this acknowledgment did not change the legal status of the enslaved or of married women, but in a military and revolutionary context it had greater prospects for both Black and white men. At the heart of the debates about and uses of military clothing is, counterintuitively, the notion of equality. Militaries are deeply hierarchical organizations in which rank and subordination are central to their functionality, and clothing is instrumental to maintaining that hierarchy, since different ranks had different uniforms.[10] Within specific ranks, though—among all privates or all sergeants—the goal was a kind of equality: each private or sergeant had garments identical to every other private or sergeant. Viewed from above, this uniformity had a disciplinary and anonymizing effect: all men within a given rank looked the same. But that outcome transpired only if authorities supplied the promised goods. When they failed, which happened often, soldiers insisted on their rights to garments of relatively equal quality and quantity. No matter on what side of revolution they fought, white and Black troops expected to experience this palpable and personal version of equity—one that was no less powerful than those found in republican decrees.

The unevenness in achieving sartorial uniformity amplified the political significance of instances when common men, especially men of African descent, did appear in full military garb. At these moments, Black soldiers were dressed like—and sometimes better than—their white counterparts, contesting racist hierarchies in visible public ways. Given the shared knowledge about and appreciation for textiles, Atlantic audiences understood the radical assertion of equality transmitted by these men through their garments. Military clothing both identified political loyalties and offered a means for many men to contribute to the ideological content of that loyalty.

MAKING UNIFORM

During the American, French, and Haitian revolutions, most textiles that clothed soldiers came from Europe. Even those in North America and Saint-Domingue relied heavily on supplies from Britain, France, and Spain, and that being so, all armies were beholden to European systems for producing and disseminating military clothing. By all accounts, the British had the most developed export-oriented textile manufactures, the largest and strongest navy, and considerable experience in conducting war in places far from home. Historians have maintained that this prowess helps to explain Britain's ascendancy in the eighteenth century.[11] But the case of military clothing shows that its administrative wizardry was, on the ground, in greater disarray than a bird's-eye view of its organizational structure suggests—and in key respects it was in keeping with the experiences of rivals. The messiness of the British case illuminates the ordeals all regimes faced as they tried to make uniforms uniform. The problems were practical, as agencies struggled to obtain a consistent product, and they were ideological, as the promise of clothing established expectations among soldiers about their governments.

Military-issued garments were more commonly called "clothing" than "uniforms" because what men wore on the battlefield was not so far removed from everyday wardrobes. By midcentury the suit was standard attire for most free men, and military dress drew on this familiar form.[12] When enlisting, the British infantryman (a soldier who marched rather than rode to battle and who comprised the majority of the army) received "a good Cloth Coat, well lined, looped with worsted Lace [a flat, woven decoration used around cuffs, collars, and button-holes]," a waistcoat (a vest), a pair of breeches, stockings, shoes, a shirt, a neck-cloth (a stiff neck band of leather or cloth), and a "good Strong Hat bound with white Tape [a narrow, woven strip of wool cloth that reinforced and decorated seams and brims]."[13] Every year thereafter, a soldier collected the same items, except instead of an entirely new waistcoat, he was issued only "the fore Part . . . , the Hind Part to be made out of that of the preceding Year."[14] Soldiers also received two pairs of shoes per year, with spare soles and heels, and mittens, caps, overalls, and other garments, as commanding officers saw fit.[15]

The parity between civilian and military apparel enhanced the value of military clothing for most men. In all armies the rank and file were caricatured as the "dregs of mankind," yet their actual composition was diverse, with large numbers of artisans—from brewers and weavers to masons and schoolteachers—filling out the ranks.[16] Compared to earlier generations, eighteenth-century free men had more items of clothing and a greater variety of garments. On the eve of revolution, the average wardrobe of a Parisian artisan consisted of between fifteen and twenty principal articles (breeches, coats, waistcoats), whereas in the previous century, a craftsman had two or three changes of daytime clothing.[17] Despite this marked growth, the addition of an entire new suit of clothing every year represented a substantial increase for a poor or middling man.[18]

The economic and sartorial impact was most impressive for Black soldiers, those who were enslaved or had been prior to the revolutions. For centuries, the master class enforced the status of enslaved people through dress. On Atlantic plantations, masters dispensed a few items annually—for men a couple of shirts and trousers (or enough fabric to sew them) of cheap, coarse material. The deliberate choice of inferior fabric and the absence of culturally significant items like coats, hats, and shoes were meant to emphasize the degraded station of the enslaved.[19] Sometimes household slaves and coachmen received better garments and cast-offs from masters' families, and whenever possible enslaved people supplemented their meager wardrobes with items bought from nearby markets, stores, and traveling salesmen.[20] In some colonies, sumptuary laws buttressed racial and sartorial hierarchies. Free people of African descent and the enslaved were prohibited from wearing certain articles and specific materials, as white men and women feared the challenges clothing could pose to racist notions of white superiority.[21] So for Black people, access to military garments represented an economic and social boon.

Recruiters knew that clothing lured newcomers, and when traveling from town to town, they wore their handsomest dress, confident in the power of clothing to seduce men to join. One sergeant sent to scout for men in Languedoc asked his captain for a new uniform, "something dazzling to make the young men envious."[22] Satirical prints play up the contrast between dashing soldiers and shabby recruits. The 1780 engraving *Recruits* shows two soldiers smartly dressed in gleaming white breeches, snappy coats, ornamented hats, and polished boots. They school three recently enlisted men in military bearing, the latter's lowly status underscored by their slovenly appearance: one man is in such dire straits that his toes peek through his shoe (figure 3.1). The sign above the tavern door points to the folly of the recruits' choice. A returned soldier in a striking red coat wears an eye patch and is missing an arm and a leg—injuries that severely limited his economic prospects, let alone his health. The loss of limbs was a high price to pay for even the most elegant coat.

While social commentators mocked both men and women for losing sense at the sight of regimentals (think of the Bennet girls from *Pride and Prejudice*), soldiers' relationship to military clothing was more complex. The lure of the French sergeant's "dazzling" uniform was not just that it was fashionable and hence appealed to men's vanity. Rather, such garments *cost* more than others. As recruiters and recruits throughout the Atlantic world understood, people invested in textiles because cloth was a durable and portable commodity that had high re-sale value. For men with limited options, and for those drawn from the artisanal classes, military clothing was a real economic takeaway—one possibly worth the gamble of enlistment.

Soldiers were quick to realize the value of military clothing because it represented one of the few tangible aspects of their pay. All armies set a daily wage rate for soldiers, but they rarely saw any of it in specie. Most compensation was gobbled up by deductions. The largest share was for food; for a French soldier in the American Revolution, for instance, provisions amounted to almost 40 percent of his wages.[23] But a whole host of other expenses were charged against soldiers' pay: contributions to the hospital, fees to the agent who sourced goods for the unit, other collective costs, and, of course, clothing.[24] Military administrators ascribed a monetary value to each garment so that governments and men knew the exact amounts deducted from a soldier's wages. In 1792 a British foot soldier paid 5 shillings, 6 pence per shirt, and 6 shillings for a pair of shoes. During the American Revolution, Congress annually set prices for Continental Army garments: in 1778 a coat was valued at $25, a vest at $9, a shirt $8, breeches $10, and so

RECRUITS.

London.Publish'd Jan.ᵗ 1ˢᵗ 1780 by Watson & Dickinson N°158 New Bond Street.

Figure 3.1. Henry William Bunbury, *Recruits* (London: Watson & Dickinson, 1780). The same year that this stipple engraving appeared on the Anglophone market, French printers copied it, giving it the propagandistic title *Recrues anglois partant pour l'Amérique* (*English Recruits Departing for America*) to exaggerate the supposed unpreparedness of British troops. (Courtesy of The Lewis Walpole Library, Yale University.)

on.[25] Bureaucrats devised neat organizational charts for keeping track of these deductions, but in practice systems were chaotic. In 1780, when a commission investigated the British army's finances, it found the labyrinth around pay so impenetrable that the committee, as one scholar has described, "abandoned its task in despair."[26]

These opaque circumstances meant that any one man's pay could be lost in a mire of accounts. Clothing was the most concrete evidence of wages that a soldier witnessed. It was palpable, belonged to him, and lasted longer than a meal. Commanding officers felt the pressure to deliver clothing, knowing that it was essential for the exercise of war and for avoiding dissent among the men. When clothing did not arrive at the designated time, it sparked discontent, and officers saw such grievances as legitimate. In March 1777, Captain Robert Kirkwood of the Continental Army read to his men a letter from headquarters stating that "the General is very sorry there should be so much foundation for the frequent complaints of the sodery, respecting their pay and cloathing, he is very sensible of these difficulties and promises them everything in his power to have them speedily redressed."[27] Perhaps the men found some humor in the unintentional pun about quick redressing, but the letter's phrasing is revealing in its recognition of the justness of the soldiers' complaints and an expressed commitment to do something about them.

The Caribbean theater shows the degree to which the acceptance of a soldier's right to clothing proliferated. After the American Revolution, the Carolina corps of loyalist and mostly Black troops was reassigned to Grenada and served throughout the Leeward Islands. Governor Edward Mathew had high hopes for the corps, seeing it as a solution to the chronic problem of manning the West Indian colonies. Since Black troops were, according to Mathew, more inured to the climate than British soldiers, they could provide the continuity necessary to protect the islands. His plan sparked debate because of the perceived threat to racial hierarchies: Mathew took it as a given that the men must be paid and clothed like other soldiers, as they had been during the War of Independence.[28] In 1788 he complained to his superiors, "The men of the Whole Corps have ever been under regular Military Stoppages, but since June 1785, have received neither Cloathing, appointments, or any allowance in lieu of them."[29] Mathew haggled with the local legislature and with the metropole to determine who would pay for their upkeep. For the year 1789 the Treasury agreed "to provide good and suitable Clothing and Accoutrements for so useful a Corps." Two years later, however, the unit's agents were pressing officials for the balance still due.[30]

On the one hand, the case of the Carolina corps points to how the right to clothing pervaded the military to such an extent that it applied to Black soldiers, a population snubbed within the army in other respects (restrictions on promotions and command, among other slights). On the other hand, it illustrates the frustrations and limited recourse of officers and men when clothing did not arrive. Toussaint Louverture sent numerous missives to higher-ups pleading for garments for his soldiers: "It is very painful for a commander who has seen his forces endure thirst and hunger, and be exposed to the greatest dangers to expel the British from the territory of Saint-Domingue, it is painful, I repeat, to behold these very soldiers deprived even of such basic clothing as would cover their nudity." Their condition grieved Louverture's "sensitive . . . heart," and the soldiers felt the physical discomfort of being poorly dressed as well as the economic hardship of not receiving their garments.[31]

Although racism exacerbated the situation of Black soldiers, problems with clothing supply affected corps throughout the Atlantic world. Almost all who served in the British, French, Haitian, and American armies experienced shortfalls, and as commanding officers knew from experience, when appeals to superiors failed, soldiers displayed their displeasure through more drastic measures.[32] John Robert Shaw, who had served with the British and then switched to the American side, joined a soldiers' march in Philadelphia to express "our grievances, such as no pay—no clothing, nor other necessities and conveniences, without which we could serve no longer." Their protest was effective as the men were immediately issued "such clothing as we stood in need of, and some money," and shortly thereafter received additional pay "with all the arrearages of clothing."[33] Other generals and their men were not so lucky. It was rumored that General Charles Lee, on the march in the winter of 1776, lost about twenty-seven hundred men (out of three thousand) "by dissertion for want of Cloathing," and Connecticut soldiers under the command of General Samuel Parsons "mutinied" repeatedly to protest their lack of garments.[34] At times, Louverture was forced to let his men "go marauding" for clothing to quell their frustration at being "naked like earthworms."[35]

To diffuse discontent, commanders had the option of compensating soldiers with money (called "arrearages"), but cash was hard to come by. When paid, officers and men still faced the problem of obtaining clothing. Men objected that government rates for garments failed to factor in wartime inflation, which sent prices soaring. In a letter to his superiors, British general James Pattison explained the difficulties of outfitting several prisoners of war who had escaped from the enemy. They "came in almost naked, having receiv'd no Cloathing for these two Years," and so he had to clothe them, "but the high Price of every Thing here [in New York City] . . . brought the Expence of a compleat Suit of Cloathing for a private Soldier to £5.3.11 1/2 Sterling."[36] Near the end of the war, an American soldier claimed that U.S. currency had depreciated so dramatically that cloth for a coat cost $2,000 per yard and the buttons to complete it $1,500.[37]

Given preexisting attitudes toward dress in the civilian world as well as the monetization of garments in the military context, military clothing had an economic value that all sectors—government officials, commanders, and common soldiers, regardless of race—recognized. Soldiers demanded clothing annually, with an eye to their present circumstances as well as to future ones, and higher-ups acknowledged clothing as a soldier's right, one of the few. This awareness placed enormous pressures on supply systems, but it had another important effect: it established the expectation that governments would furnish certain types of products. Black and white men were aware that the prices of garments varied according to their quality: the fiber (cotton, wool, linen), the tightness of the weave or knit, the fastness of dyes, the ornamentation. As governments assigned prices to articles, soldiers wanted to ensure they got their money's worth, which in turn necessitated that governments provide reasonably consistent garments.

Consistency was difficult to achieve because of the complicated coordination of suppliers, shippers, and administrators that was involved in every consignment. In the British case, no single office oversaw the regulation, acquisition, and dissemination of military clothing; several government agencies—the War Office, Treasury, Clothing Board, and Board of Ordnance—were involved.[38] In short, the process was decentralized, and the British were not unusual in this regard. The U.S. system of supply came about piecemeal during the war for independence.[39] For their part, the French did not establish a central administrative body for military clothing until 1787, and even then the process of provisioning was riddled with problems and underwent numerous overhauls in the 1790s.[40]

No matter the regime and its exact organizational structure, the collective task of furnishing clothing was enormous. In the summer of 1776, the British War Office computed the garments required for 1777, enough for forty-five battalions stationed in North America totaling roughly eleven thousand men.[41] To supply them, the British military relied on agents. The government could commission them directly, but more often it depended on the long-standing—and, in the revolutionary period, increasingly criticized—practice of awarding budgets to colonels who, at their discretion, hired agents. An agent knew the needs of "his" regiment—the particularities of its insignia and colors, the number of men, their ranks, and so forth, and he was responsible for locating, buying, and preparing for shipment the appropriate clothing for the rank and file.[42] Colonels paid their agents and pocketed whatever funds remained.

In theory this arrangement seemed sensible. Although the British textile industry had grown dramatically and become more efficient as the century wore on, the government had not yet cultivated smooth channels between manufacturers and the military. Furthermore, the Atlantic textile trade relied on agents, and so the government built on existing norms.[43] In practice, however, mechanisms of supply were complicated by the burden of accountability in charged political atmospheres. Petty corruption and late payments jeopardized the credibility of regimes. Accusations surfaced of colonels inflating the sizes of regiments and acquiring subpar clothing on the cheap. In 1795 the commander of the Second West India Regiment received over £11,000—enough to pay and outfit at least eleven hundred men, and yet reports show the regiment with only fifty-one troops.[44] Agents griped about the bureaucratic mire that hampered their best efforts. In 1777 John Ogilvie of the partnership of Ogilvie and Gray wrote to the Treasury that the previous year he had advanced over £2,000 to clothe Colonel Maclean's Corps, serving in New York. As Ogilvie explained, he had been "drawn into this Advance from a desire of forwarding the publick Service, and on a firm reliance of being reimburs'd in due time," but so far, no payment was forthcoming.[45]

While malfeasance and delays crept into the system and tarnished causes, the difficulties in assembling orders contributed to the value of clothing among bureaucrats, officers, and men. So, too, did the formidable task of shipment. Available tonnage was a constant problem. The government chartered rather than owned most transport vessels, and some merchants were reluctant to lease their ships for fear of seizures, interruptions, and other mishaps.[46] Officials also became concerned about the security of cargos. In comparison to previous imperial conflicts, clothing emerged as an even more prized commodity. Without the ability to produce significant quantities of cloth on their own, North American and Caribbean revolutionaries depended heavily on European imports—purchased, donated, or seized.[47] As a result, European armies had to expend extra effort to secure supply lines. This realization dawned on the British early in the North American conflict, when in the winter of 1776–77 a rebel cruiser captured the transport ship *Mellish,* which was loaded with clothing for eight Canadian regiments. Officials pointed to this example to argue for "the absolute necessity of sending Clothing in Ships strong enough to defend themselves from the Enemy."[48] From this point forward, the British tried to ensure that each ship carrying clothing had enough guns and troops to protect the cargo; in the case of the *Speke,* which took men, goods, and clothing to Dominica in 1777, the ship had twenty-two nine- and six-pound cannons as well as ninety seamen.[49]

Despite precautions, the fog of war exacerbated troubles. Recruits sent to the West Indies in 1780 arrived without their clothing when the vessel carrying it became separated from the convoy.[50] Ships had a hard time keeping abreast of the movements of regiments and delivered consignments to the wrong place. General Pattison groaned that the garments for Captain Stewart's Company, then in Philadelphia, had been sent to Canada, and that for Lieutenant Colonel Innes's troops went to Philadelphia rather than to Rhode Island.[51] The Southern (Continental) Army waited for a shipment of over twenty thousand suits, postponed when the vessel dismasted and had to pull into port for refitting.[52]

For all their difficulties, at least French and British forces had the advantage of moving cargo by sea. The Continental Army often needed overland transport, which was cumbersome and expensive. Wagons were scarce, as were wagoners. The work was risky, lonesome, and tedious as drivers were prone to attack, exposed to the elements, and called out day and night. Congress had a hard time hiring men for the job, and wagoners had a bad reputation for stealing goods, diverting consignments, and abandoning loads when the going got tough.[53] The inability to shift provisions from one point to another stymied operations. One Pennsylvania official grumbled about "the fifty wagon loads of cloths and ready made clothes for the soldiery" that sat "in the Clothier General's store in Lancaster" for want of transport.[54]

The intensive labor and organization of fabricating and moving military clothing added to its worth, and to a certain extent, this effort was characteristic of the eighteenth-century Atlantic textile trade, which made fabric a valuable commodity in any context.[55] But in the case of military garments, these conditions were intensified by the exigencies of warfare and by the drive for a degree of uniformity. Since the government assigned a specific price to each garment, it had to guarantee that the quality of each item reflected that price. Unlike items sold by a cloth retailer, who could adjust pricing from bale to bale as he or she saw fit, military garments received values before they were constructed. Because cloth and clothing came from so many sources, quality control was always an issue. The French and British struggled with this quest for consistency, while North American and Caribbean armies were more exposed to the caprices of supply since they were farther away from sources. Military garments needed to be roughly equal for soldiers to accept them.

The problem of quality control began at the top. A 1768 British warrant stipulated that every article should be "good," but what exactly was "good"? The orders were maddeningly silent in this regard. In 1782, a full fourteen years after the clothing regulations were published, William Fawcett in the Adjutant General's Office asked for clarification about a "sufficient quantity of Cloth for the Fore-Part of a Waistcoat." He suggested that the Clothing Board should "oblig[e] all the Clothiers of the Army, without exception, to furnish the same quantity of Cloth" as it would be an "expedient" and "effectual measure."[56] Perhaps government officials trusted in what they thought were shared understandings of quality, but the lack of specific instructions opened the door to discrepancy and fraud. While rules became more precise, this work was in progress throughout the revolutionary era.

Without clear guidelines and oversight, quality was variable at best. The American soldier Joseph Plumb Martin traveled with his lieutenant to Tappan, New York to bring back clothing for their unit, and as he packed garments for transport, his superior officer told him to "take care of my own interest[.] I accordingly picked from the best of each article what was allowed to each man and bundled them up by themselves."[57] Martin and his fellow soldiers knew that not all shirts were alike, and these differences mattered: the better the shirt, the longer it lasted, and the more a soldier felt that he was getting the value he deserved. Soldiers objected when they received inferior goods: winter items with a weave so open that "straws [could be] shot through without discommoding the threads" and other garments "which weir not fit for the Devil to waire."[58] Although the regulations were light on particulars, soldiers understood what to look for and voiced their discontent.

Some higher-ups tried to defuse frustration on this score through appeals to sacrifice. When Louverture wrote to Sonthonax about inadequate supplies for his troops, the commissioner regaled the general with instances from the American and French revolutions when poorly equipped and outnumbered soldiers emerged victorious and urged him to "remind the republicans under your command of these heroic traits."[59] According to Sonthonax, deprivation was part and parcel of wars against despotism, but such explanations had their limits, and intractable hardship led to critiques of revolutionary causes, as Nathanael Greene had predicted. Years after the war, when Joseph Plumb Martin published his memoir, he ruminated on his government's failure to regularly provide him and his compatriots with good-quality clothing, and he highlighted how that neglect led to real distress. After enumerating the shortcomings of clothing distribution, Martin launched into an indictment of the revolutionary regime: "That the country was young and poor, at that time, I am willing to allow; but young people are generally modest, especially females. Now, I think the country . . . showed but little modesty at the time alluded to, for she appeared to think her soldiers had no private parts; for on our march from the Valley forge, through the Jerseys, and at the boasted battle of Monmouth, a fourth part of the troops had not a scrip of any thing but their ragged shirt-flaps to cover their nakedness, and were obliged to remain so long after."[60] Martin sees soldiers' exposure as evidence of his country's lack of virtue. Not even the poverty of the new country, he argues, excuses the humiliation and suffering soldiers endured. Martin leads the reader to wonder what kind of woman/country would be *that* immodest, and in the eighteenth century the only possible answer was a prostitute—a far cry from the image of the United States as a virtuous lady liberty.

Martin's censure is the product of postwar reflection, but some soldiers expressed their dissatisfaction on the spot. In February 1779 a commissary arrived at a camp outside of Philadelphia with a "parcel of shirts . . . but they proved to be so little (it's said but two and half yards in [a] shirt) that [the soldiers] returned him the shirts and all, to return back as a cheat to the public."[61] The men took the high ground, locating corruption in the system (not the cause wholesale) and claiming to act in the name of the public good. Commanders feared, though, that such incidents could escalate—that soldiers would feel the injustice so acutely that they would launch more vigorous protests about their circumstances and the movements that created them.

But remonstration occurred less frequently than it justifiably could have because soldiers were well aware that shoddy garments reflected textile shortages. In ideal conditions, certain types of fabric were used for specific purposes. A fine, sturdy broadcloth was preferred for coats because its weave was so tight that it did not require hemming after cutting, while linen, since it was cooler and lighter, was favored for lining sleeves, and shalloon (a shiny wool twill) for visible contrasting areas.[62] Clothiers and quartermasters, however, did not have the luxury of choice, as stock dwindled. Nathanael Greene wrote to colleagues up and down the Eastern Seaboard to cobble together the fabrics, trimmings, gilt buttons, and other items for his own uniform.[63] If the quartermaster of the Continental Army had a hard time locating the right materials for his personal use, then it comes as no surprise that quartermasters, clothiers, and commanders faced more trying circumstances in outfitting vast numbers of men—so much so that they competed with one another for shipments. A military tribunal adjudicated a grievance between a clothier general and deputy quartermaster who both claimed a consignment of "Brabant linen" from France. One wanted it to outfit one thousand men in hunting shirts and the other to line the interior walls of tents; both argued that their requests were central to military endeavors. The two men, as the reporting officer described, displayed "some Ebulitions of Temper" that resulted in the involvement of superiors.[64] Under conditions in which suppliers competed for any cloth that was somewhat suitable, it's no wonder that they took whatever fabric they could get their hands on.

Problems with quality plagued the army's aspiration to make uniforms uniform, and this inconsistency was a point of controversy with soldiers, white and Black, who demanded products that warranted their pay deductions. From the regulations that governed military clothing to the chains of production and distribution, all levels struggled to translate uniformity from an ideal into practice. Even by eighteenth-century standards, as articulated by the warrants and by soldiers' expectations, the quest for uniformity fell short. Nevertheless, regimes kept trying during the revolutionary period, not only because they had wars to fight but also because clothing's value was central to soldiers' relationships with militaries and governments. The soldiers had a right to clothing of a particular sort, and yet given the extraordinary labor that went into obtaining it, officers were not willing to let soldiers do whatever they wanted with these garments. Throughout the wars, men and officers struggled to determine suitability.

SUITING SOLDIERS

Part of the difficulty of making military clothing uniform lay with the nature of dress itself. Unlike other elements in soldiers' kits, clothing had to suit the wearer. This suitability was literal in that the garments had to fit men of all body types, and it was figurative in that from the army's perspective, ensembles had to signal the wearer's regiment, rank, and other aspects of differentiation. From the soldier's point of view, military garments, like all other attire, had to meet his sensibilities as a wearer—to adhere, to some degree, to his notions about appearance, even within the confines of the army. Everyone from generals to common men in the field introduced variations to his dress—out of necessity sometimes, but at other moments as an expression of preference. The wrangling over suitability reveals another facet of the quest for equality in the age of revolutions, as parties negotiated the relationship between the individual and the collective, between soldiers' rights as owners and garments' intended uses in warfare.

Once clothing arrived to its destination, the first task was to check that "the Accoutrements are properly fitted, According to the size of each man."[65] Sometimes suppliers sent ready-made clothing, but in the eighteenth century, there was not a standard or sophisticated sizing system. In the British navy, slops (the term for ready-made, loose-fitting, standard-issue garments) came in just three sizes—36, 38, and 40 (according to average chest measurements), and in the French army, the *justaucorps,* or coats, were either small, medium, or large.[66] Not surprisingly, then, ready-made breeches, sleeves, and shirttails required hemming or letting down; breeches and coats needed to be taken in or let out, and so on. One colonel griped that these garments were so poorly constructed that "the People are obliged to have them sewed over."[67]

Correct fit was crucial to the performance of one's duties. As scholar Daniel Roche has pointed out, "The soldier's dress had to be tailored in such a way that the different parts would not all get wet at the same time. . . . It had to be easy to look after, simple to repair, light in weight and convenient to put on and off."[68] Rarely, he notes, did reality live up to this model, and soldiers protested ill-fitting clothing. Militaries anticipated this situation and recruited tailors and textile workers, many of whom had been displaced by the early effects of industrial expansion, especially in Britain.[69] Aware of these skilled workers among the troops, agents sent tailoring implements. When the British agent Thomas Harley fulfilled an order of fabric for provincial troops in 1777, he included almost £300 worth of thread, tape, breeches string, needles, thimbles, hooks and eyes, shears, and leather shreds (for ties or fasteners).[70] Despite this forethought and preparation, the burden of production was great. Most tailoring occurred in the winter months when action slowed, and armies used the reprieve to regroup and re-kit. Military tailors worked at a breakneck speed to alter ready-made garments and to construct new ones from whole cloth. When the British occupied Philadelphia in the winter of 1777–78, the demand for clothing was so urgent that General Pattison excused the tailors from Sunday services; they "were to Continue at Work."[71] A few weeks into the job, two of the tailors found the pace so odious that they skulked off and got drunk.[72]

There was more work than military tailors could handle, and so armies turned to locals—an economic windfall for communities. According to orders for a New York regiment in 1781, civilian tailors "were allowed" 6 shillings, 6 pence for a regimental coat; 2 shillings,

6 pence for a jacket; and 3 shillings for a pair of breeches. They received the same amount for "turning old clothes" for new purposes.[73]
These prices, though, were below going rates in the Caribbean. Charles
Moore, a tailor in Bermuda, announced that he charged 16 shillings,
8 pence for making a "lapelled cloth coat," while breeches cost 5 shillings, 4 pence.[74] Whatever their prices, tailors' services were in demand,
beyond their capacity. The Kingston, Jamaica, tailors McCallum and
McDonald were shorthanded and advertised for "five or six Taylor
Negroes," noting that "Good encouragement will be given and their
wages paid regularly."[75] White tailors frequently hired Black assistants,
which speaks not only to how the arrival of an army increased pressure
on civilian tailors but also to how knowledge of cloth and of clothes
making penetrated all levels of society. As the planter Edward Long observed, slaves were "expert at their needles," and white artisans sometimes exploited this "expert" labor for the military's benefit.[76]

In fact, the pervasiveness of clothes-making know-how helped soldiers find other outlets for modifying garments. When military and civilian tailors were overwhelmed, soldiers sought out resident makers.
In the winter of 1778, Benjamin Gilbert, in Colonel Rufus Putnam's
Fifth Massachusetts Regiment, visited several nearby artisans: he had
his coat altered at the tailor's and his hat "dressed" at the hatter's; he
took cloth to Molly Shays so she could sew him a jacket; and a woman
identified only as Lucy spun yarn and then knitted Gilbert a pair of
stockings. Gilbert paid $4 for the stockings, $1 to the hatter, 15 shillings to the tailor, and 9 shillings for the jacket.[77] From the perspective
of communities, the presence of soldiers presented economic opportunity for self-described tailors and milliners, and for diverse people,
especially women, who could construct garments.

Even with access to civilian makers, soldiers felt the strain of time
and money to guarantee that their clothing fit well. For some men,
others' services were too expensive, so they put their own sewing skills
to use for their attire. At the same time that Benjamin Gilbert commissioned various people to fabricate and repair his clothing, he sewed and
lined a pair of homespun breeches, crafted worsted buttons for himself
and another soldier, and paid to have cloth cut out in the pattern for a
pair of overalls, which he then sewed himself.[78]

The range of people who could contribute to a single suit of military clothing speaks to the shared knowledge and skills of clothing

construction across sexes, classes, and races. Many people throughout society had the know-how to assess and to produce garments, and this lingua franca around clothing contributed to its value. In the case of the army, both officers and men saw clothing as products of their labor: commanders had the task of acquiring and distributing clothing, and soldiers bought it and invested further time and care by altering garments and sometimes fabricating them. The concern with worth extended to the maintenance of clothing. Soldiers needed to keep their garments in good order for their own protection and comfort during the war, and proper care boosted the longevity of articles, particularly if a soldier hoped to continue to benefit from them in peacetime. As a result, soldiers and commanders went to extraordinary lengths to conserve clothing as best they could, but this common goal at times put them at loggerheads.

Tough conditions made preservation a constant struggle, and this fact informed uniform design. The French army preferred white garments for the color's national significance and because white quickly became dingy, fading to a yellow or gray that blended in with the surrounding countryside.[79] James Simcoe, the commander of the Queen's Rangers, a loyalist corps in Canada, argued against changing his regiment's coats from green to red. A green coat, he claimed, "if put on in the spring, by autumn it nearly fades with the leaves, preserving its characteristic of being scarcely discernible at a distance."[80] Officers weighed how circumstances in the field affected garments and tried to turn them to advantage.

While these accommodations addressed tactical aspects of wear, the rough and tumble of military life took a toll on clothing. In the heat of battle, soldiers tore garments as they ran through the landscape or met the end of a bayonet or bullet. General de Vioménil inspected the Saintonge regiment after the battle of Yorktown and concluded that it needed at least 690 jackets, 1,030 pairs of breeches, and 1,000 hats, as well as fabric and braiding for garments that could be mended—and that was just for one of the French regiments.[81] Marches could be as devastating to clothing as sieges. A British soldier in Grenada in 1796 described trudging for miles "literally up and down precipices, halfway up the leg in clay, and through a wood where I believe no human foot had ever before stepped."[82] The tenacious clay sucked the shoes off soldiers' feet, and heavy rains soaked through the men's clothes as they scaled steep hills on their hands and knees.[83]

Given these hard circumstances, officers urged soldiers to turn out "in the best manner in their Power."[84] But what exactly was "in their Power" was up for discussion, and commanders issued a slew of missives designed to preserve clothing. The concern began before the soldiers reached their posts. During a voyage transporting men to the West Indies in 1803, "the Soldiers great Coats were taken from them and washed & scrubed" and "packed . . . in Bales[.] The Soldiers red Cloths are likewise taken from them[;] therefore [they] have nothing to cover them but their Waistcoats and Shirts."[85] This decision probably did not sit well with the men because coats offered some protection from rain, and in the eighteenth century people feared the adverse health effects of being wet, even in the tropics.[86] Thomas Howard, a British lieutenant stationed in Saint-Domingue in the mid-1790s, attributed a bout of illness to "having no Mantle with me" while out on maneuvers one evening: "I got wet to the Skin; & in three Days after [I] experienced the Effects of the Climate by having a most horrid Fever which had nearly deprived me of Life."[87]

Other approaches to clothing preservation were less invasive. In 1778 General Pattison ordered that all soldiers wear linen frocks and foraging caps whenever they performed duties that might "spoil their clothes," such as serving in the hospital, cooking in the mess, standing guard duty, and searching for wood and food.[88] In the Continental Army, soldiers wore their old clothes for fatigue duty in an effort "to preserve the New."[89] The conservationist impulse came from within the ranks, too. After a rousing night out to celebrate his enlistment with other recruits, one Yorkshire man was surprised that his fellow soldiers insisted he go to bed naked, "a common custom with soldiers in order to save their linens."[90]

To safeguard their economic investment further, soldiers spent a good deal of time laundering garments. Troops hired camp followers and locals to wash and iron clothing at rates set by commanders. In U.S. camps a "plain shirt" cost 4 shillings to wash and iron, and a "ruffled" one was 4 shillings, 6 pence.[91] While hired help was sometimes available, soldiers needed to tend to their own items.[92] Coats and breeches were brushed vigorously, and stains spot-cleaned. Men washed with soap and water their linen—shirts, stockings, and kerchiefs.[93] This labor did not suffer from a gendered stigma. In domestic settings, laundry fell under women's purview, but in a military context, it was simply another task that men performed.

The attention and energy devoted to the maintenance of clothing reflected the efforts of both officers and troops to keep a specific suit of military clothing on the back of an individual soldier for as long as possible. It was an issue in which the soldiers' interests and that of their superiors often aligned. But commanders were vexed by the constant movement of clothing among men. All accepted that the loss of garments was inevitable on the march and in battle. In anticipation of a skirmish, troops jettisoned extra weight, including whatever stockpile of clothing they had accumulated. Before a march in August 1778, Benjamin Gilbert noted, "We had orders to dispose of all Cloaths more than we could carry in our Packs."[94] Sometimes the excess baggage was hauled away for safekeeping, but with varying success. In the aftermath of a contest, camps and battlefields were strewn with all manner of articles, which victorious soldiers appropriated.[95]

More problematic from the perspective of officers was the circulation of clothing within camp, and they attempted to prevent men from selling, swapping, and stealing garments. Commanders saw the marketplace for military clothing as a threat to their authority and as a potential opportunity for pilfering, price gouging, and hoarding. The army feared that such activities would elicit accusations of corruption. But soldiers viewed trading and hawking as within their rights as owners and a practical solution to the need for well-fitting garments. In sum, military clothing was both private and public, and the rank and file and commanders struggled to define what this meant for fair use.

Officers tried various means to prevent troops from selling and exchanging garments. At weekly reviews, they appraised what each man wore. A British soldier recounted that every Monday the troops turned out for inspection and "if any clothing is missing, a circle is formed, and a drumhead court martial is called and the delinquent is tried and punished according to his des[s]ert."[96] General Pattison went even further in his quest to keep track of garments, insisting that "All the Mens Coats Waistcoats & Breeches are to have the Names wrote on the Lining with Ink and a paper Pasted in the inside of each Hat with the Name Wrote on it. Their Linnen and Necessaries are to be Mark'd with the initial Letters of their Name."[97] Pattison hoped that such precautions would create clear trails of ownership, preventing an individual soldier from selling military-issued items to another and then claiming falsely that he lacked the "necessaries" due (and therefore required additional ones).

But the emphasis on an individual's possession of garments also introduced the possibilities for him to exercise other aspects of textile ownership, including sale. As much as commanders tried to curtail it, the marketplace for clothing was impossible to check. The scale and volume were too great to police thoroughly, and exchange of all sorts was part of camp life. When an officer died, his possessions were sometimes auctioned. Authorities advertised these sales, like that of the late General Poor in 1780, which included "several suits of Cloaths A Genteal Small Sward Sash Epaulets and many Other Articles."[98] These items were probably out of reach for most soldiers, but camp auctions added to the climate of circulation. Among the troops, articles changed hands for sundry reasons. Inspired by sympathy, men gave items to each other, and some speculated in clothing to augment lousy pay. In February 1776 David How, a soldier from Massachusetts, purchased three pairs of shoes for 5 shillings, 6 pence each, and the next day, sold a pair to another soldier for 6 shillings, 8 pence.[99] Swapping was common as well, as troops looked to improve the condition or fit of their garments (and therefore save on labor) or simply preferred a particular style. In April 1778 Gilbert sold a broadcloth jacket to one man for $20, and then traded jackets with another, paying him $4 to even out the deal.[100]

While the most diligent of commanders could not rein in this activity, officers did exert their power in cases of theft. Regimental order books are littered with court-martial transcripts in which soldiers are accused of stealing garments. If convicted, the punishments were significant. John Homes, a private in the American army, was charged with stealing one pair of stockings from the regimental store. No fewer than five witnesses testified at the trial, recounting in detail the circumstances surrounding the theft. Despite his protestations, Homes was found guilty and sentenced to one hundred lashes.[101]

Both the thorough procedure and the punishment were typical for men convicted of stealing clothing, whether it was a relatively inexpensive item like a pair of stockings or a more costly garment such as a coat.[102] By means of comparison, deserters also received one hundred lashes; however, an American sergeant named Obby, convicted of pilfering rum from the stores, was denied the following month's ration of liquor but still had to pay for it. Then he was taken to the parade ground, where the drum major stripped him of his coat "and put it wrong side Outwards" and returned him to the ranks.[103] These cases point to how seriously the military considered the theft of clothing. It was more akin to deserting the army than to pinching a provision, and the experience of Sergeant Obby highlights one of the reasons why: clothing carried social significance, so much so that wearing it inside out in public was a humiliation.

Government functionaries, civilians, officers, and the rank and file went to extraordinary lengths to attain and keep suitable clothing on the backs of soldiers. All worked to ensure that garments fit properly and were maintained as well as circumstances permitted. They were motivated by a shared goal of military efficacy, yet troops had the added incentive of property ownership, and certain aspects of that ownership brought them into conflict with officers. Trading and selling were among the rights of possession, but commanders attempted to check men who, they felt, went too far. At these moments, clothing—because of extant practices and shared understandings of it—brought out tensions over the right of individuals to seek this type of equality, even within a hierarchical military context. The political power of this dynamic is more pronounced when we consider what soldiers actually wore.

SARTORIAL ASPIRATIONS

The goal for armies was not just to clothe soldiers in suits but to clothe them in particular suits—to make evident, through an individual's garments, his loyalties as well as his rank and unit. Bureaucrats, in collaboration with officers and agents, devised elaborate sartorial markers of distinction that they saw as critical to effective operations and to instilling senses of pride and belonging among the troops. They proposed striking ensembles: brilliant scarlet or blue coats bedecked with gold epaulets, lace, and rows of gleaming buttons; achingly white, thigh-hugging breeches; and tall hats with feathers, ribbon, gold trim, and fur.

While the loftiness of sartorial standards was persistent, their details and execution were not stable. The decentralized process for developing uniform regulations introduced ambiguities into the precise content of the form, and conditions on the ground forced officers and soldiers to modify their expectations. Yet the discrepancies between archetypal attire and what men really wore increased, rather than obviated, the political potential of military clothing in two ways. First, it allowed a soldier an opportunity for self-expression, which underscored his ownership of the clothing and the rights that went with it. Second, when a soldier of African descent achieved the sartorial ideal, that accomplishment had a tremendous impact on Atlantic observers, who comprehended the Black wearer's claims to the economic and social value of those garments, to rights of ownership, and to equality within a military setting.

The realization of armies' sartorial aspirations was hampered not only by the mechanics of making and moving clothing but also by the confusion about acceptable designs. Piecemeal directives came from several authorities. In the British case, the War Office concocted a dizzying array of ways to distinguish one regiment from another through clothing. Although waistcoats and breeches were the same for all regiments, hats and coats bore the burden of distinction since they were the most prominent exterior garments. Consider a 1768 chart of facings—a contrasting material applied to a lapel, collar, or cuff of a coat—for the marching foot regiments. According to the schema, a British regiment could have either blue, yellow, green, buff, white, red, black, or orange facings on its red coat. What's more, each regiment claimed unique shades of its assigned color. In the case of green facings, there was "goslin," "full," "deep," "very deep," "willow," "popinjay," and "yellowish." One scholar has attempted to re-create these hues using surviving facings in the queen's collections and accounting for differences between eighteenth-century and contemporary dyes, fading, and other factors. His chart gives us the best estimation of these colors, yet in the end he laments the inability to overcome the discrepancies as "a most difficult problem!"[104] (The exclamation point is his.)

The British were not alone in these seemingly endless combinations of colors and ornamentation. They took their cues from the French, who had their own dense vocabulary of facing colors—from jonquils and camels to auroras and sky blues. In some measure the gaps in understanding are a result of the distance between our time and theirs, of our attempt to recover, as one historian has eloquently put it, "a visual sensibility different from our own."[105] Yet the subtleties in shades may have been just as perplexing then. How would agents scattered across Britain and Ireland or soldiers in Charleston, New York, and Kingston know the difference between "popinjay" and "willow"? The language of color in such fine gradations was not self-evident.

Facings were just one aspect of distinction on coats. Motifs on buttons differed from regiment to regiment, and within units their material (gilt or not) reflected rank. Epaulets, looping, and lace came in sundry colors and weaves, and their application to coats—the patterns in which they were sewn—varied, according to unit and rank. As for hats, their ornamentation—feathers, cockades, trim—changed from one regiment to the next and one rank to the next. The permutations seemed limitless and in flux, as officials tinkered with designs.

Commanders got in on the act, requesting changes and sometimes devising uniforms in their entirety. Governor Mathew, looking to promote his pet project of a permanent Black corps in the British West Indies, reported to his metropolitan superiors that he had "directed my Agents Bishopp and Brummel, to send out a complete suit of Cloathing for one mounted and for one dismounted Pioneer, according to our Ideas of Service in this Country, with distinguishing Cape and Cuff to each of the three Divisions, with the exact charge of each."[106] According to a receipt received a few months later, Mathew had settled on green jackets, "Frill'd" shirts, linen waistcoats and leggings, round hats with feathers (in either red, yellow, or green), and leather stocks and shoes with brass buckles.[107]

With so many hands involved in the design of uniforms and with so many options for differentiation, mix-ups surfaced in bureaucratic circles. In the British military, every ornament required approval by the Adjutant General's Office, and the devices were forwarded to the Clothing Board via the Comptroller's Office, which ensured that the standards were followed. Correspondence between these offices described approved changes, but at times words failed, and samples (unfortunately now lost) of the proper brim of a hat or the lace for a coat were sent as well.[108] These precautions occasionally failed to do the trick, however. In November 1784, the Comptroller's Office pointed out that in the new pattern for coats for the Twenty-Third Regiment, "the Collar was made upright which They conceive is not conformable to the General Regulation and have therefore suspended the making up of that Clothing."[109] Even the bodies that passed the regulations had a hard time keeping track of and enforcing them consistently.

Conditions on the ground impeded the implementation of designs, and commanders revised clothing protocols whenever they saw fit. Many of the alterations resulted from problems with stock. The changes could be minor, switching the color of a facing, for example, because the stipulated one was unavailable.[110] Higher-ups faced bigger problems when key garments could not be acquired at all, and some suggested other means by which to achieve a sense of sartorial cohesion. In the early days of the American Revolution, the Continental Army and state militias lacked the quantities of cloth required for complete suits. As a solution, George Washington advocated pairing hunting shirts—a utilitarian, loose-fitting, long shirt with an open neck, often in osnaburg—with trousers and gaiters (figure 3.2). Given the situation, hunting shirts were practical for the uniformity they provided and because "no Dress can be had cheaper, nor more convenient, as the Wearer may be cool in warm weather, and warm in cool weather by putting on undercloaths which will not change the outward dress, Winter or Summer."[111] Although Washington lauded their virtues and some American troops wore hunting shirts at various points during the war, he saw them as a temporary measure. Whenever resources permitted, he opted for the traditional suit. Some civilians and British soldiers mocked hunting shirts as a visible sign of the U.S. army's lack of professionalism. A British woman described a muster of the North Carolina militia: "I must really laugh while I recollect their figures: 2000 men in their shirts and trousers, preceded by a very ill beat-drum and a fiddler, who was also in his shirt with a long sword and a cue at his hair, who played with all his might. They made indeed a most unmartial appearance."[112] It was hard enough for soldiers to muster the courage for battle without being derided for their clothes in the process.

From Washington's perspective, hunting shirts fell short of the martial model, but at least they were a feasible and functional substitution. Other commanders were not so lucky, and straightened circumstances pushed officers and men to improvise. Over four thousand British soldiers captured at the battle of Saratoga marched from Massachusetts to a POW camp in Virginia. In light of their compromised clothing,

Figure 3.2. Fringed hunting shirt, 1780–90. (Museum of the American Revolution.)

General von Riedesel ordered a group of female camp followers to trim the skirts from the men's greatcoats and to recycle the excess cloth to patch their garments.[113] Higher-ups everywhere complained about men cutting up tents and blankets for clothing—further testimony to the sewing skills of soldiers, albeit to the chagrin of officials.[114] In moments of extreme distress, commanders authorized the use of whatever fabric was available to clothe their soldiers, but officers insisted that decisions about alterations were their prerogative, not their men's.

No matter how much commanders tried to check soldiers' modifications to their garments, the inability to supply them with the appropriate ones and the customs of textile ownership gave men—of all ranks and races—an opening for sartorial self-expression. Coats provide an instructive example. In an era when clothing was as crucial to identifying individuals as physical features, a man's coat was almost synonymous with his person. Most free men did not have more than a coat or two, and so one could recognize a man, literally, by his coat. Surviving examples represent disproportionately the elites, and even they are few, but many fail to conform faithfully to regulations. Consider, for instance, a British field officer's coat in the collections of the Colonial Williamsburg Foundation (figure 3.3). The coat dates from the early 1790s, when the man who wore it, Colonel Moncrieff, was appointed deputy adjutant general. While the cut of the coat reflects his new position, it bears hallmarks of uniform design from the 1770s in the arrangement of the buttons along the sleeves, the chest, and exterior pockets. The officer had served during the American Revolution, favored the look of an earlier era, and thought that, almost twenty years later, he could wear it credibly.[115]

In fact, officers from Admiral Lord Nelson to Colonel Thomas Pinckney to Governor-General Toussaint Louverture bucked clothing dictates, perhaps thanks to the privileges that came with their positions. But what about the rank and file? Knowing what common soldiers wore is a methodological challenge: few garments remain, and textual sources are anecdotal, not comprehensive. The best evidence for their actual clothing is gleaned from advertisements for deserters, and the largest available cache, of about 215 cases, comes from North America between 1776 and 1783.[116] Like advertisements for runaway slaves and servants, those for deserters enumerated garments. Perhaps some soldiers on the lam sought to disguise their status by jettisoning any article with martial associations, in the process obscuring our view of their attire. But the material resources of common soldiers were slim, and the value of garments discouraged disposal. So, while the level and reliability of detail varies somewhat, these descriptions offer the clearest contemporaneous insight into what most soldiers wore—by necessity and sometimes by choice.

Given their prominence, coats were the articles mentioned most often in the notices, and they came in assorted styles.[117] Over half of the ads used the term "regimental," "soldier," "Regular," or "uniform" to

Figure 3.3. British field officer's coat, 1790–93. (The Colonial Williamsburg Foundation. Museum Purchase.)

indicate a coat with clear military provenance, and the rest were distinguished by known types ("surtout," "watch," "frock fashion," "great"), by cut ("long," "short," "strait-bodied," "long waisted"), and by notable features ("lapelled," "quilted," "folded")—all of which were found in civilian dress, too. On the one hand, the vocabulary signals that military coats were a recognized style and that they reached some soldiers. On the other hand, the range of terms shows the diversity among soldiers' most conspicuous garment—the one that was intended to give them the most uniform appearance. Some of this variety resulted from differences between units, but it can be found within individual units as well. Of the four deserters from Captain Parke's company in Colonel Flowers's regiment of artillery and artificers, each man wears a different coat: "light coloured faced with blue," "blue uniform faced with red," "short, light coloured," and "British regimental died brown with white edgings."[118] Of the nine deserters who absconded from Captain Garzia's company of Colonel Elliot's regiment of artillery, four wore blue coats (faced with different colors), one had a "sailor's habit," another a brown coat, yet another green, one of red baize, and the last "light coloured."[119]

The predominant color of coats, when noted, was blue, with brown in shades ranging from "brownish" to "snuff" being the next most frequently mentioned color. There was a smattering of greens, grays, and even reds, and a significant number were merely "coloured": "light," "dark," or "mixed." Fifty-three coats were faced or "turn'd up" with contrasting colors at the collar, lapels, or cuffs—signs of military sartorial distinction. Type of cloth was recorded less faithfully than style or color, but there was a good deal of variation among fabrics.[120] A slim majority of coats were made of the preferred broadcloth, but there were also coats of homespun, "blanket," calico, linen, nankeen (a yellow or buff-colored cotton), camblet (or camlet, a kind of wool), fustian (a sturdy, twill-weave cotton), baize (a coarse woolen, similar to felt), shag (a cloth with a long nap), and swanskin (a twill-weave flannel).

The advertisements for deserters indicate that at least half of soldiers acquired a coat that adhered to regulations to a degree—either in color, cut, or material. These semi-conformable coats were frequently paired with nonregulation garments, though: for example, brown regimental coats coupled with a striped waistcoat or green vest, and blue regimental coats with brown linen, leather, or buckskin breeches.[121] This mixture of regulation with nonregulation stemmed partially from supply glitches, yet some soldiers' ensembles suggest that even within a military context and with limited means, men found ways to assert their own senses of style. William Bostwick of Colonel Swift's regiment in Connecticut experimented with pattern and color: "a round brim'd hat with a red and blue cockade, a pepper and salt coat, a red and white flowered vest, good leather breeches, gray stockings, flowered silver shoe buckels."[122] Sometimes the distinction lay in the details: Elin Alurd, a shoemaker by trade, had nondescript clothing but sported a pair of "long quartered shoes of waxed neats leather, closed in the inside on the grain."[123] The small pool of Black deserters shows a level of sartorial diversity and desire for self-expression similar to white peers'.

There were men like Jacob Speen, a "mulatto," from the Sixth regiment in the Continental service, who possessed some elements of the typical uniform, such as "a light brown coat turned up with white."[124] Others, such as James Anderson, "a black soldier" of the Sixth Virginia regiment, had more distinctive items. Along with his light gray coat faced with green, he sported "a small hat with a piece of bear skin on it"—an honorific reserved for members of prestigious units.[125]

With such elegant hats, spiffy footwear, and striking mix of garments, the attire of some Black and white soldiers made an impression—one that speaks to the wearer's intentionality rather than the martial model. The gap between regulations and their fulfillment allowed some men to exercise their rights over their garments and wear them in ways that they saw fit. But for every William Bostwick or Jacob Speen, there were many soldiers whose only article worth mentioning was an "old blanket" or a homespun coat with osnaburg trousers and a felt hat.[126] The pressures of want and of harsh conditions undercut the aspirations of soldiers and officers.

In the context of this variegated and often distressed clothing landscape, encounters with men who realized the sartorial ideal, or key components of it, resonated strongly. With so few men steadily dressed in regulation uniforms, those who managed the feat broadcast political statements bolder than we have appreciated. Men in uniform laid claim to the economic, social, and cultural values imbued in those textiles, which among civilians broadcast their rights as owners, and within the army demanded an equality of station—a right to be treated like any other member of their rank. Because of the lingua franca of textiles, both Black and white troops made and understood these statements, but for men of African descent, the political import was more radical, in light of the material and ideological degradation that accompanied slavery and racism.

The leading officers in the Haitian Revolution—Toussaint Louverture, Henry Christophe, and Jean-Jacques Dessalines, among others— were usually described as wearing full military regalia. In his 1805 *An Historical Account of the Black Empire of Hayti*, the British soldier Marcus Rainsford recounts first meeting Louverture. According to Rainsford, he wore a red cape; a blue jacket with red cuffs, "eight rows of lace on the arms," and large gold epaulettes; scarlet waistcoat and pantaloons; half boots; and a round hat decorated with a red feather and a tricolor cockade.[127] Before the revolution, Louverture was known on the Bréda plantation for his attention to his appearance, yet his military attire represented a significant material improvement from his earlier days—legible to all as an expensive suit.[128] It was also indicative of his authority and position within the French republican army and, like the uniforms of other officers, his had sartorial idiosyncrasies in keeping with the assembled reality of many officers' clothing. Unorthodox elements derived from personal choice, too. The red plume on Louverture's hat was a gift from General Étienne Laveaux, a sign of his esteem and friendship, but Black Saint-Dominguans would have recognized its religious significance, as feathers were part of several vodou rituals.[129]

More striking are depictions of common Black soldiers in full uniform. At times these portrayals reflect the status of white men more than that of the Black men pictured. Period prints and paintings of white officers, like those of Washington and Lafayette, show Black servants in resplendent outfits, typically bringing horses to the generals.[130] In John Singleton Copley's 1783 painting *The Death of Major Peirson, 6 January 1781,* Pompey, a servant, takes an active role in the scene, picking up a gun and killing the sniper who has felled the major, all while wearing a dashing ensemble.[131] But the sartorial grandeur of these Black men is associated with the white men to whom they attend. Despite the real dangers they faced, their expensive clothing is nearer to livery than to soldiers' uniforms—an actual practice as well as a pictorial convention across the Atlantic world.[132]

These depictions of Black troops tried to contain their political impact, but this was impossible out in the field as soldiers met. Diarists (admittedly all white) appraised the clothing of the Black rank and file, occasionally noting instances when they had a more martial appearance than their white peers. In the lead-up to the siege at Yorktown in 1781, Baron Ludwig von Closen reviewed Washington's troops, commenting on the clothing of each unit and concluding, "Three-quarters of the Rhode Island regiment consists of negroes, and that regiment is the most neatly dressed, the best under arms, and the most precise in its maneuvers."[133] Jean-Baptiste-Antoine de Verger, a sub-lieutenant in Royal Deux-Points regiment (from what is now Switzerland), sketched some of the same soldiers von Closen had seen: a Black infantryman from the First Rhode Island regiment, a musketeer from the Second Canadian regiment, an American rifleman, and a gunner from the Continental Artillery (figure 3.4). Among the four men, the white rifleman deviates the most from the martial model; the side view shows

Figure 3.4. Jean-Baptiste-Antoine de Verger, *Soldiers in Uniform* (1781). (*Prints, Drawings and Watercolors from the Anne S. K. Brown Military Collection.* Brown Digital Repository, Brown University Library, https://repository.library. brown.edu/studio/item/bdr:236977/. Digital object made available by Brown University Library, John Hay Library, University Archives and Manuscripts, Box A, Brown University, Providence, RI, 02912, U.S.A., [http://library.brown.edu/].)

not only his hunting shirt but also his pouch, axe, powder horn, and long rifle. While the attire of the Black soldier differs from that of his white peers, those differences stem from the distinctions of his unit. He, more so than the rifleman, exemplifies military aspirations in his clothing and accoutrements—equal in sartorial stature and military bearing to the white musketeer and gunner with whom he is pictured.[134]

Verger and von Closen's observations and sketches of Black soldiers did not circulate outside their journals, yet their reflections shed light on the thousands of encounters between Black and white men, who appraised one another's clothing on the battlefield, in camp, and on the march. A few images of Black troops, like those in Rainsford's work, were published and distributed among audiences located away from the theaters of war. Although Rainsford emphasizes his interactions with officers, his book includes a plate in which a Black private, the lowest-ranking soldier in the French republican army, is impeccably dressed. From his cockaded and feathered hat and smartly cut coat to his form-fitting breeches and shiny black boots, he radiates martial sophistication and manly fortitude (figure 3.5).[135] A few eccentricities signal his Caribbean roots: the large, gold hoop earring and the turban-like shape of the hat. But for anyone, a civilian or soldier, seeing the print, it would be hard to deny the fine quality of his garments and his ability to wear them appropriately, conforming to martial sartorial ideals.

The Author in Conversation with a private Soldier of the Black Army on his Excursion in St. Domingo.

Figure 3.5. *The Author in Conversation with a Private Solider of the Black Army on His Excursion in St. Domingo,* from Marcus Rainsford, *An Historical Account of the Black Empire of Hayti* (London, 1805). (Library Company of Philadelphia.)

When white men met fully uniformed Black soldiers in the field or as images of them moved through the Atlantic world, the clothing spoke volumes about these men's economic wherewithal—in terms of acquisition, maintenance, and labor—that was threaded through each garment and of their rights of possession over that clothing. Free men of African descent who served in the Jamaica militia during the American Revolution made this connection overtly. Protesting their exclusion from hurricane relief funds, they reminded the Jamaica assembly of their military service: "As good citizens, and in arms, as soldiers, they have always done, and are still ready to do, their utmost in defence of the British constitution." As concrete evidence of their loyalty, they cited their substantial outlay to clothe themselves in regimentals—a sign of putting their money where their mouths were. And for that contribution, they contended, they deserved more equitable treatment—as "citizens," no less.[136]

To claim equal status via military clothing after centuries of degradation, men of African descent advanced one of the most radical and tangible assertions of the age of revolutions. They used military rank to insist on an equality that few among the master class were ready to accept. Napoléon Bonaparte and his advisors in Saint-Domingue comprehended the revolutionary nature of uniforms when they decided that they could no longer "tolerate a single épaulette on the shoulders of these negroes."[137] Force, however, was the only way to remove them. After all, like the coats on which they were sewn, the epaulettes belonged to the Black soldiers who wore them.

For all its hierarchical pretensions, military clothing offered hundreds of thousands of men throughout the Atlantic world a material means through which to argue for equality. Identifying the fullness of this challenge now has required a rigorous reconsideration of these garments in their eighteenth-century context—what it took to fabricate, transport, and distribute them and how these factors informed people's understanding of their economic and political value. To be sure, this material articulation of equality was not the lofty notion enshrined in the Declaration of Independence or the Declaration of Rights of Man and Citizen (although for people of African descent and women these avowals fell far short). Yet the equality of military clothing was, for many men, concrete and valuable, evident in everyday life, and practical in ways that declarations were not. When, for sundry and often legitimate reasons, regimes failed to live up to their contractual obligations with military clothing, soldiers—Black and white—voiced their discontent in terms, including the language of rights, that were accepted. Governments responded to these demands as best they could to serve their own purposes of reinforcing the hierarchies that were central to armies' effectiveness. But in the process, soldiers had opportunities to see and to express themselves as worthy of a kind of equal treatment—a vision that, as men of African descent demonstrated most powerfully, had enormous political consequences.

The equalizing potential of garments could not be contained in the military sphere. In the revolutionary period many men moved back and forth between military and civilian life: when service periods expired, in brief interludes of peace, and as they mingled with local populations during deployments. Moreover, the arsenal of civilians who helped to outfit troops in ways large and small meant that many were familiar with these men and their garments. In all these situations, soldiers' military clothing—and its significance—went with them. The permeable line between the two realms indicates that dress had political resonance for civilian populations, too. Here, revolutionary authorities, similar to military leaders, had grand plans, but the people had their own ideas about the importance of these things.

4   Dangerous Trifles

PEOPLE IN THE eighteenth century loved to accessorize. They added yards of ribbons to garments and wigs, folded handkerchiefs in elaborate ways, and studded their ears, wrists, necks, and fingers with jewelry. They tacked tassels and buckles to their breeches and shoes, peppered waistcoats and coats with buttons, swung swords from their waists, and stuck feathers in their hair and hats. Makers churned out these novelties by the millions, offering consumers boundless options for indulging in ornament, and satirists had a field day mocking the deluge of "geegaws" that overran attire.

Following such critics, we usually categorize these items as trifles—frivolous embellishments of and afterthoughts to more substantial articles of clothing. But the pervasiveness and affordability of many accessories gave them tremendous potential for personal and political meaning. Well before the revolutionary era, individuals of all ranks adopted accessories whenever they could to express their senses of style and self. Elites had greater spending power and hence more opportunities to bedeck themselves with little fineries. And yet accounts of ribbon trimmings appeared in descriptions of runaway slaves as well as in high-end French fashion magazines. For actors across the social spectrum, small sartorial gestures had big impact, helping to distinguish a person from others.

Accessories reflected the new as they freshened up garments to speak to current modes and to personal taste. It was easier and cheaper to swap out a ribbon or set of buttons than it was to replace an entire gown or coat. In this way, accessories had a responsiveness that clothing did not, and individuals put this flexibility to political ends in the age of revolutions. As one French newspaper remarked, "It is with . . . rosettes, ribbons and caps, that one disperses tyrants."[1] This clever observation may have been in jest, but it indicates just how noticeable the phenomenon was then. And for us now it raises the question as to how and why accessories, in particular, became an influential means through which so many people engaged in revolutionary politics. To comprehend this development, we must begin by appraising why makers were primed to take advantage of the novelty of Atlantic revolutions and the specific ways in which they did so. As they considered whether to incorporate allusions to revolutions in their wares, manufacturers assessed the likelihood of profit against the economic and political risks of production. Their calculations were informed by the conventions of their media with both fabrication and consumption, and by their location in the Atlantic world. In comparison to other goods, such as decorative wares, accessories makers—including those in Britain—found it economically and politically safer to incorporate revolutionary motifs into their items, albeit within certain limits, because of period standards for these things.

That said, the materials of and habits surrounding accessories shaped their political resonance. Even the most blatant of accessories—ones emblazoned with republican slogans, personages, or scenes—were not straightforward badges that proclaimed the wearer was for or against revolution. Rather, people's interpretations of and reactions to accessories were influenced by eighteenth-century understandings of how each type within the genre functioned: the different expectations for medallions versus ribbon or buttons versus feathers. Context mattered, too. As accessories moved geographically and among diverse populations, they took on new significance. Who wore a particular item, how, where, and when, figured into its meanings for the bearer and for witnesses. One of the era's most iconic accessories—the cockade—demonstrates how the race, class, gender, and place of the owner imparted unforeseen importance, and controversy, to these items.

A closer look at the making, distribution, and display of revolutionary accessories helps us to appreciate what eighteenth-century actors signaled when they wore their politics on their sleeves. Accessories were forceful professions of revolutionary zeal, and so their very presence among ordinary men, women, and people of African descent provides insight into how these sectors insisted on their right to take part in political movements. However, the power of accessories derived not from their ideological transparency but from their mutability. As they traveled from one site to another, accessories became a means through which various people affected the terms of political participation. Their experiences with these objects contributed to, rather than simply reflected, the ideological content of these items and, by extension, of the movements they represented. The changeability of accessories influenced the tumultuous nature of revolutionary politics—at once full of democratic possibilities as participation widened, and full of uncertainty as observers evaluated and sometimes worked to check its effects.

TRADING IN NOVELTY

The storage cabinets of the Musée Carnavalet, the museum of the history of Paris, are teeming with small things—drawer upon drawer of cockades, medallions, snuffboxes, and buttons, all dating from the French Revolution. What's impressive is not just the number of items that have survived but also the incredible variety of forms and designs. They range from small fabric rosettes and austere metal buttons with succinct slogans to audacious cockades embellished with glittering sequins and minutely rendered medallions of the execution of Marie-Antoinette. Some are the work of professionals, others are handmade, and still others exhibit qualities of both.

While the Musée Carnavalet's trove is unique as a collection, the articles within it are indicative of a larger phenomenon. These items proliferated throughout the Atlantic world because of well-established production and sartorial practices of accessories. By the mid-eighteenth century, they were already versatile and pervasive objects, able to respond to trends at competitive prices. Two prominent types of accessory manufacture—ribbon and the related industries of medallions and buttons—shed light on the supply and distribution sides of personal adornment. These accessories were popular in both senses of the word: they were desirable and often inexpensive, and as a result they reached broad segments of Atlantic consumers. Their modes of fabrication and dissemination encouraged this popularity, and these factors explain why accessories lent themselves so easily—and so powerfully—to political expression in the revolutionary period.

Manufacturers did not launch headlong into rolling out revolution-themed accessories. They were aware that political subjects had possible negative consequences for their businesses, and so they looked for ways to enter the market securely. Their strategies depended on the types of accessories they made: the conventions of ribbon were distinct from those of medallions and buttons. Their locations also informed their decisions, as politics at home affected abilities to weigh in on revolutionary developments elsewhere.

As a rule, accessories traded in variety. Producers of other goods, such as fabric and ceramics, offered an array of choices for eighteenth-century consumers, but with articles like ribbon and buttons the scale of diversity was greater because for makers they required smaller investments in materials and in time. Manufacturers priced their goods to capture a spectrum of consumers. In the Anglophone Atlantic, silk ribbon typically cost only 1 shilling per yard, and although a ceramic cameo medallion could fetch as much as a guinea (21 shillings), the majority were around 5 shillings each. Given that the average annual household expenditures for English laborers ranged from 500 to 1,000 shillings, a length of silk ribbon or a small medallion was a feasible discretionary purchase for many individuals.[2] The low cost reflected a competitive market in these industries: England and France supported robust ribbon manufactories in Coventry and Saint-Étienne, respectively, supplying both home and empire.[3] In the eighteenth century Birmingham emerged as a major producer of a whole range of small metal goods, while Paris was a hub for French button manufacturing.

Accessories appealed to men and women, although some commentators then (and our erroneous preconceptions now) cast them as feminine items. Ribbon, for example, became a trope in critiques of women's attire and their supposedly insatiable craving for buying and wearing it. A 1777 ode to the bride "Chloe" in *Gentleman's Magazine* lampoons the artifice of women's dress, from the cork bolstering her posterior to the pounds of pomatum whitening her hair to the "ten yards of gay ribbon to deck her sweet skull." The poet warns her husband "never to undress her" or "you'll find you have lost half your wife."[4] Thanks to the lavish application of accessories like ribbon, some women were more fabric than flesh.

To be sure, the forms of women's garments (gowns, bonnets, corsets) welcomed the incorporation of ribbon more readily than those of men, but both sexes used it frequently. Ribbon was a familiar embellishment because it was as much a fastener as an ornament. As author Michel-Réné Hilliard d'Auberteuil remarked about colonial Saint-Domingue, everyone from officials to merchants to townspeople were "covered with . . . ribbons."[5] Some men tied their queues and shoes with lengths of ribbon, and it decorated men's hats and secured women's bonnets and caps, edged handkerchiefs and lapels, circled necks and waists, and dangled medallions, cameos, and other adornments.[6]

Anecdotal and visual sources testify to the assorted applications for ribbon, not only between the sexes but also among people at all social levels. Most strikingly, some enslaved men and women appropriated ribbon in their dress in ways that attracted attention from creole and European viewers and that served Black people's own senses of sartorial expression.[7] Late eighteenth-century images by Nicolas Ponce, Agostino Brunias, and others show free and enslaved women of African descent trimming their hats, necks, and handkerchiefs with ribbon (figure 4.1). While these portrayals are idealized, other observers corroborated the conspicuous use of ribbon. In 1783 a German soldier passing through Saint-Domingue noted that enslaved people sold produce at urban markets and spent the profits on "some finery, or other trinkets" like "the most beautiful ribbon," which gave "them the satisfaction of being different from their poor comrades."[8] Advertisements for runaway slaves in the Caribbean and the United States mentioned ribbon details on garments, such as one for a young enslaved barber in Kingston, Jamaica, who wore a "fustian coattee lapelled and edged with blue ribbon."[9]

Men and women also wore medallions, which included cameos, where the decoration was built up on the surface, and intaglios, where the design was engraved or embossed into the surface. In the late eighteenth century, medallions were part of the rage for all things classical. Some medallions, about an inch or so in size, were mounted as jewelry; they appeared in women's hairpins and hatpins, brooches, and bracelets, and they were worn as pendants and rings by both sexes. Slightly larger medallions adorned scent bottles, seals, and snuffboxes.

COSTUMES
DES AFFRANCHIES ET DES ESCLAVES.
des Colonies.

Figure 4.1. Nicolas Ponce, *Costumes des affranchies et des esclaves des colonies*, from *Recueil de vues des lieux principaux de la colonie françoise de Saint-Domingue* (Paris, 1791). Notice the use of ribbon in the women's dress: the woman to the left selling produce has a bow at the front of her cap, while the woman to the right has a large ribbon that wraps beneath her jaw and is tied at the top of her head. (There is perhaps another tied around her throat.) Additionally, ribbon nips in the waist of the woman at the center, and a large medallion hangs from her necklace. (Courtesy of the John Carter Brown Library.)

All were, in a sense, a type of jewelry, but one not as dear as that of precious stones and metals. As one manufacturer put it, "We can make heads with color'd grounds [cameos] cheap enough for any body," and because of their lower price point, they found their way into the sartorial arsenal of men and women.[10]

Men's garments, especially coats and waistcoats, were more conducive than women's attire for buttons. Like ribbon, buttons were functional closures, but they were also small platforms for display, and they could be very showy.[11] One commentator declared 1786 the year when the "mania of buttons" "reigned" in Paris. Men "not only wore them of an enormous size, as large as crown pieces, but they painted on them miniatures, and other pictures."[12] A humorous discourse in a U.S. magazine mocked "Will Toilet," who admitted, "The number of scutcheon buttons on my coat, was of more importance to me than the confederation of thirteen states."[13] Men, as much as women, had their own weaknesses when it came to accessories.

As the send-ups of men's fascination with buttons and women's love of ribbon intimate, accessories featured in politicized conversations that condemned luxury. Reformers decried the money spent and the indulgence of vanity that these trinkets allegedly promoted.[14] Women neglected their domestic duties in the pursuit of small fineries, while men shirked public obligations. In some cases, the quest for accessories shaped men's decisions about their responsibilities. One report from London lauded Charles Fox, the controversial Whig politician, for his opposition to a proposal to tax ribbons and gauzes. With tongue firmly in cheek, the author noted that Fox's "triumph in Westminster, was considerably facilitated by the efforts of the ladies, and he owes it in justice to the sex to protect them from the heavy oppressions" of ribbon taxes.[15]

Sartorial doomsayers warned that obsessive consumption of these trifles frayed the moral fiber of the population, and eventually the entire nation would unravel. Some revolutionaries employed this argument in their attacks on standing regimes, identifying the luxury of monarchs and their courts as signs of political corruption, and notions of simplicity, particularly with attire, formed a component of some articulations of republicanism. But in comparison to other items that attracted censure on this score, most accessories were relatively inexpensive. It was the fact that they were "cheap enough for any body" that led to their purportedly voracious consumption, as individuals bought more yards of ribbon, more sets of buttons, and yet more medallions in the race to distinguish themselves from others.

Although producers of accessories might take issue with the aspersions cast on their wares, they encouraged broad consumption not only with savvy pricing but also by offering a range of styles to tempt any taste. The medium, however, affected the manifestation of this variety.

With ribbon, diversity came from playing with fiber, color, weave, and width. Manufacturers made ribbons of several types of thread and in innumerable hues, and they could be fat, skinny, and every thickness in between. The tightness of the weave (the number of stitches per inch) affected its appearance, as did weaving patterns. U.S. retailers delineated, for instance, between padusoy ribbon (a kind of silk grosgrain) and sarsenet ribbon (a silk twill used for linings), among others.[16] When the Philadelphia mercantile firm of Dutilh and Wachsmuth imported a box of silk ribbons worth about £784, it itemized the contents by quality ("coarse," "fine," "extra fine," and "best"), by size ("broad" and "broader"), and by style or decoration ("galloon" and "black pearl edged").[17] Certain ribbons were designated for specific functions. Caribbean vendors advertised "cockade," "fashionable," "fancy," and "hair" ribbons.[18] While these terms reflect the florid language of publicity, they point to particular applications ("hair" and "cockade") or suitable occasions for use ("fancy").

In the case of medallions and buttons, variety resulted from their distinctive materials and modes of manufacture. The industries were closely related. Manufacturers of metal buttons, like Matthew Boulton, also produced medallions and fabricated the mountings for those of other materials; Josiah Wedgwood collaborated with Boulton to set ceramic cameos in metal frames. Both accessories came in assorted materials: buttons could be wood, bone, or ivory, and at times covered with cloth or leather; they were found in metal, glass, ceramic, and a combination of these materials, too—with painted or engraved scenes on paper under glass and mounted on metal. Medallions were either metal (precious or base) or ceramic.

The characteristics of these materials affected their sartorial impact— the shininess of metal versus the color of cloth or ceramic. But makers took advantage of the flat surfaces of buttons and medallions to introduce other aesthetic elements. Whether cameo, intaglio, or painted, motifs ran the gamut, as seen in Wedgwood's popular ceramic medallions. Starting in the early 1770s, Wedgwood produced heavily in this area with his jasper, a matte, biscuit-like body available in several colors that sought to mimic the pottery of antiquity. (It is still in production today.) Designs were abundant: flowers, cherubs, classical scenes, commemorations of important occasions, and portraits of historical, fictional, and contemporary individuals. By 1788 he offered almost

eleven hundred different cameos and intaglios, suggesting not only that
his customers had a plethora of options but also that Wedgwood witnessed profits sizable enough to sustain such an ambitious inventory.[19]
Although they demanded some investment to model figures and scenes
for the molds, the medallions could respond to the times, incorporating
the newest stylistic trends and marking noteworthy recent events and
personages with minimal economic risk because of the small size and
relatively low fabrication cost. Pressing clay into a mold was simpler
and swifter than the throwing, molding, decorating, and multiple fir-
ings required of a teapot.

What Wedgwood discovered for his medallions held true for other
accessories, too: because manufacturers already offered an assortment
at reasonable prices, they had the capacity to react quickly to new fashions, including politics. In fact, these industries depended on this ability. As Wedgwood noted, "Novelty is a great matter in *slight* articles
of taste."[20] Production times varied from industry to industry, though.
Wedgwood complained to a Birmingham metals manufacturer that his
coat cameos took longer to produce than those of metal: "We cannot
make these as you make metal ones with a stroke"—an allusion to the
stamp decoration of some metal buttons.[21] Even with these disparities,
all producers had to act as swiftly as their materials allowed because
some opportunities were fleeting. In 1779 Wedgwood asked his partner,
Thomas Bentley, why he had not yet sent an image of Augustus Keppel. Keppel, a British admiral and politician, had just been acquitted
by a court-martial and had emerged a national hero: "We should have
had [his image] a month since, and advertised it for pictures, bracelets, rings, seals etc. after presenting a ring, or polished seal of him to
each of the thrice worthy court martial. Seriously we must have him
in some or all of these forms soon, or it will not be worth while in any
point of view to have him at all."[22] To profit from the wave of support,
Wedgwood had to seize the moment—before enthusiasm waned and
pocketbooks snapped shut.

The flow of Atlantic trade compounded the pressure to make items
promptly. Many accessories manufacturers were oriented toward the
export market, and they had to get their goods to merchants in time
for seasonal shipments. When Benjamin Franklin died in 1791, a London merchant wrote repeatedly to Wedgwood, urging him "to hasten
the Medallions of Dr. Franklin as the last ship this Season will sail

beginning of next week."[23] If Wedgwood's products missed the boat, he and his contact would have to wait months before sending another consignment, at which point the funerary fervor might have dissipated and consumer desires diminished.

Although the ribbon industry did not bear the burden of producing representations, it did have to react to the caprices of color preferences. Every season, sometimes every month, magazines described the quintessential outfits of *la mode* for men and women, detailing the trendy cut and colors of the main garments and complementary accessories. According to the *Bermuda Gazette*, women's "morning dress" in London for April 1797 consisted of a "*Cabriolet* bonnet of light green velvet, tied under the chin with a white ribbon; light green satin ribbon, in half plaits on the tops of the crown, surrounded with a band of white satin in large plaits, crossed with pink-coloured satin ribbon; large rosette of pink ribbon in front, and small one behind."[24] Only the elite could manage this elaborate head covering, with the requisite three colors of ribbon—and be prepared to change it in the afternoon. Because of the affordability of ribbon, though, women of lesser means could participate in the latest fashions by incorporating au courant colors, weaves, or fabrics as part of their dress. Their application may not have been as extravagant, but the preference for specific colors at particular moments put pressure on manufacturers to produce ribbons in coveted shades—and fast. One English account ridiculed a 1775 craze among members of the French court to possess accessories that were the color of the queen's hair; "Such was the continued demand, that some of her *majesty's hair* was actually obtained by *bribery*, and sent to the Gobelins, to Lyons, and other manufactories, that the exact shade might be caught."[25]

The reigning paradigm for accessories consumption, as with decorative wares, was emulation—that royal and aristocratic modes would trickle down to the populace domestically and throughout the empire. And as the article in the *Bermuda Gazette* reveals, people in the Atlantic world noted metropolitan styles, even if word about them arrived a few months after the fact. But manufacturers were also subject to the whims of Atlantic customers. In an order to a London firm, a merchant in the Virginia backcountry balanced residents' established preferences for certain types of ribbon ("pink" and "double satin") with the possibility of enticing them with new colors.[26] Regional inclinations could buck trends set by manufacturers and metropoles, inducing ribbon makers to keep capacious inventories.

Given extant practices and pricing, accessories manufacturers—perhaps more than any other sector—were poised to incorporate the emblems, colors, and personalities of revolutions into their lines and to get them into the marketplace swiftly. While manufacturers were keen to benefit from political fashions, they were cognizant that their products had ramifications. Novelty, as Wedgwood emphasized, did not mean triviality. Makers had to weigh the economic and political costs of fabricating goods with explicit revolutionary allusions, and when they did decide to offer such articles, they had to adapt them almost continuously, as each twist and turn of events inaugurated new colors, emblems, and individuals for celebration and for condemnation.

The first issue, whether to produce politically themed accessories or not, was less problematic for manufacturers in the country where the revolution was occurring. It is not surprising that French manufacturers churned out a slew of items that celebrated their revolution. They did so to a lesser degree during the American Revolution, too, in acknowledgment of their alliance. The question was trickier for makers not in revolutionary sites but with Atlantic reach, like Britain. They had to determine whether to craft items that endorsed revolutions in North America, France, and Saint-Domingue—to appeal to customers in those overseas markets and to those at home sympathetic to these movements. Whereas producers of decorative wares generally avoided blatant political overtures, makers of accessories (including men like Wedgwood and Boulton who also made housewares) reached a different conclusion. The lower price point, speedier fabrication time, export orientation, and functions of accessories mitigated the risk, and so items with political references became a tempting prospect.

The specific type of accessory mattered in this calculation. For ribbon manufacturers in Coventry, the choice was less fraught. The political significance of specific colors did not obviate their use in other venues. While Americans wanted black ribbon to create cockades that signaled their independence from Britain, other Atlantic buyers continued to wear it for mourning and additional purposes. Although the combination of red, white, and blue (the "tricolor") became synonymous with the French Revolution, the individual components were still popular alone and in sundry arrangements.

For accessories with greater narrative potential, like medallions and buttons, the call was harder. Wedgwood is a helpful test case for gauging how manufacturers navigated the decision with discretion. Sometime in 1777 he produced an oval intaglio, about an inch in diameter, of Franklin's rattlesnake: the "Join or Die" emblem. Franklin had originally invented the motif for his ill-fated Albany Plan of 1754, and in the 1770s it reemerged as a symbol of North American resistance. Wedgwood's rattlesnake intaglios were not for popular consumption, though. In a letter to Bentley, he advised, "It will be best to keep such unchristian articles for private trade."[27] The word "unchristian" points to his awareness that others saw the motif as objectionable. Most likely, they were passed by hand among American partisans in his circle.

During the war for U.S. independence, Wedgwood continued to weigh the possibility of producing American-themed wares for the public market. In late 1777 he contemplated introducing a medallion of George Washington, but worried that "many circumstances may make it highly improper *for me & at this season* to strike Medals to his honor."[28] As his emphasis demonstrates, Wedgwood was sensitive to his official standing as the queen's potter and to the fact that the British had just suffered their first major defeat to the Americans at Saratoga in October. Moreover, Wedgwood felt ambivalent about Washington, confiding to Bentley that he seemed "at this time more absolute than any Despot in Europe."[29] That winter, however, Wedgwood enthusiastically worked up medallions of Benjamin Franklin (figure 4.2). Although Franklin's prominent position in U.S. independence was well known, his recognition as a scientist in international circles perhaps made his visage less contentious. Nevertheless, Wedgwood disguised Franklin's identity as the "Grand Duke of Muscovy" around the factory to avoid unwanted attention.

After the war ended, Wedgwood became more open and diverse in his offerings of American revolutionary luminaries. He publicized medallions of Washington, Franklin, and Lafayette, among other patriots, as part of the "Heads of Illustrious Moderns" series ("modern" denoting everyone from Chaucer forward). That said, many Britons still smarted from the loss—the nation's first defeat in decades, and at the hands of their own colonists, no less. But the sheer range of Wedgwood's medallions in "Illustrious Moderns" deflected rancor. American Whigs were in the catalogue, alongside several Tories: King George

Figure 4.2. Medallion portrait of *Benjamin Franklin,* 1777–80. Wedgwood
produced several different medallions of Franklin. This version is based on the
Jean-Baptiste Nini portrait made famous during Franklin's time in Paris. Note
the last name stamped below the rendition so that consumers could more easily
identify the sitter. (Jean Baptiste Nini, original modeler, Josiah Wedgwood &
Thomas Bentley partnership, Staffordshire, England, United Kingdom, 1777–80,
Stoneware and ormolu, 1958.1175, Bequest of Henry Francis du Pont, Courtesy
of Winterthur Museum.)

and Queen Charlotte, of course, but also William Franklin, Benjamin's estranged loyalist son, then living in England. In this way, Wedgwood protected himself, using the vast scope expected of the genre to sell renditions disagreeable in some circles but not in others.

For all these precautions, the topsy-turvy character of revolution sometimes left accessories manufacturers treading a delicate line between politics and profit. In France firms faced the problem of what seemed like an ever-changing array of emblems. Passé motifs were not just unfashionable; they were criticized vehemently as being anti-revolutionary. On the one hand, these shifts provided a chance for more profit, as some consumers updated their accessories to correspond with the latest political iteration. On the other hand, makers were exposed to reprisals for selling goods with outdated emblems. In the winter of 1789 one manufacturer advertised a line of buttons that "was gilt with a fleur-de-lis and the motto, live free or die" and was "all the more patriotic" because it was not made of "English metal."[30] Others offered versions of the Declaration of the Rights of Man and Citizen fitted for snuffboxes and medallions, miniature engraved cockades also suitable for snuffboxes, and medallions with the "tables" of the 1790 Constitution.[31] Makers capitalized on the notoriety of certain individuals—duc d'Orléans, Lafayette, and the now enlightened king—and put their faces on accessories. Almost all these motifs and men fell out of favor: the fleur-de-lis, long tied to royalty, went by the wayside; another constitution was ratified; and new regimes denounced many figures affiliated with the early days of the revolution. Manufacturers and dealers could be left with heaps of unmovable stock—or worse, in the tense political climate, vigilant authorities and angry patrons could call into question the political loyalties of producers and vendors.

Circumstances were heated in the home countries of revolution, but their repercussions were felt elsewhere, too. Although he was hesitant about the French Revolution's aims, Matthew Boulton rode the waves of its political tide as he attempted to capture opportunities. In the summer of 1789, a procurement official for the French army commissioned Boulton to produce buttons for the new National Guard uniforms, and he created copper medallions featuring the revolution's heroes. He experimented with small currency for the new French Republic, but after August 1792 this venture halted abruptly when the government banned the trade in coins. Boulton had to recall his shipments and unload a large quantity of copper at a loss. Émigré counterfeiters approached him about engraving plates for fake *assignats* (the controversial currency of the revolutionary government), but Boulton refused. In 1803, however, he fulfilled an order for buttons with fleurs-de-lis in honor of the future Louis XVIII.[32]

Wedgwood also seized on the windfall of the political turn in France. While he had been reticent to incorporate revolutionary emblems in his decorative wares, Wedgwood came to a different conclusion with his cameos. To some extent, his decision reflected his personal views. As he wrote to his Lunar Society associate Erasmus Darwin, "I know you will rejoice with me in the glorious revolution which has taken place in France. The politicians tell me that as a manufacturer I shall be ruined if France has her liberty, but I am willing to take my chance in that respect, nor do I yet see that the happiness of one nation includes in it the misery of its next neighbour."[33] In Wedgwood's estimation, "The diffusion of liberty through any nation will add to the security and happiness of the neighbouring ones."[34] Like many other Britons in the summer of 1789, he saw the French Revolution as an attempt to adopt a constitutional monarchy, and hence to become more like the British.

In addition, Wedgwood's choice was shaped by consumers' expectations for accessories; customers tolerated a degree of novelty with them that they did not with dinner- or teaware. And so, with an eye to both French and British markets, Josiah Wedgwood Jr. asked his father, ten days after the storming of the Bastille, "Do you not think it would be proper to get some snuff box tops with the Duke of Orleans head on them[?] You have no doubt seen in the papers that the French have recovered their liberty & that the Duke is a very great favourite with the popular party."[35] Four days later, Josiah Jr. reported that work on medallions of the duke and Jacques Necker, the French finance minister, was under way. He proposed a more emblematic scene as well: "Do you choose to have anything modelled of the same size which should relate to the late revolution in France & to the support given to public credit by the national assembly? What do you think of a figure of Public faith on an altar & France embracing Liberty in the front?" As usual, he stressed the need for speed: "We ought to do something & that quickly."[36]

In 1790 and 1791 Wedgwood rolled out medallions of Necker and duc d'Orléans as well as other leading lights of the movement like comte de Mirabeau, Jean-Sylvain Bailly, Lafayette, and Louis XVI, hoping these items would sell well in Britain and in France.[37] But Wedgwood was no fool. He continued to celebrate uniquely British events and personalities—even those less than enthusiastic about the revolution across the Channel. In 1789 he issued a medallion marking the restoration of George III's health (after a bout of madness), and in 1790 he made one of Edmund Burke.[38] Wedgwood's prudence paid off when open endorsement became more dangerous as the British found themselves at war with France in 1793. During this phase of the French Revolution, many of the men immortalized in Wedgwood's cameos had fled or died, and he did not make medallions of prominent Jacobins such as Robespierre or Danton since the war thwarted trade to the Continent and there was little prospect of selling such items in Britain.

For all his care, Wedgwood did provoke controversy, both intentionally and unwittingly, with his medallions during the Haitian Revolution. In the late 1780s Wedgwood joined Thomas Clarkson's campaign to end the British slave trade, lending financial support and his aesthetic sensibilities. In 1787 Wedgwood proposed, designed, and produced a seal for the Society for the Abolition of the Slave Trade, and the image became an emblem for Atlantic abolitionist groups for decades (figure 4.3). He crafted the device in jasper cameos that were distributed to abolitionists in Britain and abroad, and they set them in bracelets, rings, hairpins, and snuffboxes. The medallions had an emotive impact on viewers; Benjamin Franklin maintained that "contemplating the figure of the Suppliant" had "an effect equal to That of the best written pamphlet in procuring favour to these oppressed people."[39] Years later, Clarkson recalled, "At length the taste for wearing them became general, and thus fashion . . . was seen for once in the honourable office of promoting the cause of justice, humanity, and freedom."[40]

The design shows the expanse and limits of British abolitionism. Although the slogan draws attention to the common humanity of master and slave, the scene depicts the enslaved man as submissive, pleading for rather than demanding liberation.[41] In this era Clarkson and his contemporaries fought against only the slave trade, not slavery itself. Wedgwood, in letters to acquaintances exhorting them to back the cause, stressed the need for "mild treatment and . . . assistance as might be procured from the introduction of machines and free labour" to sustain plantation agriculture.[42] The emphasis was on measured action

Figure 4.3. Slave medallion, Josiah Wedgwood, ca. 1790. (The Colonial Williamsburg Foundation. Museum Purchase.)

among white people for a freedom that would be given slowly to enslaved people, not reclaimed by their own hands.[43]

While the device reflected the circumscribed agenda of British abolitionism, its circulation during the Haitian Revolution was credited with much more radical goals. As proslavery observers looked for ways to explain the uprising in the French colony (with justifications that did not challenge slavery), they blamed abolitionists for their heated rhetoric and for their provocative medallions. Bryan Edwards, in his 1797 *An Historical Survey of the French Colony in the Island of*

St. Domingo, claimed that antislavery agitators distributed pamphlets and, more damningly, "the society caused a medal to be struck, containing the figure of a naked negro, loaded with chains, and in the attitude of imploring mercy; thousands of which . . . they found means to disperse among the negroes in each of the sugar islands, for the instruction, I supposed, of such of them as could not read."[44] Edwards argued for a direct link between the alleged circulation of thousands of these medallions and slave unrest in Saint-Domingue—and perhaps elsewhere in the Caribbean.

Similar stories spread about medallions with other types of antislavery content that reached the enslaved. In the fall of 1791, the *Daily Advertiser* of Kingston had "authentic information" about the revolt in Saint-Domingue. The report asserted, "In the first of the engagements one of the Chiefs of the Rebels being killed, there was found about his neck a medal of San Gregorie, a Saint in the Romish calendar; and it appeared in evidence that this medal was worn by the negro as the portrait of his patron the Abbe [abbé Grégoire]; the similarity of the name giving countenance to the conceit."[45] Saint Gregory, a medieval pope, is best remembered for bringing Christianity to England, while abbé Grégoire was a leader in the French abolitionist group Société des amis des noirs. The implication was that the enslaved had transformed a Catholic token into a revolutionary talisman.

Whether the "rebel" leader wore this medal is impossible to substantiate, as is the author's explanation of the "chief's" association with the image depicted. What's more, this account, as well as that of the sudden delivery of anti–slave trade medallions, attributes the actions of the enslaved to white abolitionists, failing to acknowledge the political ideology of Black people. But the focus on these things suggests an interesting point of intersection between European-manufactured medallions and the sartorial practices of Black people, namely, that some wore amulets around their necks (figure 4.4). Often called gris-gris, they originated in West Africa, and in the New World could be comprised of assorted natural and crafted items, each with specific meaning: slips of paper with verses, buttons, plants, and bone, among other articles.[46] Some enslaved people prized these amulets, gathered in a small pouch, for their protective capabilities, and they were instrumental for participants in slave rebellions, emboldening them to fight when the odds were stacked against them. In Saint-Domingue amulets

A Rebel Negro armed & on his guard.

London, Publib'd Dec.r 1.st 1794, by J.Johnson, S.t Paul's Church Yard.
53

Figure 4.4. *A Rebel Negro Armed & on His Guard*, plate 53 from John Gabriel
Stedman, *Narrative of a Five Years Expedition against the Revolted Negroes of
Surinam* (London, 1796). This plate was also issued as a single print in December
1794 by J. Johnson in London (who printed the 1796 edition of the book, from
which this image is taken). Stedman describes the rebel as wearing, among other
items, "a Superstitious *Obia or Amulet* tied About his Neck, in Which case he
Places all his hope and Confidence." (Library Company of Philadelphia.)

had another spiritual dimension because of their affiliation with vodou, which provided one ideological framework and organizational structure for the revolution.[47]

While white commentators did not comprehend the sophisticated religious significance of amulets, they were aware of them and tried whenever possible to analyze their contents and purported power. When the Swiss artist and collector Pierre Eugène du Simitière traveled to Saint-Domingue in 1773, he acquired a line from the Koran written, as he affirmed, "in my presence by a Negro Mondinga." The gris-gris was one of the "curiosities" in the collection at his American Museum, which opened in 1782.[48] During the Haitian Revolution, accounts related instances when African-made amulets empowered enslaved people. A white creole soldier described the execution of a Black man who "gave the signal [to the firing squad] himself and met death without fear or complaint." On searching the victim's body, the men found that "on his chest he had a little sack full of hair, herbs, bits of bone, which they call a fetish; with this, they expect to be sheltered from all danger; and it was, no doubt, because of this amulet, that our man had the intrepidity which the philosophers call Stoicism."[49] For all his condescension, the narrator acknowledges that the amulet motivated the man to an extraordinary act of bravery.

The medallions manufactured in Europe were, to be sure, different from the amulets made by people of African descent, and white producers like Wedgwood did not figure on the enslaved as part of their consumer base. Nevertheless, mass-produced medallions like the ones with the anti–slave trade motif or with the image of Saint Gregory had revolutionary potential for the enslaved because they slotted into their extant material culture practices. They were amulets of another sort, and in contrast to the intentions of white makers and white abolitionist buyers, they had the capability to promote radical change at the hands of Black people. To what degree these medallions circulated is hard to verify, but the recognition (even among the disdainful master class) of their power to inspire military action in the name of freedom speaks to a shared understanding of the revolutionary capacity of accessories: they could be tools in the battle to overturn the status quo.

Accessories had great capacity to engage overtly with revolutionary themes. The fast fabrication, penchant for variety, and reasonable production costs meant that many manufacturers—including those in countries opposed to revolution—were willing to take some risks.

But these gambles were calculated, as manufacturers were mindful of the economic and political pitfalls of their engagement with revolutionary wares. While makers weathered the unpredictable nature of revolutions—their shifting ideological content and their disruptions to trade—they managed to distribute thousands upon thousands of articles to Atlantic consumers. Despite their forethought, they could not have anticipated all the meanings these items attained, as the anti–slave trade medallions show. Perhaps this unpredictability is not surprising with a niche item like abolitionist cameos, but it was also central to the most prevalent accessory of the age: the cockade.

ACCESSORIES IN MOTION

The accessibility of accessories was a boon to revolutionaries, who sought to disseminate their messages widely. They hoped that these "trifles" would rally support for their causes and instigate revolutionary action elsewhere. But as these small things dispersed outside of their home contexts, their connotations were much less fixed than some revolutionaries wanted. Cockades, because of their prominence and pervasiveness as revolutionary accessories, reveal how movement affected political content. When they surfaced in new sites, cockades became enmeshed in local contests with actors and agendas that differed from those at their points of origin. These circumstances introduced new meanings for cockades, ones that were not necessarily in sync with those of revolutionary leaders and that show how they were sites of contest for determining the scope and terms of political participation.

The cockade was, and still is, one of the most familiar emblems from the age of revolutions. A rosette of ribbons generally measuring a couple of inches in diameter, a cockade was pinned to a hat or bonnet, or to a lapel or gown. The most recognizable today is the tricolor cockade—the combination of red, white, and blue ribbons that was the badge of French and French Caribbean revolutionaries. But cockades in a spectrum of colors and configurations abounded. Within individual nations, they were intended to indicate partisan loyalties, as rival factions and their adherents adopted distinctive cockades. These emblems spilled out into the Atlantic as well, and people wore cockades to endorse revolution, or the status quo, elsewhere. In the 1790s, for example, disgruntled planters in Saint-Domingue rejected the tricolor and took up the black cockade to curry British favor, while white Democratic Republicans in the United States embraced the tricolor to celebrate French achievements (although not Haitian ones).[50]

Through cockades, historians have found a quick way to locate the ideological outlook of sundry types of people—the enslaved, women, and average folk—on the revolutionary spectrum. But these interpretations fail to explain why cockades as a form were popular vehicles for personal political expression in the revolutionary period. Answering this question requires a closer look at cockades as commodities—how they were made, sold, and bought—and at the cultural and social practices associated with them. A deeper contextualization of cockades as eighteenth-century things sheds new light on their import. Rather than repositories for straightforward partisan messages, cockades were open to numerous interpretations as diverse populations interacted with them.

Thanks to the vigorous ribbon industry, cockades were widespread before the age of revolutions. Men of means fastened cockades to their hats, and they appeared in fashion magazines as components of ornate women's headdresses.[51] Although these confections targeted the elite, the lower classes adopted cockades, too. A small black-and-white cockade is among the collection of mementos desperate mothers left for their children at London's Foundling Hospital.[52] Some pre-revolutionary cockades had political applications. During heated campaigns in Britain, a candidate's supporters would sport cockades to broadcast their allegiance. When John Wilkes was elected to Parliament in the late 1760s, "every inhabitant of the town [Middlesex], appeared with a blue cockade in his hat, interwoven with the words *Wilkes* and *Liberty.*"[53] One man lamented that his entire family was "election mad" over a race in Westminster: "The boys have got huge blue cockades, and the girls blue and yellow, or orange, which occasion perpetual hostilities among us."[54] No doubt exaggerated for comic effect, these episodes nevertheless point to how cockades were seen as articles with political resonance.

In the late eighteenth century their popularity and their politicization reached new heights. They turned up everywhere, from the United States to the Caribbean to Europe, and in great numbers. While it is impossible to calculate quantities with precision, people made and bought many cockades. At the outset of the French Revolution, they were in such demand that the Anglophone press claimed that French residents had spent "nearly a million livres" on cockades.[55] The sum is probably inflated, but the hyperbole suggests how noticeable the scale of the phenomenon was, despite the distance. Furthermore, cockades were a constant in the era. They were associated with all three revolutions, and even in France, where political regimes and emblems fell out of favor swiftly, the tricolor cockade persisted—from the Girondins and Jacobins to the Directory and beyond.[56]

The continuity of cockades meant that many people looked to profit from selling them, and so there were numerous outlets to buy them. French consumers could purchase tricolor cockades in shops, by subscription, and on the streets (figure 4.5).[57] In U.S. cities, hatters, milliners, and general dry goods retailers advertised cockades for sale alongside other imported goods, and in the backcountry, stocks of ribbon (the most common material for cockades) were a mainstay in shopkeepers' inventories.[58] In the Caribbean, urban residents had access to cockades and ribbon in stores and outdoor markets, and dry goods merchants sent out enslaved traveling salesmen to hawk wares from plantation to plantation.[59]

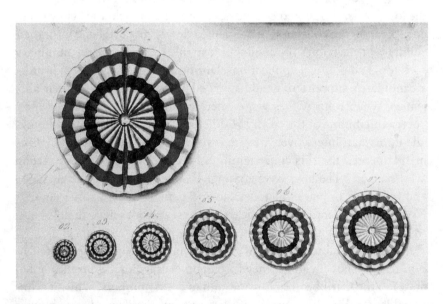

Figure 4.5. Cockades in French peddler's trade catalogue, ca. 1806–13. (Courtesy, the Winterthur Library: Joseph Downs Collection of Manuscripts and Printed Ephemera.)

The fabrication of cockades was open to everyone, professional and amateur alike. Some enterprising producers scaled up manufacturing to meet consumer demand. In 1790 one merchant announced in the weekly journal *Révolutions de Paris* that he offered a cockade with a depiction of the French Constitution at its center surrounded by a tricolored ribbon, available in several sizes. He pitched his product to members of the National Guard and noted that the price depended on the amount of ribbon selected.[60] Meanwhile, in the United States in the late 1790s, purveyors offered miniature silver eagles to embellish cockades, and one New Yorker advertised, "Those who object to the expense of procuring the silver Eagles, are informed, that at Newark, very handsome ones are manufactured at a shilling each, then why not in this town?"[61] Proto-industrial production of cockades, or their constituent parts, could help drive down prices.

These cockades drew on specialized trades like printmaking and silversmithing, but they could be fashioned by anyone with basic sewing ability. In the eighteenth century this included a lot of people: women of diverse backgrounds, but also enslaved men, soldiers, and sailors. Individuals created them for personal use, to peddle in the streets, or to sell to shopkeepers, similar to other types of outwork. The raw materials for cockades—ribbon, but sometimes wool and leather—did not require a significant upfront investment, and consequently, people at all levels of society in the Atlantic world could fabricate cockades to express their own political affiliations and for economic benefit.

The broad pool of makers resulted in a wide variety of cockades, as did the adoption of certain colors by different regimes. North Americans began their revolution sporting a black cockade and then designed a new one (black and white), sometimes called the Union cockade, to reflect the alliance with France in 1778.[62] In the late 1780s one needed an orange cockade in Holland, and in the 1790s such was found briefly in Suriname and Curaçao as well. The green cockade thrived in revolutionary Ireland, while Polish patriots donned blue and green; the Swiss colors were red, white, and green.[63] But the rules for the color of cockades in any single place were not necessarily fixed. In Martinique, for example, the "National Cockade" reigned in the late 1780s, but a few years later counterrevolutionary forces insisted that the white cockade be worn, only to revert to the tricolor again when republicans prevailed.[64]

Specific colors reverberated with significance, although their exact meanings were debated. Camille Desmoulins credited himself with the idea that residents wear cockades when storming the Bastille in July 1789. He recalled that he initially decided on green because of its associations with "hope" and with duc d'Orléans, who at the time was viewed as a champion of government reform. A few days later, the color was changed to a combination of red, "to show that we were ready to shed our blood," and blue, "for a heavenly constitution." In 1793, though, Desmoulins claimed that he asked the crowd whether the blue referred to "Cincinnatus, colour of American liberty and democracy."[65] While Desmoulins's association with the U.S. cause is revisionist, it points to an awareness in some quarters of the transatlantic implications of cockades and the room for interpretation—and dispute—at the most basic level of color.

Cockades embraced modification and personalization beyond color. Extant examples attest to the responsiveness of the form: some included revolutionary scenes and icons printed on paper or fabric, while others were embroidered with hand-stitched slogans, miniature liberty caps, sequins, and other flourishes.[66] Although surviving cockades privilege the most elaborate and unusual renditions, the practice of alteration was ubiquitous enough to catch the eyes of authorities. Occasionally revolutionary regimes saw this variety as disruptive and attempted to regulate the look of cockades. Oversight was easier to enforce in some sectors than in others. For the military, specifications for cockades were included in uniform codes. In the United States, cockades should be "stiffened with pasteboard" to make them more visible in the field, and commanding officers could check, during inspections of soldiers' dress, that the stipulation was carried out, at least when circumstances permitted.[67]

Variability was tough to police among the populace, though, and surveillance came from above and below. Some revolutionaries denounced cockades that were too small as well as those that were too big. Others cast suspicious eyes on where a cockade appeared on a wearer's body, interpreting some sites—like a woman's breast or the left versus the right side of a man's hat—as subversive. Still others balked at the addition of feathers, beads, and sequins to cockades, alleging that they reduced a noble emblem to a flashy adornment.[68] In Paris in the spring of 1793, reports maintained that a group of *sans culottes* took affront at ribbon cockades, decrying them as elitist and demanding that citizens wear ones of wool or leather. They confronted people in the streets accordingly.[69]

The charged climate surrounding the look of cockades was cause for concern for those navigating Atlantic politics: the wrong cockade in the wrong place (or none at all) could provoke outrage or land one in prison. Benjamin Johnson, an American Quaker traveling to France in the mid-1790s, remarked dryly, "My curiosity to see a little dirty Flemish town was not strong enough to overpower my apprehension of being insulted for not wearing a cockade, I therefore staid at home also, pretty much in our chamber."[70] Johnson's caution was more the rule than the exception. Even ambassadors and foreign agents, who were legally exempt from wearing cockades in France, took them up in the name of safety. As James Harris, First Earl of Malmesbury, explained while on a diplomatic mission to the French Directory, "The wearing of the national cockade is . . . so unpleasantly enforced by the populace, that it is impossible to appear in [the streets] without it."[71]

France was not an outlier. When newspapers reported on cockades in specific places, they did so as a kind of warning. The press counseled that it would be "extremely dangerous to refuse wearing" the newly adopted green cockade in Ireland, and one risked being "ill treated" if one walked in the streets of Amsterdam without an orange cockade. In Martinique during one of its republican phases, "every person, American or native—to avoid incurring the displeasure of the people, are obliged to wear the National Cockade."[72]

The language about cockades—that of "danger," "displeasure," and "apprehension"—points to a characteristic that in an age of revolutions set cockades apart from other politicized accessories: its affiliation with the military. Mounting or taking the cockade, as it was called, marked the moment when civilians became soldiers, choosing sides and staking their lives on that decision. One slang phrase for acquiring an officer's commission was "to buy [a] sword and cockade."[73] The centrality of the cockade to military life was symbolic and practical. At a time when uniforms were not uniform, armies and navies relied on cockades as a quick and cheap way to identify soldiers and sailors. During battle, prominently displayed cockades helped to distinguish allies from adversaries or, within one's own camp, to incorporate foreign mercenaries and to differentiate among divisions.[74]

As cockades became a more noticeable presence among civilians, military connotations went with them. Although cockades operated as symbols of political conflict by demarcating camps, they contributed to generating that conflict because of their association with war. One newspaper described a cockade as "a provocation" to which people reacted aggressively, lobbing verbal insults and, in some cases, ripping off others' cockades.[75] The position of cockades on the wearer heightened the stakes of this violence. In the eighteenth century an attack on one's headgear—be it a hat, bonnet, or wig—was a grave insult that necessitated retaliation.[76] Cockades, then, became doubly charged, promoting, it seemed, ceaseless cycles of reprisal.

Revolutionary regimes knew of cockades' militaristic association and at times actively encouraged it. Starting in the summer of 1792, when war and fears about internal security loomed, French officials invoked the tricolor cockade as a visible sign of the merger of the categories of "citizen" and "soldier."[77] The 1793 French Constitution proclaimed that "all French were soldiers," and this emphasis on the importance of military service to citizenship persisted during the Directory.[78] The National Assembly went on to decree that "every cockade, other than that with the national colours, is a sign of rebellion."[79] As a result, during the Terror (1793–94), when the revolutionary tribunal published lists of men and women condemned to the guillotine, they were often accused of, along with other crimes, "trampling the tricolor underfoot."[80] Years later this indictment still held sway. In 1798, when Léger-Félicité Sonthonax appeared before the Council of Five Hundred (a body within the French legislature) to justify his actions while commissioner in Saint-Domingue, he alleged that André Rigaud, the rising leader in the south, "had trodden under foot the Republican cockade, and hoisted the standard of rebellion."[81] To dishonor the cockade—or to wear a different one—was treasonous and punishable.

While the French government was the most vehement in this regard, cockades resonated as militant items in other areas of the Atlantic, too. As Sonthonax's testimony reveals, metropolitan controversies played out in the colonies. In early 1793 discord overwhelmed Pointe-à-Pitre, Guadeloupe, when residents wearing the tricolor cockade came to blows with those sporting the white.[82] In Jérémie, Saint-Domingue, some colonists pinned black cockades on their hats in anticipation of joining invading British forces: "Nothing but the want of red cloath prevents their all being in uniform."[83] In both instances, wearing a cockade signaled a readiness to fight for one's political loyalties.

The militarism of cockades took on distinctive connotations in the Caribbean because of the presence of Black people. Several reports listed cockades as part of the arsenal for slave rebellion in the West Indies. This was a new development as cockades were not affiliated with slave insurrection—rumored or actual—before the age of revolutions. In Martinique, patriots supposedly hoarded "muskets, regimentals, and national cockades, which were to be distributed among the negroes they expected would rise."[84] In response to tumultuous events nearby, Governor Clugny of Guadeloupe declared that "any slave who wore the cocarde would be whipped in the public square."[85] Despite such deterrents, cockades and their militarism spread among free and enslaved Black people, including to islands outside the French empire. In 1795 a New York newspaper related that "a Conspiracy has been discovered among the blacks at Dominico. In possession of the Ring-leaders were found fire arms, ammunition and French cockades."[86]

These accounts cast cockades as essential elements for armed rebellion—as crucial as guns and ammunition—and some white U.S. observers feared the consequences of Caribbean examples. A man in Charleston, South Carolina, writing under the pseudonym "Caution," described how "some free negroes have been seen on board the French vessels with the national cockade; what effect must this produce on our slaves[?] . . . Have we not every reason to fear it will make them very restless in their present situation?"[87] Black men's tricolor cockades signaled not only their desire for liberty and equality but also their willingness to act with force to realize them.

The connection between militarism and cockades had important implications for women, as well. Some commentators waxed rhapsodic about the loveliness of white women with cockades. At a fête in Portsmouth, New Hampshire, "the ladies to exhibit their patriotic enthusiasm, wore upon their caps the national cockade which made a very beautiful appearance and lively impression upon every susceptible spectator."[88] Men and women in Le Cap in 1798 marched together holding oak branches in their hands and wearing "tricolor ribbons" on their hats.[89] In these orchestrated scenarios, women's cockades operated within established gender and class norms. Their cockades attracted men to the wearers and, by extension, to republican campaigns.

This innocuous association was difficult to sustain, however. Throughout the revolutionary era, the question arose as to whether women should be allowed to wear cockades because of their militarism. Early on in the French Revolution, stories circulated about intrepid women who bore arms and cockades in the name of political transformation.[90] These were patriotic tales meant to rally people to action, but there was uneasiness in some sectors about cockaded women's political and physical power.[91] For French officials and for many Atlantic observers, this tension snapped in what became known as "the war of the cockades," when women, in Paris and elsewhere, clashed on the streets over the emblem.[92] A U.S. newspaper recounted an episode in Les Halles in which a group of women "flogged" a female passerby and tore off the national cockade she wore. The victim, on leaving the market, had "hardly proceeded 600 yards farther, when she was again attacked by another furious set of women, who beat her for appearing without a cockade!" The rancor had reached such a pitch by the fall of 1793 that the "streets, squares and market-places, were strewed with ladies' hats, caps and bonnets."[93] Women were damned if they did wear cockades, and damned if they didn't.

Outbursts over cockades were often cast as the lamentable results of unruly, unthinking mobs—a familiar trope in the early modern period. While collective violence was a crucial part of revolutionary action, this explanation dismissed the possible political impulses behind that violence. One influential ideological strand from the age of revolutions tied one's rights to freedom and citizenship to one's willingness to fight, and potentially die, for them. A virtuous man fought for liberty and in the process proved himself worthy of the reward.[94] Gender and racial hierarchies denied white women and enslaved people this capacity, and it was one justification for their continued political and social subjugation. When white women and people of African descent wore cockades, they claimed the militarism seen as elemental to enjoying rights, which many observers, including many revolutionaries, were unwilling to accept and looked for ways to check.

Even among white men, those who, in theory, enjoyed the full ability to act on a cockade's militarism, these accessories bred polarizing and combative tendencies that, in the eyes of some commentators, were getting out of hand. In the lead-up to the American Revolution, civilians adopted the cockade in protests against imperial policies. In the 1775

London engraving *The Alternative of Williams-Burg,* members of the crowd sport bow-shaped cockades on their hats as they force three men to sign a boycott pledge (figure 4.6). Many of the cockaded men brandish weapons menacingly: one at the center wields a long knife, and another, a formidable pair of scissors. Even the child wears a sword, albeit a toy one, at his waist. The less than flattering portrayals of the self-declared patriots (the hooked nose of the woman, the gaunt and haggard faces of the men) make it clear that this is a pro-British print. While the British had an interest in dismissing American demonstrations as the work of misguided mobs, the significance here is that they used cockades, paired with weapons, as visual cues to do so.

Critiques of cockades and their militarism shaped the ways political opponents cast each other. But fears about the violence cockades stimulated—especially other nation's cockades—occurred within national contexts as country after country was dragged into the revolutionary wars. The *Freeman's Journal* of Philadelphia reported in the summer of 1781 that "numbers of Englishmen" died in a riot in Amsterdam; as a result, "no man who speaks the English language is permitted to walk the streets, without our [the American] union cockade in his hat."[95] Britain had just declared war on the Dutch Republic, so perhaps the retaliation was to be expected. Yet Americans, in order to distinguish themselves from other English speakers and to travel safely in Amsterdam, needed to wear the correct cockade.

Neutral countries felt the violent backlash of cockades. In the United States in the 1790s, many Democratic Republicans embraced the tricolor cockade, while Federalists called for the black—or, as their foes claimed, the British—cockade. Fights broke out in Charleston, Norfolk, Philadelphia, and New York when one group spotted the other's cockades and tried to remove or deface them.[96] Frequently the protagonists were identified as sailors, soldiers, visitors, or immigrants; in other instances, they were American civilians, and these were considered more problematic.[97] Commentators in both parties lamented this development: "Citizens have no business with cockades; it is a military emblem which ought only to be worn by a soldier. To wear it as a badge of distinction is indiscreet and improper, it ought to be discountenanced by the citizens at large."[98] As political violence escalated in New York City, another writer, supposedly "an Old Continental officer," pleaded with the youth to "lay aside your cockades until the voice of your country

Figure 4.6. *The Alternative of Williams-Burg,* attributed to Philip Dawe (London: R. Sayer & J. Bennett, February 6, 1775). (Library of Congress, LC-USZC4-5280.)

may give you a call, which God forbid may ever happen to our happy land."[99] Cockades were understood as a bellicose incitement to violence, and if they spread among civilians, then civil war could result.

For all the disruption caused by tricolor and black cockades in the United States, Americans had a hard time giving them up during the French and Haitian revolutions. In the midst of the fervor, some proposed devising an entirely new cockade, but these revisions failed to catch on.[100] Among those who wore political cockades, they stuck with either the black or the "red and blue"; both sides declared these were "American" colors, yet as one Philadelphia editor pointed out, because of parallels with the British and French ones, these cockades led to "misconstruction[s] of the views of the wearers . . . and excite[d] disorder."[101] The debate became so contentious that one militia commander exclaimed with exasperation: "It is much to be regretted that we are yet to be informed what is the true American National Cockade, or whether there really is any."[102] It seems that the United States, at least where cockades were concerned, could not break away from the broader Atlantic context and remained shaped by the two nations—Britain and France—that, from a U.S. perspective, dominated the political discussion.

These examples of men and women throughout the Atlantic world donning cockades and taking to arms demonstrate the boldest translation of ideals into action. Cockades were powerful things for the ways they could gather people to act on their political loyalties, and revolutionary leaders relied on this capacity to propel their endeavors. But time and again, the accessibility of cockades as a commodity, combined with their militant connotations, extended the sphere of political participation in ways that made some revolutionaries and their opponents uncomfortable. With a simple bit of ribbon, women, the enslaved, and the "wrong" kind of white men could appropriate the ideals associated with cockades—when authorities thought these sectors of the population were not ready (or never would be ready) for political power.

In this mode, cockades were visible signs of revolutionary ardor, a profession of one's commitment to ideals. As William Cobbett, an outspoken Englishman who emigrated to the United States in the 1790s, declared, "The handwriting at the bottom of an address is seen but by few persons, whereas a cockade will be seen by the whole city, by the friends and the *foes* of the wearer; it will be the visible sign of the sentiments of his heart, and will prove, that he is not ashamed to avow those sentiments."[103] Cobbett suggests "those sentiments" were evident, as have many historians since, yet the debates over the militarism of cockades indicate that observers struggled to fix clear meanings to cockades as they moved in the Atlantic world. That flexibility and capaciousness were appealing to those looking to expand revolutionary possibilities.

Specific colors had national significance, but the points of overlap— where two or more nations adopted the same colors—resulted in confusion, or at the very least argument. Was a red and blue cockade French or American? Was black British or American? Was the tricolor French or Haitian? Embellished cockades provided some ideological precision. Rather than, for example, endorsing the French Revolution writ large, they celebrated specific aspects of political transformation. The cockade with an image of the French Constitution backed that moment of revolutionary reform, the version of the constitution passed in 1790. The addition of eagles to black cockades underscored their Americanness and celebrated federalism.

At times, though, these elements made cockades difficult to decipher with certainty as they surfaced in different places. In 1793 some British prisoners escaped from revolutionary Saint-Domingue to Baracoa, Cuba, and they brought with them a cockade that they said had been in the hands of Black "rebels" in the French colony. Documents describe the cockade's decoration in some detail: "a little heart of grain bordered in gold, on one side a fleur-de-lis in the center, on the other an inscription, also bordered, that reads *Constitution*."[104] The trio of symbols recalls a phase of the French Revolution when demands for constitutional monarchy drove political reform. In 1790 and 1791 French faïence manufacturers produced wares painted with three flaming hearts (representing the three orders), slogans like "The Nation, the Law, the King" and "Constitution," and fleurs-de-lis, among other emblems. These designs fell out of favor with the execution of Louis XVI and the Jacobin turn. The appearance of this cockade in Saint-Domingue in the summer of 1793 is a bit of a puzzle. By then the Jacobin commissioners Sonthonax and Polverel led the colonial government, and so the cockade found by the British men was out of step with current events—in France and on the island.

Observers familiar with the range of French revolutionary iconography would have interpreted this cockade as a device that endorsed the legitimacy of monarchy, albeit with some republican elements. In this vein, the cockade complements readings of the Haitian Revolution that derided the ideological credentials of the enslaved by claiming they had been—and still were—on the side of monarchy. They described the slave revolt as "a Counter-Revolution" in which enslaved people "believed in the Imprisonment of the King, that he had issued them Orders to arm themselves, and to restore him to Liberty."[105] Opponents to the French republican regime trotted out such arguments when they spoke of Toussaint Louverture and other Black leaders' alliances with the Spanish in the early 1790s.[106]

For the formerly enslaved, however, these symbols had different meanings. As historian Ada Ferrer points out, in Haitian vodou the heart would come to represent Erzulie, the deity of love and beauty. Perhaps the heart already had this affiliation by the late eighteenth century, and the cockade could have referenced that spiritual power for practitioners. As for the fleur-de-lis, Black revolutionaries knew of its association with the French king. Throughout the colonial period, official decrees and sites of authority, such as courthouses, featured the motif, and a slave convicted of stealing or running away was branded on the shoulder with a fleur-de-lis.[107] But not all allusions to royalty were negative for enslaved people, nor were their connotations limited to what white commentators at the time speculated. Several scholars have shown that enslaved people in Saint-Domingue (and elsewhere) had distinct ideas about kingship based on experiences in West Africa, and these understandings contributed to the organization and goals of Black revolutionaries during the Haitian Revolution and beyond. What's more, enslaved people had their own view of the French king and his intentions. According to legend, participants at the Bois-Caïman ceremony of 1791 were galvanized to rise up in part because they thought that masters had ignored royal stipulations to reduce the working days for slaves.[108] As a sign of his loyalty to the king, Jean-François, one of the earliest leaders of the insurgents, wore the "cross of Saint-Louis" on his uniform, while those of his guard were decorated with fleurs-de-lis.[109] The flexibility of symbols, and in this case their ability to incubate other meanings, gave cockades enormous ideological and political power—well beyond what makers intended.

But as several observers noticed at the time, the opposite was also true: cockades were badges of conformity that signaled the limits of political identification and political practice. When the American bookseller Benjamin Johnson reached the French coast in the mid-1790s, he noticed that "every passenger on board" except for himself and his Quaker companions had cockades with them, either on their hats or in their "pockets ready to put on." Some volunteered to share their extra cockades with Johnson. He declined, and they proposed that if he did not want to wear one, he should have "a bitt of three coloured ribband" to show any official who might stop him.[110] His shipmates, on approaching France, put on cockades to avoid trouble, whether they believed in the ideals tied to them or not. French laws enforced this obligation. The government mandated that foreigners wear the cockade while in the country and that people in all newly incorporated territories embrace the emblem, too. There is, in the very absolutism of these decrees, a tacit recognition that wearers might not espouse the cockade's principles.

The coercive aspect of cockades raises questions about their appearance in other settings where power was at play—for example, in households with individuals in subservient positions. In 1795 the Philadelphia jeweler Claudius Chat offered a $25 reward for his runaway French apprentice, Hustache Mabian, "who had on when he went off, a middling high crowned hat with a national cockade."[111] Joseph Jacobs, a Flemish man indentured to a tailor in Baltimore, also took to his heels, sporting a "round hat with the national cockade mounted," and Michel, a "black boy" on the lam, "used to have a black cockade on his hat."[112] Often scholars interpret these cockades as signs of the wearers' political leanings, and this could be the case. Yet it is just as possible that masters insisted on cockades for dependents, using servants as vehicles to advertise the patriarchs' political loyalties.[113] In the age of revolutions, wearing a cockade could be as much about compulsion as expression.

Revolutionaries maintained that these directives—at the national and household levels—were didactic. They purportedly helped wearers inculcate the republican values that the cockade encapsulated. When Victor Hugues, governor-general of Guadeloupe in the mid-1790s, requested that his superiors send thousands of cockades for distribution among Black soldiers, he argued that cockades were "little stimulants that produce great effects."[114] Others suggested, though, that the obligation surrounding cockades undercut their enlightened associations. As one critic asserted, "It is . . . an act of tyranny to compel a man to wear a cockade." It was "oppressive" and tended "only to make hypocrites. . . . The result is, that an external badge, and *not principle*, becomes the test of a good and faithful citizen."[115] According to these commentators, the violation was two-fold: revolutionary regimes undercut their republican foundations by forcing citizens to put on cockades, and this coercion resulted in lip service to, rather than authentic espousal of, enlightened ideals. In short, the cockade became banal. One American Federalist pointed out that for "young men" in New York, "the wearing of the cockade in common is regarded as useless and insignificant."[116] Others scorned the facile link between republicanism and cockades: "No nation can subsist a moment without a cockade. Religion, virtue, morals, education, every thing good and happy, depends on a cockade!"[117] The exterior manifestation through the cockade, not the virtues themselves, had emerged as the means to measure men.

Banalization was problematic, but the bigger fear for revolutionary regimes was that their cockades could hide ideas and agendas that worked actively against the political projects they endorsed. Evidence for this deceit abounded. Sometimes the culprit was vanity. In Britain and the United States, observers mocked their "*cockaded* heroes" who played the soldier but whose courage went only as deep as the ribbon they wore (figure 4.7).[118] An English report skewered a coxcomb with his red-heeled shoes and "white sattin muff over his pretty, delicate, tender hands" who wears a cockade and "would wish to pass for a soldier."[119] One American dialogue ridiculed a "fantastical Chap" for his "*British cockade*" and velvet shoes—the latter a telltale accoutrement of gout sufferers. When a veteran of the American Revolution asked the "Chap" how he had come by his ailment, whether through the "fatigues of patriotism, or hardships of war," he responded that it was by "drinking the President's [Adams's] health on St. George's day last, and partly running about to promote the election of Mr. Jay."[120] The "Chap's" "fatigues" and "hardships" were a far cry from those of a real soldier.

These exaggerated cockaded characters mocked military puffery and political pretense, but the cockade-as-charade argument had less humorous applications. U.S. newspapers featured scores of anecdotes

Pray Sr. do You Laugh at me

THE MARTIAL MACARONI.

Pubd. according to Act of Parlt. Novr. 6th. 1771 by MDarly 39 Strand.

Figure 4.7. *The Martial Macaroni* (London: M. Darly, November 6, 1771). One of the characters in Darly's popular macaroni series of etchings, the "Martial Macaroni" wears, along with other outlandishly sized accoutrements, a flamboyant cockade that dwarfs the hat, swallowing it in tentacles of black silk ribbon. The caption reinforces the visual lampoon: "Pray Sir do you laugh at me?" Clearly, the answer is yes. (Courtesy of The Lewis Walpole Library, Yale University.)

about men who used cockades to cloak their misdeeds—to escape from prison, to take out credit, to steal, to seduce young women.[121] In these scenarios, a man employed the cockade to inveigle his way into someone's confidence and to exploit him or her. One report objected that in London "apprentices, clerks, and tailors . . . when out of the sight of their masters and acquaintance, impudently hoist a cockade, and commit the most ungentleman-like actions."[122] Because cockades were so accessible, almost anyone from any class could masquerade as someone worthy of the emblem.

According to critics, these duplicitous schemes had deleterious effects, especially on women. They fell victim to the wiles of cockaded men so often that one newspaper posted a false marriage advertisement as a warning. Addressed to the "ladies," the advertisement purports to be written by a "Gentleman, who has lost a considerable fortune by drinking, wenching and gambling" who seeks to wed a "foolish young girl or liquorish old dowager, with an independent fortune." He lists his attributes as "a perfect adept . . . of the tea[-]table," "beauty," and "entitled to wear a red coat and a cockade." He "would promise to make any woman happy—for a MONTH—and miserable all her life after."[123] Men, too, were burned by the confidences cockades elicited. During the American Revolution, a Continental soldier met several men who posed as fellow combatants but were "itinerant traders." When the soldier asked one of them "why he wore a cockade, he said it answered for a pass."[124] This "pass" allowed them access to troops, whom they swindled by selling marked-up goods. In another instance, French émigrés wearing national cockades manned a British frigate. When they encountered a Boston vessel, the captain, thinking the frigate was French, told the crew that he was really bound for Bordeaux, although his paperwork claimed he was headed to Hamburg. Tricked by the émigrés' ploy, the Boston vessel was taken into British custody.[125]

As egregious as these deceptions were, the worst, in the eyes of revolutionaries, were cockades' capacity for ideological treachery. One report carped about Americans "who left *America* reputed aristocrats" then suddenly, upon arrival to France, "talk of nothing but Liberty, Equality & Fraternity, &c mount the cockade, and sing *ca ira*, in full chorus."[126] Another professed that the same was true in reverse: hardened French aristocrats who sought refuge in the United States "are now eager to put up the national cockade, and never are without it a single moment."[127] Relocation allowed for reinvention simply by adopting an outward trapping of political sentiment. The availability of cockades, as far as cost and supply, made this fraud easy. As firebrands in the French Assembly pointed out, it was a fundamental problem of having revolution wrapped up with small things: "The word *Republican* is impressed upon the cockades of our revolutionary hypocrites, on the buttons of their coats, in the very lids of their snuff-boxes! In short (with them) republicanism is every thing, and its principles every where prevalent, except in their own hearts."[128] Accessories like cockades had the flexibility to let anyone anywhere appear republican, thereby subverting, if not outright mocking, the principles they were supposed to represent.

The banalization of cockades provided an opening for more radical critiques, though. After witnessing a Caribbean colonist residing in New York beat an enslaved person with a plank, one U.S. commentator remarked, "This Frenchman appears to me to be one of those who, while they honour the republic with their mouth, and decorate their hats with the national cockade, retain all that despotism so predominant in the West Indies, in their hearts." The author pivots from this specific episode to a more general observation: "Facts speak louder than words, and let a man's professions be what they may, I cannot believe he has any real regard for genuine republican principles, so long as he violates the strict law of nature, in depriving his fellow creature of that liberty which every man undoubtedly has right, and a capacity (if properly cultivated) to enjoy."[129] The editorial dates from 1795, a year after slavery had been abolished in the French Caribbean. The only reason the master can continue to keep a slave and to treat him with such impunity is because he migrated to New York. The author hints that the real hypocrisy exists in the United States, whose laws abet the deprivation of Black people's liberty. A man of "genuine republican principles" must support gradual manumission, then up for consideration in New York and finally passed in 1799.

Cockades were anything but frivolous bits of ribbon. Their Atlantic ambits during the age of revolutions demonstrate the factors at play— the extant practices and ideas associated with them as well as the location and profiles of wearers—that lent cockades changeable political currency. On the one hand, compulsion could make them banal, and on the other, they encouraged individuals to act publicly and forcibly on convictions. For women, the enslaved, and free people of African descent, this latter expectation offered an opportunity to take change into their own hands and on their own terms. Both ends of the spectrum were problematic for revolutionaries, as these small things disrupted the ideological cohesion to which their movements aspired.

From the battlefields and parlors of Europe to plantations and ports in the Americas, accessories were a means through which many people engaged in politics—and not always in ways that manufacturers, political leaders, and elites envisioned. Context, especially location and wearer, mattered for how these articles became politicized, as did the cultural conventions of items. The political resonances of cockades, medallions, buttons, and other embellishments were unstable, but that mutability gave them power as they moved among places and people. Accessories laid bare the intimate texture of the social pressures of political affiliation—whether banal or radical or any point in between. And in the ideological and sometimes violent contests that raged over their meanings, they reflect the messiness of actors' endeavors to comprehend revolutions as they transpired in far-flung corners of the Atlantic.

In his attempt to explain the reasons for the American Revolution, Josiah Wedgwood used an extended metaphor in which apparel elucidated the power dynamic between mother country and colonies. Britain, the parent,

> had driven out the brat [the North American colonists] in its infancy and exposed him in an uncultivated forest to the mercy of wild beasts and savages without any farther inquiries after him, 'till we imagined he might be brought to render us some essential services. We then took him again under our parental protection; provided him with a straight waistcoat, and whenever he wriggled or winched, drew it up a hole tighter, and behaved so like a step-mother to our son, now grown a very tall boy, that he determined to strip off his waistcoat, and put on the togs [clothes] at once, and is now actually *carrying fire and water through the whole empire* wherever he pleases.[130]

One cannot help but wonder if, in Wedgwood's imagination, some of that young man's adult garments included the potter's cameo buttons. Regardless, his allegory underscores that jettisoning one's old clothes and putting on all new togs was no easy feat for revolutionary nations. This literal and figurative circumstance reveals why accessories and military clothing were so important in the age of revolutions. They held economic and personal worth, and they had political value as revolutionaries challenged the status quo. Producers, distributors, and consumers turned to these items to test the limits of new notions about these new nations in the making. The characteristics of a genre shaped its resonance: military garments opened up discussions about equality, whereas accessories raised issues of liberty and of the scope and means of political inclusion. Another set of objects—maps, prints, and wax figures—grappled with the "*fire and water*" of Wedgwood's description, the wars that erupted in sites throughout the Atlantic world and the actors who carried them out.

III
SEEING REVOLUTIONS

WHEN WE FOLLOW the spread of news during the age of revolutions, we usually look to two routes: word of mouth and print culture. In the stories people relayed to one another, and in the accounts published in newspapers and pamphlets or handwritten in letters and bureaucratic reports, individuals discussed the revolutions as they happened.[1] While these channels were crucial for disseminating information about and opinions on actors, events, places, and ideas, contemporaries wanted to *see* the revolutions. The impulse for visualization came from several quarters: competing sides of the era's political and military contests; professionals, amateurs, and dealers in the arts; and popular demand.

The upshot was a veritable explosion of visual culture. The prodigious volume reflects how the technologies and markets for maps, prints, and other articles had developed during the eighteenth century so that such profusion was possible. It stemmed as well from the intense interest the revolutions generated in their home countries and abroad, and that interest was expressed in a range of visual styles. There were iconographic images of principles, allegorical interpretations of the rise of new republics, and commemorations of key moments, sites, and personages. A fair share of this visual culture, though, translated the here and now of revolutions into depictions. Similar to pamphlets, newspapers, and other printed texts, these renditions attempted to keep pace with developments to explicate the who, what, where, when, and how of this watershed.

The chapters in this part examine three important and popular media for seeing revolutionary news: maps, prints, and wax sculptures. Within these genres, they concentrate on examples that crossed borders, and this aspect is tricky for these objects. Maps and prints are notorious (among scholars at least) for being difficult to track with specificity. We lack detailed registers that would help us to trace these items as they moved from makers to sellers to consumers. Few printers left thorough records, those for booksellers are not much better, and probate inventories for individuals normally fail to list the titles of the maps and prints under valuation.[2] Following the ambits of wax sculptures is hampered by the paucity of records from creators and of extant examples of their compositions.

Even with these limitations, it is worth exploring the circulation of these goods as much as possible because they were instrumental to how people saw—and did not see—revolutions as they occurred. Maps, prints, and wax figures made revolutions visible for Atlantic audiences, frequently bringing clarity and precision to narratives. The interdependence between visual and textual news is not surprising, given how the technologies, publishers, and markets for maps and prints overlapped with those of newspapers, pamphlets, books, and broadsides. Of course, texts are things, too, and are occasionally analyzed as such, but our interest here is how the imagery of maps, prints, and wax sculptures contributed to people's understandings of revolutions in unique ways. Despite their close relationship to printed texts, they did not stay faithful to language-based accounts because the process of transforming them into visual culture was not straightforward. As artists picked what to represent, what to leave out, and how, their decisions yielded portrayals that at times diverged from texts. For intelligibility, visual depictions were necessarily selective, as were written and oral versions. Yet the practice of choice in visual renditions worked differently than in linguistic ones, and each medium had distinct characteristics. The conventions of the form, the proclivities of creators, the sites of production, and the perceived preferences of consumers—all these factors shaped how a map, a print, or a wax figure portrayed revolutionary news.

As a result, each genre engaged with discrete facets and consequences of the revolutions. Maps were essential tools in fighting revolutionary wars, but they also relayed the territorial outcomes of battles to Atlantic audiences. In so doing, they validated, and sometimes denied, the spatial alterations wrought by campaigns. Prints showed revolutionary people, both individuals and collectives, in action, and the nature of these portrayals—who exactly was rendered, how, and when—contributed to discussions about the application of popular sovereignty in the United States, France, and Haiti. Finally, wax figures dwelled on violence, re-creating dramatic episodes, like the execution of Louis XVI and the assassination of Marat, that compelled viewers to entertain whether the means and human costs of achieving revolutionary change were legitimate.

As mapmakers, printers, and wax sculptors visualized the revolutions, they fostered powerful experiences for those near and far from the action. They literally influenced who and what people saw of the Atlantic revolutions, and how they did so. But these things also generated blind spots—aspects that makers could not depict and that audiences refused to see. These things were at once conduits for and obstacles to revolutionary change, influencing which transformations people were willing to accept at the time and which they rejected.

5 Cartographic Contests

IN PERIOD PORTRAITS, revolutionary-era leaders often hold or stand near maps. Washington, Louverture, Bonaparte, the list goes on—all had portraits with maps as prominent symbolic devices. The maps in these pictures call attention to the nations or empires with which the men were associated, sending a clear message to audiences about the power of the sitter over that terrain. As scholars have demonstrated, maps and the cartographic practices that produced them were political ventures, concerned with claiming and perpetuating dominion.[1] The very ways a place was represented on a map argued for a specific vision of national or imperial sovereignty. Artists and their subjects appropriated the ideological function of real maps by including them in portraits, and in doing so they suggest that the legibility of maps went beyond the elite. After all, a map's ability to project power in a painting was effective only if viewers were familiar with the medium.

The maps illustrated in these portraits were most likely props in artists' studios or imagined renditions rather than items owned by the subjects. These men, however, did need actual maps for their work in warfare, diplomacy, and governance. Maps were made and consulted in anticipation of and during battles, to negotiate boundaries at peace conferences, and to explain the outcomes of those battles and negotiations. Their centrality to these important undertakings inspires two basic questions: How did people acquire maps during the age of revolutions, and how did they use them in their political endeavors?

The answers to these deceptively simple questions offer a fresh perspective on the power of maps as objects. While the ideological significance of maps emphasizes their national contexts, their distribution and applications shed light on their Atlantic attributes. This is particularly the case for published maps because they were reproduced in larger numbers and were more widely disseminated than manuscript maps. The process of creating and retailing maps relied on transnational exchanges of people, commodities, and information, and, like other consumer goods, maps were made, distributed, and sold with international markets in mind. These Atlantic aspects of printed maps were not necessarily at odds with nationalist and imperialist political ambitions. As a printed map circulated, it normalized territorial claims when, for example, other countries acknowledged the cartographic assertions of an empire by incorporating its interpretation of borders, place-names, and other details into their maps. The national and international influences on mapmakers and their wares were indispensable and regularly reinforcing.

That said, in the late eighteenth century, the production, movement, and consumption of maps had the potential to disrupt the territorial aspirations of nations and empires because maps were instruments of revolutionary wars. Armed forces employed maps of different types in pursuit of military and political objectives. Borrowing from eighteenth-century French terminology, some were *cartes,* which provided overviews of terrain; others were *plans,* which focused on a single locale (a port or region, for instance) and projected its future spatial possibilities.[2] Finally, battle maps presented retrospective cartographic renditions of what had happened on the field.

Regardless of the specific form, these maps worked toward the goal of transforming Atlantic spaces via warfare in two ways. First, maps performed concrete functions on the battlefield and on the high seas, as armies and navies looked to them for crucial information to devise and execute their campaigns. Second, one goal of these wars was to dispute the very national and imperial dominion that maps asserted, and so maps had political salience, too. These two features led not just to the use of extant maps but also to a proliferation of the practice of mapping. The problems militaries experienced with available maps led them to question their purported authority and to try, almost constantly, to create better ones. Meanwhile, revolutionaries crafted new maps to reflect their ideological aspirations. Seeking to revise the political organization of their world, they redrew its maps.

The pervasiveness of mapping afforded opportunities for assorted sectors of the population to capitalize on this mode of cartographic knowledge. The possibilities on this front come to the fore most strongly with people of African descent. Black actors understood terrain in ways that did not rely on European-style maps and mapping, and throughout the revolutionary period, they deployed that knowledge to advantage. But Black armies adopted Western cartography as well because they decided it was expedient for their military and political aims. In Saint-Domingue, maps helped the Black army to scale up its campaigns when it organized, grew, and coordinated its maneuvers with French republican officials. Maps had an ideological benefit, too, showing white observers that men of African descent could implement European tools as well as, and sometimes more effectively than, their white peers. Many white accounts highlight the guerilla tactics of Black soldiers (which were important), but white readers concluded from these biased descriptions that Black men were not "honorable" soldiers because of their unorthodox use of spaces. For Black armies, then, employing and adapting maps contributed to combating racist hierarchies.

The radical potential of maps and mapping among men of African descent was intelligible to white audiences because different constituencies exercised the power of maps to promote their visions of what revolutions should mean. And yet the conventions of maps as things—the structures that surrounded their production, distribution, and consumption—affected how various perspectives were and were not represented and disseminated. They perpetuated some aspects of revolutionary spatial change and hindered others, and in the process, maps revealed the extent to which diverse actors could and could not reimagine and accept the transformation of political spaces in an age of revolutions.

MAPS AS AN ATLANTIC ENTERPRISE

Eighteenth-century maps were either manuscript (drawn by hand) or printed (engraved or etched and published). Both types could result from surveying terrain or by collating already available information from assorted sources; sometimes a map combined the two methods. The time and labor involved varied, even among those produced by the same means. For maps based on eyewitness appraisals, a soldier could sketch a quick map in the field during a reconnoitering mission, while a professional surveying team might spend months in a specific area, at extraordinary cost, to determine its contours as precisely as possible. In 1784, for instance, the French cartographer M. de Chastenet-Puységur tarried for a year with his team, recording measurements for an enormous pilot atlas of Saint-Domingue. After the expedition concluded, it took another three years to create and publish the resulting maps.[3]

A compilation map, however, did not require a cartographer to leave his desk. He synthesized material from engineers' surveys, travelers' accounts, and reports from boat pilots, as well as maps drawn or printed by other makers. In his 1802 printed map of Saint-Domingue, J. B. Poirson explained that his work drew on "the hydrographic map of Chastenet-Puységur, on the diverse topographic sections of the interior of the island published by Phelipeau; the map 'itinéraire' of the two principal routes from Cap Français to Santo Domingo by Daniel Lescallier, taken down in 1784; and on many manuscript maps."[4] The process of assembly could be as simple or as complex as the mapmaker and the market could bear, from a perfunctory retouching of an existing map to a multi-year process. Compilation mapping was the forte of some of the most famous makers of the eighteenth century: men like Jacques-Nicolas Bellin and Guillaume and Joseph-Nicolas Delisle in France, and Emanuel Bowen, Thomas Jefferys, and William Faden in England.[5]

Both modes of mapmaking encouraged exchange of cartographic intelligence across national lines, but there were structural limitations that influenced the production of printed maps. Cartographers relied on many people—Indigenous and enslaved, sailors and soldiers, elite, middling, and lower sorts—to provide information for manuscript maps of North America and the Caribbean. But in the early modern period, Native and Black actors did not have access to the means of production for published maps, and maps were beyond the abilities and wherewithal of most white North American and Caribbean printers. There was the occasional maker, but in general, the dearth of skilled engravers and the prohibitive cost of copperplates, paper, and labor hampered the development of extensive printed mapmaking in the colonies, and so most published maps that circulated in the Atlantic came from Europe.[6]

These origins shaped their pretensions. European maps of the Americas claimed vast territories, and the peoples and resources therein, in the name of empire. The long-winded, pompous titles and obsequious dedications celebrated the supposed power and prominence of European nations. Florid language, paired with decorative motifs, announced imperial designs for these regions: people of African descent laboring for well-heeled Europeans, merchant and naval ships plying the seas, bales and casks of lucrative commodities, and all manner of exotic flora and fauna (figure 5.1). Through these trappings, cartogra-

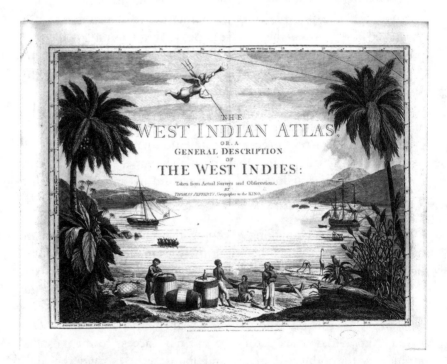

Figure 5.1. Title page of Thomas Jefferys, *The West Indian Atlas* (London: Sayer & Bennett, 1771). This title page features all the tropes of imperial aspirations for the Caribbean and asserts the accuracy of the maps therein. (Library of Congress, Geography and Map Division, LC-USZ62-46098.)

phers argued for the eminence of a specific nation: Britain, or France, or Spain, and so on.

This jingoistic bluster obscures the fact that cartographers, sellers, and buyers were much less jealous in their dealings with one another, even when at war. During the American Revolution, British printer William Faden sent at least four cases of maps, including several of North America and the Caribbean, to Jean-Nicolas Buache de La Neuville, *géographe du roi* in Paris and assistant keeper of maps for the French navy. The same month that France signed a treaty of alliance with the United States, Faden mailed Buache more maps, this time of Rhode Island, Newport, and New Jersey. It is unclear if these maps helped the French to plan their attack on Rhode Island in August 1778, but Crublier d'Opterre, an engineer who traveled with General Jean-Baptiste Donatien de Vimeur, comte de Rochambeau (the commander of French land forces in North America), owned a copy of Faden's map of New Jersey. Buache returned Faden's favors in kind. One of Faden's French contacts maintained, "M. Buache has procured for me everything that you have asked for up to now in the way of maps from the Dépôt de la Marine; [he] asks me to tell you that he will not refuse you anything from this Dépôt provided that you, on your side, send us what we ask for in the way of things published in England."[7] Buache, for example, shipped to Faden an atlas of North American charts, and George III, hydrographer Alexander Dalrymple, and the secretary of the Admiralty used them to appraise possible campaigns. Repeatedly, cartographers and their clients within governments set aside national rivalries—and overlooked the ideological affectations of maps—in their quests for the best spatial intelligence available.[8]

Rather than indicating political fickleness, the transnational movement of maps exposes the nature of the business. Eighteenth-century monarchs desired up-to-date maps for the knowledge they contained and the tactical advantages they might afford, but government backing for the industry was weak. French cartographers had more institutional support than did British ones. Despite his enthusiasm for maps, George III sponsored few mapmaking expeditions, and men appointed "geographer to the king," like Faden, received the title but no monetary compensation.[9] Not surprisingly, makers, purveyors, and consumers of printed maps looked across national lines, regardless of the political landscape, for the cartographic information they needed to succeed.

Additionally, cartographers were not exclusively interested in making maps of their own territories. It was standard practice to draft maps of regions under the control of other states. In any given year, Thomas Jefferys, a London-based mapmaker, was as likely to offer a map of "the bishoprick of Paderborn" in Germany or "the isle of Cuba" as he was "the great, direct and cross roads through England and Wales."[10] And while maps might impose clear lines of possession, spaces were contested and shared in practice. During the Seven Years' War, Bellin published *Description geographique des isles Antilles possédées par les Anglois*. The atlas appealed to French officials, who saw British Caribbean islands as prospective spoils of the war; however, Bellin described his work as a service to all vessels sailing in the region. As he declared in the preface, "It is useful for all commercial nations to know with precision the areas controlled by their neighbors, their extent, their commerce and their strength."[11] He complained that the British had not produced good hydrographic maps of the Caribbean, and since the waters there affected multiple empires, he was not going to let the question of jurisdiction prevent him from filling in the gaps.[12]

As Bellin's explanation emphasizes, accuracy was central to the cartographer's endeavor. Mapmakers and publishers advertised that their goods incorporated the most reliable and newest knowledge. In their 1775 catalogue, the London firm of Sayer and Bennett showcased their ambitious "General Atlas . . . describing the whole Universe; being a complete and new Collection of the most approved Maps extant; corrected with the utmost Care, and augmented from the latest Discoveries."[13] While this atlas was mostly comprised of compilation maps, Jefferys's *West-Indian Atlas* (also available from Sayer and Bennett) was "taken from actual Surveys" and paired with "an authentic Historical Account."[14] Some works were accompanied by long descriptions of the mapmakers' methods as a testament to their thoroughness. Chastenet-Puységur's pilot of Saint-Domingue begins with an eighteen-page narrative that details his calculations at sixty different sites in the colony.[15] Makers and publishers also promoted the accuracy of their maps by highlighting their prestigious precursors, including those from abroad. Sayer and Bennett's world atlas was "an Improvement on the Maps of D'Anville and Robert," two respected French cartographers.[16] Map publishers saw the authority of their products resting on the twin pillars of pedigree and newness.

These criteria contributed to the decision to print a specific map. All maps started as manuscript maps, but not all manuscript maps were published. One modern inventory of plans of the siege of Yorktown tallies over one hundred manuscript maps, with only around thirty printed.[17] A publisher (who was sometimes but not always the map-maker) weighed whether a manuscript map was marketable enough to warrant the effort.[18] Publishing a map with a certain level of detail entailed a substantial financial investment, especially during periods of war, like the revolutions, when printing supplies became more expensive. The price of fine-quality copper skyrocketed as navies used it to bottom ships, and premium paper went through periodic shortages as military mobilization increased pressure for rags. But the biggest outlay for publishers was labor. Maps were a specialty among engravers and etchers, and although a single maker's name appeared on a printed map, several pairs of hands went into one plate. An assistant drew the outline, another focused on topographic features, and still another did the lettering.[19] The costs added up.

If done well, the conversion of a manuscript map into a published one demanded time. The plates for a grand project such as Chastenet-Puységur's and Jefferys's splendid, large-scale atlases could take years to engrave; a single plate, depending on its size and detail, required anywhere from a few weeks to several months. On the speedier end of the spectrum, William Faden produced a plan for Fort Sullivan, South Carolina, six weeks after Sir Henry Clinton's defeat there in 1776, and later that year, he needed only four weeks to publish plans of British victories on Long Island.[20] For all his hustle, Faden's maps of American revolutionary sites appeared after the battles had taken place. Sometimes, however, government officials wanted multiple copies of a manuscript map more quickly, and they discovered it was swifter to assign men to copy a map by hand than to convert it to a plate for numerous printings. One staff member at the Dépôt de la Marine remarked, "Two people can copy fifty plans or designs while six will not [be able to] make four [printed] maps that demand a great deal of work, discussion, attempts, and arrangements."[21] The lengthy collaborative process of printing maps did not suit every application.

Since the transformation of a manuscript map into a printed one was often costly and cumbersome, map publishers found it easier to copy a previously published map. They would revise it a bit, freshen up its aesthetics, and claim it was in keeping with the "latest observations."[22] International connections were critical to supplying mapmakers and dealers with "new" material. British mapmakers bought printed French maps, copied, and sold them, sometimes without changing the text from French to English. The practice was so widespread that in 1778 two French dealers, looking to acquire recently published British maps, requested, "Do not send new maps which you could have copied from our French ones, since we would make nothing of them here."[23]

Although copying was a convention of the trade, at times it became politicized. Both during and after the U.S. war for independence, some North American printers took pride in copying and selling versions of British maps (instead of offering the British maps directly to consumers), declaring the practice more "patriotic."[24] The French also leveraged the political implications of pirating British maps. In 1779 M. Le Rouge, *géographe du roi,* issued a series of beautiful maps of at least a dozen Caribbean islands. The title for each proudly announced the map's provenance, and many were "translated" from Jefferys's 1775 series published in London.[25] Jefferys's status as a premier mapmaker lent prestige to these editions, but their release in French, shortly after that nation had seized Dominica from the British (1778) had political aspirations as well. They allowed French mapmakers and viewers to conceptualize other British islands in the West Indies as potential French possessions and provided cartographic intelligence to officials and militaries interested in making that aspiration a reality.

The acceptance of copying meant that the same maps were published repeatedly—a trend at odds with the purported newness of maps and with representations of revolutionary developments. Take, for example, Bellin's *Carte de la partie françoise de St. Domingue,* made for the French navy in the 1760s. Over the next several decades, it was reissued in France as well as reproduced elsewhere. As late as 1814, the Philadelphia printer Mathew Carey presented a version of the Bellin map, listing the original French title and Bellin attribution above his English translation: "A Map of the French Part of St. Domingo" (figure 5.2). Makers and sellers like Carey did not advertise these editions as historical maps of places (although there was a trade of older maps by famous makers). Rather, with a few changes, they were sold as up to date. Carey added some information of interest: he noted, "Places burnt by the Negroes are coloured Yellow," a clear reference to the Hai-

Figure 5.2. *A Map of the French Part of St. Domingo* (Philadelphia: Mathew Carey, 1796[?]). This example dates from the 1790s, but Carey issued the map well into the 1810s with no alterations. (Library Company of Philadelphia.)

tian Revolution. That said, Carey did not alter any of the place-names to acknowledge the changes that had occurred on the island between the 1760s and 1814; he continued to call the nation "St. Domingo," not "Haiti," the town "Le Cap Français" instead of "Cap Henry," and so on. Such choices had ideological consequences; in this case, it was part of the larger trend to refuse to recognize formally the independence of Haiti or to consider its revolution as a revolution.[26]

Map production in this era reflected the specific demands of maps as objects—what it took to create them with the technologies and materials available. Atlantic networks of trade and news supplied essential information to mapmakers, and these connections persisted when mapmakers of rival nations went to war. But their cosmopolitan efforts paid off only if they sold their wares. After all, printed maps were goods, and mapmakers sought to reach a substantial number of consumers—not just government officials and other mapmakers—to see a profit. The typical print run for a single map was between two hundred and three hundred copies and, as with production, an Atlantic view informed map dealers' understanding of their market.[27] Their strategies to make maps available to consumers of varied wherewithal and in sundry locations contributed to the wide circulation of maps, and this breadth mattered practically and ideologically during the age of revolutions.

In places like London and Paris, map sellers were usually in the printing trade. They were engravers, stationers, book- and print sellers, and printers, and this held true in North America and the Caribbean, too. The merchandise in printers' shops could be a bit of a jumble. At the Imprimerie Royale in Cap Français, one could find books, leather portfolios, quills, seals, lined paper for music, and paints as well as maps of Louisiana, Saint-Domingue, Cuba, and other Caribbean islands.[28] In North America, maps turned up for sale among other imported items. In 1775 the New York City shopkeeper Richard Sause marketed maps alongside cutlery, jewelry, and hardware, while in the early 1790s, a Savannah firm offered maps in addition to fabrics, shoes, and ceramics. Maps were sold by portraitists, cabinetmakers, and upholsterers, and could be bought at taverns, inns, coffeehouses, and auctions.[29]

Some of these ventures represented one-off speculations—the case of an artisan or importer seizing the opportunity of a map windfall. But the diversity of venues was a common rather than an unusual mode of sale. The assorted retail settings for maps underscore how they were consumer goods, not rarefied items exclusively for elites, and their spread was promoted by a range of pricing.[30] During the eighteenth century, maps had become more affordable for Atlantic buyers. A modest map cost as much as a deck of playing cards, a yard of silk ribbon, or an unbound novel. Size was an important factor in determining price. In England, a one-sheet map made from one plate at small to medium scale cost between 6 pence and 2 shillings, while larger maps—either from a folio-sized plate or a multi-sheet map from several plates—ran anywhere from 4 shillings to 3 guineas (63 shillings). An atlas started at £1 and could rise as high as £6. Meanwhile, in France, small, single-sheet maps sold for between 10 and 20 sous, and atlases ranged from 30 to 100 livres. Even high-end buyers looked for deals, though, by signing on as subscribers to grandiose mapping projects.

The 1791 *Recueil de vues des lieux principaux de la colonies françoise de Saint-Domingue* cost 36 livres for subscribers to the entire series or 48 livres if one chose to buy separately, "in sheets."[31] Color, too, influenced price. In 1775 Sayer and Bennett listed their wall maps in two versions—uncolored and colored, with the cost of the latter double that of the former. Similar trends governed the French map market, and in both countries, sellers charged more for imported maps than for locally produced ones.[32]

On the other side of the Atlantic, evidence for pricing is scant. A few North American records suggest that while retailers marked up prices for imported maps as much as 25 percent, they were still reasonable for some consumers. John and Betsy Ross, who had just struck out on their own as upholsterers in Philadelphia, possessed, as of January 1776, one map of "the Seat of Civil War in New England."[33] Toward the end of the war, Philadelphia bookseller Robert Bell offered several maps by popular British mapmakers in his 1783 catalogue: Jefferys's *New Map of Nova Scotia, and Cape Britain, with the Adjacent Parts of New England and Canada* cost $2, while his *The Island and Colony of Cayenne* went for 50 cents. One could purchase Robert Sayer's *A New General Chart of the Atlantic or Western Ocean by Mr. Fleurieu* for $4.[34]

These prices put maps in reach of the middle classes throughout the Atlantic world, and maps appeared in other contexts that aided their social and geographic distribution. Jefferys's *New Map of Nova Scotia,* for example, was first published in the book *The Natural and Civil History of the French Dominions in North and South America.*[35] Maps appeared in all sorts of volumes—atlases, pilots, and tomes on geography, of course, but also histories, travelers' accounts, and other narratives. Periodicals featured small maps to complement articles. Between 1731 and 1833, *Gentleman's Magazine,* a trendy British periodical, included at least fourteen maps or plans of various sites in the Caribbean alone. Maps decorated public spaces as well. In North America, they were found in statehouses, taverns, public libraries, and other high-traffic settings.[36]

While these venues abetted the dissemination and familiarity of printed maps, the process of drawing maps permeated sectors of everyday life. Officials and surveyors drew plat maps on deeds to demarcate property lines, sailors sketched shoreline views, and city planners drafted designs for new neighborhoods. Maps had become so prevalent in Atlantic culture that the language of mapping shaped modes of writing fiction and poetry.[37] They informed casual descriptions, too. Attempting to convey the effects of ringworm, one soldier in the Caribbean explained, "These Spots are surrounded with a kind of hard, Scrufulous border, that makes them look in my opinion, something like *land-Maps.*"[38]

Although the making of printed maps was a specialized trade based mostly in Europe, mapping as an activity and maps as consumer goods were transnational and popular in important respects. From the exchanges of knowledge that informed their production to the circuits through which they moved to the venues in which they were sold, maps and their makers relied on and were oriented toward the Atlantic as much as an individual nation or empire. This orientation was central not just to the creation and marketing of maps but to the work they did. As concerns about accuracy and newness (or, at the very least, lip service to both) indicate, maps were vital for representing Atlantic spaces and for navigating them—tasks that were imperative to revolutionary wars. Their military application heightened demand for maps in this period, and their use in the field reveals both the potential and pitfalls of cartography in campaigns for revolutionary change.

USEFUL CARTOGRAPHIES

It bears remembering that a map made for one context was not automatically useful in others. Mapmakers decided what (and what not) to include on a given map based to some degree on its anticipated purpose.[39] Maps of the same region varied because map users needed certain types of information to achieve specific aims: mariners required nautical notations, property owners wanted details on land features, monarchs insisted on crests and other testaments to their power. A single map might answer to several applications; however, it could not fulfill all possibilities. A map was necessarily selective in order to function well.

During the age of revolutions, the most pressing demand for maps was for the military. Scholar Jeremy Black has noted that all wars rely on "a close understanding of the spatial dimension of force and a control of the territory itself," and maps aided both endeavors.[40] In the late eighteenth century, military and government leaders saw maps as central to military tactics. They had become a standard item in every officer's kit, and in war zones cartographic knowledge circulated through the ranks and among civilians. Yet the utility of maps for planning and executing battles had its limits. Users in the field cultivated a healthy skepticism about what maps depicted—a dynamic that tempers assertions of the overwhelming authority of maps. At the same time, actors' suspicions help to explain the pervasiveness of mapping; they felt the impulse to map almost constantly to achieve representations that were more effective practically and ideologically.

According to the leading military strategists of the day, maps were indispensable to warfare. Frederick the Great, seen as *the* expert on such matters, proclaimed, "Tactics become a useless art if it is not adapted to the terrain," and military handbooks, which thrived and were shared across national and linguistic boundaries, repeated this refrain.[41] Maps supplied military strategists with knowledge of the landscape so that they could locate the enemy, plan troop movements, and decide on points of attack and defense. Maps did so efficiently, bringing together in one image material that would take pages of text to describe. Since some European generals had never set foot in North America or the Caribbean before they arrived for war (and high-ranking government officials never would), maps provided insight into unfamiliar areas. But even locals needed maps. While George Washington knew parts of his native Virginia and had trained as a surveyor, he desperately collected cartographic information for other areas. How was he to find, he wondered, the "cross roads between Sussex and Morristown" if they were not "laid down on my pocket Map"?[42] Consider another native to his revolutionary terrain, Toussaint Louverture. Although he had spent most of his life in northeastern Saint-Domingue and was famous for his epic rides crisscrossing the colony, maps would have proved a convenient way to acquaint himself at a glance with the geography of Hispaniola.

Given the consensus among military tacticians on the utility of maps, soldiers in all armies sought them out. Maps were not issued to officers, and so they had to buy their own. As soon as war loomed on the horizon, government officials and military men scrambled to acquire the latest maps of probable war zones. Supply was always an issue in the Americas, and U.S. revolutionaries felt this problem acutely. Because of the lopsided nature of map production, state legislatures, military leaders, and members of the Continental Congress lamented the dearth of available maps of North America. In November 1776, Washington complained that not only did he lack adequate maps to plan his campaigns, he had "in vain endeavoured to procure them."[43] Jefferson tried to obtain maps for General Horatio Gates but met with little success. As the Virginia Assembly acknowledged regretfully, "During the time of war the importation of books and maps shall be *hazardous*"—and hence elusive.[44] They were so coveted that Washington directed his spies to pilfer maps at every opportunity, and other commanders were also on the lookout.[45]

From the comfort of the metropole and headquarters, government administrators and high-ranking officers preferred large multi-sheet maps. Admiral Richard Howe, for instance, purchased over seventy charts of New England and Nova Scotia for which he paid around £265 to the Swiss-born, British-trained mapmaker Joseph Frederick Wallet Des Barres.[46] Because of their size, though, such maps were inconvenient for troops on the move, and more often, officers invested in small bound collections of maps. As one publisher of these "pocket atlases" professed, "Surveys and Topographical Charts being fit only for a Library, such Maps as an Officer may take with him into the Field have been much wanted. The following Collection forms a PORTABLE ATLAS OF NORTH AMERICA, calculated in its Bulk and Price to suit the Pockets of Officers of all Ranks."[47] Sometimes these atlases were more portable in name than in function. From its title alone, Sayer and Bennett's 1776 *American Military Pocket Atlas Being an Approved Collection of Correct Maps, Both General and Particular, of the British Colonies; Especially Those Which Now Are, or Probably May Be the Theatre of War* seemed the ideal assortment of maps for an officer in action. But it was nicknamed the "holster atlas" because it was too large for the real pocket of a man's coat.[48]

Size issues aside, pocket maps provided an overview that helped soldiers orient themselves in foreign terrain. When Captain John Gabriel Stedman, a Scots Brigade officer, got lost during a march in Suriname in the 1770s, he "in the Middle of this Distress Recollect[ed] that by the Map the River Pirica was due W[est] from us I Determined to Lose no more Time but to Set forward Without Delay." Nevertheless, he found it hard to locate north in the pouring rain without a compass; luckily, "the Black Boy [traveling with him] Put me in Mind that on the S[outh]

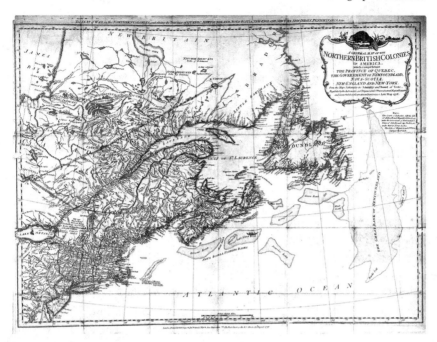

Figure 5.3. *A General Map of the Northern British Colonies in America,* from *The American Military Pocket Atlas* (London: R. Sayer & J. Bennett, [1776]). This pocket atlas features six maps: North America, the West Indies, the Northern Colonies, the Middle Colonies, the Southern Colonies, and Lake Champlain. While the octavo volume measured about 10½ by 8¼ inches, each map folded out—this one's full size is 20½ by 27½ inches. (Library of Congress, Geography and Map Division.)

Side, the Barck of the Trees Was Smoothest—This Was a Luckie Hint and off we Set through Thick and Thin."[49] Stedman's recollection of the map allowed him to identify his general location, but he required additional information (from an enslaved person) to navigate through the landscape.

Stedman's situation was exacerbated by the lack of a map and compass, but even with map in hand his abilities would have been hampered. The scale of pocket atlas maps meant that they had narrow practical applications (figure 5.3). With scales as high as 150 miles to the inch, these maps lacked the textured detail that was imperative to military maneuvers on the ground. Larger maps had their problems, too: inconsistency of scale, diverse points of reference (for instance, various prime meridians), unreliable norths, and obsolete information. And whatever their size, maps contained a lot of blank spaces, which commanders sometimes interpreted as easy terrain but, as soldiers discovered all too frequently, was not.[50]

Representing environments accurately was difficult, and topographic maps, which aspired to the most detailed depictions of landscape, left much to be desired. Eighteenth-century maps were dire in their portrayals of mountains, as the French and the British realized in the Caribbean.[51] On period maps, uniform, decorative peaks dot the interiors of Saint-Domingue, Dominica, and elsewhere, but give no real sense of the mountains' sizes. In contrast, maritime maps incorporated data about the depths in and around shorelines because this was relatively easy to measure with a weighted line. Calculating the height of mountains was a much more involved process. Occasionally mapmakers added brief descriptions to try to put them in context. One 1794 map noted that the Hotte Mountains in southwestern Saint-Domingue were "the highest in this part," but exactly how tall they were was unclear.[52] A map of Dominica from the late 1770s features a border that runs along the base of the mountain range to demarcate "the cultivated and inhabited lands" from "the uncultivated and entirely abandoned" areas.[53] While this boundary might be helpful for prospective planters interested in settlement, it mattered little to militaries tracking foes in the interior.

During the attempted French reconquest of Saint-Domingue, General Donatien-Marie-Joseph Rochambeau (the son of the leading French general in the American Revolution) described how the lack of good knowledge of the mountains resulted in devastation for his army: "The hills and . . . mountains [were] nearly always inaccessible [and] offered sometimes a sharp rock, lacking in vegetation, and sometimes an immense forest of prickly wood and strong and torturous creepers, wrapped from branch to branch, making access impenetrable."[54] Time and again, officers and soldiers complained about the brutal landscapes of the Caribbean and North America: the impassable rivers and mountains, thick forests, and roads that were roads in name only. As one officer recounted, the men "waddled through Water and Mire above our hipps, Climb'd over heaps of fallen trees, creep'd underneath them on our bellies."[55] Maps provided very little concrete insight to prepare armies for these challenges that affected their efficacy.

Military officials were aware of the deficiencies of extant maps and quick to note outright mistakes. Washington, Jefferson, and Thomas

Gage, among others, all criticized the "blunders" and absences in maps of North America.[56] When they could, armies brought along professional surveyors to produce more finely grained renditions of militarily significant landscapes. During the American Revolution, the Continental Army had forty-nine cartographers on the payroll, and the British had ninety. The sheer amount of territory overwhelmed both outfits, and the processes of surveying and mapping were often too slow to keep pace with maneuvers.[57]

More efficient were reconnoitering missions, when scouts explored the landscape, recording observations and swift calculations to refine the cartographic information on published maps. Washington kept a printed pocket map that he updated with annotations gleaned from reports by troops, guides, and messengers.[58] In the field, though, conditions were less than ideal for even quick mapmaking. A second lieutenant in the British engineer corps noted apologetically of his hand-drawn plan of Portsmouth that it "was done in a Great Hurry & partly by Candle Light," which explained the "Indifferent Drawing." A Hessian officer admitted that his map of Paulus Hook, New Jersey, was "drawn by guess."[59]

The open discussion qualifying the utility of maps suggests that actors knew of their deceptive authority. Maps peddled in power, but the approach to them in military contexts indicates a constructive distrust of what maps depicted and how much one should take them at face value. They used maps as tools—with discretion. This sensitivity is expected perhaps among the highest-ranking officers, but it reflected a larger trend in military training in the late eighteenth century. As map scholar J. B. Harley has observed of the American Revolution, "Rather than rigidifying national differences in mapmaking, [the war] intensified the movement of men, ideas, and techniques that gave rise to the common characteristics of military mapping."[60] In other words, the practice of and attitudes toward maps and mapping were Atlantic in character, and although elites dominated the discourse, cartographic culture was broader. The experiences of people of African descent demonstrate this phenomenon most vividly, as they, whenever possible, put the practical and ideological power of maps and mapping to radical ends.

For centuries, masters in the Americas tried to curtail enslaved people's access to maps, fearful that they would abet escape and rebellion. But cartographic knowledge was impossible to restrict completely because all people possess capabilities for spatial representation. As archaeologists have shown, West Africans had ways of distinguishing between political territories, and these modes informed enslaved people's spatial organization of New World landscapes.[61] For some newly arrived Africans, the ecologies of American environments were reminiscent of their homelands, contributing to the comprehension and navigation of their surroundings. Enslaved people carved out clandestine areas within rural and urban landscapes—to gather privately, to hide out temporarily or permanently, and to hunt and forage for food. By some accounts, the Haitian Revolution began at Bois-Caïman, a surreptitious religious ceremony among enslaved people that took place in the interstices of plantations on the northern plain. Throughout the Americas, people of African descent developed distinct visions, understandings, and approaches to moving through the spaces of slavery in ways that subverted their oppressors' spatial plans.[62]

There were points of intersection between Black and white cartographies, too. Some masters depended on slaves' geographic savvy. Owners of rice plantations in the southern colonies of North America relied on the task system, in which individual enslaved people tended certain plots. The arrangement worked only if both parties shared a cartographic conception of the lay of the land. At times members of the master class acknowledged the superior geographic know-how of people of African descent. Caribbean maroons were feared for their knowledge of, as planter Bryan Edwards put it, "every secret avenue of the country; so that they could either conceal themselves from pursuit, or shift their ravages from place to place."[63] This intelligence was formalized, to some extent, in British treaties with Jamaican maroons that delineated their territory from that of colonists and stipulated that maroons maintain roads between specific towns across the island. To negotiate with British officials about these spatial parameters, maroons needed not only firsthand experience in the actual landscape but also a familiarity with its presentation on maps.

Cartographic knowledge among enslaved and free African-descended people came to the fore in the age of revolutions in various ways. Given the power asymmetry at the heart of map production, surviving examples of maps made by people of African descent are rare, but evidence of their existence comes from the testimony of José Antonio Aponte, a free Black carpenter in Cuba who, inspired in part by the Haitian Revolution, planned a rebellion in 1812.[64] When Spanish authorities raided his house, they discovered a cache of books. His library included at least two works with maps, a guide to Cuba and a history of Rome, so clearly he knew the genre.[65] But the prosecutors were more concerned with a volume of paintings in his possession. Aponte created some of the drawings in the book, and his collaborator, Trinidad Nuñez, painted others. Many were compiled from locally available engravings and even printed fans, brought together in layered collages until the image depicted what Aponte desired.[66]

The work is missing or has not survived, but we have some knowledge of it because Aponte was pressed to explain each page, and his inquisitors dutifully recorded the details. He described it as a "Historical Book," but there was no text. Rather, Aponte narrated as he showed the pages to listeners. Several incorporated maps—some hand-drawn, perhaps others printed and pasted. Officials were curious about those of Havana, and they asked him repeatedly why he chose to portray specific buildings in and routes through the city. Aponte claimed that he had done so for his own amusement, but officials suspected the maps were tools for coordinating rebellion.[67] Whether they were or not, the authorities believed that Aponte could have used maps to instruct other free Black and enslaved men. In other words, the master class accepted the capacity for spatial abstraction and for its visualization in maps by people of African descent and thought their skills could aid in strategizing for and carrying out an insurrection.[68]

Many of Aponte's followers lived in and around Havana, so the streets, sites, and landscape were most likely familiar. But Aponte's spatial and ideological ambitions were greater. Historian Ada Ferrer has contended that Aponte's book "was a history of the world reconceived, a new universal history in which Black men ruled."[69] As part of that project, his book contained representations of distant places: picture 27 was a map of Europe, Africa, and Asia, and although what histories Aponte told in relationship to the map are unknown, his listeners, through the image alone, gained a global spatial awareness (if they did not have it already). The first illustration of the volume showed the creation of the world and the Garden of Eden, featuring the rivers Euphrates, Nile, Ganges, and Gihon. These four rivers deviate from those named in the book of Genesis, but they center the origins of the universe in places where people of color predominated.[70] In both plotting rebellion and mapping the long *durée* of history, the renderings in Aponte's book employed the military and ideological power of maps.

Although extant maps drawn by African-descended people are few, their activities during the revolutionary wars provide additional proof of their understanding of European cartographic practices. Isolated episodes shed light on the dissemination of military mapping among Black civilians. In 1775 General Gage, then in Boston, sent out two soldiers to map the nearby countryside. They disguised themselves as rural folk, "with brown cloaths and reddish handkerchiefs round our necks," but a Black woman saw through their ruse. As the soldiers reported to Gage, the woman "said she knew our errand was to take a plan of the country; that she had seen the river and road through Charlestown on the paper."[71] She identified the map, knew that mapping was a key military activity, and recognized the representation of Charlestown on the map. This incident is especially noteworthy because in this period cartography was seen as more the purview of men than women, white or Black.

The anecdote intimates the possible breadth of awareness among people of African descent of military cartography, and this awareness had developed long before the revolutions. Throughout the eighteenth century, Black men were fixtures among European troops stationed in the Caribbean. In the French and British West Indies, men of African descent—free and enslaved—served as pioneers (in construction), artificers (artisans/mechanics), infantrymen (foot soldiers), and cavalrymen (on horseback), and in these capacities they engaged in all manner of work for which spatial knowledge was crucial.[72] Throughout Stedman's *Narrative of a Five Years Expedition against the Revolted Negroes of Surinam,* Black men figure centrally as his unit traverses the landscape. One plate enumerates the order of a march through the forest: "Two Negroes with Bill hooks to open a Path" led the group, and more Black men were distributed throughout the line, carrying provisions, ammunition, and sick and wounded soldiers (figure 5.4). Although under the direction of white officers, these Black men, who comprised one-quarter of the total number of people on the march, participated in coordinated movements of troops, for which protocol recommended maps.[73] Also recall that when Stedman became lost with a Black servant, it was their shared understanding of cardinal direction (both knowing north) as well as the Black man's superior knowledge of local flora that enabled them to find their way back to camp. Whether hauling supplies, constructing fortresses, building roads, or couriering

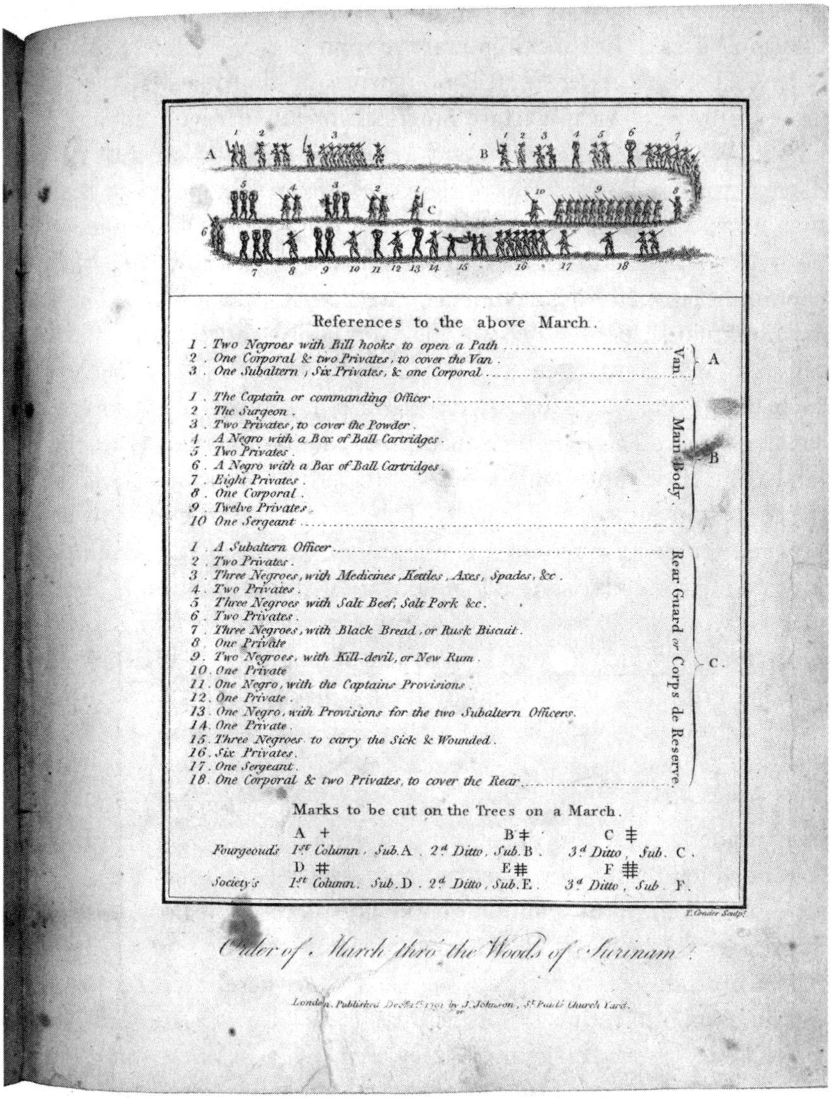

References to the above March.

1 . Two Negroes with Bill hooks to open a Path ....
2 . One Corporal & two Privates, to cover the Van .
3 . One Subaltern , Six Privates, & one Corporal .... Van } A

1 . The Captain or commanding Officer............................
2 . The Surgeon .
3 . Two Privates, to cover the Powder .
4 . A Negro with a Box of Ball Cartridges .
5 . Two Privates .
6 . A Negro with a Box of Ball Cartridges .
7 . Eight Privates .
8 . One Corporal .
9 . Twelve Privates .
10 . One Sergeant .... Main Body. } B

1 . A Subaltern Officer ....
2 . Two Privates .
3 . Three Negroes, with Medicines, Kettles, Axes, Spades, &c .
4 . Two Privates .
5 . Three Negroes with Salt Beef, Salt Pork &c .
6 . Two Privates .
7 . Three Negroes, with Black Bread, or Rusk Biscuit .
8 . One Private .
9 . Two Negroes, with Kill-devil, or New Rum .
10 . One Private .
11 . One Negro, with the Captains Provisions .
12 . One Private .
13 . One Negro, with Provisions for the two Subaltern Officers .
14 . One Private .
15 . Three Negroes to carry the Sick & Wounded .
16 . Six Privates .
17 . One Sergeant .
18 . One Corporal & two Privates, to cover the Rear .... Rear Guard or Corps de Reserve. } C.

Marks to be cut on the Trees on a March.

	A +	B ‡	C ‡
Fourgeoud's	1st Column . Sub.A .	2d Ditto . Sub.B .	3d Ditto . Sub. C .
	D #	E ‡	F #
Society's	1st Column . Sub.D .	2d Ditto . Sub.E .	3d Ditto . Sub . F.

Order of March thro' the Woods of Surinam.

London, Published Dec.r 1st 1791 by J. Johnson, St Pauls Church Yard.

Figure 5.4. *Order of March thro' the Woods of Surinam*, plate 20 from John Gabriel Stedman, *Narrative of a Five Years Expedition against the Revolted Negroes of Surinam* (London, 1796). As this plate illustrates, enslaved people were integrated into the formal order of marches: at the front "to open a path," interspersed through the main line carrying boxes of "Ball Cartridges," and in the rear guard hauling medical supplies, camp equipment, provisions, and the sick and wounded. (Library Company of Philadelphia.)

messages, some men of African descent had exposure to the conventions and uses of European military mapping.

Given these experiences, it is not surprising that Black soldiers integrated European-style warfare practices into their revolutionary campaigns. While West African tactics remained essential, men of African descent were willing to appropriate those from Europe when it suited their aims. The strongest evidence comes from Saint-Domingue, where both African- and island-born men exhibited their knowledge of European military methods, including those that relied on maps. The leaders Boukman, Georges Biassou, Jean-François, and Jeannot had been seized as war captives in Africa and sold into New World slavery. As such, they were acquainted with European military innovations, like cavalry, that had already been incorporated into warfare in their homelands, and they implemented these strategies in the earliest moments of the contest in Saint-Domingue.[74] When Louverture and his army joined French republican forces in the mid-1790s, he consulted the same military manuals as his white contemporaries, those that emphasized the utility of maps. He tasked French engineers with designing forts and blockhouses, which resulted in scores of manuscript plans, some of which were realized (built no doubt by Black men). Louverture also hired surveyors to evaluate the terrain for military campaigns and for agricultural development.[75]

Because of the Black army's huge size (numbering at least 50,000 men) and its increasing professionalization, maps were handy tools for coordinating the positions and movements of soldiers. They would have been helpful for maintaining the army's chain of hospitals and its impressive courier system. In fact, communications ran so smoothly that according to one French engineer, "Nowhere is correspondence delivered as promptly as in Saint-Domingue." Louverture was a stickler for precise planning of military maneuvers, asking for as much topographical information as possible and giving exacting instructions to his generals—all of which maps and mapping facilitated.[76] In the mid-1790s, the Black army established a cordon, a network of armed strongholds, stretching from La Tannerie, near the border with Santo Domingo in the northeast, to Laferrière in the northwest. During the Seven Years' War, white colonists had proposed a similar measure, and although their plans never came to fruition, Black troops adopted the strategy in the 1790s, taking over abandoned plantations and turning them into a chain of fortified posts.[77] Whether Black soldiers were cognizant of these earlier proposals, or whether they reached the same tactical conclusion themselves, the scale of the endeavor demanded a degree of spatial organization for which maps were vital. For the cordon to work well, the camps had to be spaced at regular intervals, communication sustained along the entire line, and activities coordinated. Cartographic renderings—acquired or handmade—were imperative to its creation and maintenance.

The case of people of African descent shows the ways that war accelerated the circulation of maps and the practice of mapping in the age of revolutions. Not every foot soldier—white or Black—owned a map or possessed the training necessary to create a detailed one. But focusing on the practical work of maps reveals the broad contours of their Atlantic dissemination. Officers, on the one hand, saw maps as indispensable, and on the other, questioned their accuracy. The tension between the two encouraged mapping, as soldiers looked for better cartographic information. As a result, maps and mapping stood at the heart of military enterprises in North America and the Caribbean, and people of African descent, like Aponte in Cuba and soldiers in Saint-Domingue, capitalized on the pervasiveness of maps to pursue their own agendas. At times, though, the drive for cartographic precision within militaries came into conflict with the other work of maps— namely, their political claims.

PAPER BATTLES

The pressure for more and better maps was driven not just by pragmatic concerns of conducting war but by politics as well. As Aponte's book illustrates, maps had narrative power, and militaries and regimes exploited this quality. Maps were a means of accounting for the successes and failures of revolutionary wars. Victorious armies celebrated their conquests by renaming key features and redrawing borders on maps to signal their new political allegiances, while military officers relied on cartography to justify their actions to superiors and to the public at large.[78] In both arenas, maps were sites of contest, ones that differed from textual accounts because of their characteristics.

Among the prerogatives of a triumphant army or navy was the power to change the names of territories won, to establish new boundaries, and so forth, converting, for example, in the case of the patriots, British North America into the United States of America. Only six months after the Treaty of Paris was signed, the Connecticut goldsmith and counterfeiter Abel Buell issued the first printed map of the "United States of North America," with its flag incorporated into the elaborate cartouche.[79] During their revolution, the French embraced the political power of cartographic projects. When the regime decided to rational- ize the organization of provinces into departments and to introduce a new system of measurement, these policies compelled revisions to the national map. The seizure of real estate from aristocrats, royals, and the clergy affected the cadastre, a map that recorded property owner- ship for taxes and other administrative purposes. Finally, as the French Revolution abandoned the monarchical past, royalist names of places, streets, and buildings were (or were supposed to be) replaced with re- publican ones.

The translation of these transformations into new, workable maps of France was uneven at best in the 1790s because of the rapid pace of political change within the government, incessant war, and meager funding.[80] Despite shortcomings in execution, the impulse to update French maps to reflect current events and ideological shifts shaped the cartography of the colonies, too. The urge was not strictly a metropoli- tan imposition. From 1793 onward, actors in Saint-Domingue modi- fied places and their cartographic representations in ways that best suited their political imperatives. Often military victories led colonial revolutionaries to rename sites. In the fall of 1799, Louverture com- missioned a map of Aquin, a town in the southern region of the island under André Rigaud's control. The War of the Knives—the fierce con- test between the two generals' armies—had begun just a few months before, but Louverture was already imagining the spatial transforma- tions his triumph would inaugurate. Drawn by the engineer Sonis, the map proposed republican names for the town's principal streets, like Rue de l'Égalité and Rue du Peuple, and one of the main thoroughfares was christened Rue Louverture.[81]

Louverture's cartographic intentions for Aquin were in keeping with trends throughout the colony. In Le Cap, the republican administra- tion replaced ancien régime terms with revolutionary ones. A manu- script map from 1800 includes both names for each contested site— the old ones in red and the new ones in black: Champ de Mars/Place de la Fédération; Rue Royale/Rue Nationale; Rue Dauphine/Rue de l'Égalité.[82] Hand-drawn maps for other areas in Saint-Domingue show similar aspirational changes: Fort-Dauphin remodeled as Fort-Liberté, and Port-au-Prince as Port-Républicain, among others.[83] In the case of the Cap Français map, these changes were part of the physical and political "reconstruction" of the city, but the dual notation indicates that this renovation was incomplete. In the thick of revolutionary war, it was difficult to implement these updates on maps, let alone on the ground, yet the drive to do so persisted in cities and in the countryside. As planters fled or died, military leaders seized estates, and the administration hired land surveyors to map their boundaries and identify their new owners.[84]

The 1801 Constitution articulated the full scale of the spatial and political ambitions for the colony. The first two articles demarcate "the Territory" of Saint-Domingue, including all of Hispaniola and several nearby islands, and the former was a controversial claim. While Spain had been defeated in Santo Domingo in 1795, the region had not been integrated into the French republican system; most glaringly, slavery persisted there. On his own initiative, Louverture invaded the eastern part of the island in 1800, a move that affronted Bonaparte and his appointees, who wanted to subvert the colonial experiment with abolition.[85] Following closely on the heels of the new Constitution of 1801, the law of July 13 enumerated the administrative divisions of "departments, arrondissements, and parishes," creating, among other units, a department around Gonaïves named Louverture, and Crête-à-Pierrot, a fort east of Saint-Marc in the Artibonite River valley, became Fort Louverture.[86]

While men of African descent were drawing and describing a new cartography for the island in a mode that white audiences would recognize, most of these alterations failed to appear on published maps. Part of the problem was structural. Because most maps were printed in Europe rather than in the colonies, revolutionaries in Saint-Domingue did not control published cartographic renderings of their own island. What's more, the swift tempo of spatial change outstripped the production speed of the mapmakers. Even government-sponsored cartographers could not keep up with the shifting borders, names, and owners—in the colonies or at the metropole.[87]

In Saint-Domingue, racism was an influential factor, too, and the selective changes that did make it onto European printed maps reveal how white makers and audiences wrestled with representing

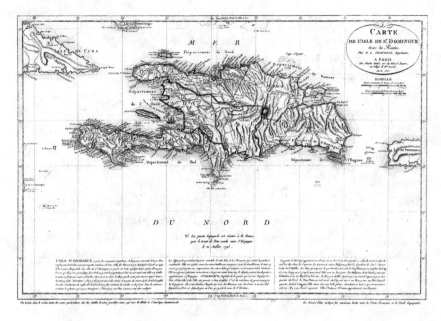

Figure 5.5. *Carte de l'Isle de St. Domingue avec les routes par P. L. Griwtonn, ingénieur* (Paris, 1801). (Courtesy of the John Carter Brown Library.)

revolutionary spatial transformation wrought by Black men. A prime illustration of this struggle is the 1801 reissue of P. L. Griwtonn's 1760s map of the island (figure 5.5). The 1801 version included elements that indicated French dominion over the entire island, an achievement of the Haitian Revolution. It divided Hispaniola into five departments—North, West, South, "l'Engano" (Inganno), and Samaná—and these designations follow the Council of Five Hundred's 1797 administrative reorganization of the colony. The first three had long been the names for regions in Saint-Domingue, but in this new iteration, their boundaries expand east to subsume portions of former Santo Domingo. Inganno and Samaná split the remaining eastern part of Hispaniola into roughly south and north.[88] This spatial integration had existed on paper prior to the 1800–1801 campaigns, yet it was the Black army that translated the council's cartographic plans into reality. The map seems to acknowledge this feat, but, significantly, the new departments are imposed on a map that is overrun with pre-revolutionary detail, so much so that it appears as though an engraver reworked the original 1760s plate. Cities bear their pre-1793 names. The western portion of the island is labeled "A la France" and the east "A l'Espagnol," and the old border between the two colonies is evident as well. Only a note floating in the sea south of the island confirms that the French and Spanish parts have been "reunited," thanks to the treaty of 1795.[89]

The awkward combination of pre-revolutionary and revolutionary elements stands out in the three-paragraph history at the bottom of both the 1760s and 1801 versions of the map. It recounts the "discovery" of Hispaniola and its partition into French and Spanish sectors, and remarks that "the Jacobins, the Capuchins, the Carmelites and other religious groups, performed priestly functions in all the Antilles." Before the revolution, "Jacobins" referred to Dominican friars, but by 1801 the more famous Jacobins were those associated with the French Revolution. The appearance of the label alongside some of the religious sects that revolutionary Jacobins reviled makes the politics of the map difficult to read. The rushed revisions to the 1760s plate point to a pressure to issue something quickly; perhaps the printer anticipated interest from buyers wanting to follow General Leclerc's 1801 invasion. The choice of updates, though, is telling. The 1801 Griwtonn map celebrates the acquisition of the whole island as of 1795 but is ambivalent about the republican regime and the Black soldiers who accomplished it.

The difficulties in reckoning cartographically with the political consequences of revolutionary wars are borne out in another form: the battle map. Long before the late eighteenth century (and continuing thereafter), maps were produced as companions to written accounts of battles, offering a convenient visual guide so that readers and viewers unfamiliar with the location could "see" the conflict as it unfolded. But they also put forward specific versions of events, and an examination of the genre demonstrates some tensions over legitimacy brought about by revolutions.

Between 1775 and 1795, over two hundred battle maps from the American Revolution were published, and collectively they reveal conventions that held true of the genre throughout all three revolutions. Some maps appeared fast on the heels of a battle. A map depicting the battle of Bunker Hill in 1775, with the British and American positions marked, was printed just four days after the first written accounts arrived in London. In such instances, mapmakers and sellers sought to profit from the novelty of the moment. Some battle plans, however, came out months, even years, after the event. Their publication was frequently motivated by the desire to commemorate a notable conquest. In general, map sellers preferred victories by their home nations, which sold better. In the months following Yorktown, the French celebrated the allies' success with the publication of lavishly detailed maps. But in some cases, battle maps made sense of disastrous defeats. Generals commissioned fresh surveys of places where they had lost to accompany their written justifications. They sought to rehabilitate tarnished reputations through these accounts, hoping that maps would bolster their cases among government officials and the public.[90]

No matter when in relation to the actual episode they were printed, battle maps were in conversation with textual and verbal narratives. Audiences had already heard or read about the campaign, and the maps helped individuals far from the center of action to visualize the space, at least cartographically. Similar to written accounts, battle maps emphasized the role of eyewitnesses. In the 1776 *A Plan of Boston, and Its Environs: Shewing the True Situation of His Majesty's Army* (in October 1775), London printer Andrew Dury addressed "the public," averring, "The principal part of this Plan was Survey'd by Richard Williams, Lieutenant at Boston—and sent over by the Son of a Nobleman to his Father in Town by whose Permission it is Published." The inscription highlights not only Williams's presence at the battle but also his rank and connections to men of substance—all of which testified to his reliability. That said, the printer's yearning to compile supplemental cartographic information was irresistible; he mentioned, "The Original has been compared with and Additions made from Several other curious Drawings."[91]

Unlike a print of a battle scene, which usually presents a snapshot of a moment, a battle map narrates several stages of a conflict at once. Published maps of the siege of Yorktown provide a case in point. Philadelphia printer Robert Scot engraved a plan of the battle, produced shortly after the seminal showdown in October 1781, at the behest of Sebastian Bauman, a major in the New York, or Second Regiment of Artillery (figure 5.6). Bauman was a military engineer, born and schooled in Germany, who drew his map based on surveys taken a week after the battle had concluded.[92] Dedicated to General Washington, the map

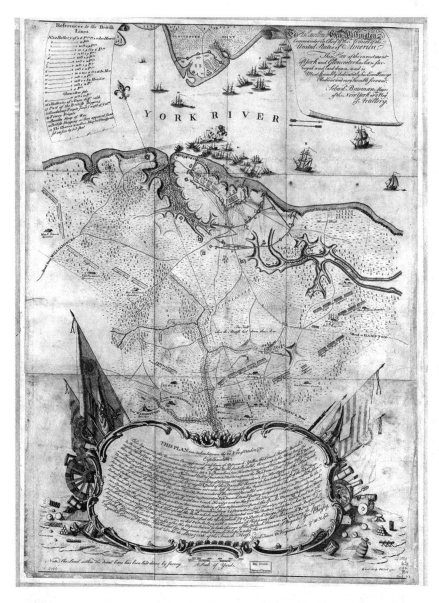

Figure 5.6. *To His Excellency Genl. Washington, Commander in Chief of the Armies of the United States of America, This Plan of the Investment of York and Gloucester Has Been Surveyed and Laid Down* (Philadelphia: Robert Scot, 1782). (Library of Congress Geography and Map Division.)

marks the positions of French, American, and British forces; the placement and size of cannon; the locations of the hospital as well as Washington's and Rochambeau's quarters; and the "Field where the British
laid down their Arms." The plan is dotted with the letters A through R,
and a lengthy key explains the significance of each. A demarcates the
"exterior works evacuated in the night of the 9th of Sept," while I indicates "Part of the 2nd Parallel thrown up by both Armies on the night
of the 11th [of October]." K tracks the size and position of the artillery
used on the 15th and 17th, and so on. The map, through the letters,
presents the sequence of the siege, allowing the reader to connect the
narrative of the battle to a representation of the place.

The verbose and celebratory key and cartouche declare the American sympathies of the maker and patron. But the literary indulgence
of Scot's map was a variation on a common theme across the Atlantic.
Printed French and British plans of Yorktown also presented several
stages at the same time. William Faden's 1781 *A Plan of the Entrance
of Chesapeak Bay, with James and York Rivers* depicts the positions of
the British army, the French and American armies, and de Grasse's fleet.
Notably, it restricts its version of events to the "beginning of October,"
avoiding the climatic surrender. Faden, as geographer to the king, probably wanted to avoid immortalizing British defeats, but as a mapmaker
and seller, he sought to appease public curiosity to learn more about the
controversial battle. Interestingly, in his spatial narration, Faden alludes
to an event that happened years earlier, describing Norfolk as "Burnt
January 1st 1776."[93] This caption references how Lord Dunmore, then
governor of Virginia, evacuated the city after facing off with patriots
in December 1775. Dunmore torched a few buildings as he departed,
but in his wake, patriots set fire to the rest of the town and blamed it
on the governor.[94] Faden's throwback to the initial days of the struggle
provokes at least two interpretations. On the one hand, it shows how
little had changed over the war: the Americans drove Cornwallis out of
Virginia in 1781 as they had Dunmore in 1776, suggesting the folly of
the British endeavor in North America. On the other hand, connecting
Yorktown to the unscrupulous behavior of Virginia patriots in 1776
hints that perhaps the Franco-American victory and revolutionaries'
ideals were not as meritorious as the winners claimed.

Scholars have argued that printed battle maps appealed to active and
armchair military strategists—men who wanted to review the sequence

of military maneuvers and to debate the prowess and shortcomings of a war's generals and admirals. Ever the map enthusiast, Frederick the Great followed the course of the American Revolution from a collection of maps in his palace in Potsdam. (He apparently relished Hessian defeats.)[95] But women tracked the revolutionary wars, too, and they celebrated fantastic victories and lamented crushing defeats. When Admiral Nelson won the battle of the Nile in 1798, the November issue of *Lady's Magazine* featured a frontispiece of his fleet, a brief biography, and extracts from his dispatches.[96] Middle-class women stayed abreast of clashes between soldiers elsewhere. In late 1789 the same magazine carried articles about the Garde du Corps at Versailles and the actions of soldiers in Saint-Pierre, Martinique, and Port-au-Prince, Saint-Domingue.[97] Given how war pervaded these decades and how many women of various means were tied to men—brothers, husbands, sons, friends—who fought in these wars, there is no reason to believe that battle maps fascinated men only.

The hundreds of surviving battle maps of the American and French revolutionary wars attest to their popularity. By comparison, contemporary maps of battles from the Haitian Revolution are lacking, even though the British and French published battle maps of West Indian triumphs at other moments. During the American Revolution, Buache published *Carte de la Dominique, prise par les François le 7 septembre 1778,* with an inset of the plan of attack on the island, each step enumerated in the key.[98] A few years later, a London publisher gloated over the British victory at the battle of Saintes (in Dominica in 1782) with an elaborate view of the positions of every ship (identified by name) of the French and British fleets on the morning of the battle.[99] And while other modes of military cartographic planning and documenting occurred in Saint-Domingue, there are no printed maps that narrate military battles there—not even between 1793 and 1802, the years when the French were most optimistic about the prospect of incorporating the colony and all its inhabitants into the empire on republican terms. There are no battle maps, for instance, of the successes of Rigaud's and Louverture's forces against British troops in the mid-1790s, or of victories in Spanish Santo Domingo in 1794, although both theaters, among many others, were vital to establishing French dominance on the island.[100]

One battle map—printed well after the end of the Haitian Revolution—explains the general rule of absence by showing how the

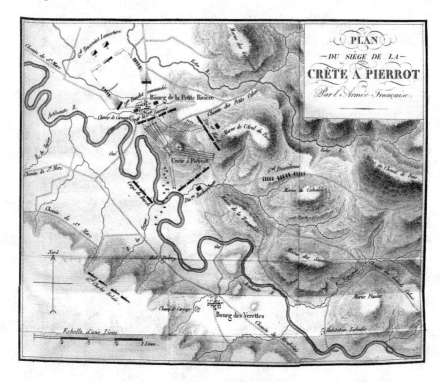

Figure 5.7. *Plan du siège de la Crête à Pierrot par l'armée française*, from Pamphile de Lacroix, *Mémoires pour servir à l'histoire de la révolution de Saint-Domingue* (Paris, 1819). (John Hay Library, Brown University.)

conventions of cartographic representation challenged racial hierarchies. The map depicts the siege at Crête-à-Pierrot/Fort Louverture in March 1802, but it dates from 1819, appearing in Pamphile de Lacroix's *Mémoires pour servir à l'histoire de la révolution de Saint-Domingue* (figure 5.7).[101] Lacroix served as a chief of staff for General Jean Boudet during the Leclerc expedition, and wrote a two-volume history of the campaign. In this episode, French troops marched on the garrison held by Louverture's troops. According to written accounts, the steep terrain led to a ghastly siege, with the French losing over one thousand men before the Black army escaped. The French took the fort, but at tremendous cost and without crushing Louverture's forces.[102]

The map refers to the fort by its earlier name, Crête-à-Pierrot (instead of Fort Louverture), denying the Black revolutionaries' naming preference. That said, it marks out the lines of Generals Dessalines and Louverture's troops as well as those of the French generals, using the standard cartographic shorthand of diagonally bisected rectangles. Directional arrows chart the flow of combat between the two armies. Noticeably missing from the map is any indication that the French army fought forces comprised of free men of African descent. The conventions of the genre thwarted inclusion of such qualifiers. On battle maps, men were represented through abstract symbols: rectangles, clusters of squares, and lines marked their positions and their numbers. In this way, battle maps had an equalizing power, reducing all men to the same pictorial units regardless of affiliation and, in this case, regardless of race. But the singularity of this Haitian Revolution example indicates that it was a type of equality that few European and American mapmakers were willing to concede.

The problem of the form, at least from the perspective of white mapmakers and audiences, becomes clearer when compared to published descriptions of battles during the Haitian Revolution. Many from the period are laden with geographical references so precise that readers needed maps to follow them fully. Consider M. Gros, *An Historick Recital, of the Different Occurrences in the Camps of Grand-Reviere, Dondon, Sainte-Suzanne, and Others, from the 26th of October, 1791, to the 24th of December, of the Same Year.* Published in Baltimore in 1792–93, the eyewitness account is littered with place-names, which are italicized for emphasis. Some, like Fort-Dauphin and the Cape, were familiar to North American readers, especially those in Baltimore who traded with merchants in those ports. But the majority are at the level of camps and plantations: Delpuech, Lacul-de-Samedi, Villate, Escrevisses, and Ancelin, among others.[103] Although these may have appeared on topographical or plat maps of the region, few turned up on any printed map of Saint-Domingue available in the United States. The author included them, though, because he felt that this geographic specificity testified to the veracity of his narrative and bolstered his overall goal of presenting "a more exact Judgment on the real Cause of our Misfortunes."[104]

As with some battle maps, Gros's narrative is a justification of the white colonial army's losses. But Gros derived crucial explanatory power for his defense in his portrayals of the Black soldiers he encountered. In his estimation, they were not proper troops; rather, their movements were the "March of the Incendiaries" and the "Approach of the Vagabonds." He recounts one battle at a plantation in which white forces, "after a Resistance of five Hours," had to flee. While the white creole outfit was defeated, it was, in Gros's telling, the Black soldiers who were "cowardly Assassins" because they "dared not pursue them [the colonists]." The aftermath of battles underscored the supposed unworthiness of the opposition. According to Gros, "We . . . found Eight and Twenty of these Scoundrels promiscuously heaped together, among whom, were four Mulattoes." The failure of the Black soldiers to bury their dead honorably seemed yet more evidence of their shortcomings.[105]

In *An Historick Recital,* Gros blames various actors, including incapable white Frenchmen, for the state of the war in the colony, and occasionally he notes the judiciousness of some Black leaders. Frequently he casts the Black soldiers as the pawns of white, *gens de couleur,* or Spanish commanders. But for all his reliance on geography to substantiate his account, the translation of a single battle into a map would obscure the racist perspective that informs his analysis of the fighting in Saint-Domingue. In Gros's estimation, the Black soldiers did not deserve to be represented in the same mode as their white adversaries. The abstraction of people into symbols concealed differences that Gros felt were crucial. While this perspective is expected from someone who rejected the aims of French and Haitian revolutionaries, even white actors sympathetic to these goals could not bring themselves to print battle maps of the war in Saint-Domingue. Such maps, because of the customs of the genre, had the capacity to challenge hierarchies that neither the most revolutionary of white-led regimes nor their most vociferous detractors were willing to overturn.

The New-York Historical Society owns a miniature portrait of Toussaint Louverture painted on ivory and measuring just over six by five inches (figure 5.8). Louverture is depicted in profile and half-length (from the waist up). Portraits in this period featured sitters in different sizes: full-length, three-quarters (down to the knees), half-length, bust (with or without hands), or simply the head.[106] The latter two were more typical because they were easier and cheaper to produce, and so the half-length portrait of Louverture implies substantial investments from both buyer and artist. Those investments increase if the miniature

Figure 5.8. Unidentified artist, after Nicolas Eustache Maurin, *Dominique Toussaint L'Ouverture (1743–1803)*, after 1832. Watercolor on ivory, 6 ¼ × 5 ¼ in. Purchase, The Louis Durr Fund, New-York Historical Society, 1956.123. (Photography © New-York Historical Society.)

was executed in Saint-Domingue during the general's lifetime, when access to ivory, paints, and an artist of ability were dearer because of the war.[107]

The half-length pose provides an opportunity to show off Louverture's exuberant military dress to fullest effect. He wears a deep blue coat emblazoned with gold braiding, buttons, embroidery, and epaulets, and the coat's red cuffs and collar are decorated with gold as well. Brilliant white lace peeks through the cuffs and collar, and a tricolor sash circles his waist, the hint of a golden sword hilt hanging from it. A black bicorn hat with gold edging, button, and fastener; a small tricolor

cockade; and tall red and white plumes complete the look. Every element of his appearance speaks of decorum, wealth, and authority.

With his hands he unfurls a map, and its title, in tiny script, is just
discernable: *Carte de L'isle de St. Domingue*. Like portraits of other
revolutionary leaders, Louverture's map signals his work as a general
as well as his political power: he holds Saint-Domingue literally and
figuratively in his hands. But the contest over the cartographic representation of revolutionary spaces raises the question, Which map
of Saint-Domingue is Louverture holding? The title is generic: many
French maps of the colony began with the phrase "map of the island of
Saint-Domingue." Only the qualifiers that came afterward, the name of
the cartographer, date, dedication, and so forth, distinguished one map
from another. Without the short title, though, the subject of the painted
map is difficult to identify. The miniature map's wavy lines might suggest regional borders, rivers, or mountain ranges of Saint-Domingue,
but the outline of the island is not distinct. Given the medium, it is
unreasonable to expect the artist to depict the cartography clearly, let
alone reproduce a specific map.

Nevertheless, its pictorial ambiguities reflect the status and use of
actual maps in the revolutionary period. Although printed maps were
more detailed than the one in the miniature, they, too, were shot
through with inaccuracies, absences, and sleights of hand. Actors—
from the elite to the enslaved (and some, like Louverture, who were
both)—recognized that maps were at once powerful and exasperating
tools on the ground and in the public sphere. Their utility was appealing to militaries, as maps helped to navigate spaces and to coordinate
maneuvers, and they were important to governments, normalizing the
representation of places from particular political perspectives. In the
hands of revolutionaries, maps could contribute to making the Atlantic
world anew.

Yet at times the shortcomings of maps frustrated these ambitions.
When maps failed to depict spaces correctly or in enough depth, militaries could not act effectively. And when maps had to portray the
achievements of actors whose agendas reached the revolutions' most
radical conclusions, mapmakers struggled to portray those spaces in
those terms, or ignored them altogether. In other words, maps, because
of their characteristics, ran into problems with the intersection of people, spaces, and politics, and their overwhelmingly white, European

creators stopped short of embracing fully the spatial transformations wrought by revolutionary wars.

If maps and mapping reveal the unevenness in achieving and charting spatial change, the world of prints—the nearest counterpart to printed maps—was preoccupied with the people who brought about those changes. Printmakers and their audiences tried to identify the who's who of revolutions as they appeared on the international scene, and their visualizations of "the people" brought to the fore questions about the legitimacy of political actors and their claims to sovereignty.

6   People in Print

IN SEVERAL RESPECTS, eighteenth-century prints share a good deal with maps. Europe produced most prints that circulated in the Atlantic world, and consumers found them for sale at the same places where maps were available: assorted stores and auctions. Prints also appeared in periodicals and books, but this was neither technologically nor commercially viable on a grand scale.[1] More often they came in single sheets for display (framed, framed and glazed, or neither) and sometimes were gathered in portfolios and volumes. As with maps, the cost of prints varied according to the quality of the image, its size (the larger it was, the more expensive), and additional decoration, such as color. Overall, like other consumer goods, prints became more afford-able in the eighteenth century, with prices for "common" prints ranging from 1 to 3 shillings in London and 10 to 15 sous in Paris, or about a third of a laborer's daily wage.[2]

Yet prints diverged from maps in ways that mattered for visual culture in the age of revolutions. First, the multiple methods for printmaking (engraving, etching, mezzotint, and so forth) allowed printmakers to respond to current events more quickly than mapmakers could. Second, prints did not perform the practical work of navigation that maps did, so they were displayed in domestic settings and some public venues. Finally, and at the risk of stating the obvious, maps and prints treated different subjects. Prints had a wider field of topics (people, places, events) and styles (allegories, emblems, caricature).

These distinguishing features shaped prints as revolutionary objects, and political imperatives added urgency to this type of visualization. Historian John Brewer contends, "For the ardent revolutionary the Revolution must not only happen; it had to be seen to occur, its images and messages inscribed again and again on revolutionary participants and observers alike."[3] Just as a copperplate fixed a picture onto paper, eighteenth-century revolutionaries believed that images made impressions on the minds of the populace and that these impressions encouraged people to act.[4] This understanding of the power of pictures inspired not only supporters of revolutions but also those who objected to, were ambivalent about, or were economically motivated by them. As a result, European makers published prints that expressed an array of political views through numerous themes and modes: portraits of notable figures, scenes of battles, landmark episodes, satires, and iconographic representations, among others.[5]

The perceived necessity of visualizing revolutions resulted in a staggering volume of output. Thousands upon thousands of individual political prints were published in these decades, and because of the reproducibility of the form, each subject was reprinted many times over. Although these prints frequently targeted local audiences and were preoccupied with national affairs, they also weighed in on international issues. French and British makers published prints about the American Revolution, and British and American printers issued ones of the French Revolution. To a lesser extent, European and American artists portrayed aspects of the Haitian Revolution.

Despite the striking range, quantity, and Atlantic character of political prints, the number about the Haitian Revolution is significantly smaller, and the topics and styles are less diverse. This relative lack stems in some measure from the fact that there were few printmakers in Saint-Domingue, and so period engravings reflect the perspectives of white, usually European, outsiders. Without a doubt, racism influenced their renditions. As anthropologist Michel-Rolph Trouillot argued regarding texts, the Haitian Revolution failed to fit white observers' political and racial categories, and therefore was written about in terms that depoliticized the motivations of Black people.[6] Although these accounts were discriminatory in content, their magnitude was abundant, as newspapers and eyewitness accounts tracked the twists and turns of events in Saint-Domingue.[7] By comparison, the dearth of visual representations implies that white printmakers thought that Atlantic spectators were more limited in what they would tolerate seeing than in what they would read or hear about developments in the French colony.

That said, observers did visualize the Haitian Revolution for public consumption, and one significant element is portrayals of people of African descent. Scholars, evaluating these depictions alongside those from other eras, have shown how these decades affected the long and checkered history of representations of Black men and women.[8] But images of revolutionaries in Saint-Domingue were also in conversation with renderings of their political contemporaries in North America and France, since the question of actors was central to picturing all three revolutions. With each, observers wondered who exactly were "the people," did they deserve to rule, and were their new leaders legitimate. Political theorists had been pondering the parameters of popular sovereignty for centuries, but the late eighteenth-century revolutions translated theories into action and in a variety of ways.

Revolutionaries wanted to be seen in order to bolster their case for the validity of their movements, and audiences wanted to see these people as they took stock of these claims. Makers had to determine whom to portray and how, and this was not a clear-cut process. To some extent, their decisions were informed by pragmatic factors like structures of production and the perceived market as well as the predilections of individual artists. But their political calculations come across strongly in two categories: renditions of specific figures and portrayals of crowds. Images of individuals and collectives abounded in the aftermath of revolutions, but this chapter concentrates on prints that captured personages and groups when they entered the public stage—the world of caricature, portraits, and scenes rather than iconographic and commemorative prints. It privileges single-sheet prints instead of those in books because the former had greater potential for distribution abroad and for public viewing.

This focus is crucial for analyzing how artists and broad swaths of viewers understood these new faces of popular sovereignty as they emerged. In their choices of subjects and modes of representation, printmakers participated in contentious debates about which revolutionaries warranted acknowledgment and to what degree their demands and actions were justified. Because of the conventions of the medium, prints lent a kind of legitimacy to those portrayed. The individuals and collectives selected as subjects for prints reveal the unique stakes of illustrating revolutionary people, Black and white, and these stakes were distinct from those of texts. Looking at depictions across the three revolutions uncovers visual absences—from North American intellectuals to French Jacobins to Haitian leaders—that occurred at specific moments and for particular reasons. These instances throw into relief how prints, on the one hand, propelled new visions of "the people" and, on the other, tamed some of the most radical elements of the expanding call for popular sovereignty by making certain people unseeable.

MOVING PICTURES

The technology of printmaking is fundamental to understanding the Atlantic circulation of prints and their content. While woodcutting was a long-standing and durable method for transferring pictures onto paper, intaglio printing—that of incising an image into a copperplate— was the favored means in eighteenth-century Europe. There were several intaglio techniques, and the mode affected not only a given print's aesthetic qualities but also the speed at which the print was produced, its price, and the numbers of copies made. These were significant considerations for political prints, where timeliness and dissemination mattered to artists, vendors, and customers.

Engravings took the longest amount of time to execute, requiring an engraver to cut each line into the plate at the appropriate depth and spacing. Consequently, they were the most expensive, but from a printer's point of view, these were sometimes worth the investment because engraved plates best withstood repeated pulls at the press, with some lasting for decades. Etchings, mezzotints, aquatints, and stipples were faster to fabricate, at rates that varied anywhere from three to ten times quicker. An etcher drew the design on a ground with a burin and then applied acid to bite the lines into the copperplate below. Aquatint was used in conjunction with etching: an etcher outlined the image and then aquatint created tones through the application of an acid-resistant resin so that large areas were worked swiftly. For mezzotints, the entire plate was roughened with a toothed tool and the design scraped onto the ground by smoothing down the textured plate, giving mezzotints their signature velvety black. The initial roughening (known as "rocking") was not skilled labor, which lowered the price and accelerated the speed of production. Finally, stipple, invented in London in the early 1770s, involved outlining the subject and then creating tonality by filling in the outline with clusters of dots of different thicknesses. Stipple had the advantage that it was receptive to the addition of color. As with mezzotints, assistants handled much of the in-fill dotting, reducing the price and increasing the pace of fabrication.[9]

With their distinct levels of investment in capital and labor, these diverse methods allowed publishers to present prints at assorted prices to appeal to consumers whose wherewithal ranged from small to great. But subject was just as important to attracting buyers, and in the eighteenth century, the possibilities seemed limitless. The London firm of Sayer and Bennett organized their 1775 catalogue of prints by size and then by subject. Among their large prints alone were renditions of Johann Zoffany paintings; portraits of royals, statesmen, judges, and beauties; "humorous subjects"; cattle and horses; "sea pieces"; "naked figures"; "sporting" and "scripture" pieces—to list a few categories.[10] The small prints included equally varied subjects. Sellers tried to offer something for everyone: men and women; the well-heeled, middling, and laboring; the pious and the louche; and all buyers in between.

Political prints were a subset within this capacious range, and thanks to techniques like etching, aquatint, mezzotint, and stipple, publishers could react promptly to recent events—an advantage when aspiring to pique the public's interest. From a publisher's perspective, though, politics was a tricky topic for two reasons. First, many political prints responded to the moment, so they had less capacity for reproduction in the long term. Some were in vogue briefly, only for as long as the news was new, and then faded from view, so a printer had a short period to turn a profit.[11] Given the labor and resources required for an engraving, many timely political prints (versus, for example, commemorative or iconographic ones) were etchings and mezzotints. The outlay was less, and a publisher recouped his expenses when he sold half of the run; the rest was profit. Still, some sought guarantees. In April 1794 a French etcher by the name of Courcelle proposed an anti-British caricature and wrote to the Committee of Public Safety to request support. He suggested that the committee purchase fifty impressions at

10 sols each, which he calculated would cover his production costs of 25 livres.[12] Even with a relatively modest printing project, Courcelle wanted financial assurance from officials.

Courcelle's case points to the second reason political prints were chancy. As his application to the Committee of Public Safety hints, he was concerned about cost *and* content. In all countries, censure was a real threat if authorities deemed the subject of a print unsuitable. The level of risk depended on nation and moment, but across Europe, observers saw Britain as having the most permissive attitude toward political topics, especially in artists' use of satire, a mode that flourished in the Georgian era. Commentators interpreted publishers' bald ridicule of leaders as indicative of British liberty, and within Britain many lauded humor as an expedient and nonviolent means to release social and political tensions. Some aspirant and prominent public figures angled with popular artists to appear in their caricatures, seeing them as pathways to fame.[13]

British visual liberties had Atlantic ramifications. In France publishers relied on the indulgence granted to British prints to skirt local censors. On occasion they gave domestically produced, politically critical images false imprints, stating that they had been published in England and merely copied in France. For all the praise of British license, though, authorities there routinely hauled in printers for questioning over disparaging works. They came under scrutiny most acutely during the French Revolution.[14] In 1792 the Association for Preserving Liberty and Property against Republicans and Levellers (also known as the Reeves's Association after its founder, the magistrate John Reeves) set out to guarantee that "all libelous publications . . . be withdrawn from the windows of those shops in the habit of caricaturing the King and his Ministers."[15] With backing from the government, the association contributed to the suppression of dissent at unprecedented levels. Even in Britain, political themes were more perilous in comparison to others.[16]

Given these two factors, some printmakers and publishers avoided political prints altogether. The renowned London firm of Laurie and Whittle, for instance, refrained from printing them.[17] But for many the lure of political subjects was irresistible: they offered instant novelty, which some makers, sellers, and consumers sought, and moreover the form, with its capacity for speed, abetted it, which meant that printmakers could beat artisans working in other media to the punch.

However, publishers still had to decide *which* topics to represent and how. Many British political prints described the nitty-gritty workings of Parliament, with references to men little recognized outside of inner circles, while in France they focused on Paris and the intrigues of the court. In this way, a considerable number of political prints spoke to interests that were national, not Atlantic.[18]

But as revolutions and their wars affected so many countries and colonies in the final decades of the eighteenth century, foreign political squabbles caught the attention of outsiders—and not just those in elite circles. International affairs became local news and vice versa. In fact, British satirical prints reached their zenith in the early 1790s *because of* the French Revolution.[19] Printmakers in Britain and elsewhere commented on political developments overseas, often to consider what they meant for life at home. These prints were outward facing, too, as makers looked to sell their renditions of international events abroad.

The exact contours of this Atlantic circulation of political prints are difficult to determine, however. Reliable numbers are lacking, but anecdotal evidence suggests that political prints coursed through the Atlantic marketplace for works on paper. Prior to the revolutionary period, print sellers looked for opportunities to vend wares overseas— usually landscapes, reproductions of well-known paintings, fashion plates, and so on. Take the case of British dealers. Despite healthy domestic and colonial outlets, ambitious London-based print publishers courted Continental buyers, particularly retailers and merchants who might buy prints wholesale. With the French market in mind, Robert Sayer compiled a lavish edition of William Hogarth's engravings under the title *Les satyres de Guillaume Hogarth,* and in 1768 Sayer and his new partner, Thomas Jefferys, traveled to Paris with a selection of their stock of prints, maps, and the Hogarth volume in the hopes of establishing business connections with French retailers. After six weeks, officials chased the two men out of town for selling "indecent" prints. The raid was less about pornography (by French standards, their images were hardly lewd) and more about politics, as Sayer and Jefferys's maps touted the imperial glories of Britain—an impolitic move in light of the recently concluded Seven Years' War. Despite their ignominious departure, the professional contacts Sayer and Jefferys cultivated in Paris proved profitable in the coming decades.[20]

Sayer and Jefferys's stint on the Continent was brief, but other British printers stayed longer. John Haines set up shop in Paris in the

1770s, importing from London at least ninety-five packages of prints between 1776 and 1790, with a hiatus between 1780 and 1783 when the war between France and Britain and high import duties hampered trade. Notwithstanding logistical and political hindrances, ex-pat English as well as French sellers offered British prints during the American Revolution, as seen in advertisements in the French publications *Catalogue Hebdomadaire* and *Mercure*. Notices gesture to a large assortment of subjects among these imported prints but name only a few specific titles—and sentimental ones at that. A couple political scenes are mentioned, such as engravings of Benjamin West's *The Death of General Wolfe*.[21] Like the original painting, the print illustrated a romanticized Wolfe expiring on the battlefield during his victory at the battle of Quebec. Although West completed the work in 1770, it was in the early 1780s that affordable print versions landed in Parisian shops. Whereas Sayer and Jefferys's pro-British, post–Seven Years' War maps ran afoul of authorities, the tables were turned a decade or so later. The French crowed about their triumph over their archenemy in the American Revolution, and Wolfe's death was no longer the end of the story in the contest between France and Britain for European dominance.

Finally, print publishers cracked the Continental market from a distance. William Holland and S. W. Fores produced several prints of French revolutionary events with an eye to London and Parisian outlets; in Holland's case, his creations occasionally had titles in both English and French, a sign of his international aspirations.[22] John Boydell promoted high-end engravings of Old Master paintings through catalogues, issuing French-language versions in 1779 and 1783. In 1787 Valentine Green did the same, and another print publisher named Torre (of Italian origin but located in London) kept a Paris branch in the 1780s.[23] Meanwhile, the London-based firm of Colnaghi distributed a French catalogue in 1793 that listed, among other prints, scenes from Louis XVI's last days and noted that "they took responsibility for mailing [their prints] to the provinces and abroad."[24] In the throes of war, the messieurs Colnaghi were confident their wares would arrive to the Continent and beyond.

Even without foreign branches and catalogues in other languages, publishers made headway abroad. In the 1780s one observer remarked on the "great quantities" of British caricatures that arrived "to Germany, and from thence to the adjacent countries." He found this "singular and ridiculous, as very few of those who pay dearly for them, know any thing of the characters and transactions which occasioned such caricatures. They laugh at them, and become merry, though they are entirely unacquainted with the persons, the manners, and the customs which are ridiculed."[25] In an effort to elucidate what was lost in translation, the Weimar-based magazine *London und Paris* had regular features on "Englishe Carricaturen" and "Pariser Carricaturen" that highlighted the latest political prints in both places, complete with narrative explanations and small reproductions.[26] Through these means, British and French prints circulated far and wide.

Political prints alighted in the colonies, too, but pinpointing exactly which ones, how many, and when is hard. Newspapers reveal glimpses into the compositions that reached North America. The British print *The State of the Nation An: Dom: 1765 &c,* which underscored North American hostility to the Stamp Act, was for sale in Boston and Philadelphia in 1765.[27] In the summer of 1783, John Swanwick advertised a shipment of goods from England, France, Holland, and Germany, among which were "a few Coloured and Mezotinto Engravings, Emblematical of the return to peace to America," as well as some mezzotints of Thomas Paine.[28] North American engravers copied British prints, mainly those critical of imperial policies. Paul Revere pirated *The Able Doctor, or America Swallowing the Bitter Draught* from the April 1774 issue of *London Magazine* and produced one thousand copies of it for the Boston periodical *Royal American Magazine* in June that same year (figure 6.1). In August a Philadelphia engraver published a version of the same scene under the title *The Persevering Americans, or the Bitter Draught Return'd.*[29]

When it came to pirating, American engravers were in step with their European peers. Copying the works of others was a crucial component of any printer's business, one about which they had few qualms and at times celebrated as a service. In the 1760s an English firm specializing in low-end prints announced that it was "copying new sorts from the various inventions of the best French, Dutch, and Italian prints."[30] Artists realized there was little they could do. Benjamin Wilson, who had etched *The Repeal (of the Stamp Act)* in 1766, observed that within five days of publication, plagiarized editions surfaced on the London market, and soon they appeared in Philadelphia as well.[31] British printmaker John Dixon's *The Oracle* became the basis for a well-known German print titled *The Tea-Tax-Tempest or the Anglo-American*

Figure 6.1. Paul Revere, *The Able Doctor, or America Swallowing the Bitter Draught*, engraving from the June 1774 issue of *Royal American Magazine*. (Courtesy, American Antiquarian Society.)

Revolution, which was subsequently copied by a French publisher and then another British one. There are numerous other examples, but the point here is that such copying would have been impossible if original and knock-off versions were not moving through the Atlantic world.[32]

Direct evidence of political prints in the Caribbean is sparser. Newspaper advertisements reference images in general terms: "Prints with or without frames," "Prints in gilt frames," and "Prints, framed and glazed."[33] A few notices draw attention to general topics. At the Montego Bay printing office, one could find "some capital naval prints, neatly framed and glazed," while a dry goods importer in Kingston described "an elegant few beautiful proof impression prints, among which are four views of the East India Company's shipping in gold burnished frames."[34] In the face of this paucity of detail, our understanding of the circulation of political prints in the Caribbean comes from negative evidence, of authorities looking to prevent the distribution of prints that might encourage instability, especially slave rebellion. In 1796 Bryan Edwards complained about the dissemination in Jamaica of prints depicting the oppression and resistance of enslaved people, and in Cuba and Caracas in the 1790s, officials tried to thwart the entry of all printed materials, textual and visual, that referenced French politics. When the Spanish took over Fort-Dauphin, Saint-Domingue, briefly in 1794, authorities confiscated any French printed work.[35]

Although the Caribbean ruling elite were concerned about the circulation of political prints, their movement was tough to police. Most were small and portable, about the size of a single sheet of paper, and thanks to these traits, they traveled through personal, not just mercantile, channels. Consider documented North American examples. From London, Benjamin Franklin mailed cards with his print *Magna Britannia Her Colonies Reduc'd,* to his wife Deborah, his sister Jane, his partner David Hall, and Joseph Galloway.[36] Franklin sent other political prints, too, including *The Repeal.*[37] While encamped in Cambridge, Massachusetts, in early 1776, George Washington received from a friend a British-made mezzotint of himself.[38] Given the ways through which items of all sorts flowed in the Caribbean, and the diverse people—from the enslaved to the elite—who facilitated the traffic in goods, political prints had plenty of opportunities to spread in the islands.

Anecdotal sources testify to the Atlantic dispersal of political prints, but the scale is elusive. Shipping records and inventories are frustratingly silent on the question. At best, they note general quantities of prints, with no information about their subjects. The technique of fabrication, however, gives a sense of the printing capacity of a single plate and therefore a single image. An engraving could sustain 4,000 copies, with some degradation to the image after the first 1,500 to 2,000 prints, while the typical run for an etching was about 1,000. Aquatint plates yielded anywhere from 500 to 750 decent prints. Mezzotints lasted for about 100 to 150 good impressions, and stipple around 1,000. With all methods, retouching lengthened the life of a plate but compromised the quality of the printed image. Tenacious publishers could squeeze 10,000 to 20,000 impressions out of a repeatedly reworked plate.[39] In sum, one image could have as few as 100 copies or as many as several thousand in circulation. Add pirated versions to these figures and the possible volume at any one time increases significantly.

Similar to other types of visual and textual media, prints had a public side. In urban areas, they were posted in shop windows to catch the attention of passersby. London publishers immortalized scenes of residents of different backgrounds transfixed by and reacting to the prints on view.[40] At times displays were unabashedly political. For the opening day of his store in Philadelphia in 1790s, William Cobbett staged a spectacle:

> As my shop was to open on Monday morning, I employed myself all day on Sunday in preparing an exhibition that I thought would put the courage and power of my enemies to the test. I put up in my windows, which were very large, all the portraits that I had in my possession of *kings, queens, princes* and *nobles.* I had all the English ministry, several of the bishops and judges, the most famous admirals, and, in short, every picture that I thought likely to excite rage in the enemies of Great Britain. Early on the Monday morning I took down my shutters. Such a sight had not been seen in Philadelphia for twenty years. Never since the beginning of the rebellion had anyone dared to hoist at his window the portrait of George the Third.[41]

Cobbett enjoyed political controversy and saw the eye-catching exhibition of prints as a provocative means to incite it.

Other public venues displayed prints. In his scrapbook of revolutionary prints and newspaper clippings, Pierre Eugène du Simitière recorded that *The Repeal* "came from London to Philadelphia, and was put up at the coffee house there the day the news arrived of the Stamp-act being repealed."[42] Prints decorated taverns, barbers' shops, and offices. In 1802 a traveling engraver observed, with dismay, that in the waiting room of the Calais passport office hung "the masterly caricatures of [James] Gillray, ridiculing the chief personages of the English administration."[43] Some print sellers rented out collections to clients. S. W. Fores in Piccadilly advertised that "Folios of Caracatures" could be "lent out for the Evening," so that hosts could entertain families and guests.[44] Prints were shown in museum exhibitions, on their own or with other types of objects. For only a shilling, one could visit "Hollands Exhibition Rooms [in London, where] may be seen the largest Collection in Europe of Humourous Prints."[45] In the early 1790s, Holland and his competitor Fores touted that their rival exhibition rooms featured the latest French prints.[46]

While prints were not a mass medium in the modern sense, more people in the Atlantic world had the chance to see political images—both domestic and foreign—than the print-run numbers suggest.[47] European publishers sought out international markets for their products despite the political, economic, and logistical disruptions of war, and through copying and presentation in public and domestic settings, images had the ability to reach diverse audiences. Within this vast field, though, print makers and sellers had to choose what to depict about their tumultuous political times and how. Their decisions on this score reveal not only the views of artists but also what sellers thought consumers wanted.

PORTRAYING NEW MEN

Portraits were a major sector of the print market before the revolutionary period, with publishers offering expensive and reasonable renditions of a host of notables: kings, queens, aristocrats, politicians, judges, preachers, military officers, actors, writers, famous beauties. The range appealed to assorted tastes, and print sellers balanced the demand for the standard roll of prominent figures (monarchs and the like) with people who had lately garnered the public's interest.[48] In the latter category, individuals from the age of revolutions soon turned up in print sellers' stock.

In the crux of political upheaval, portraits of individuals took on new importance within revolutionary regimes and beyond. Artists sought to depict the audacious actors who claimed the reins of government—men (always men) who in the past were not associated with the halls of power and so had not been the subjects of openly distributed printed portraits. Atlantic consumers assessed a sitter's character through his physical features, pose, clothing, and other accessories, and in the process, observers appraised the political movement with which that person was associated. Revolutionaries were conscious of the stakes of their appearance in the world of print, and whenever possible they crafted their portraits to convince the public of their fitness to rule.[49] But the process of portrayal was often out of their hands, especially when artists decided from a distance whom to represent and how. As print portraits from all three revolutions demonstrate, makers wrestled with personifying ideological radicalism, concerned with the ways that prints legitimatized individuals and their arguments.

When it came to renditions of revolutionaries, there was a heavy emphasis on generals and politicians.[50] During the late 1770s and early 1780s, print sellers in France and Britain advertised prints of leading North American patriots. In 1780 Blaizot in Versailles and Chéreau in Paris opened a subscription for a series of twelve portraits of the American "Generals, ministers and members of Congress best known in Europe."[51] While not all of the portraits were ready for sale, the seven available included military leaders General Charles Reed and Baron von Steuben; Silas Deane (diplomat to France); John Dickinson (author of *Letters from a Farmer in Pennsylvania* and member of the Continental Congress from Pennsylvania); W. H. Drayton (representative to the Congress from South Carolina); Charles Thomson (secretary of the Congress), and "Le Gouverneur Morris" (then member of the Congress from New York, but notice the "Le"). Blaizot and Chéreau also tendered a portrait of Benedict Arnold, sold separately from the series but for the same price.[52] Some of these men are instantly recognizable even today; others, like Drayton and Thomson, less so. European printmakers found it difficult to determine prominence from afar, particularly in the early days of the revolution. Washington, Franklin, and John Paul Jones were obvious candidates for portraits, but the importance of other actors was less evident from across the Atlantic.[53]

Then there was the practical problem of acquiring reliable likenesses. Between 1775 and 1777, Sayer and Bennett issued ten mezzotint portraits of Americans: the generals Benedict Arnold, Horatio Gates, Charles Lee, Israel Putnam, John Sullivan, George Washington, and David Wooster; commodore of the Continental Navy, Esek Hopkins; the president of the Continental Congress, John Hancock; and Robert Rogers, who commanded a ranger unit that volunteered to fight for Washington and, when spurned, sided with the British (figure 6.2). But no one in Britain (or the rest of Europe, for that matter) had seen these men in person, with the possible exception of Rogers, who visited England in 1775. Nor were their images in international circulation. As early as 1775, some American printers offered mezzotints of their rising leaders, and during the war du Simitière sent to Paris for engraving his collection of drawings of American statesmen and military officers, some of which were taken from life. In 1783 the British firm of Wilkinson and Debrett published du Simitière's works in a volume titled *Portraits of Generals, Ministers, Magistrates, Members of Congress, and Others, Who Have Rendered Themselves Illustrious in the Revolution of the United States of North America.*[54] While American-made and more accurate renditions eventually arrived abroad, there was a lag time, and the result in the case of Sayer and Bennett was a series of wildly inaccurate likenesses.

Figure 6.2. *George Washington, Esqr.* (London: C. Shepherd, after Wilkinson, September 9, 1775). Mezzotint. (© The Trustees of the British Museum.)

Although print portraits were sometimes speculative, they were not necessarily derogatory—even when the subject was a purported enemy. Sayer and Bennett, for example, depicted American leaders with the honorific trappings and noble postures of generals. When Washington saw the print of himself from this series, he was pleased that he "made a very formidable figure," although the resemblance was off.[55] French makers also produced images of their allies, some taken from British prints, that emphasized their respectability.[56] Perhaps more surprisingly, printers in Britain avoided visual send-ups of Washington, Franklin, and other notable Americans. Reservations about the war, in some quarters, help to explain why printers shied away from mocking portrayals. Washington, for instance, enjoyed a fairly good reputation in the British press for the duration of the war.[57]

British printmakers preferred to satirize their own military and political leaders during the American Revolution, blaming their missteps for the war's unsuccessful trajectory.[58] (Of course, British printers offered plenty of laudatory portraits of victorious generals and admirals.) When identifiable Americans had cameos in British satires of the colonial crisis or the revolution, they were not the men under scrutiny. Two prints from 1783, *The Blessings of Peace* and *A Political Concert*, feature Benjamin Franklin, but he serves as a foil to criticize British ministers and military men. To be sure, plenty of people in Britain condemned what they saw as the treasonous actions of the colonists, and portraits of American revolutionaries sometimes became flashpoints for venting that frustration. In August 1776, while the Sixty-Ninth Regiment of Foot was in Lincolnshire awaiting deployment, groups of officers on two separate occasions visited two different print shops and destroyed portraits of Israel Putnam and Charles Lee posted in the windows.[59] In the heat of the moment, "they all declared, with horrid imprecations and threats, that if any more [of the portraits] should appear in that place, they would send the common soldiers to break the windows, nay even to pull down the whole house."[60] But the account in the *London Evening Post* condemned the lawlessness of the perpetrators. The author mocked their bravery when faced with paper renditions of the enemy and doubted their abilities should they meet Lee and Putnam in the flesh.

Portraits of American revolutionaries in Britain, then, put faces (if sometimes dubious ones) on their foes, and yet that process was less about demonizing Americans and more about accounting for how the British had mishandled the colonies before, during, and after the war. The focus on the ministry, on the one hand, was a means to disparage the British government, but on the other hand, it evaded visualizing the intellectual implications of the patriots' war, which critiqued not just individuals in power but the very form of British government itself. Few of the ideological contributors to the U.S. revolution received the attention of a portrait in Britain or France. Franklin's image was, it seems, everywhere, but he was a known entity before the revolution and was celebrated at the time more for his scientific and diplomatic accomplishments than for his intellectual influences on independence.[61] By contrast, engraved portraits of Thomas Jefferson and John Adams did not surface until after the revolution, despite their crucial roles in shaping its ideological underpinnings. Their absence may signal problems with supply or perceived lack of prominence. But it also indicates a sidestepping of discussions of republicanism—a tendency visible in British press coverage of the war, and one that many French officials embraced as well.[62] Print portraits emphasized the military, diplomatic, and administrative actors in the revolution, those who were less intellectually threatening to European standing orders.

Portraits and caricatures by Anglophone printers during the French Revolution demonstrate a few similarities to the U.S. case and some marked differences. If British printers were hesitant to ridicule specific Americans, they were willing to do so with several high-profile figures of the French Revolution. Some prints were sympathetic to select French leaders, but the satires stand out for the way they show the uncertainty of political reactions to events in France. In the early years of the revolution, British printmakers lampooned the French king for his ineffectiveness. He became ever fatter, bumbling, and slovenly as printers derided his economic mishaps, his botched flight from Paris to Varennes, and his cowardice and overall ineptitude. During the war between Britain and France, French generals received similar treatment, with their traits exaggerated to comic and political effect. Napoléon Bonaparte and Louis Lazare Hoche, among a few others, garnered the lion's share of disdain: Bonaparte is squat, while Hoche is spectrally skinny.[63]

On one level, these satires delegitimized the French project and looked to promote anti-French sentiment at home. As propaganda for the war effort, these prints indict the French regime from the bungled attempt to establish a constitutional monarchy through Bonaparte, and every iteration of government in between. Yet the prints are more ambiguous than one might expect. Louis XVI's outsized physical features, for example, are reminiscent of contemporary caricatures of George III, creating a parity between the two monarchs and their incompetence as rulers. Prints also mocked British generals and leaders alongside French ones, which intimated that the conflict was as troubling for

British actors as for French ones. And historian John Richard Moores has contended that the fixation with condemning French generals was sympathetic to the French population. By showing them under the sway of wanton figureheads, the British proposed that the French, as a people, were redeemable.[64]

Although British printmakers had a heyday with several French notables, the absences are as important. Despite the open hostility toward Jacobins in textual appraisals, printers created very few portraits or caricatures of them. London publishers issued medallion portraits of Maximilien Robespierre in stipple shortly after his execution in the summer of 1794, and a broadside with a teary-eyed portrait of the deceased Camille Desmoulins circulated in 1795.[65] Jean-Paul Marat appeared after his murder, but usually in conjunction with his assassin, Charlotte Corday.[66] Conspicuously, these images were disseminated after the men's deaths, not while they exerted power in France.

In Britain there was a reticence to portray these men when they dominated the government, and the reasons behind this reluctance stem from some characteristics of the medium. If portraits and caricatures were a means by which individuals looked to establish their legitimacy and standing, then British publishers repudiated Jacobins' claims to govern by refusing to depict them. While individual Jacobins were discussed and derided in the press, they were not immortalized in print when they were active in the state. That said, allusions to, if not exact likenesses of, famous Jacobins turned up in prints. In the 1793 etching *Citizen Coupe Tête in His Misery,* a sans culottes family feeds on bones in their home, and on the wall above the fireplace hangs a trio of indistinct sketches of "Marat Pain[e] Robertspi[erre]" (figure 6.3). Some Jacobins' infamy persisted in images throughout the decade. Gillray's *The Shrine at St. Ann's* (1798) incorporates a bust of a demonic Robespierre, and in his *The Arms of France* (1803), specific Jacobins are listed, sarcastically, among other "French worthies."[67]

When printmakers looked to put recognizable faces on Jacobins, they turned to well-known figures of the British political opposition. In May 1794 the publisher Hannah Humphrey released an unusual suite of etchings by James Sayers under the title *Illustrious Heads Designed for a New History of Republicanism in French and English Dedicated to the Opposition.* The collection purported to portray foremost French radicals, but the actual renditions are of British opposition

Figure 6.3. Thomas Ovenden, *Citizen Coupe Tête in His Misery* (London[?]: J. Downs, 1793). Hand-colored etching. (© The Trustees of the British Museum.)

politicians given French names. The portrait labeled "Robespierre" is Charles James Fox, that of Bertrand Barère (an outspoken supporter of the Terror) is Richard Sheridan, that of Jacques-Pierre Brissot is James Maitland, the Eighth Earl of Lauderdale, and so on. The series lacks finesse in its political attributions. Brissot, although described on the print as a "citoyen actif & Sans culotte," was affiliated with the Girondins, opposed Robespierre's regime, and was guillotined because of it. Clearly, the goal was to discredit the British political opposition by branding them all "Jacobins." As the banner held by the devil on the frontispiece proclaims in Latin, "With the name changed, the story applies to you."[68]

One person who drew outsized ire in Britain was Thomas Paine. In the 1780s and early 1790s, British publishers had sold printed portraits of Paine, and some reached the U.S. market. As the French Revolution radicalized, however, visual satirists gleefully seized on Paine (rather than specific French Jacobins) as the incarnation of Jacobin radicalism. Paine, to a certain extent, attracted this fury because of his outspoken critiques of the British government. The publication of the first part of *The Rights of Man* (1791) repudiated Edmund Burke's tract *Reflections on the Revolution in France,* while the second part of Paine's work (released in February 1792), caused an uproar in Britain because of its call for the end of monarchy and of the House of Lords. In December 1792, a British court tried Paine in absentia and convicted him of libel. Having fled England for France, Paine was elected to the National Convention. He served there until December 1793, when the Jacobins imprisoned him because he had argued against the execution of Louis XVI.

Given his political profile, it is no wonder British satirists latched onto Paine, but what's important is how they did so. While several artists caricatured Paine throughout the 1790s, consider a trio of prints by James Gillray. The first, *The Rights of Man* (1791), shows "Tommy Paine, the little American Taylor," measuring the Crown (a literal crown) for "a new pair of Revolution-Breeches." With tape in hand and an enormous pair of scissors at his hip, a raggedly dressed Paine (so how good of a tailor can he be, anyway?) mutters to himself about the difficulties of clothing such a large "Bauble." In the 1792 etching and aquatint *Tom Paine's Nightly Pest,* Paine sleeps on a bed of straw, with his coat for a blanket and his bare feet peeking out (figure 6.4). He

Figure 6.4. James Gillray, *Tom Paine's Nightly Pest* (London: H. Humphrey, December 10, 1792). Hand-colored etching. (Courtesy of The Lewis Walpole Library, Yale University.)

dreams of the "charges," "pleas," and "punishments" leveled against him, as a frightened devil flies out the window, dropping the bow that it had used to play "Ça Ira" on a violin. In 1793 Gillray made *Fashion Before Ease,* in which Paine (who was formerly a stay-maker) attempts to lace Britannia into an ill-fitting corset.[69]

In all three images, Paine sports a tricolor cockade on his hat, and other symbols of the French Revolution abound. *The Rights of Man* is "Humbly dedicated to the Jacobine Clubs of France and England," and in *Tom Paine's Nightly Pest,* his head rests on a tricolored pillow. Artists like Gillray used Paine to point to the danger of Britons embracing "French" principles. By bringing the ideals of the French Revolution to British shores, Paine threatened the political system from within.[70] However, the extreme hyperbole in Gillray's prints and those of some of his contemporaries signals that he was criticizing the intensity of British reactions to Paine as much as he was Paine himself. *Tom Paine's Nightly Pest,* which was issued around the time of Paine's libel trial, is histrionic in its references to his purported misdeeds. In front of the three faceless judges unfurl long scrolls that enumerate Paine's crimes and penalties. Among the charges are "Libels, Scurrilities, Lies, Perjuries, Rebellions, and Treasons," with the corresponding punishments being "Corporal Pain, Contempt, and Detestation." Isaac Cruikshank's *Wha Wants Me,* also from December 1792, takes a similar tack. It features Paine with dagger in hand and a starburst of crimes radiating from his body, including "Cruelty, Equality, Madness, Anarchy, Murder, Treason, Rebellion, Perjury, Atheism, Misery, Famine, National & Private Ruin, Ingratitude, Idleness, Treachery, Injustice."[71] The charges seem exaggerated for the author of, according to Gillray's print, "The Rights of Farthing Candles proving their Equality with the Sun & Moon And the Necessity of a Reformation in the Planetary System." Both prints (as well as others) lampoon Paine as ridiculous. In so doing, they ask why the judges—and the government they represent—are taking Paine so seriously, hinting that his critics were as susceptible to irrational political frenzy as the target of their attacks.

The obsession with Paine as the incarnation of French radicalism resonated in the British Caribbean as well. Throughout 1793 white colonists in Barbados, Grenada, and Jamaica staged public spectacles that denounced the French Revolution by burning effigies of Thomas Paine. One event in Savanna-del-Mar, Jamaica, made clear the ways that Paine, in some Anglophone minds, represented all French radicals. According to a newspaper report, the Paine effigy wore a "red bonnet (the distinguishing cap of the Jacobins), on the front of which was written, in black characters, 'Brissot—Marat—Robespierre—Egalite [duc d'Orléans].'" As a band played "God Save the King," the organizers set the effigy alight and, filled with gunpowder, it exploded, "to the great entertainment of a vast number of spectators."[72] In this instance, the effigy embodied Paine as well as notorious (from the British view) French revolutionaries, and the crowd had the pleasure of blowing up all five at once.[73]

U.S. printmakers also avoided portrayals of French Jacobins. In part the oversight was structural: in the 1790s, the output of political prints in the United States paled in comparison to those in Britain since the industry was less developed. Nevertheless, Paine proved useful in

American political prints, where he was linked to Democratic Republicans, particularly Thomas Jefferson. Most often Paine is portrayed as abetting designs for Jacobinesque anarchy. The earliest, *A Peep into the Antifederal Club* (1793), places Paine at a meeting of Democratic Republicans, whose members listen as Jefferson exhorts them to follow him in "knocking down" the government. Paine, scissors in hand, points out that the Black man next to him, "Citizen Mungo," will surely join Jefferson, since "he has nothing to lose." In *The Providential Detection* (ca. 1797–1800) Jefferson kneels before an "altar to Gallic despots" on which burn copies of various texts, including Paine's *The Age of Reason*. Finally, in *Mad Tom in a Rage* (ca. 1801), Jefferson, disguised as a devil, helps Paine as he topples a column inscribed "Fed[era]l Gov[e]rn[men]t G[eorge]. Was[hington] J[ohn]. Ada[ms]." The pair struggle with the task, but Paine avers, "With the assistance of my Old Friend & a little more Brandy I will pull it down."[74] Similar to their British peers, American printmakers sidestepped depicting Jacobins outright, preferring to invoke their power by domestic association.

Printmakers throughout the Atlantic world were discerning in representing individuals from the American and French revolutions. As the case of the American Revolution illustrates, the problem of distance influenced some choices as publishers were unable to distinguish, from across the ocean, which men were eminent and what they looked like. Politics, too, affected the decisions of publishers who, in both the United States and Britain, shunned depictions of Jacobins. These practical and ideological factors put their approach to portrayals of Haitian revolutionaries in a new light. In the 1790s British and U.S. printmakers did not publish images of men tied to the Haitian Revolution. No matter their racial identification or their political leanings, none of the prominent players—from Ogé to Louverture to Dessalines, or from Sonthonax to Laveaux to Leclerc—turned up in Anglophone prints. French printmakers also slighted some important individuals from the colonies, while others, like Ogé when he was in Paris, paid for the making of their own portraits. Printed portraits of Louverture and of Étienne Victor Mentor (a Black deputy from Saint-Domingue to the Council of Five Hundred), however, were produced in France, and a print of Louverture was made in Germany as well.[75] The French and German renditions of Louverture from the 1790s were not drawn from life, although Mentor was in Paris for several years.[76]

While racism helps to explain the evasion of major African-descended actors in the 1790s, a few prints surfaced at the tail end of the Haitian revolutionary war. Atlantic politics shaped the timing and content of these depictions. Consider the sudden spate of printed portraits of Toussaint Louverture that began around 1802. Several appeared as plates in biographies that were interested more in tracking the military and political battles on the island than in narrating his life with any degree of veracity.[77] In 1802 two British printmakers issued single-sheet portraits of Toussaint Louverture, and in both images he is presented with the honors afforded to respected military men. One etching, by John Kay in Edinburgh, shows Louverture full-length, in uniform, with his sword raised to direct well-dressed troops in the background. Another etching, printed by the London duo of Williamson and Parsons, renders Louverture in half-length (again in military regalia), identifies him by his official title of "Governor of St. Domingo," and purports to derive from an original drawing. The print was reasonably priced—1 shilling uncolored, or 1 shilling 6 pence colored—a sign of the makers' desire to reach consumers.[78]

Why the sudden urge to visualize Louverture in 1802? After all, he had been well known in Britain in the 1790s thanks to extensive press coverage of affairs in Saint-Domingue. But with the Leclerc expedition the British public understood Louverture in new terms, namely, as an adversary of Napoléon Bonaparte. This connection is evident in several prints that paired Louverture with Bonaparte after the Treaty of Amiens expired in the spring of 1803, which was also when Louverture died. They use Louverture's arrest and incarceration as yet another example of Bonaparte's crimes. In several images, Louverture is referenced only by name. On the left side of the 1803 print *The Arms of France*, a monkey (a common trope for France in British prints) sits atop a pile of books (by Rousseau, Voltaire, and, of course, Paine), and below that is a prison window, with chains hanging along the sides and the name "TOUSSAINT" above it.[79] Meanwhile in the 1808 etching, *The Progress of the Emperor Napoleon*, "Toussaint" is on the list of "Murders" that decorate the back of the emperor's new throne.[80] In these instances, Louverture's name is enough to condemn the French leader.

In two prints from the early 1810s, Louverture takes the form of a specter haunting Bonaparte. While the print is not a portrait, Louverture's head is visible alongside those of other ghosts, and it is distorted.

In *Bony's Visions or a Great Little Man's Night Comforts*, his face, exaggerated and in profile, is attached to a bird's body, while in *Buonaparte! Ambition and Death!*, his mouth gapes in a horrifying scream. In both prints, Louverture's face is darker than those of his counterparts, but his race, and racism, are not necessarily the basis for further facial distortion. The other ghosts—all white men—are portrayed with dreadful features: some are missing eyes, one has a metal-like grill for a mouth, still another's hair sticks up from his skull at odd angles. Louverture's grotesque appearance, like that of the other victims, is in service to a gothic vision of Bonaparte's mental torment.[81]

The most portrait-like rendition of Louverture in these scenarios comes from an etching from 1804, *The Corsican Usurpers New Imperial French Arms*, where a full-length depiction is part of a fake coat of arms for Bonaparte (figure 6.5). Nero and Caligula stand at either side of the shield, which pins the pope facedown on the ground. A Janus-faced bust of Bonaparte and a crowned devil top the escutcheon. The shield is divided into eight scenes: two are filled with skulls and crossbones, but the others contain scandalous episodes of Bonaparte's rule. In one, labeled "Jaffa," French soldiers shoot at bound Turkish prisoners, and in another, titled "The Plank," men walk the plank of a vessel flying the French tricolor. But Louverture is the only individual in any of the sections who speaks. Dressed in an officer's uniform and standing in his prison cell, he asks, his chained arms and legs outstretched, "Is this French faith?" He is turned to his right, as if he is addressing the people in the neighboring frame, in which the pope kisses Bonaparte's feet.

These portrayals of Louverture present him with other wronged individuals of heinous episodes—all victims of Bonaparte's tyranny. Louverture is among a cohort of white men: duc d'Enghien (who was court-martialed and executed for designing against France), Jean-Charles Pichegru (who was accused of plotting against Bonaparte and died in prison), Captain Wright (a purported royalist agent), and Johann Philipp Palm (a Nuremberg bookseller who published a tract critical of Bonaparte and was shot for it). These men resisted Bonaparte's rule, and commentators found it important to include Louverture among them. As one London newspaper put it, Louverture's arrest and death fix "as deep a stain upon the character of Bonaparte as any of all the atrocities which have marked his reign."[82] Some accounts in the British press worked to dismiss negative and racist reports about Louverture

Figure 6.5. Charles Williams, *The Corsican Usurpers New Imperial French Arms* (London: S. Fores, 1804). Hand-colored etching. (© The Trustees of the British Museum.)

that Bonaparte's government had perpetuated—ones that accentuated Louverture's alleged treachery, ignorance, and crudeness.[83] One article boasted, "We feel a pleasure in being able to vindicate the conduct of this great and good man, and to repel the calumnies that are so widely spread respecting it."[84]

In these visual representations Louverture gains a kind of equality—that of an equal victim. But they stop short of the bolder rhetorical moves in the British press. Some texts cast Louverture not only as a target of Bonaparte's fury but also as a leader on par with other worthies. A few months after his death, the *Morning Chronicle* printed an ode to "General Toussaint" written by William Joseph Denison, Esq., a banker, politician, and sometime poet. Condemning the Leclerc mission, Denison highlights Louverture's exalted station: "You've gain'd the statesman's fair and just renown, / The warrior's laurel and the martyr's crown. / You'll share the palm with KOSCIUSKO's name, / With TELL and WASHINGTON's immortal fame; / The paths of glory equally you trod, / Like them you spurn'd Oppression's iron rod."[85] In Denison's estimation, Louverture is a martyr for freedom like other, white but noticeably not French, men.

Harnessing the ghost of Louverture to Bonaparte checked Louverture's more radical potential. It was also in keeping with the visual culture of the abolitionist movement, which emphasized the victimization and passivity of the enslaved.[86] (Remember Wedgwood's anti–slave trade medallion.) Moreover, these images underscore the uniqueness of Toussaint Louverture—as a man and as a leader of a revolutionary antislavery movement. One print from 1808 (the same year as the British and U.S. abolition of the African slave trade) alludes to Louverture's continued influence (figure 6.6). Titled *Johnny Newcome in Love in the West Indies*, it is one in a series in which Johnny Newcome, a white Englishman, arrives to the Caribbean and indulges in sex, gluttony, and general debauchery. This example, organized in six frames in cartoon-like format, follows Newcome falling in love with an African woman and hiring an obeah practitioner to help him to seduce her. He succeeds, and they have numerous children whom, at the end, Newcome abandons to return to his "Native land." The last frame of the print features headshots of his nine mixed-race offspring, one of whom, Hector Sammy Newcome, is described as "a child of great spirit, can already Damnme Liberty and Equality and promises fair to be the Toussaint of his country." This print, as with others in the collection, peddles racist stereotypes, so much so that the equation of Hector Sammy Newcome with Louverture is understood as ludicrous. In this telling, Louverture is one of a kind, minimizing the threat of other people of African descent rising.

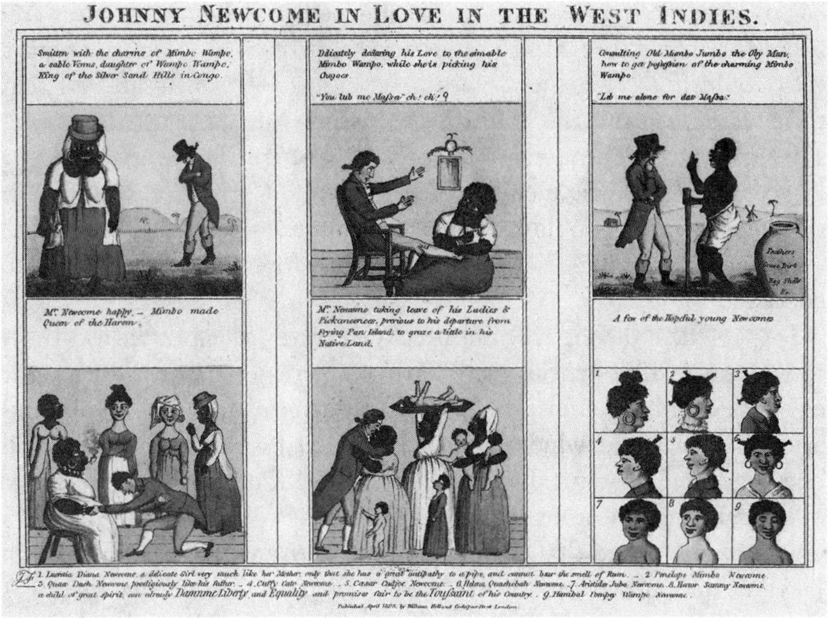

Figure 6.6. *Johnny Newcome in Love in the West Indies* (London: William Holland, April 1808). Aquatint with etching, hand-colored. (Courtesy of The Lewis Walpole Library, Yale University.)

The decision to represent Louverture on these terms attempted to curb the radicalism of the Haitian Revolution in another important way. While Louverture ruled when Leclerc's army invaded, Jean-Jacques Dessalines and Henry Christophe, among others, led the charge that defeated the French army and declared independence in 1804. The Anglophone press chronicled their achievements, but these men did not appear in print portraits made abroad until several years after the founding of Haiti. Jean-Louis Dubroca's 1805 racist "biography" of Dessalines included plates of its subject, but they are the exceptions that prove the rule.[87] The account has one image of him on a throne, and in another, he is decapitating a white woman. These depictions were meant to denigrate Dessalines and the new nation. Yet this was a hazardous gamble because in the hands of people of African descent, such images could inspire radical action. José Antonio Aponte's book of drawings, for instance, had portraits of Louverture, Dessalines, Christophe, and Jean-François, some copied, as Aponte testified, from engravings.[88] Perhaps well aware of this political volatility, white publishers preferred to picture Louverture most often as a victim because they could not bring themselves to visualize the victors and all that their victory meant: the end of slavery, rights for men of African descent, and an independent state comprised of free Black people in the Caribbean. Portraying men like Dessalines and Christophe would have acknowledged their political movement, an admission that few white observers, in the immediate wake of Haiti's founding, were willing to concede.[89]

For all their distinctive interpretive features, the printed portraits of Haitian revolutionaries were part of a broader concern during the age of revolutions as printers worked to determine which revolutionaries to depict and which to avoid. Printed portraits—even satirical ones—granted a political and ideological legitimacy to their subjects, a legitimacy that Britons were reluctant to bestow on some American revolutionaries, and that Britons and North Americans denied French Jacobins and most Haitian revolutionaries. Seeing these new men was a dangerous business, more so than writing or reading about them. The dynamics of recognition were more troubled with visualizations of revolutionary collectives.

THE PEOPLE IN ACTION

If portrayals of revolutionary individuals were a fascination and a quandary in the visual culture of this period, so, too, was the other end of the spectrum—the crowd or, less flatteringly, the mob. The crowd had been a fixture of early modern society and its visual culture, but it became a formidable political force in the eighteenth century. Its power crested in the U.S., French, and Haitian revolutions in that the actions of people out of doors were instrumental in all three. In the historiographies of the U.S. and French revolutions, "the people" have long been central to discussions of popular sovereignty. While less explicit in the literature and not considered in the same terms, the political power of the collective shapes the Haitian case as well, where the deeds of rebelling slaves, *gens de couleur,* and *petits blancs* in Saint-Domingue share some features with their U.S. and French peers. Even in Britain, the masses exerted noteworthy political influence, so much so that one commentator called them "ye mobility," an antagonistic counterpart to and check on the nobility.[90]

Prints captured the rise of this political and social force, but they are not faithful studies of actors or their actions. Depictions lack the specificity in recording social makeup and behavior that would allow us to "see" the people and their practices. Instead, visual culture cast the crowd and its activities in particular ways for specific ends. Often violence to property or to persons stood at the center of these representations, and the animating issue in these scenes was whether the violence was merited. Although crowd violence was always extralegal, it was sometimes viewed as natural justice—a valid response to an unfair situation that formal institutions had failed to rectify. In the revolutionary period, the question of what constituted an injustice was debated vigorously: were, for instance, North American colonists truly oppressed by the stamp tax, and therefore did tax collectors deserve tarring and feathering? The stakes of these discussions were high, as popular responses became part of calls for sweeping change. Crowds' targets had the potential to move from discrete perpetrators or sites to a more general critique of corruption within political and social systems that warranted dramatic overhaul. The visual culture of crowds participated in this argument over the legitimacy of popular protest. Printmakers located outside these movements presented different versions of the people—some endorsing, others damning, and still others ambiguous. An examination of these visualizations reveals how they contributed to promoting and circumscribing acknowledgments of the sovereignty of the masses.

In the case of North America, crowd activity figured most conspicuously in prints of the colonial crisis. Some portrayals emphasized participants' respectability. Consider François Godefroy's *Origine de la Révolution Américaine* from 1784, one of a series of sixteen engravings that illustrates episodes from the revolution. In this rendition people gather to watch the tarring and feathering of John Malcolm, a customs officer, in January 1774. Malcolm pleads as they hoist him high for punishment, but the onlookers are serene; no one is crying out for blood. A few well-dressed women in the foreground regard the scene, dogs frolic, two boys scamper near the cart, and others assemble in the street or lean out from windows in nearby buildings. In its architecture and the dress of the people, the scene is more akin to a French country fair than an instance of extralegal violence in North America. The caption stresses the Bostonians' restraint: the crowd was "moderate . . . in their vengeance."[91] The scene is presented as an unequivocal example of righteous retribution—one outside the courts, to be sure, but still the just action of a reasonable people.

This kind of interpretation is expected from the French in the first flush of victory over the British. But other printmakers mapped European respectability onto North American participants in political protest, too. In 1778 the Augsburg artist Franz Xaver Habermann created a series of *vues d'optiques* about the British North American colonies. Habermann had an international market in mind for the prints, which were published with German and French titles, and because they were projected via a device called a zograscope, there was a public display dimension as well. Some are views of the streets and ports of Boston, New York, and Philadelphia which, with their ornate buildings, look more like grand European cities than New World outposts.

In one of Habermann's images, a crowd dismantles the statue of George III in New York City in July 1776 (figure 6.7). While referencing an actual incident, the print takes some liberties: the statue of George III is standing (rather than on horseback), and men of African descent dominate the foreground, pulling on ropes attached to the statue in order to bring it down. The white actors and onlookers are dressed, as in Godefroy's print, like genteel Europeans, but the Black men are bare-chested, wearing kerchiefs around their heads and loose-fitting, exoticized trousers. The implication is that they labor under the direction of others: in other words, the enslaved are not "of the people" who perpetuated this political act (since they are, by legal definition, not people). And yet they are central to the scene and help to place this event—more than architecture or the clothing of white observers—in the Americas.[92]

It comes as no surprise that British prints usually had a contrary take on the crowd in North American protests. Members have a more rough-and-ready appearance—in their dress, facial expressions, and posture—than they do in Continental renderings. The 1774 print *The Bostonians Paying the Excise-Man, or Tarring and Feathering* by Philip Dawe is typical. In the foreground, a group of Americans have just tarred and feathered a taxman and are forcing him to drink from a teapot. The men leer at their victim, enjoying the pain and humiliation they inflict. A sailor, recognizable by his short jacket and kerchief, looks particularly pleased as he clenches his fist and wields a club menacingly. The tax collector peers out at the viewer with a pained expression,

Figure 6.7. Franz Xaver Habermann, *Die Zerstörung der Königlichen Bild Säule zu Neu Yorck/La destruction de la statue royale a Nouvelle Yorck* (Augsburg, ca. 1776). Etching. (© The Trustees of the British Museum.)

inviting identification with him, not the colonists. In the background, another gang of men dumps a cargo of tea overboard. The disreputable mob assails both people and property, and their appearance and deeds call into question their fidelity to the very rights they claim to defend.[93]

While Dawe's *Bostonians* features men exclusively, other British representations incorporated women and people of African descent into the crowds, much like their European peers, but to different ends. In 1775 Sayer and Bennett published Dawe's mezzotint *The Alternative of Williams-Burg* (see figure 4.6), in which a ragtag armed crowd forces merchants to sign a nonexportation agreement. Two women stand out: the first, haggard and frowning, with a hooked nose, holds an infant, while another child next to her carries a flag with "liberty" written across it. Located in the foreground, at the side of the frame, she regards the scene with grim approval. The other woman is in the middle, just behind and to the left of a knife-toting, pipe-smoking fat man overseeing the coerced signatures. Only her face is visible, but she averts her gaze from the spectacle. Her fine features and sad expression testify to her sensitivity and dismay. In their disparate appearances and reactions, the women work to elicit the viewers' condemnation of the crowd's objectives. To approve is to relate to the harpy, and to reject is to connect with the concerned woman.

The Alternative of Williams-Burg also includes a Black man, his face discernible next to the woman at the center. He watches the incident unfold, eyes wide, lips slightly parted. He is among the crowd but, as with the woman next to him, he is not participating in the action. Unlike the example of the Habermann print, the primary purpose of this man of African descent is not to mark it as a colonial scene. As the numbers of Black Londoners grew in the eighteenth century, they had become a noticeable presence in portrayals of "the people of out of doors," and some depictions were sympathetic.[94] *The Alternative of Williams-Burg* follows this mode, as the Black man is astonished at what he witnesses. In Matthew Darly's *A View in America in 1778,* the role of the African-descended man is even more pronounced. A white man wrapped in furs, with an obvious eye disorder (and hence not seeing clearly), spots a pompous military officer ignoring a group of poorly clad and ailing troops, gesturing instead, with a sweep of his arm, to one well-dressed soldier. In the foreground a man of African descent stares out at the viewer; he has been pelted with cannonballs that litter the ground. Most scholars have interpreted the white men as Americans and concluded that the print is a commentary on their lip service to liberty while soldiers suffer and die in miserable conditions and Black people are enslaved. At the same time, though, Darly's work raises questions about the British military's inability to vanquish this seedy army.[95] Either way (or perhaps both), the Black man makes the visual link with the observer, pointing out the folly and absurdity of the conflict and of its celebrated ideological underpinnings. His position as the lowest on the social ladder, whose members were constant targets of violence, underscores how transparent this condemnatory conclusion should be.

These British portrayals reflect the views of those critical of the colonies, but they are a symptom of a growing ambivalence about the political power of crowds in general—in fact or in print. Prior to the age of revolutions, British visual culture celebrated the crowd, illustrating its members with humor and a certain degree of respect. While participants could be troublesome, raucous, and downright wrong, they were seen as evidence of British liberty. These depictions mixed high and low, male and female, Black and white, satirizing one and all, and they took comfort in the ability of the classes to rub elbows, laugh at their foibles, and mete out natural justice while maintaining social and political stability.[96]

Around the time of the American Revolution, British confidence in the crowd faltered. Homegrown crowd action began to fade from visual culture after the Gordon Riots in 1780 and when calls for political reform in Britain gained momentum in the earliest days of the French Revolution. At the very moment when "the people" exerted their political will more forcefully out in streets throughout the Atlantic world, crowds and their behavior were increasingly suspect in British prints.[97] This ambivalence sneaks into Gillray's 1779 *Liberty of the Subject*. Published during heated debates over the impressment of civilians to serve in the navy, the print shows a crowd coming to blows with a press gang that is seizing a tailor to haul him to sea. The ironic title for the scene suggests that one of the liberties of a British subject is having his liberty abrogated. But the feeble response of the cringing tailor, who fails to fight, and the violent reactions of two women who brandish sticks and grab the hair of the gang leader, raise doubts about the character of the subjects as well. Gillray plays both sides of the controversy to brilliant and uncertain effect, demonstrating the wavering virtue of the people and their government.[98]

The French Revolution posed more insistently the question of the role of the people out of doors and their visual representation. Initially, the French Revolution seemed to dispel doubts across the Atlantic world about the integrity of the crowd. The storming of the Bastille elicited what one scholar describes as a "veritable frenzy" of celebratory Bastille-related prints.[99] A Swiss visitor to London remarked, "All the printshops were filled with caricatures of events in France."[100] This congratulatory visual outpouring over the Bastille's demise stemmed from decades of seeing it as a bulwark of despotism. Philosophes, novelists, and other commentators had cast the Bastille as a physical manifestation of arbitrary power since the king could imprison anyone there indefinitely, without grounds. Stories had spread about how its secret cells were crammed with innocent captives withering away in darkness and squalor.[101] When the people of Paris set about liberating the prison's victims and tearing the building down, observers in Britain, the Caribbean, and the United States rejoiced. In their view, the focus of the people's outrage could not have been more appropriate, and therefore the crowd's actions indicated the trueness of its moral compass.

The only problem with visualizing the storming of the Bastille was that the actual seizure failed to live up to expectations. Just seven people were rescued from inside its walls; however, both visual and textual accounts were so invested in the draconian vision of the Bastille—and the noble cause of the people to eradicate it—that they exaggerated aspects, and even invented incidents, to toe the preferred interpretive line. French, British, and U.S. prints emphasize the overwhelming scale of the edifice in comparison to the people who besieged it. Its imposing stone walls make it appear impenetrable, lending valor to the crowd's undertaking and its success. The people are organized, cheerful, and dedicated to the task. Prints also show members of the crowd breaking into cells to free prisoners. One frequently reprinted scene was the liberation of comte de Lorges who, the story went, had been shackled in his cell for thirty-two years. But he did not exist; he was a fictional composite of all the tales that had circulated for years about the Bastille's residents. Yet the prints needed such a character because his extreme suffering accentuated the courage and principles of the rescuers.[102]

The visual culture of the Bastille reveals how artists shaped their depictions of crowds to argue for the legitimacy of the people's endeavors. The overwhelming Atlantic consensus around the Bastille was a short-lived phenomenon, however. As the French Revolution radicalized and the people became more demanding politically and more violent in their efforts to realize those demands, prints produced outside of France cast their deeds as horrible. Print publishers fixated on negative portrayals of French mobs to show how far people on the streets had gone astray. Gillray, Cruikshank, and other popular British artists depict barefoot and sometimes bare-assed *sans culottes* murdering aristocrats and priests. The perspective of their scenes is close enough to see individual faces, which are outrageously distorted, with cavernous mouths and bulging eyes, and they wear an aspect of gruesome delight as they threaten their targets. Some prints go so far as to portray crowd members consuming the body parts of their victims, relishing limbs, entrails, and hearts. After the declaration of war between France and Britain in 1793, printers set similar scenes on British streets, suggesting the terrors that a French invasion would bring to the home front.

These British images had French counterparts. Between 1791 and 1792, counterrevolutionaries turned to caricature as a means to undercut the republican project. Approximately 150 caricatures were produced during this period, covering an array of subjects. Several portray crowds' wanton and cannibalistic violence, but the appearance of the people is less vicious and the visual effect less visceral. In *Les braves brigands d'Avignon* (1791), smartly dressed men with wild hair and hideous mouths chew on arms and legs, while Jean-Baptiste Jourdan (a commander in the French revolutionary army who had, incidentally, fought in the battle of Savannah and in the West Indies during the American Revolution) strides over a pile of dead bodies.[103] But perpetrators and victims share classical features. French artists sympathetic to the Jacobin phase of the revolution, such as Jean-Louis Prieur, did not shy away from portraying crowd violence either. In his famous series *Tableaux historiques de la Révolution* (which was also printed in Germany, Belgium, and the Netherlands), Prieur presents the people pillaging elite houses, tearing down a statue of Louis XIV, and preparing to hang Joseph-François Foulon (controller-general of finances under Louis XVI) *à la lanterne* (figure 6.8). Prieur pays attention to individuals in the crowd, picturing men, women, and children from all social backgrounds, as indicated by their attire. Yet in their physical traits and demeanor, they are never distorted; they are simply ordinary people, performing the work necessary to bring revolution to fruition.[104] In comparison to contemporaneous British prints, the people, even while committing violent acts, are more subdued, almost proper.

British printmakers portrayed the people of the French Revolution with a zeal for outlandish horror, savoring macabre and shocking detail. This characterization of the mob persisted—and, somewhat counterintuitively, increased—after the Jacobins were overthrown in the summer of 1794. The French Terror continued in British visual culture throughout the 1790s, although as an actual revolutionary phase, it had ended in the republic. This sleight of hand was essential for two political and ideological purposes: first, maintaining support for the war against France in the face of mounting domestic hardships, and second, continuing to cast the French Revolution and its perpetrators

SUPPLICE DE FOULON A LA PLACE DE GREVE .
le 23 Juillet 1789

Figure 6.8. *Supplice de Foulon à la Place de Grève, le 23 Juillet 1789*, plate 21 from *Collection complète des tableaux historiques de la Révolution française* (Paris: between 1789 and 1804). Jean-Louis Prieur, artist; Pierre Gabriel Berthault, etcher. This image depicts the attempted hanging of Joseph-François Foulon in the Place de l'Hôtel-de-Ville in Paris in the summer of 1789. Allegedly the rope broke three times, and the crowd ended up decapitating him. His head was then paraded around town on a pike, the mouth stuffed with grass, hay, and excrement. The violence of the episode is, however, sanitized by the elegance of Prieur's rendition as well as the tame portrayal of the crowd, the fine buildings, and the distant perspective of the action. (Library of Congress Prints and Photographs Division, LC-USZC2-6490.)

as misguided. British printmakers applied these characteristics of crowd portrayals to homegrown opposition (those who might rally around Fox, Paine, and the like) and to the Irish Rebellion of 1798. Consistently in the 1790s, British printmakers found representations of collective "Jacobins" a convenient mode to discredit people out of doors in France, at home, and beyond.[105]

But similar to some print portraits from this era, their extremism gives an observer pause. What seem like the most judgmental prints, such as Gillray's *Un petit souper a la Parisienne* (1792) or *Promis'd Horrors of the French Invasion* (1796), contain a good deal of ambiguity. By reveling in the lurid, these prints indicted the British government's war furor—its voracious fearmongering in an attempt to annihilate the opposition, a strategy that curtailed British liberty, which the war against France was supposed to preserve.[106] There is humor in these portrayals, too—in the exaggerated features, the absurd gestures, the clever visual and verbal puns. A viewer was just as likely to chortle as to gasp, and their power in this regard accounts for the popularity of this golden age of British caricature.

In prints of the American and French revolutions, depictions of the crowd ranged from the romanticized to the nightmarish. This scope suggests how the power of the people was a moving target, which provides a useful context for appraising portrayals of the Haitian Revolution. At first glance, the sensationalist mode—that often deployed for Jacobin crowds—seems most apt for visualizing biased contemporary reports of the Haitian Revolution. After all, written accounts of the slave rebellion propagated stories of babies skewered on pikes, white women raped over the dead bodies of their husbands, fathers, and brothers, and so on.[107] But prints of revolutionary Saint-Domingue are selective in the crowd action they represent. The greatest number of prints—although they comprise only a handful—concentrate on the temporal bookends of the revolution: the battles at Cap Français (in 1791 and 1793) and the campaign for independence in the early 1800s. The Le Cap engravings, as a group, emphasize the violence that Black people enacted on white residents and their property. They downplay, or ignore altogether, the brutal acts of white men against African-descended men, women, and children.[108] The prints have titles like *Révolte des Nègres* and *Vue des 40 jours d'incendie* and render the furor of a mob unleashed. Fires rage and smoke billows as Black men, armed with axes, knives, and bludgeons, attack respectably attired white people. Black men and women destroy buildings and appropriate clothing, jewels, swords, and other goods.

The Le Cap engravings cast the slave owners—not the enslaved—as the victims, and the tenacious repetition of these images had political consequences. Despite noteworthy episodes in subsequent years, visual culture harped on Le Cap. Atlantic observers read about the abolition of slavery and citizenship for freed men, and about Black soldiers defeating invading British forces, but they saw pejorative images of the burning of Cap Français. In the mid- and late 1790s, the visual culture of the Haitian Revolution refused to keep pace with developments, and so the extraordinary achievements of that period were associated visually with racialized destruction.

That said, the dogged recurrence of these images posits that audiences were not so easily convinced. There are subtle differences among the prints, especially in the portrayals of white people, that demonstrate makers going to some lengths to persuade viewers to their vision of the revolution. A case in point is a 1797 German engraving of the slave rebellion in 1791 (figure 6.9). The explanatory caption takes pains to identify the place as the "Französchen [sic] Kolonie St. Domingo," and in the background stand palm trees and curious houses with conical rooftops—an effort to evoke a tropical setting. But the white actors look as though they have been plucked from an early modern northern European genre painting: the women wear stereotypical head coverings, and the men sport tight suits. The parity in the clothing of the besieged Saint-Dominguan colonists and that of the intended German-speaking audience encourages the viewer to identify with the colonists (rather than the enslaved who, oddly, wear frock-like garments). An image titled *Cruauté des Nêgres* from an 1803 Swiss almanac creates a similar connection through setting. At the center, a group of Black men wearing only loincloths assails a well-dressed white man. But the murder occurs in a room with a tiled floor, arched doorway, and portraits and a decorative map on the walls. The interior finishes read more northern European than colonial Caribbean, again transforming the foreign into something familiar for Swiss audiences.

These less than faithful details could be attributed to a lack of knowledge about the look of people and places in Saint-Domingue. But the artists could have invented fanciful clothing (as they did for the enslaved) or used known French styles. They, however, chose to introduce recognizable local elements, driving home—at least for the Germans and the Swiss—the anti-French message of their images: the French Revolution was horrible for individuals and property in Saint-Domingue, and thus one must fight it on the Continent.[109] These

Vorſtellung der auf der Franzöſchen Colonie St. Domingo von denen ſchwartzen Sclaven eingebildete Franzöſchen democratiſche Freyheil, welche ſelbige durch unerhörte Grauſamkeit zu erwerben gedachten. Sie ruinirten viele hundert Coffe. und Zucker-Plantagen und verbranten die Mühlen, ſie metzelden auch ohne Unterſchied alle Weiſe die in ihre Hände fielen, dabey ihnen ein weiſes Kind zur Fahne dienle, ſchändelen Frauen und ſchleplen ſie in elende Gefangen. ſchaft, 1791. allein ihr Vorhaben wurde zu nichte.   93.

Figure 6.9. *Vorstellung der auf der französchen Kolonie St. Domingo von denen schwartzen Sclaven eingebildete französchen democratische Freÿheit* (ca. 1797). Engraving. (Archives départementales de la Gironde, cote: 61 J 66/170.)

choices also reveal how creators could not rely on racial identification alone to convince audiences to condemn the Haitian Revolution. Given European rivalries, printmakers did not take it for granted that viewers would see themselves in French colonists.[110]

The violence in these prints aimed to undercut the political legitimacy of the actions of the enslaved, yet the stylistic portrayal of the people and the violence they experience is reserved in comparison to British depictions of French Jacobin crowds. The viewer witnesses crowd violence in revolutionary Saint-Domingue at a remove. Unlike the prints from the American and French revolutions, the faces of the perpetrators and their victims are more sketches than full-fledged caricatures. They do not register the bloodlust, alarm, disappointment, shock, and other emotions envisaged in prints of revolutionary violence in North America and France. In one surviving rendition with a greater degree of detail (*Pillage du Cap*, discussed in chapter 2; see figure 2.2), people of African descent have exaggerated traits that pander to racist stereotypes; that said, in this engraving as well as the others, there is none of the bloodshed and gore that characterize prints of other revolutionary crowds.

So the unexpected question is, Why didn't prints of the revolutionary crowd in Saint-Domingue revel in explicit violence? It was an available style, and in the late eighteenth century, publishers knew that violence, including the violence of slavery, sold. Historian Karen Halttunen has coined the phrase "the pornography of pain" to encapsulate the pleasure audiences took in seeing, hearing, and reading about horrific things in the guise of sympathizing with one's fellow man or woman.[111] Both sides of the slavery debate explored this mode. In an attempt to generate solidarity with slave owners, newspapers, histories, and novels trafficked in the physical and sexual violence of the Haitian Revolution.[112] Meanwhile, the emerging visual and material culture of antislavery frequently focused on the pain slave masters exacted on Black people's bodies.[113] Some British artists who composed ghastly caricatures of anonymous Jacobins engraved arresting prints that engaged with the violence of the slave trade and slavery. In 1791 Gillray published *Barbarities in the West Indias,* which visualizes testimony given in Parliament about an English slave driver who boiled an enslaved man alive in a vat of cane juice. Isaac Cruikshank's 1792 print *The Abolition of the Slave Trade* shows sailors stringing up an almost naked enslaved woman in order to whip her—again inspired by a real episode.[114] As with many of Gillray and Cruikshank's works, the message is equivocal. It is unclear whether the makers endorse or parody the cause of abolitionists, but there is no denying the graphic and intimate character of the violence. The perspective and scale of the prints draw viewers closely into each scene.

The comparative detachment of Haitian revolutionary scenes reflects, to some extent, different national and artistic styles. The only renditions of the collective endeavors of enslaved men and women published during the Haitian Revolution come from France, Germany, and Switzerland—not Britain, which had a bolder tradition. Yet even taking these aesthetic conventions into account, French and German printmakers hesitated to chronicle the Haitian Revolution as it occurred, as the scarce number of imprints indicates. They were extraordinarily discerning in what they chose to visualize from the revolution because the very composition of the crowd in Saint-Domingue—one comprised of men and women of African descent—posed an ideologi-

cal challenge about who were legitimate political agents and what constituted legitimate collective action.

The absence of British and North American prints of the Haitian
Revolution as it unfolded lends further weight to this conclusion. In
1794 a Parisian engraver, lately emigrated to Philadelphia, proposed to
produce a print of "the massacre of 771 French men, murdered the 7th
July at Fort Dauphin in the Island of St. Domingo," but whether he did
so remains unknown.[115] A few British prints refer obliquely to enslaved
people taking up arms. In 1792 Richard Newton produced *A Real San
Culotte!!*, in which a Jacobin stands with one foot on France, the other
on America, straddling Britain in between. The man is divided in half:
one side is a white Jacobin, holding a dagger dripping with blood; and
the other side is a black, devil-like figure, complete with a spear, amulet,
and smock. The black half has its hoof planted on America, and so perhaps alludes to rebels in Saint-Domingue.[116] References to "St Domingo"
also appeared in prints from 1803, listed alongside other theaters of war
where Bonaparte's conduct was suspect. Isaac Cruikshank in *The New
Consular Waltz* depicts seven women using a blanket to toss Bonaparte
in the air. Each woman levels an accusation, including one who cries,
"*You sent my Sweetheart to St Domingo!*" While a clear reference to the
Leclerc campaign, the charge is less about the power of Black soldiers
and more about a rumor that Bonaparte had deployed to the island
soldiers he deemed troublesome, with the knowledge that, thanks to
tropical warfare and yellow fever, most were unlikely to return.[117]

Not until after the revolution did British and North American publishers offer prints that pictured collective action in Saint-Domingue—
usually for pro-slavery ends. The absence was not simply a matter of
ignoring the endeavors of the enslaved during the Haitian Revolution
since it was discussed in detail in other realms. Rather, the comparisons
to the visual culture of other revolutionary crowds are instructive. For
all their supposed barbarism, French and North American crowds in
prints retained their political legitimacy among both proponents and
opponents of these revolutions. The people out of doors in the U.S.
and French revolutions may have been, by British estimates at least,
erroneous and reprehensible, but they were still acknowledged political
agents.

If British and American printmakers represented revolutionaries in
Saint-Domingue in the same visual terms (even grotesque ones), then

the parallel implied that free people of African descent and the enslaved had a similar claim to political action—a conclusion that white Britons, with their own Caribbean colonies and their invasion of Saint-Domingue from 1794 to 1798, and that white Americans, as supporters of slavery, wanted to avoid. The visual association would have opened the door to abolitionist readings that went beyond what white antislavery activists at the time condoned. As scholar Marcus Wood argues, the visual culture of late eighteenth-century abolitionism presented the enslaved "as cultural absentee, . . . as a blank page for white guilt to inscribe," not as agents determined to end slavery.[118] Black soldiers during the Haitian Revolution challenged this construction, and so in visual culture, the other available modes for representing "the people" would have created a parity between the actions of the formerly enslaved and those of other revolutionaries—an equivalency that white printmakers and their white audiences refused to entertain. For them, select individuals from the Haitian Revolution, like Toussaint Louverture, could be made to fit available genres, at least after his death. But the "people" of the Haitian Revolution lay outside the realm of the representable.

Among all Atlantic revolutionaries, those in Saint-Domingue demanded most emphatically to be understood as people—as individuals and as collectives with legitimate political claims. They had to overturn slavery (which defined them as property, not as humans) and racism (which cast them as inherently inferior) to achieve their goals. And because of structural inequalities in the making of prints, actors in revolutionary Saint-Domingue lacked access to the means to produce and disseminate their own images of "the people." That said, the Haitian case is an extreme instance of a more general debate in the era about who were "the people," were their assertions valid, and were they fit to rule. Prints of revolutionary individuals and revolutionary crowds wrestled with the problem of whom to represent and how. The political climate at their points of origin—Britain versus France, North America versus Germany, and elsewhere—influenced publishers' options, and so, too, did artists' styles. Yet across the Atlantic, printmakers struggled with the power visualization gave to subjects. Prints afforded a legitimacy to revolutionaries' claims to popular sovereignty, and in so doing, contemporaries thought that they had the potential to inspire others, including people of African descent. Moreover, makers had to consider what audiences—imagined as international and white (but in practice not restricted to them)—would bear. Prints were commercial goods, and although horror may have sold, there were limits to what white consumers would stomach and pay for.

The political implications of visualization were contentious in the world of prints, but representations of revolutionary-era people took on new dynamics when rendered in three dimensions. Some of the same individuals immortalized in prints appeared as life-size sculptures that were staged in evocative tableaux in public venues. And similar to prints of crowd action, sculptors explored the ramifications of political violence for Atlantic societies. Yet artists' specific choices of subjects and the conventions of the form expose a related but different set of interpretive challenges for observers coming to terms with the mechanisms for and meanings of revolutionary change.

7 Terrible Amusements

MADAME TUSSAUD, WHOSE wax museums attract millions of visitors today, got her start during the French Revolution. She apprenticed under her uncle, Philippe Curtius, who ran one of the most stylish wax museums in Paris. While there, she was a frequent witness to the political violence of the late 1780s and early 1790s: she crossed riots in the streets, watched as crowds attacked the Bastille, and saw the blade of the guillotine fall repeatedly. Tussaud also claimed that the government called upon her whenever someone notable died to cast that person's head. In her capacity as a wax artist, she supposedly held Maximilien Robespierre's "severed head in her lap," handled Jean-Paul Marat's "still warm . . . and bleeding body," and modeled a likeness of Princesse de Lamballe from her decapitated head "whilst surrounded by the brutal monsters, whose hands were bathed in the blood of the innocent."[1]

Tussaud took creative license with her past, and so the details of her memoirs, including the grisly conditions under which she fashioned her figures, are suspect. However, we do know that in 1802 she arrived in England with several wax heads of famous individuals who had died between 1793 and 1794: Louis XVI, Marie-Antoinette, and Robespierre, among others (figure 7.1). Although Tussaud's fantastic success and longevity as a wax artist are exceptional, her choice of subjects for exhibition was part of a broader phenomenon. In the last quarter of the

Figure 7.1. Madame Tussaud's wax renditions of the heads of Louis XVI and Marie-Antoinette. This image of their display dates from the early twentieth century, but Tussaud purportedly modeled these heads immediately after the executions of the former French king and queen and brought them with her to London, where they have remained ever since. (Getty Images.)

eighteenth century, artists in the Atlantic world staged shows of life-size wax sculptures that featured revolutionary deaths prominently.

Exhibitions like Tussaud's were one of many popular amusements. In the eighteenth century the term *amusement* could have negative connotations, implying idleness, frivolity, or lack of discipline.[2] But just as often, amusements were seen as acceptable, even beneficial, diversions that provided relaxation and enjoyment. This pleasure derived from encounters with the merry, the droll, or the bizarre in venues that ranged from theaters and halls to taverns, gardens, and parlors. With their graphic representations of violence, wax displays of revolutionary deaths played with the darker end of the spectrum, and they did so in very public ways.

Tussaud's terrible amusements, and others like them, provide unusual insight into how people in the Atlantic world comprehended and experienced certain types of revolutionary violence at a distance. Lately historians have called for a reinsertion of violence into our narratives of Atlantic revolutions. Coercion, displacement, war, and extermination marked colonialism from the beginning; however, at the end of the eighteenth century, these elements had a new cast as hundreds of thousands perpetrated and fell victim to violence for causes that were revolutionary. This violence was not only a consequence of conflict but a force that shaped politics, ideology, and society as well.[3]

Wax shows engaged with these issues by helping people to see and deliberate over two violent novelties, most evident in France and Saint-Domingue. During the French Revolution violence came in diverse forms at various moments, yet wax artists fixated on the Terror (1793–94). They emphasized aspects that they thought would be striking to Atlantic observers: what became its iconic instrument (the guillotine), the volume of executions and their pace (so many people and so quickly), and the high profiles of some victims (aristocrats, royals, and self-avowed revolutionaries).[4] As for the Haitian Revolution, slave insurrections had occurred over the centuries, but with the emancipation decrees in 1793–94, enslaved people's armed struggle for freedom and rights changed from a rebellion against authority into a campaign to apply French laws. As a result, some French republican sectors saw as legitimate the subsequent violence in the colony, as Black men fought those resistant to realizing emancipation and citizenship on the ground. This acknowledgment of the validity of Black militancy, albeit partial and temporary, was something new.

These transformations in the French Atlantic world had significant ramifications for Anglophone observers, who wrestled with the consequences of this political violence for their societies. Newspapers, periodicals, and firsthand reports were influential sources of information, and maps and prints contributed to these discussions, too, the former by visualizing military campaigns and the latter by portraying collective action. But terrible amusements, with their three-dimensionality, elicited a strong combination of cognitive, emotional, and physical responses. Of course, works on paper are three-dimensional objects as well, yet eighteenth-century makers did not exploit that characteristic in the content they conveyed. For wax artists, it was essential to their craft.

Wax figures stirred from audiences a range of reactions that defy clear categorization as "for" or "against" the revolutions with which they were affiliated. Practitioners aimed to transfix viewers with the medium's intense realism, and when these conventions were applied to depictions of death, they offered audiences powerful and distinctive experiences of revolutionary violence. Two often-reproduced deaths—those of Louis XVI and Jean-Paul Marat—bring to light different facets of the Terror's impact abroad. With the execution of Louis XVI, spectators faced the implications of the demise of this monarch and the use of the guillotine. In the case of Marat's assassination, attention focused less on the target than on its agent, Charlotte Corday, and so visitors confronted women's participation in revolutionary violence.

While wax tableaux of famous French revolutionary deaths appeared frequently in Britain and the United States, those of the Haitian Revolution did not. One example elucidates why: a wax rendition of Toussaint Louverture. Although it does not re-create a death scene, the context surrounding the sculpture reveals the ways that white supremacy affected white audiences' thresholds for seeing revolutionary violence, even when only implied, and suggests its resonance for Black viewers as well. As with the portrayals of Louis XVI and Marat, part of the power of Louverture's sculpture derived from its life-size scale, and this attribute is put into perspective by contrasting wax figures as a genre with another terrible amusement that was fashionable in Britain: miniature guillotines. Made of bone by French prisoners, these toys underscore how size and setting informed observers' perspectives on violence.

Together, these terrible amusements allow us to see how some types of political violence in the French and Haitian revolutions entered the everyday lives of people far removed from the center of action. They took the conversation out of the realms of battlefields, rarefied intellectual debate, and party politics and into entertainment halls and homes. With this change of location, these objects created what we might think of as a virtual experience of violence. Visitors to U.S. and British wax museums did not observe these actual deaths; yet they did have potent encounters with revolutionary violence that for some viewers felt remarkably real.

This engagement was circumscribed by what makers chose to represent and how. With the emphases on certain aspects of the Terror in France and on Black-on-white violence in revolutionary Saint-Domingue, late eighteenth-century terrible amusements promoted a tendency to highlight specific violent episodes and actors from the revolutions and to let them stand in for a much more complex landscape of violence—a tendency that, like Tussaud's waxworks, persists in popular perceptions of revolutionary violence to this day. In their selective and graphic portrayals, these terrible amusements had a reductive quality that sometimes, despite makers' intentions, cast doubt on the purportedly enlightened aims of revolutions.

WAXING REVOLUTIONARY

When Tussaud arrived in England, she was one of the latest practitioners of a familiar art that was centuries old. The Egyptians, ancient Greeks, and Romans all produced wax figures for both religious and secular purposes, and the practice persisted in medieval and early modern Europe with funeral effigies for royals and other dignitaries. Scientists and doctors used wax sculptures for anatomical study, celebrating them as vehicles for reform. Dr. Abraham Chovet, for instance, began his career in London teaching medicine from anatomical waxes, moved to the Caribbean, and ended up in Philadelphia in the 1770s and 1780s.[5]

In the eighteenth century displays of life-size wax sculptures emerged as a form of popular entertainment. These shows were trendy and affordable, occurring in amusement halls in London and Paris and in their smaller-scale incarnations in North America and the Caribbean.[6] Philippe Curtius's *salon de cire* at the Palais Royal in Paris illustrates how grand these spaces could be. The staging of his exhibitions, complete with expensive furniture and props, ornate architectural detail, and dramatic lighting, set off his works to maximum advantage and drew customers from all sectors of society.[7] Artists with less capital rented rooms, employed those of patrons, or set up in taverns, hotels, and other venues to showcase their talents.[8] Exhibitions often went on tour as the need for profit spurred makers to hit the road. An artist would enter a town, post advertisements in local newspapers, stay for a month or two until ticket sales slowed, and then move on to another city.[9] The dislocation wrought by revolutions exacerbated this propensity to migrate. The most well-known example is Madame Tussaud, but throughout the period scores of wax sculptors traveled abroad with their wares for economic and even ideological reasons.[10]

Whatever their magnitude, eighteenth-century wax exhibitions featured an array of notables. Artists portrayed statesmen, aristocrats, and beautiful women; historical, literary, and biblical characters; what we might call ethnic types (a Chinese man, a Native American woman, and so on); and allegorical representations (maternal love and childhood innocence, among others). The diverse subjects reveal attempts to appeal to wide audiences, and to encourage people to visit repeatedly, wax artists crafted renditions of individuals who had lately captured the public interest. The chance to see these luminaries, one advertisement proclaimed, "must be highly gratifying to all, who, having heard of the fame of their characters, wish to see . . . their persons."[11]

Wax figures, like print portraits, helped to fulfill this desire to see the new and newsworthy, yet they created a distinct viewing experience because of the startling realism of the medium. Wax has an uncanny ability to imitate the look of human flesh to a degree that prints, paintings, or sculptures in marble or alabaster cannot. This quality, along with actual hair and clothing, intensified the realism and individuality of a wax figure (figure 7.2).[12] Promotional copy highlighted the provenance of clothing especially, sometimes advertising that the person had worn the garments now on the wax rendition.[13] Failing that, some artists employed seamstresses who could reproduce the appropriate fashions. This attention to detail was more pronounced in London and Paris, where wax artists commissioned leading dressmakers to re-create garments; however, Reuben Moulthrop, a sculptor in East Haven, Connecticut, hired two seamstresses to sew clothing specifically for his works.[14] For maximum impact, artists felt that each element of a sculpture—its attire, hair, and physical traits—had to ring true, even for those who would never see the living person.

The hyper-mimicry of wax sculpture created compelling encounters for viewers. Spectators regularly professed that they had mistaken the figure for a real person. In a letter to his local paper, "Columbus" described a visit to an artist's studio where he thought a wax rendition of the Virgin Mary was an actual woman. Not until, at the artist's urging, he touched the woman's "solid, cold" hand did "the curtain of delusion disappear."[15] In the opinion of some commentators, the realism of wax sculptures made them more honest than other forms of visual

Figure 7.2. Patience Wright, *William Pitt the Elder, Earl of Chatham*, 1775. Wax sculpture. (Copyright: Dean and Chapter of Westminster, London.)

representation. One newspaper article praised a waxwork exhibition in New York City for its faithfulness to portraying people as they were rather than how they might aspire to look: "Here, as in a mirror, we see man in his natural and best appearance and attire, entirely divested of those ornaments and trappings, which . . . are but too apt to flatter, if not mislead the human eye." In the reviewer's estimation, the accoutrements, poses, and garments typical of paintings and prints obscured the "majesty" of the individual.[16]

This sincerity was a key component of the edifying aspects of wax figures. Unlike other deceptions that were offered up as visual puzzles to delight audiences, these sculptures were less about ferreting out the ruse and more about giving oneself over to the experience.[17] When a spectator did so, practitioners maintained that he or she would have important revelations, and this argument was in keeping with emerging notions about vision.[18] Although the reliability of the senses was questioned in this period, many philosophers, scientists, and theologians touted vision's ability to discern truth through reading and observation. As a result, the early modern era witnessed an explosion of print and of instruments (microscopes, glasses, and telescopes) that enhanced the power of seeing.[19] The setting for wax figures facilitated this penetrative viewing. A spectator could look at a wax sculpture with an intensity and open scrutiny that civility, status, and other social mores prohibited in interactions with a living person. While only select members of the French populace watched the royal family eating dinner at Versailles, visitors to Philippe Curtius's *salon de cire* in Paris or to the waxworks in Cap Français, Saint-Domingue, could linger over representations of the royal family, taking in and appraising all the details, without committing offense.[20]

Visual discoveries, for all their appeals to reason, had an emotional impact as well, one that wax artists exploited in specific ways.[21] Through their work, they played with ideas concerning man's capacity to identify with fellow men. Sympathy was celebrated as a virtue of enlightened individuals and societies, believed to be fundamental to building republics as it nurtured connections and good will among citizens.[22] In the case of wax sculptures, practitioners contended that viewing their work would "afford the most agreeable sensations."[23] These "sensations," according to performance historian Joseph Roach, amounted to a "vivid intimacy" in which audiences connected with not only the individual rendered but also the qualities, events, and other attributes associated with that person.[24]

In light of practices surrounding and attitudes toward wax figures, it is not surprising that late eighteenth-century Atlantic revolutionaries surfaced in displays. Some artists saw their inclusion as an opportunity for visitors to participate in the debates of the day. No one embraced the political possibilities of the medium more heartily than Patience Wright. The daughter of a radical Quaker from Oyster Bay, Long Island, Wright began working in wax as a means to support her children after the death of her husband. In the eighteenth century, elite and middling women practiced wax modeling, which was considered a fitting art for them, particularly when in miniature (fruit, flowers, cameos), and a few women became professional practitioners.[25] Wright's sister, Rachel Wells, joined her in this venture. In the early 1770s the two women pooled their resources and established two waxwork exhibitions—one in Philadelphia and the other in New York, and they had a studio in Charleston, South Carolina. At these sites, they displayed life-size sculptures and busts of esteemed men like the evangelist George Whitefield and author John Dickinson.[26]

By all accounts, the sisters had success with their enterprise, so much so that Patience Wright, like other North American artists of the time, decided to try her luck in London. She landed there in 1772 during the colonial crisis. Wright identified with the emerging patriot movement—by going to London, she hoped to further not only her career but the republican cause as well. She set up shop in the trendy neighborhood of Pall Mall and parlayed her folksy, if not brash, personality and her impressive sculptures into a thriving business. Her ties to Benjamin Franklin and others well placed in the London scene eased her entrée into elite circles; the king and queen sat for her several times. Rubbing elbows with royals and aristocrats only stoked Wright's enthusiasm for the patriots. She used her proximity to influential men to gather information for revolutionaries, sending dispatches to contacts in North America and in Paris. Legend has it that Wright occasionally stuffed her letters into wax busts that she sent abroad—a quite literal politicization of her work.[27]

Wright achieved notoriety for her zealous opinions and political activities, but she thought of her art as the main vehicle for disseminating republican ideology.[28] In her showroom she segregated her renditions of patriots from those of aristocrats and royals, and when anyone complimented her republican figures, she remarked, "My good friend, you may behold those men's hearts in their faces."[29] Their visages reflected their principles, and in Wright's estimation, her work helped people understand ideas in a way that was simpler to access and more persuasive than any treatise or text. To this end, she pestered Benjamin Franklin to sit for a bust, copies of which she wanted to send to major European leaders.[30] His face, honestly portrayed, would make the patriot cause transparent and convincing to those still on the fence about whether to support the rebelling colonists. And perhaps, she postulated, it could spread republican revolution throughout Europe.

With their realistic likenesses of revolutionaries, some wax artists hoped to sway audiences to this side, but the reception of their work was less straightforward than they anticipated. Some viewers were unconvinced. When Mrs. Cradock, a middle-class Englishwoman on a tour of Paris, visited Curtius's salon with her husband in the 1780s, she noted of Franklin, Rousseau, and Voltaire that "the workmanship was so good that the very character of these famous, though baneful, men was conveyed by their appearance."[31] Curtius, who was known for his republican sympathies, perhaps intended to celebrate the trio, yet Mrs. Cradock remained steadfast in her loyalties. Patience Wright's comportment ignited controversy that tarnished her intended political message. Her location, at the heart of the very empire she derided, almost guaranteed critique, but even fellow patriot Abigail Adams, who met Wright at her London studio, thought her repugnant, dubbing her "quite the slattern" and "the queen of sluts."[32] The insults are gendered and politicized: a respectable woman of ardent republican sentiments would be as offended by "queen" as by "slut."

Adams's vehement reaction may have stemmed as much from her dislike of Wright's art as of her exaggerated personality. A few years before, John Adams had written to Abigail of the creepiness of Rachel Wells's gallery in Philadelphia, where he felt as if he were "walking among a group of corpses."[33] He was unnerved by the suspended motion of the figures: some laughed, others cried, and still others walked, sat, or stood. Their poses, combined with their hyperrealistic features, fostered a morbid mood. John Adams was onto something. For some visitors (although clearly not for Abigail and John Adams), the creepiness was part of the allure. They enjoyed the thrill of dabbling safely in dark matters and, aware of these less lofty impulses, artists regularly staged re-creations of infamous murders.

Wax's eerie ability to evoke life and death resulted in interpretive ambiguities in the age of revolutions, when notorious political deaths appeared in exhibitions. While wax sculptures could be vehicles of republican ideology, they also demonstrated, especially when arranged in graphic tableaux, the grave costs of translating ideas into action. The political takeaways of these deaths were not necessarily evident, and the exhibitions, with their astounding realism, forced audiences to discern who was a vile murderer, who was a martyr to a lost cause, and who was a heroic agent of revolutionary change.

GUILLOTINING A KING

Given the conventions of the genre, wax figure exhibitions were apt venues for exploring violence associated with the Terror. When the Terror began in earnest, wax artists were quick to reconstruct some of the most controversial deaths for visitors. The execution of Louis XVI in January 1793 initiated the trend. The novelty of Louis's death was not that it was an execution per se. In this era, public executions of criminals were commonplace in the Atlantic world. In New York alone, almost seventy people were hanged between 1776 and 1796 for crimes ranging from counterfeiting, forgery, and robbery to arson, rape, and murder.[34] These were often massive events, drawing large crowds comprised of all sectors of society. But the execution of a king by guillotine was unique in the annals of capital punishment, and wax artists sought to profit from the public's fascination. In their reconstructions of the scene, they amplified two thorny aspects of the actual event: who was being executed and how. These issues had political significance in the United States and Britain, not only contributing to appraisals of the end of monarchy in France but also calling into question the allegedly enlightened means through which it happened.

During his trial and execution, the French revolutionary regime insisted on calling Louis XVI Louis Capet. It was crucial to the government's endeavor to desacralize and delegitimize monarchy. But wax displays of the execution referred to him as "king." Such a stance is expected in Britain, where the defense of monarchy was central to denunciations of the French Revolution.[35] Less predictably, it persisted in the United States as well. Reuben Moulthrop notified the New Haven public "that he has moddelled in Wax, a striking Likeness of the KING OF FRANCE in the Act of losing his Head under the GUILLOTINE, preserving every Circumstance which can give to the Eye of the Spectator a realizing View of that momentous and interesting Event."[36] Employing the monarch's title—in capital letters, no less—was in part a marketing ploy, for Moulthrop and other wax artists understood that what was extraordinary about this execution, compared to others, was the status of the victim. But the choice betrays some political ambivalence, too. After all, Louis XVI was a familiar face in the United States. The visual culture of the American Revolution had celebrated the U.S.-French alliance, and the king was a pivotal personage in those homages. After independence, Americans continued to honor the French monarchy with a pair of magnificent state portraits of the king and queen that hung in the congressional assembly room.[37] In light of this recent past, it was hard for Americans—even the most radical among them—not to see Louis XVI as a king.

In both the United States and Britain, the title was critical to the drama of the scene. It played up the disjuncture between the traditional treatment of a monarch and the circumstances of his death. First there was the question of his appearance. Thanks to widely circulated written accounts, Moulthrop and other artists knew that Louis did not wear royal trappings to his execution. Reports described that before ascending the scaffold, he removed his coat and met his fate "with his neck and breast bare," wearing "a clean shirt and stock, white waistcoat, black florentine silk breeches, black silk stockings, and his shoes were tied with black silk strings."[38] This state of undress in public was unthinkable for an eighteenth-century king and contributed to signaling just how revolutionary the event was. With their faithful re-creations, the wax displays made this visible for audiences who were used to appraising status through attire.

Then there was the effect of the execution on Louis's body (see figure 7.3). On this score, Daniel Bowen's waxwork reveals how far artists were willing to go to present the episode in all its gruesomeness. An advertisement for his Philadelphia show tells visitors what to expect from his version of Louis XVI's death: "When the last signal is given . . . the king lays himself on the block, where he is secured. The executioner then turns and prepares to do his duty, and, when the second

Figure 7.3. James Gillray, *The Blood of the Murdered Crying for Vengeance* (London: Hannah Humphrey, 1793). Gillray's print features torrents of blood, but not even his arresting portrayal of Louis XVI's execution approaches the overwhelming realism of wax displays of the event. (Beinecke Rare Book and Manuscript Library, Yale University.)

signal is given, the executioner drops the knife and severs the head from the body in one second. The head falls in a basket, and the lips, which are first red, turn blue."[39] Automata formed part of Bowen's display, and while this was unusual, his attention to detail (of lips turning from red to blue, for instance) is in keeping with the overall impulse of this medium and its adherents: to bring hyper-specificity to the death of this man.

By reconstructing Louis's execution so meticulously, wax artists invited viewers to deliberate whether the punishment fit his alleged crime. This debate was already raging in print. Many Britons decried Louis's fate, and Thomas Paine, who had debunked monarchy in *Common Sense* (1776), argued that his death was unjust because of his endorsement of the American Revolution.[40] But the wax displays made the execution an emotional experience for visitors, and their visceral reactions informed political appraisals. Critics worried that wax show audiences would not condemn his execution; rather, they would see it as grounds for celebration or as a casual entertainment. William Cobbett complained in a local paper of Bowen's exhibition: "The queen of France, the calumniated Antoinette, was the first foreigner . . . that advanced a shilling in the American cause. Have I ever abused her memory? . . . It was not I that guillotined her husband, in an automaton, every day, from nine in the morning till nine at night, for the diversion of the citizens of Philadelphia."[41] Cobbett argued that the distasteful exhibition desensitized audiences. The relentless repetition (twelve hours each day) and its placement among other amusements caused Americans to forget that to a certain extent they owed their independence to the French king and queen.

Others defended the didactic potential of visual representations of the execution. London printer William Lane offered an engraving, *Massacre of the King of France,* for 3 pence. The "very cheap" price was intentional so "that this horrid and unjust Sacrifice . . . should be known to all classes of People, and in particular to the honest and industrious Artisan and Manufacturer, who might be deluded by the false and specious pretenses of artful and designing persons." He felt it his duty to ensure that "the conduct of France, in their destruction of Monarchy . . . be publicly and universally known."[42] Lane emphasized that people needed to see the carnage for themselves—if only in simulacrum—to comprehend the terrible price of revolution. If Lane thought that prints had the power to make the horror more real, wax tableaux were more convincing in this respect.

The reactions of audiences, however, were hard to shape consistently, even within the same crowd. A London newspaper recounted an episode in which a woman, upon seeing a Louis XVI wax figure guillotined at a local show, "could express her feelings only by broad unfeeling laughter." Whether this laughter was gleeful or nervous is unclear, but the ambiguity is the problem; emotional responses to the displays were unpredictable and therefore, in the minds of some, politically dangerous. In this instance, other spectators censured the woman, and as the newspaper was careful to note, some women in attendance "were so distressed at the bare representation of such an outrage to human nature, as to leave the room in tears"—a reaction that the editor felt was more appropriate for an "Englishwoman."[43] The story suggests, though, that responses were unreliable.

The instability of reactions points to a fundamental tension with the shows: that they were amusements. As such, some detractors contended that their instructive power was at odds with the need to entertain. This issue surfaced not only around Louis XVI's death but also around his mode of execution. Hangings were the typical means of capital punishment in the Atlantic world; guillotine-like machines had been used in Europe in the past, but they were rare.[44] With their conspicuous and recurring application in revolutionary France, people were eager to see this technology in action. One newspaper summed it up bluntly: "It is presumed the curiosity of the Public will be gratified by the View and the Effect of an Instrument like that by which [Louis XVI] suffered."[45]

There was an ideological element to the guillotine as well. Its adoption in France had resulted from an extended campaign among self-proclaimed enlightened individuals who touted the humanity of the machine. Penal reform movements in Britain and the United States got their start during this period, and in light of French arguments, the question arose as to whether the guillotine might be a less cruel form of capital punishment.[46] Proponents maintained that the criminal died swiftly—a mercy for the subject and spectators, as both experienced less anguish. Moreover, mechanization spared the executioner the stigma traditionally affiliated with his profession.[47] These claims had Atlantic resonance, and guillotine displays like that of Louis XVI's death were a chance for individuals to weigh the benefits and drawbacks of the machine.

Consider the impressions of John DePeyster, a member of the New York elite, who saw a guillotine at the Tammany Society's museum in 1794. He wrote to his brother-in-law, Charles Willson Peale, that the guillotine had "a figure on it, of a Man who has his head Severed from his Body,—Verry Natural—but the most frightfull-awfull sight that can be Imagined."[48] His revulsion stemmed less from the act of execution and more from the method: "I . . . Coencide in opinion with every Man, who condem's the publick Exhibition of such a Machien in a Country where it is hoped it will never be put in Use,—Especially when it has a Corpse on it, in the Attitude and appearance of Reallity."[49] The mere sight of the guillotine at work, even in a wax simulation, endorsed violence by the same means.

In the early 1790s Peale pondered whether he should acquire a guillotine for his museum in Philadelphia, and DePeyster discouraged him in the strongest of terms. A guillotine in a museum was like stopping in "a Summer House" to discover "five or Six hooks to it, to hang Men on by the Neck."[50] Men like DePeyster thought of a museum as a place where people could better themselves by what they encountered there, becoming more virtuous citizens to sustain the U.S. republican experiment.[51] A guillotine in such a setting, DePeyster underscored, transformed a site of uplift into a killing field. The other exhibitions could not temper the guillotine's impact: he claimed that during his visit, it "drove every other Consideration from me."[52]

Other attendees must have thought similarly because the caretaker of the Tammany Society's museum tried to mitigate negative reactions by keeping the guillotine separate from the rest of the exhibitions and by offering to show it with or without the body. The advertisement explained almost apologetically, "When the Machine is seen alone, nothing appears horrible."[53] Yet for some the problem was not the body: it was the machine itself. The replacement of human with mechanical action—one of the merits of the guillotine—heightened anxiety.[54] Early modern capital punishment relied on lengthy spectacle as a clear demonstration of state power. The scaffold was the stage for a drama that took time to perform, including speeches, appeals, and other rituals.[55] While dreadful, this prolonged practice was essential for crowd catharsis, a sense of justice achieved. With the guillotine, the pace of the executions accelerated exponentially. In the case of Louis XVI, the London Magazine reported, "the short length of time in which he appeared on the scaffold, and the interval of the fatal blow, was no more than two minutes."[56] The deadly speed, accuracy, and durability of the guillotine promoted repetition. While far fewer individuals died by guillotine than in the French revolutionary wars, the numbers of people killed at a single public execution shocked some commentators. At early modern hangings, one or two victims was standard, but guillotine executions could feature well over a dozen people. An English observer, Mary Russell, remarked with horror that sixteen men were decapitated in thirteen minutes.[57] Critics claimed that such tempo and volume numbed onlookers: "The Parisians have been too long familiarized to the sight of blood, to be affected by seeing it stream from *only* twenty-one bodies at a time!"[58] The machine's bloodlust seemed insatiable, as did that of the crowds at the executions, and some wondered if the killings would ever stop.

The guillotine's association with Louis XVI's execution and with the Terror more generally discouraged penal reformers outside of France from adopting it. Without doubt, graphic wax displays also convinced elite men like DePeyster, Cobbett, and Lane to reproach the revolution that embraced it. Some may have reached the same conclusions without ever seeing the wax tableaux, but the exhibitions, more than newspaper accounts or engravings, brought mixed and wider audiences closer to the experience of Louis XVI's execution. In the process, they opened a Pandora's box of reactions as visitors laughed or cried, were curious or revolted. These emotional and physical responses to the guillotine introduced greater uncertainty into Atlantic observers' views on the revolution that had produced such a spectacle in the first place, questioning whether the means compromised the legitimacy of the ends.

THE BEAUTIFUL ASSASSIN

Some of the same factors were at work in the wax tableau depicting the assassination of Jean-Paul Marat by Charlotte Corday. In contrast to Louis XVI, Corday captured public interest from a position of obscurity, but her case became the first in a series of high-profile trials, and subsequent executions, of eminent women with assorted political affiliations. The year 1793 brought the guillotining of Olympe de Gouges, Madame Roland, Madame du Barry, and Marie-Antoinette, among others. These deaths were reported in the U.S. and British press; however, only Corday's example was transformed into a wax display in North America. At first glance, the choice of Corday over, for example, Marie-Antoinette, is surprising. Marie-Antoinette was a queen, and so the elements that made her husband's death noteworthy applied to her as well. But from the perspective of wax sculptors, the similarities were a drawback: Marie-Antoinette's execution lacked novelty, whereas Corday's had it in spades. She was a prime candidate for a wax figure because she murdered Jean-Paul Marat. The displays staged the assassination, and since Corday was an agent rather than a victim of violence, these exhibitions brought to the fore the provocative question of women's involvement in revolutionary violence. Women wearing cockades sparked similar concerns, but with Corday, the episode and its profound effect on the French Revolution brought out new aspects in the debate over the scope of women's political participation.

The standard account of Marat's assassination goes something like this: in early July 1793, Corday, a twenty-four-year-old woman from Caen, traveled to Paris with the goal of killing the man whom she blamed for what she saw as the French Revolution's errant path. Marat was a vocal mouthpiece for the rising tide of radical sentiment; self-styled as "the friend of the people," he published a newspaper of the same name in which he denounced those whom he felt had betrayed the revolution. As a deputy in the National Convention, Marat had the power to convert words into action, and under his influence scores of his political enemies were imprisoned or, if lucky, fled. Corday intended to kill Marat at the national festivities on July 14, but on reaching Paris, she learned that illness confined him to his apartment. On July 13, Corday visited his building twice and was denied entry. Undeterred, she sent a note to Marat stating that she had information worth his time. Falling for the ploy, Marat agreed to see Corday, whom he received while soaking in a rented bathtub to relieve a skin condition. She pulled out a knife she had purchased earlier and stabbed him in the chest. He died almost instantly, and Corday was seized by neighbors, arrested by officials, and taken to prison. She stood trial on July 17 and was beheaded the same day.[59]

The murder and trial captivated publics at home and abroad, and French officials attempted to make Marat the focal point. Marat's funeral, orchestrated by the artist Jacques-Louis David, was an elaborate affair that venerated him as a republican martyr. But for all the pomp and ceremony surrounding Marat in Paris, Corday upstaged him outside of France. Audiences were intrigued by this heretofore unknown woman, and newspapers throughout the Atlantic world rehearsed whatever details they could learn about her story.[60]

Visual representations highlighted the assassination scene, and wax artists followed suit. In the United States, renditions of "the unparalleled

Figure 7.4. Isaac Cruikshank, *A Second Jean d'Arc or the Assassination of MARAT by Charlotte Cordé of Caen in Normandy on Sunday, July 14, 1793* (London: S. W. Fores, July 26, 1793). Published shortly after the assassination, Cruikshank's print forgoes the bathtub but emphasizes the spilling of blood and Corday's respectability through her attire and pose. (Courtesy of The Lewis Walpole Library, Yale University.)

murder of Marat, by Miss Cordie, in France" soon appeared.[61] At Bowen's Museum in Boston, she was depicted "holding the bloody Dagger over the dead Body of MARAT." According to accounts, Corday's single blow had gone straight to the heart, unleashing torrents of blood, so for wax artists the opportunity for reproducing gore was obvious (figure 7.4). Advertisements suggest that sculptors indulged in this vein: the assassination was "placed in a separate Apartment, and may be viewed or not, at the pleasure of the Company."[62] As with the guillotine, squeamish visitors could avoid the garish scene, while those who braved it could luxuriate in the lurid representation.

Wax re-creations of Corday relied on the same dynamics that were at work in representations of Louis XVI: hyperrealism, the spectator's ability to linger, and the relationship between pleasure and horror. But in this instance a woman stood at the center of action, one who transgressed gendered expectations by perpetrating a violent political crime. On one level, Corday offered yet another example for the lively trade in crime fiction and "true crime" stories that had an eager readership in the eighteenth-century Anglophone world. Of these narratives, those of a "female Offender," one period commentator declared, "excites our curiosity more than a male."[63] Female killers could be cast sympathetically. At their most radical, authors critiqued patriarchy and its social, economic, and legal supremacy that left women with few options.[64]

In general, however, accounts of female murderers were cautionary tales, warning readers to safeguard their virtue through vigilant conduct. During the age of revolutions, republicanism became a component of the definition of that virtue, at least for some. Although war and lawmaking were ostensibly a man's business, the rhetoric of revolution opened up possibilities for women to act. In France the vocal— and on occasion very physical—participation of white women was initially commended, but around the time of Marat's assassination some revolutionaries worked to rein in women's political activity and sequester their contributions to the home. These efforts were never entirely successful, and the regime's rhetoric became increasingly shrill, as evidenced by the harsh denunciations of renowned women.[65] Officials subjected Corday to damning accusations, yet these stubbornly refused to stick—in large part because of the way she managed the aftermath of her crime.

The influence of gender in interpretations of Marat's assassination is apparent in U.S. wax displays. Despite the universal condemnation of murder and attempts by some republicans to check women's political engagement, exhibition promoters described Corday as "beautiful" and "tragical." The juxtaposition of these adjectives with the vivid reconstruction of the assassination scene created a cognitive tension between the sympathetic protagonist and her heinous deed. It is worth examining each term closely to see how it shaped audiences' understandings of this instance of revolutionary violence. First, Corday the "beautiful." While Louis XVI's face was recognizable internationally long before his execution, Corday's was not, and she sought to change that by requesting, from prison, that an artist render her portrait. She couched her appeal cleverly: "I would like to leave this token of my memory to my friends. Indeed, just as one cherishes the image of good citizens, curiosity sometimes seeks out those of great criminals, which serves to perpetuate horror at their crimes."[66] Corday played to the regime's desire to stress the "horror" of her act, but the portrait by Jean-Jacques Hauer undercut that "horror" by highlighting her beauty.

Although there was some variation, a few tropes recur frequently enough to indicate how Corday looked—in wax and other media. Most show her as young and slim, with long locks, a serene face, and elegant stature. Madame Tussaud, who claimed that she called on Corday in jail, remembered that she was "tall and finely formed; her countenance had quite a noble expression; she had a beautiful color, and her complexion was remarkably clear; her manners were extremely pleasing, and her deportment particularly graceful."[67] Her clothing accentuated her beauty. On the day of the murder, she wore a stylish but sensible dress, a tall black hat decorated with jaunty green ribbons, a pink scarf, and gloves.[68] In Hauer's prison portrait she wears a different set of clothes—a white bonnet and simple gown, which showed her good taste and modesty. In both scenarios, her attire is suitable for a woman of her background.[69]

Since wax artists adhered as faithfully as possible to written accounts, their reconstructions of the assassination no doubt reproduced these features. Rather than an enraged or deranged murderess, spectators encountered a self-possessed, lovely woman—with knife in hand. For the French revolutionary regime, Corday's beauty was a problem. It stood in stark contrast to Marat's physical deformity: Corday had found him in the bathtub because he sought relief for a chronic skin ailment that compromised his body and health. In an age when outward appearance was thought to manifest one's inner character, Corday's beauty and Marat's disease muddied the waters of culpability.[70] His bodily corruption could be interpreted as an external manifestation of perverted principles, and although she was caught red-handed, her beauty, in contrast to his malady, hinted that perhaps not all was as it seemed.

French authorities tried to counteract this interpretive tendency in two ways: they characterized Corday in negative terms, and they focused public attention on Marat. At a time when marriage was expected for women of Corday's age, officials cast her as an "old maid" to insinuate that she was deviant, and some proposed that she was not a woman at all. Marquis de Sade denounced her as one of "those mixed beings to which one cannot assign a sex, vomited up from Hell to the despair of both sexes."[71] He demanded that "all those who have dared to present her as an enchanting symbol of beauty should be stopped."[72]

But these negative textual descriptions did not translate into an outpouring of unflattering visual portrayals, and so some revolutionaries directed audiences to ignore Corday altogether. After Robespierre visited Curtius's wax tableau of Marat and Corday, he entreated the crowd in line outside to concentrate on Marat, "our departed friend, snatched from us by an assassin's hand, guided by the demon of aristocracy."[73] David, in *The Death of Marat,* painted three months after the assassination, removed Corday completely in an effort, as art historian Helen Weston has contended, to negate her power. He also reinvigorated Marat's body, giving him a manly torso, strong arms, smooth skin, and a saintly aura.[74]

In most portrayals, though, the erasure of Corday was impossible to sustain. It is telling that even Curtius, in the heart of revolutionary Paris, included her in the scene. Marat and Corday were inextricably linked in the public mind, and people wanted to see the woman who had managed this feat. The demand meant that her beauty was replicated in prints and in North American waxworks, introducing seeds of uncertainty into what the French revolutionary regime had hoped to make into a simple morality play.

But beauty alone was not enough to cast her, rather than Marat, as the "tragical" person in the scenario. While the definition of *tragedy* changes over time and by context, the term designates, at its most basic, a sad event that precipitates a feeling of loss. In drama, the tragic mode incites sympathy for the sufferer from the audience, which experiences catharsis at the play's conclusion.[75] The case of Corday and Marat draws on both the event definition (the assassination occurred) and the dramatic one (its reproduction in wax tableaux). Despite all Jacobin propaganda to the contrary, Corday, not Marat, emerged as the object of sympathy for many in the Atlantic world, and this had political repercussions.

Wax displays of Corday and Marat were shaped by her actions in the immediate aftermath of the assassination. Newspapers in Britain and the United States reported extensively on her trial and execution. A few early articles were unfavorable, but they were the exception in the Anglophone press, where her conduct was framed positively. Observers at her trial remarked that she "struck every person with respectful awe, and the idea of her as an assassin was removed from every mind."[76] Corday maintained the same poise before the guillotine: "You would have said, when she was conducted to the scaffold, that she was marching to a nuptial feast; she appeared with a gay air and smile on her lips, and a modest deportment without affectation." Even the executioner was "profoundly penetrated with grief at the mission he had to fulfill."[77] Details of her decapitation were fodder for myths: when the executioner showed her head to the crowd, he allegedly slapped her face. Onlookers recoiled from the disrespectful treatment, which also "restored to her cheeks their former animated glow," an effect reminiscent of tales of saints and martyrs. Although people cried, "Vive la république!" some accounts concluded that "the spectators dispersed less impressed with the recollection of her crime, than of her courage and beauty."[78] Corday could not have performed better had she been following a script. Her actions were beyond reproach—so much so that they hinted that the assassination was justified, too. Thanks to her impeccable death, Corday instigated debate about whether her murder of Marat was truly criminal.

In the United States, Corday's conduct struck a chord, and she was held up as an exemplar, albeit an imperfect one. A 1798 "sketch" of Corday began with a preface pointing out that "even though she stopped the impious breath of the diabolical Marat, [she] cannot be praised for her deed. Let us look only at the brighter parts of her picture, and draw a veil over the images of terror and blood." The article speaks effusively of Corday, revisiting reports of her fortitude and calm. It closes with a reflection on the assassination, declaring it wrong but insisting that Corday's act was "the least culpable and most disinterested instance that can be imagined; and the whole behaviour of Marie Charlotte Corde exhibits a benevolence of intention and heroic firmness of mind, that perhaps has never been surpassed by woman or by man."[79] This was not exactly a scathing condemnation.

Elsewhere the praise was even less qualified. In 1796 a "party of Ladies" in Newburyport, Massachusetts, marked President Washington's birthday by raising "a few glasses" to give five "truly sentimental and highly republican toasts." The first two were for Washington and his wife, and the fifth had religious overtones. However, the third and the fourth reveal the power of Corday's example. The third appealed to "the fair patriots of America" who shall "never fail to assert their

Independence which nature equally dispenses," while the fourth was for Charlotte Corday, with the hope that "each Columbian daughter, like her, be ready to sacrifice their life to liberty."[80] The toasts celebrate women's capacity for "independence" and cite Corday as a model for acting on that independence. Such sentiment is easy to express when the threat is distant; after all, they were not in France. Nevertheless, there was a radicalism in the appropriation of Corday as a model because it demanded exceptional public action.

In light of these admiring stories about Corday's execution, the promotional language of "tragical" for the wax displays predisposed viewers to sympathize with the assassin rather than the victim. In so doing, wax displays critiqued the Jacobin government of the French Revolution. But there was another way to read the "tragic" nature of Corday's story, one that neutralized Corday as a political actor: France did not witness the immediate peace that she intended Marat's death to inaugurate. Convinced that France was awash in counterrevolutionary conspiracies, the Jacobins pursued their enemies with ferocity, using the memory of Marat as one justification for their efforts. As a few reports pointed out, Marat's assassination was disastrous for the so-called Girondins, the group of politicians Corday had supported. Unlike Corday, "the leaders of the Girondists" (all men) knew better than to let "their passions so far . . . blind their judgments, as to encourage a murder that must excite odium against themselves and strengthen the hands of their opponents."[81] This appraisal rested on long-standing notions about how women fell prey to their emotions, resulting in poor decisions, and perhaps for some spectators at U.S. wax exhibitions, this explanation tempered the radical nature of Corday's act. From this perspective, wax displays of the assassination implied that if Corday, for all her virtue, beauty, and strength, fell short in her daring venture into public politics, then it was impossible for other women to achieve better through similar means. For some, Corday was the ultimate cautionary tale, showing how awful the consequences could be if women in the Atlantic world engaged in politics and political violence.

Representations of Corday had more staying power than those of Louis XVI. Depictions of the assassination of Marat continued well into the 1800s, while those of Louis XVI and the guillotine stopped in the late 1790s. The persistence of Corday can be explained by the variety of readings that the assassination sustained: it was an inspiration and a warning, it was titillating and lamentable, it was transgressive and reassuring. Perhaps more any other figure, Corday encapsulated the unexpected dynamics of revolutionary violence in the Atlantic world and how its means constantly tested and reinforced the boundaries of transformation.

THE AMERICAN "MOOR"?

If Louis XVI and Charlotte Corday demonstrate the graphic extent to which violence could be represented, an example from the Haitian Revolution signals some important limitations. In 1803 two enterprising American wax artists, Davenport and Bishop, took their show on the road, and the exhibition included several revolutionary personages and scenes that were at this point standard: Washington, Adams, Jefferson, Bonaparte, and the assassination of Marat, among others. Also listed was "the black general TOUSSAINT, late governor of St. Domingo, taken from an original painting."[82] This show is the only one in the United States with a sculpture of Toussaint Louverture, and tracking its route illustrates how makers and audiences avoided even attempting to delegitimize the violence affiliated with the Haitian Revolution through this medium. In the Louis XVI and Corday tableaux, hyperrealism undermined observers' impressions of the Jacobin phase of the French Revolution, but in the case of the Haitian Revolution, it had the potential to lend renditions of its revolutionaries tremendous power, especially in a slave society.

Davenport and Bishop opened their exhibition in February 1803, and significantly, their itinerary over the next year encompassed "free" and slave states. Starting in Elizabethtown, New Jersey, they moved on to Carlisle, Pennsylvania, and by June they stopped in Baltimore. Sometime over the summer the partnership between the two men ended, but Davenport joined forces with a new business associate, Mr. Street (the brother-in-law and former partner of Reuben Moulthrop), and the same show, with a few additions, was staged in Providence, Rhode Island, in September.[83] Of these states, Pennsylvania had passed gradual emancipation legislation in 1780, and New Jersey would do so in 1804. While a gradual manumission law went into effect in Rhode Island in 1784, Providence merchants had been active in the transatlantic slave trade for generations, and as for Maryland, there were few signs of slavery abating any time soon. The show's circuit meant that slaveholders, abolitionists, and some free and enslaved Black people had opportunities to see the sculpture.

Mention of Louverture appeared in advertisements for each city and always in the same concise phrasing, indicating that residents already knew of him. Other sculptures, even white ones, were identified at greater length: for instance, there was "the late Gen. Butler, who fell in St Clair's defeat, represented as wounded in his leg and breast, and the Indians rushing on him with their tomahawks."[84] The brevity of Toussaint Louverture's introduction reflects, in part, the timing of the show. Through extensive newspaper coverage that year, audiences learned that Louverture languished in an isolated prison near the Swiss border, and as early as January 1803, reports from London, reprinted in April, claimed that he had died.[85] The rumor was premature, but by the time it reached the United States, it was true. Louverture had met his end in April 1803.

At this moment and as with Louis XVI and Corday, Louverture's figure was a type of effigy, a likeness of a man who had just died, which was a traditional use of this art form. What stands out about Louverture, though, then and now, is that he was a man of African descent, and while Black figures were not the majority of wax sculptures, they turned up regularly in late eighteenth-century displays. In 1772 Wells's interpretation of the return of the prodigal son incorporated two Black servants "inwaiting." In the 1790s and early 1800s, museumgoers could see "Domestic Discipline" (a depiction of an old woman whipping an enslaved girl) as well as "Mungo, disciplined by his Master" and "Cuffee, in high life."[86] In 1803 the Columbian Museum in Boston presented a scene from Shakespeare's *Othello* with the title character and his wife.[87]

These representations of Black people were mainly disparaging. Mungo was a character in the eighteenth-century British play *The Padlock,* in which a pair of white lovers employ the West Indian house slave as their go-between. Subsequent authors picked up on the typecasting, and Mungo became a shorthand to refer to any enslaved man handling his master's surreptitious affairs.[88] Cuffee also surfaced in lampooning caricatures, where the joke was the contradiction between a name that denoted enslaved or recently free status and the pretension to the "high life" (figure 7.5).[89] For most white American onlookers the

Figure 7.5. *"Cuffey Near Him" . . . "Grasps His Hand!"* from *The Echo, with Other Poems* (New York, 1807). (Library of Congress, LC-USZ62-78129.)

effect of these portrayals in wax displays was comic and reassuring, especially to those who feared the social and political consequences of gradual emancipation in the northern states. Although not the intended audience, some free and enslaved Black people attended museums, too, either of their own accord or by accompanying masters and mistresses.[90] For them such wax tableaux were yet another reminder of the violence and degradation they encountered at the hands of white people and how it could be construed as "entertainment."

Of these other Black wax sculptures, the character Othello is the closest parallel to Louverture. Both men were generals in racist worlds, but the waxwork of Othello from 1803 is complicated by the context of the Haitian Revolution. Hyperbolic accounts of Black men murdering white women in Saint-Domingue were rampant, and the scene from *Othello* in the Columbian Museum plays on this trope. The artist chose to represent the moment when Othello ponders killing his wife. In the play he smothers Desdemona, but in the wax tableau, he hovers above her with a knife. A similar reinterpretation took place in Britain around the same time—not in wax but in a series of paintings and then prints commissioned by John and Josiah Boydell (figure 7.6). Displayed in their Pall Mall gallery, the works portrayed

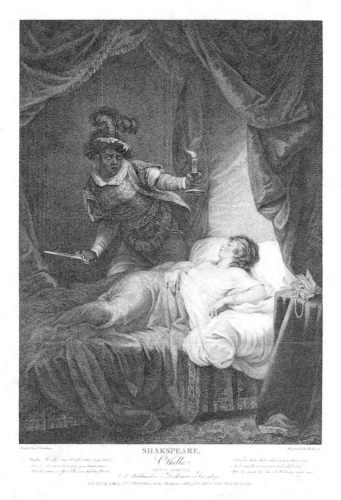

Figure 7.6. *Othello, Act V, Scene II, a Bedchamber, Desdemona in Bed, Asleep,* from *A Collection of Prints, from Pictures Painted for the Purpose of Illustrating the Dramatic Works of Shakespeare, by the Artists of Great-Britain* (London: John & Josiah Boydell, 1803). (S52801 no 93. Used by permission of the Folger Shakespeare Library.)

vital scenes from Shakespeare's plays, and for *Othello* there were two versions of the famous murder. In both he carries a dagger.[91] Perhaps the American sculptor was familiar with the Boydell prints; regardless, in Britain and in the United States, new renditions of Othello's killing of Desdemona were reminiscent of stories and prints of rebel slaves armed with cutlasses from the cane fields exacting revenge on white people.[92]

Some features of the advertisement suggest that Davenport and Bishop's Louverture sculpture avoided the more obvious racist tropes employed with these other figures. First, they declared that their representation was based on a painting. There were a few disparaging portrayals of Louverture in French propaganda for the Leclerc campaign, but in general Anglophone visual culture avoided denigrating portrayals. Next, Davenport and Bishop described him as a "general" and "governor" of Saint-Domingue. These terms might have been deployed sarcastically, along the lines of the stock character of Cuffee. Certainly, the notice flags Louverture's race: he is the "black general"; he is called only by his first name (like many enslaved and freed men); and he is not listed with the canon of other revolutionaries. Instead, he is lower down in the lineup, wedged between the "Salem Beauty" and "the Road to Ruin."

And yet Toussaint Louverture had been a legitimate general and governor, and Americans knew it. Throughout the 1790s they had followed news from the island, and toward the end of the decade, the United States had become increasingly implicated in affairs there. In the late 1790s John Adams had negotiated a trade agreement with Louverture, and the United States had been complicit in the governor-general's move to oust Rigaud and to consolidate control over the colony. Some congressional representatives had argued that a treaty with Louverture was the best defense against the spread of war from Saint-Domingue to the United States. Even those who balked at this line of reasoning, like Thomas Jefferson, were appalled by the enormous size of the Leclerc expedition, fearing that North America was next on Bonaparte's list of New World reconquests. During the final phase of the Haitian Revolution, when the formerly enslaved were fighting for independence, Jefferson turned a blind eye as U.S. merchants continued to trade with Black forces, thereby helping to undermine Leclerc's mission.[93] Most coverage of these developments appeared in newspapers, and yet Black Americans were as aware of them as white residents. They kept apprised of events from accounts read aloud or discussed from these same newspapers and from stories shared by Black sailors and refugees from the colony.[94]

There is a final significant aspect of Davenport and Bishop's Toussaint Louverture wax sculpture that implies it differed from other Black wax figures: the absence of violence. As the tableaux of Louis XVI's execution and Marat's assassination demonstrate, artists relished gory realism, and the Haitian Revolution seems primed for maximum effect in this regard. The very selection of Toussaint Louverture (versus other individuals or scenes from the revolution) denotes an effort to sidestep the issue of violence in Saint-Domingue. Unlike Louis XVI and Charlotte Corday, Louverture was not associated in the public mind with one violent act; other Haitian revolutionary leaders became infamous for specific deeds—most notably Dessalines for ordering the mass execution of hundreds of white inhabitants in early 1804.[95] But for all the violence of the revolution under Louverture's leadership, there was not a discrete, well-known episode that the waxwork could re-create.

On the one hand, this unusual sculpture of Louverture points to a halting recognition of the Haitian Revolution and the authority of one of its leaders. In a similar manner to print portraits, the timing of the exhibition (after his death) diffused some of the more radical overtones of the representation. On the other hand, the choice of Louverture posits that the Haitian Revolution, with its violence initiated by Black people to achieve freedom and rights, could not be represented in this medium—at least for white audiences. A wax rendition of that violence, with its power of mimicry, might make the self-determination of Black men and women all too real in a society still rife with slavery and racism.

What's more, the short life of the sculpture reveals that even this nonviolent portrayal proved too much for white viewers to bear. By early 1804 Davenport and Street had parted ways, and Street continued with the exhibition, now under the auspices of N. and E. Street. The two Streets (presumably relatives) set up shop in New York City, where they stayed for several months. While the collection expanded to about seventy or eighty sculptures, many were holdovers from the 1803 show. Toussaint Louverture is conspicuously absent, and near his former place in the lineup is an addition: "a scene from Shakespear's tragedy of Othello."[96] The change denotes a substitution; the artists transformed the wax figure of Louverture into Othello and placed him in a tragic "scene." Although which one is unclear, the switch signals that it was safer to stage a tableau from *Othello,* using the cultural authority of Shakespeare to justify the three-dimensional, life-size portrayal of a militant Black man, than to show Toussaint Louverture, the revolutionary general and contemporary.

It is perhaps no coincidence that the alteration came in 1804, when Haiti declared its independence. Louverture had met his end already, but his prediction that the campaign for liberty in Saint-Domingue would triumph without him had been borne out under Dessalines, Christophe, and others. While Charlotte Corday's representation pointed to, in at least one reading, the tragedy of her failure, Louverture's indicated success that, importantly, was achieved by people of African descent taking up arms. The implication was that other Black people, including Black Americans, had the ability to do the same. Even though violence was not explicit, Louverture the wax figure was too terrible of an amusement for white Americans.

For Black visitors to Davenport and Bishop's initial show, the wax rendition of Louverture must have been arresting and inspiring. It was rare for a man of African descent to be depicted with some degree of dignity in public sculpture. One wonders how openly they could stand before the Louverture figure or express their reactions to it, given the majority of white museumgoers in their midst. For those who saw the Streets' version the following year, the substitution of Othello for Louverture was perhaps a disappointment, and yet Othello, like Louverture and the other leaders of the Haitian Revolution, was still a strong, resolute Black man, fighting a world pitted against him.

SCALES OF VIOLENCE

Wax representations of distinct episodes of violence provoked debates about the means of achieving revolutionary aims and the ways those means challenged social, gender, and racial hierarchies. More so than written accounts or prints, this genre translated the news into the now by creating violent experiences that provoked emotional, physical, and intellectual reactions among audiences. Their confrontational three-dimensionality was instrumental to this effect, but another type of terrible amusement—miniature bone guillotines—suggests a different mode in the late eighteenth century for exploring these same issues. In the process, they provide a useful counterpoint to the stories of revolutionary violence encouraged by life-size wax figures by drawing our attention to the importance of scale and setting.

Constructed from animal bone by French soldiers and sailors imprisoned in Britain during the 1790s and early 1800s, the miniature

Figure 7.7. Toy guillotine, 1796–
1816. (© Victoria and Albert
Museum, London.)

guillotines proved, like wax figures, popular items among consumers
(figure 7.7). Extant examples usually measure no taller than two feet,
with some not even a foot high, and each has an operational guillotine,
complete with blade, victim (with a detachable head), executioner, a set
of stairs leading up to the platform, and soldiers on guard. The more
elaborate models include two or three tiers and are decorated with
turned railings, pierced galleries, and ornamental finials. Some bear
evidence of polychrome painting. Unlike the wax sculptures in exhibition halls, miniature guillotines ended up in people's homes. Their
ultimate destination raises the question, What made these miniature
guillotines—crafted from bone by enemies—desirable items in British
parlors? The answer lies, as is hopefully predictable by now, in the
qualities of these revolutionary things.

Throughout the eighteenth century, French prisoners were common sights in Britain and vice versa. During their numerous wars, both nations housed captives while waiting to broker prisoner exchanges. Prior to the Napoleonic era, these swaps were frequent, and so internment was relatively short. Before release, officers enjoyed the privilege of parole; they lived among locals in designated towns, which eased the pressure for space in prisons. But at the end of the century, this system broke down. The rate of prisoner exchange slowed considerably because of changing French attitudes toward war that dispensed with ancien régime procedures.[97]

The British, as a matter of principle or obstinacy, continued to operate under eighteenth-century rules, and as a result, around two hundred thousand French soldiers, including some Black men from the West Indies, ended up in Britain at some point during the revolutionary and Napoleonic wars.[98] Facilities for POWs, called depots, had been used in previous conflicts, but their capacity fell short of demand. New accommodations were constructed, and soon every major port—London, Liverpool, Bristol, Portsmouth—had one depot and sometimes more. But workers could not build facilities fast enough, and some POWs were stuck on unseaworthy ships known as hulks: makeshift and by all accounts hellish floating jails. As of 1806 there were twenty hulks in operation, and the total grew to fifty-one by the end of the Napoleonic wars.[99]

These accommodations made economic sense on the home front, as depots emerged as hubs of market activity. Resident tradespeople, shopkeepers, and farmers experienced a surge in customers for their goods and services, since the Transport Office (the government branch in charge of running the depots and hulks) contracted suppliers in the vicinity of each prison to feed and clothe inmates.[100] Prisoners found opportunities at these markets as well. According to the terms of their confinement, inmates could sell handmade goods. Authorities believed this concession dissipated acrimony among the prisoners. If detainees earned money to buy products that eased their detention, then they would be less likely to riot. This calculation involved some risk in that prison markets fostered fraternization between inmates and city inhabitants. To minimize disruptions, authorities controlled the prison market as much as possible, regulating its days and times, spatial organization, and points of entry.[101]

Officials were also concerned about what prisoners fabricated and sold. Certain types of wares were banned—straw work and pornographic objects—because, in the case of the former, they competed with local industry, and in the latter, they allegedly imperiled residents' morals. Officials raided and destroyed caches of banned objects from prison workshops, yet plenty still reached the marketplace, thanks to demand.[102] As one British agent complained in 1797, Portsmouth inhabitants feigned going to church and sneaked over to the nearby Portchester prison market "to buy straw hats and other forbidden articles manufactured by the prisoners."[103] National loyalties and religious obligations went only so far, it seemed, when consumers thought they could get a bargain.

Prison markets traded in novelty as well as deals, and prisoners offered sundry ingenious wares despite straitened circumstances. In most instances, they were not provided with raw material and tools needed to produce goods so they had to make do with what was available, an all too frequent circumstance for soldiers and sailors. Although short on supplies, detainees did have a lot of time to collect viable material and to transform it into something saleable.[104] As for the animal bone in miniature guillotines, it was readily available and familiar to prisoners. Inmates received a daily ration of beef or mutton from which the bones could be salvaged, and repurposing bone was common in the eighteenth century.[105] Sailors and soldiers whittled bones into powder horns as well as decorative and handy items like swifts (for winding yarn), busks (strips tucked into the front of corsets), and pipes—a genre of things known collectively today as scrimshaw; and they employed bone char (a by-product of bone carbonization) to maintain leather equipment. Bone turned up in civilian life, too: sections of baleen (hornlike plates from the mouths of baleen whales) gave ladies' corsets their stiff shape; bone bobbins were tools in the production of a fine lace called bone lace; and bone was wrought for buttons, knobs, handles, and ornaments of all kinds.[106]

Given the ubiquity of bone wares and the accessibility of bone, French POWs' use of this material was sensible. It did require extensive preparation, however: the bones were first cleaned by boiling, which had the benefit of generating glue. Then the bones were scraped, dried, and smoothed. Less adept inmates broke down the processed bone into different sizes so that deft turners and carvers could model the pieces.

Both processes demanded some skill, as detainees looked to minimize waste in order to maximize profits. After figuring and polishing, the pieces were bleached, most likely with sulfur (a disinfectant in prisons), to achieve an ivory-like whiteness, and finally, if possible and desirable, the works were painted.[107]

Finished bone products ranged from the simple—apple corers, snuff spoons, and pipe tampers—to the impressive: mirror frames, watch stands, model ships, and guillotines. POWs chose these items with British consumers in mind.[108] Compared to the typical artisan or shopkeeper, these men felt an urgency to sell their wares; sales translated into immediate benefit for their daily existence. One visitor to Norman Cross Depot (near Peterborough in Cambridgeshire) had been assured that bone work "put many pounds into the pockets of several" of the most skilled prisoners.[109] Although the smaller pieces were inexpensive, the more ambitious bone work, such as guillotines, had a more select clientele as the labor involved drove up the price. The number and range of surviving items in museum collections indicate that there was a healthy market for both tiers of wares.

In a sense the guillotines were the most distinctly French of the bone work wares, showcasing an instrument adopted only in the French empire—and dramatically so. As the guillotine was a potent symbol of the French Revolution, both prisoners and their British buyers might see it as a reminder of why Britain and France were at war, a rallying cry to patriotism that worked for both camps. But the scale and function of the guillotines introduce other meanings.[110] Bone work guillotines were toys in the eighteenth-century sense in that they were intended to amuse adults as much as children. Toys were didactic, demonstrating how something, normally an innovation like a guillotine, worked. Yet they also promoted narrative, opening up an imaginary world in which the player dictates the plot.[111] With guillotines, the inclusion of characters—the sentries standing guard in addition to the victim and the executioner—alluded to spectacle and prompted the spinning out of a story. Unlike the wax renditions of Louis XVI's death, which strove for an exact re-creation of the event, the toy guillotines allowed the owner to invent the tale, one that could differ from reports and official records. The miniature guillotines afforded owners a chance to reenact this form of violence from the French Revolution to suit their whims— a prospect that perhaps explains why bone work guillotines had an eager British market.

Consumers' reflections on their miniature guillotines are hard to come by, but the experiences of Elizabeth and Eugenia Wynne, the second and third daughters of an elite Englishman, shed some light. Living in Italy in the 1790s, the family socialized with French exiles, and in their diaries, the teenage girls remarked on violent episodes from the revolution. They expressed relief when they heard rumors of the royal family's escape, and then dismay at the executions of the "unfortunate" king and queen. In 1796 Elizabeth, known as Betsy, dined with the king's former valet, who recounted scaffold scenes in detail: how Louis XVI's neck "being so fat his head did not fall at the first stroke and he was heard [to] scream," while Marie-Antoinette was "quite a skeleton" so that "all her members trembled." But from the sisters' point of view, the guillotine could have its benefits. They rejoiced when they learned of "the monster" Robespierre's demise, noting that his death "will at least diminish the great number of persons that were *guillotiné* at Paris[,] that was about 50 every day of all ages."[112]

In Naples Betsy met and fell in love with a British naval officer, Captain Thomas Fremantle. They married, and she accompanied her husband on ship, witnessing several skirmishes in the Mediterranean. Eventually the couple disembarked in Portsmouth so that the captain could recover from an injury sustained at sea. One day in 1797, Betsy and her husband visited the prisoners' market at nearby Portchester Castle, where the inmates "are very industrious and make all kind of little works. We bought a Guillotine neatly done in bone."[113] Just a year before, she had shivered at the horrific stories of death by guillotine, but now she had purchased a model one for her home. The miniature guillotine referenced the recent past and gave Betsy—and others—some control over that past. Its scale curbed its violent associations to such an extent that it could decorate her parlor. If only, a few years later, she had gone to Madame Tussaud's exhibition, too.

In the United States and Britain terrible amusements enabled experiences with Francophone revolutionary violence in everyday life. These things focused on the Terror and Black-on-white violence—selections that, while new to eighteenth-century observers, did not reflect accurately the scope, agents, and victims of this violence. From the outset, makers' choices had a reductive impact as they sought to find the most eye-catching subjects to attract people through their doors. When consumers interacted with these objects, they contended with violence physically, and these sensations were different from encounters with print culture and from the actual moments that these objects represented. The materials, conventions, and makers' aesthetic, economic, and ideological judgments shaped how these episodes were rendered and received. During DePeyster's visit the full-size guillotine's terror ran rampant, while in Betsy Fremantle's parlor miniaturization tamed it. Both results, in their own ways, cast doubt on these forms of violence and the revolutions that embraced them. But such conclusions were not a given. These objects yielded a range of responses and informed the processing of violence in ways that were experiential and experimental, as Atlantic observers lived the revolutions in real time and space.

More broadly, wax displays brought together and leveraged the political power of many of the things explored in this book. In staging their tableaux, artists drew on print portraits to capture the visages of famous revolutionary-era figures, and they traded on viewers' knowledge of those prints to promote the accuracy of their renditions. They translated visual and written depictions of attire into actual clothing and accessories, and in so doing took advantage of spectators' understandings of garments and their meanings. It is not hard to imagine, for example, the Louverture wax figure wearing a military uniform, complete with cockade. Some wax artists incorporated props, like guillotines, in their vivid re-creations, and perhaps Marat's murder scene included furniture, decorative wares, or even a map tacked on the wall to signal its domestic setting. While their precise content remains elusive, the waxworks allow us to contemplate how revolutionary things operated across genres to produce multifaceted experiences and interpretations of landmark ideas, events, and people of the age.

Conclusion
What Remains

IN THE CENTRAL passage of George Washington's house at Mount Vernon hangs the main key to the Bastille, the infamous French prison stormed by the people of Paris in July 1789. Set behind glass in a gilt-wood case, the large iron key has decorated the hall since Washington's retirement from public life in 1797. Before then it graced his two presidential residences, the first in New York City and the second in Philadelphia. In fact, from the moment Washington received the key it stayed with him, and since his death in 1799 it is one of only a handful of items that has remained continuously at Mount Vernon from Washington's time to ours.

His acquisition of the Bastille key is the stuff of legend. Washington accepted it as a present from marquis de Lafayette, to whom it was presented right after the fortress fell. A hero of the American Revolution, Lafayette had just been appointed commander in chief of the National Guard, a new citizens' militia whose search for arms had led to the destruction of the prison (and whose uniform Vincent Ogé purchased, wore, and carried with him to Saint-Domingue). Lafayette sent the key along with a drawing of the Bastille to Washington in recognition of their personal and political ties: "It is a tribute Which I owe as A Son to My Adoptive father, as an aid de Camp to My General, as a Missionary of liberty to its patriarch."[1] He entrusted the items to Thomas

Paine, who was in Paris but intended to travel to the United States. Paine got only as far as London, however, when he cancelled his trip, and at the end of May 1790 he placed the "trophies of Liberty" in the care of John Rutledge Jr., a South Carolinian sailing home after touring Europe.[2] The gifts finally arrived in New York in August, and Washington thanked Lafayette for "the token of victory gained by Liberty over Despotism."[3]

For over two centuries, Washington's Bastille key has been displayed as a material witness to the revolutionary era. The fact that it survives when so many things from this tumultuous period did not is remarkable. Its persistence is, to some extent, thanks to its physical characteristics. Metal does not degrade to the same degree as cloth, wood, or paper, and so from the start the key had chances better than other media of lasting beyond its moment. But its survival is as much a product of social and political factors as of material ones. Like many objects that have remained from the age of revolutions, the Bastille key belonged to a wealthy white man. The upper classes had more items, usually of finer quality, and given these conditions, these items endured more often than those of the lower sort. Perpetuation was not just a question of quantity and quality; it stemmed from elite dominance. Their material culture bounty reflected the profits they derived from the subjugation of others, and, in turn, material culture was one way through which they exerted their power and sustained the hierarchies from which they benefited. This dynamic outlasted the revolutionary period even as actors from below used objects to challenge the status quo and as they destroyed many things, like the Bastille, that had abetted their oppression.

This book has employed the millions of things from this era that do not remain—alongside some that do—to understand the political possibilities of material culture for various people in the late eighteenth century. It has argued that things became politicized through acquisition and context, as well as through ornamentation and affiliation, and it has maintained that objects were dynamic contributors to contests over fundamental concepts like equality, popular sovereignty, and legitimacy. In making these assertions, this book has approached the problem of object disappearance through a close examination of materiality and by focusing on types of things that cut across class and race, and that moved across borders. To the first end, each chapter has appraised what was feasible for a given medium: the locations and the scales at which objects were produced and the circuits through which they spread. And it has explored the social practices surrounding and the decisions made during fabrication, distribution, and consumption, all of which affected what was available to whom and on what terms. Second, by analyzing things shared among the American, French, and Haitian revolutions, this book has brought groups underrepresented in extant collections into the central narrative about the impact of material culture in these transnational movements. Their inclusion has expanded the cast of actors and objects and has imparted fresh perspectives on the items that do remain, coaxing new meanings from old things. Taken together, these interventions yield a new materialist history of the age of revolutions, one that shows how material culture was not just illustrative of political debate and action but essential to the content of both.

At its core, this endeavor begins from the assertion that what survives results from circumstance and choice. Certain items do not last because use compromised their integrity: they simply wore out. But other objects were saved, or not, through selection. People determined, within their means, what they wanted to keep, and then worked to preserve those things. For the age of revolutions this process happened in ways that bear the hallmarks of that period but that also continue to resonate in our present. With this in mind, we conclude by considering, briefly, some of the afterlives of revolutionary things—those that do not remain and those that do, to contemplate the power of material culture in political life.

Although many nonelite populations suffer from a proportional lack of representation in museum collections, one of the most glaring absences is that of people of African descent. This disparity is borne out in the stark discrepancy between the amount of surviving objects for the Haitian Revolution and that for U.S. and French counterparts.[4] Far fewer things have endured with a clear provenance to Saint-Domingue, and this situation is one of the consequences of the plantation system, the nature of the war, and the ostracism of Haiti as an independent nation, among other factors. In other words, this erasure is an outcome of the revolutionary period that was, outside of Haiti, produced deliberately by early collectors and cultural institutions until very recently.[5] Entertain this counterfactual: if Toussaint Louverture had sent

Washington a key from one of the many notorious plantations on Saint-Domingue, would it have been exhibited and saved proudly as a "trophy of liberty"?

Today, museums and other organizations are seeking to redress this legacy by combing the artifact market for items with links to the Haitian Revolution and by sponsoring archaeological projects on the island.[6] They also try to highlight revolutionary Saint-Domingue in interpretations of existing collections.[7] While this work is crucial, the enormity of the task of rectifying the structural inequalities in archives and museums demands many approaches. This book has pursued categories of objects that, although the material remains may persist only for the U.S. or French revolutions, the documentary record indicates they were present among Haitian revolutionaries, too. To be sure, during centuries of enslavement and beyond, Black people drew inspiration for political action from objects with African origins such as drums, weapons, amulets, and other items, and these were instrumental to revolutionary campaigns. But they also took advantage of, whenever expedient, things common to American and French revolutionaries.

Racist observers denied this point of material intersection, doubting that people of African descent had the intellectual capacity to appreciate "European" material culture. And yet throughout the period, commentators were continually confronted by Black actors employing the same things for their own political ends. At times white bystanders attempted to disguise Black know-how with ridicule, but their mockery was a form of acknowledgment. Locating these objects now requires a combination of historical and material cultural methods. Assorted archival sources help us begin to find what does not remain, yet records have drawbacks, reflecting what white authors did and did not want to notice about Black men and women. That said, they identify a broader array of objects among people of African descent than surviving material evidence.

The significance of these things lies not just in the fact that Black men and women acquired them. Rather, their importance springs from what that procurement meant for people of African descent and to what purposes these objects were put. These aspects come to light only when we take seriously the materiality of eighteenth-century things. The reclaimed objects in this book varied within a given medium (not all coats were the same) and between media (coats versus cockades).

Historians tend to skate on the surface of these differences, and some view discussions of the nuanced distinctions within genres of material culture—say, between engraving methods or fabric weaves or ceramic bodies—as "antiquarian" affairs. While historians ferret out fine gradations of meaning in texts and even individual words, many fail to bring similar intensity to their analysis of things.

This is a missed opportunity because these differences mattered to actors at the time and influenced the political potential of objects. Only by evaluating the materiality of things in all their eighteenth-century subtlety can we comprehend the depth and breadth of how people knew the material world and harnessed it for their political goals. People of African descent, like their white peers, were aware that military garments had a political capacity distinct from that of Queen's ware and of confiscated furniture, and they deployed the possibilities of each medium as best they could. But there were limits to the power they could exercise on the Atlantic stage via objects, as seen in prints of the Haitian Revolution that were rarely produced in or imported to Saint-Domingue, or in printed maps that ignored Black achievements. An object-centered approach indicates with greater precision what Haitian actors looked to accomplish through this material culture and the extent to which people outside of Haiti were, and were not, willing to make this revolution material and why.

This method of object retrieval keeps the Haitian Revolution in conversation with material culture trends in North America and Europe, and in so doing it reframes what does remain—the caches of revolutionary things in museums and collections today. This approach uncovers novel facets of meaning for these items, and the emphasis on all three revolutions shakes up the contexts in which these objects are normally couched. Most frequently, surviving objects speak to national histories, and this interpretive bent, like the lopsided nature of collections, has its roots in the age of revolutions. One goal of American, French, and Haitian revolutionaries was to create new nations, through independence or transformation, and as part of these projects people turned to material culture to contribute to the invention of national heritages. Revolutionaries hoped that items associated with their movements would become relics, cherished because of their ties to these formative moments, and that they would serve as a mode through which future generations would honor their nation's origins.[8]

This aim led to certain propensities in what kinds of things were saved and the narratives that were told about them, as best documented in the U.S. and French cases. In the United States they became central to national mythologizing. Jefferson mused that the portable desk at which he wrote the Declaration of Independence might be "carried in the procession of our nation's [hundredth] birthday, as the relics of saints are in those of the Church."[9] (Now at the Smithsonian Institution, it is unclear if the desk was ever in a July 4th parade.)[10] While self-congratulatory elites took the lead, the impulse to conserve likely relics pervaded the ranks. Crowd members picked up and stashed pieces of the statue of George III destroyed in New York City and gathered tea that washed ashore after the Boston Tea Party. Families passed down items owned by revolutionary ancestors, eminent and humble, and in the nineteenth century collectors and amateur historians raided graves, battlefields, and attics to discover and then revere objects from this watershed.[11]

In France the making of relics mirrored a more contentious debate over its revolution and the nation it attempted to create. Observers then, and scholars ever since, have emphasized the destruction wrought by French revolutionaries, but the urge to preserve things was there from the outset as well. After the fall of the Bastille, Pierre-François Palloy, the Parisian building contractor in charge of dismantling the prison, repurposed the rubble into "patriotic relics": small renditions of the fortress sculpted from its stones, medallions of metal from the prison, pebbles set in rings, and so forth.[12] But as the revolution evolved in political complexity, relics became more varied. Individuals rescued objects affiliated with every political camp, including the ancien régime. They scoured stalls and stores of bric-a-brac vendors as well as trash heaps and wrecked buildings, salvaging government papers, prints, assignats—and even Marat's bathtub and Corday's skull. Sometimes preservation efforts were politically motivated, in that collectors identified with a side; others were inspired by a sense of public duty to conserve history as it happened.[13]

Whether they slotted easily into budding myths or were incessantly contested, revolutionary relics helped to tell stories about late eighteenth-century endeavors to establish republics. In this manner, these things complemented an outpouring of new nationalist material culture that flourished after the revolutions, especially in freshly minted independent states. Indeed, inhabitants in the Americas demonstrated the worthiness of their countries through material culture. In the United States, emblems of the nation—eagles, stars, and arrows, among other tropes—ornamented foreign- and locally made items, such as buttons, textiles, furniture, and ceramics, while paintings and popular prints acclaimed members of the revolutionary generation.[14] Although fewer relics survived in Haiti, its leaders nurtured a postwar nationalist material culture. When the country divided into north and south in 1806, Henry Christophe and Alexandre Pétion asserted the authority of their respective regimes in part through objects and architecture. Each man built a grand estate and filled it with goods that signaled the prestige of his government and of Haiti generally. Christophe imported from England his carriage, state portrait, and regalia, emblazoned with evocative symbols, and filled the main chamber of his palace with fine French furniture. Pétion stressed links between the French and Haitian revolutions by designing a flag that alluded to a shared past: red and blue stripes with a coat of arms at the center that featured a cannon and pikes around a palm tree topped with a Phrygian cap.[15]

In this vast field of politicized things, early aficionados prized the provenance of revolutionary-era objects, believing that an item owned by a specific person, witness to a remarkable event, or from a noteworthy site joined observers to that individual, moment, or place in an experiential way. Over time the power of relics arose from their ability to conjure intimate ties to an increasingly distant age, and this capacity reinforced bonds to the nation. They also provided evidence for professional and lay historians' accounts of the period. John Fanning Watson, a businessman with a passion for history, published in 1830 *Annals of Philadelphia,* which drew on his collection of souvenirs from revolutionary war battlefields and celebrated the city's role in the American Revolution. In 1867 Jules Champfleury, the director of Sèvres, used his trove of revolutionary faïence as the basis for his narrative of the French Revolution, maintaining that the ceramics offered matchless insights into "patriotic aspirations."[16]

The privileged status of relics persists today. As antiques market trends illustrate, verified provenance to a revolutionary person, place, or episode adds to an object's economic worth. A key from the Bastille or a set of buttons from Toussaint Louverture's coat garners more interest and higher prices than anonymous eighteenth-century examples.

What's more, the preservation efforts of predecessors have shaped some of our most respected repositories. From the Bibliothèque nationale de France and Musée Carnavalet in Paris to the National Archives in Washington, DC, and the new Museum of the American Revolution in Philadelphia, relics form the cores of their revolutionary-era collections, and thereby contribute to the goal of national stewardship.

These narratives about relics and postwar material culture elucidate the formation of the political cultures of individual states. But this book has contended that things from the revolutionary present have other, long overlooked contributions. Interpretations of their national significance reflect the confidence of hindsight, a confidence that late eighteenth-century actors lacked. This book has pursued the present-ness of revolutionary things, when encounters with them were not yet filtered through such histories and when they had not yet become relics. As a result, we see them in the heat of their moment—with all its instability and possibility, confusion and promise. Situating revolutionary things in their present shows how these objects were active in seminal contests of the period. Wherever their place of production, maps, uniforms, and pillaged goods were crucial to warfare, while all the objects examined in the preceding pages—from decorative tableware to wax figures—influenced debates over who enjoyed the rights aspirant republics pledged to secure.

These struggles reverberated in the United States, France, Haiti, and across the wider Atlantic world. All three revolutionary wars were international in scope, and national and inter-imperial clashes over the rights of citizens were informed by and affected Atlantic arguments over to whom republican ideals should apply. In this scenario, the displacement of things, whether intentional or accidental, matters deeply: what things moved where, when, and into whose hands shaped how various people understood what was happening in their world and how they responded to these developments. The transnational distribution of objects occurred before national narratives of revolutions were in place, and consequently they reveal key aspects of these movements as lived experiences for diverse actors, including those sectors that revolutionaries sought to exclude from the nation. Millions of goods participated in these currents, and they introduced opportunities to press for—and to silence—claims in ways that were related to, but distinct from, texts. In their materiality and centrality to daily life, objects afforded individuals across the ranks compelling modes for political expression and action. The process was in constant flux, and in the end the outcomes were mixed. In some instances things assisted in widening revolutionary agendas, and in others they bolstered stubborn hierarchies.

Recovering the materiality, circulation, and political dynamism of objects in their eighteenth-century present gives us a greater appreciation for the power of things among assorted populations then. But it is also instructive for scholars now. While many arguments in this book speak to the specificities of this era and its historiography, its approach aims to build new bridges between material culture specialists and historians. This endeavor is imperative because most people today encounter history through material culture: at museums, landmarks, memorials, and historic sites, and in their virtual incarnations. Unlike classrooms (or, alas, history monographs), these cultural institutions attract people of all ages throughout their lives. Material history is apparent in our quotidian landscapes, too: in the statues erected in parks, the names given to buildings and streets, the wall plaques and roadside markers that designate historic sites.

"Seeing" history affords people the chance to connect with the past viscerally. In so doing, it allows them not just to marvel at what survives but to ponder as well the consequences of what does and does not remain. Historians need to engage more dynamically with objects in our scholarship so that we can take fuller advantage of the materiality of history in our present. By delving deeply into the significance of things in the past, we can generate more thoughtful, collaborative conversations with those making and consuming public history about what these objects mean today and what they could mean in the future. For the uneven legacies of the age of revolutions are still with us. And perhaps by equipping ourselves with a better understanding of what remains, what does not, and why, we can come to terms with the unrealized promises of the period's most admirable ideals of liberty, equality, and solidarity.

Notes

INTRODUCTION

1. John D. Garrigus, "Vincent Ogé 'Jeune' (1757–91): Social Class and Free Colored Mobilization on the Eve of the Haitian Revolution," *Americas* 68, no. 1 (July 2011): 33–62.

2. I am grateful to John Garrigus for generously sharing his transcript of Ogé's testimony. Extrait des minutes du Conseil Supérieur du Cap, 1791, dxxv 58, dossier 574, Archives nationales, Paris.

3. Sarah Knott, "Narrating the Age of Revolution," *William and Mary Quarterly* 73, no. 1 (January 2016): 3–36.

4. Rebecca L. Spang, *Stuff and Money in the Time of the French Revolution* (Cambridge, MA: Harvard University Press, 2015), 18.

5. Many thanks to Michael Kwass for his thoughtful insights into this relationship.

6. Leora Auslander, *Cultural Revolutions: Everyday Life and Politics in Britain, North America, and France* (Berkeley: University of California Press, 2009), 3, 7–8.

7. Tom Stammers, "The Bric-a-Brac of the Old Regime: Collecting and Culture History in Post-revolutionary France," *French History* 22, no. 3 (2008): 309.

8. Quotation from Leora Auslander and Tara Zahra, "The Things They Carried: War, Mobility, and Material Culture," in Auslander and Zahra, eds., *Objects of War: The Material Culture of Conflict and Displacement* (Ithaca: Cornell University Press, 2018), 5; Jane Bennett, *Vibrant Matter: A Political Ecology of Things* (Durham: Duke University Press, 2010); Bruno Latour, *Reassembling the Social: An Introduction to Actor-Network Theory* (New York: Oxford University Press, 2005); Frank Trentmann, "Materiality in the Future of History: Things, Practices, and Politics," *Journal of British Studies* 48 (April 2009): 283–307.

9. Janet Polasky, *Revolutions without Borders: The Call to Liberty in the Atlantic World* (New Haven: Yale University Press, 2015), 3, 5; Alan Taylor, *American Revolutions: A Continental History, 1750–1804* (New York: Norton, 2016), 8.

10. Katherine Carté, *Religion and the American Revolution: An Imperial History* (Chapel Hill: University of North Carolina Press, 2021); Laurent Dubois, "An Enslaved Enlightenment: Rethinking the Intellectual History of the French Atlantic," *Social History* 31, no. 1 (2006): 1–14; Jane Landers, *Atlantic Creoles in an Age of Revolution* (Cambridge, MA: Harvard University Press, 2010); Brendan McConville, *The King's Three Faces: The Rise and Fall of Royal America, 1688–1776* (Chapel Hill: University of North Carolina Press, 2006); Julius S. Scott, *The Common Wind: Afro-American Currents in the Age of the Haitian Revolution* (London: Verso, 2018); John Thornton, "African Soldiers in the Haitian Revolution," *Journal of Caribbean History* 25, nos. 1–2 (1991): 58–80.

11. Karen Kupperman, *The Atlantic in World History* (New York: Oxford University Press, 2012), 122.

12. Arjun Appadurai, ed., *The Social Life of Things: Commodities in Cultural Perspective* (Cambridge: Cambridge University Press, 1986).

13. Wim Klooster, *Revolutions in the Atlantic World* (New York: New York University Press, 2009), 5–7.

14. Latour, 63–86.

15. Bill Brown, "Thing Theory," *Critical Inquiry* 28, no. 1 (Autumn 2001): 1–22; Ian Hodder, *Entangled: An Archaeology of the Relationships between Humans and Things* (Chichester, UK: Wiley-Blackwell, 2012); Trentmann, "Materiality in the Future of History," 289–90.

16. Hodder, 8; Trentmann, "Materiality in the Future of History," 299–300.

17. Bronwen Everill, *Not Made by Slaves: Ethical Capitalism in the Age of Abolition* (Cambridge, MA: Harvard University Press, 2020); Jonathan Eacott, *Selling Empire: India in the Making of Britain and America, 1600–1830* (Chapel Hill: University of North Carolina Press, 2016). On the consumer revolution more generally, see T. H. Breen, *The Marketplace of Revolution: How Consumer Politics Shaped American Independence* (New York: Oxford University Press, 2004); John Brewer and Roy Porter, eds., *Consumption and the World of Goods* (New York: Routledge, 1994); Cary Carson, *Face Value: The Consumer Revolution and the Colonizing of America* (Charlottesville: University of Virginia Press, 2017); Cary Carson, Ronald Hoffman, and Peter J. Albert, eds., *Of Consuming Interests: The Style of Life in the Eighteenth Century* (Charlottesville: University of Virginia Press, 1994); Neil McKendrick, John Brewer, and J. H. Plumb, eds., *The Birth of a Consumer Society: The Commercialization of Eighteenth-Century England* (Bloomington: Indiana University Press, 1982); Daniel Roche, *A History of Everyday Things: The Birth of Consumption in France, 1600–1800* (New York: Cambridge University Press, 2000); Frank Trentmann, *Empire of Things: How We Became a World of Consumers, from the Fifteenth Century to the Twenty-First* (New York: HarperCollins, 2016).

18. Manuel Covo, "Commerce, empire et révolutions dans le monde atlantique: La colonie française de Saint-Domingue entre metropole et États-Unis" (Ph.D. diss., École des Hautes Études en Sciences Sociales, 2013).

19. Ken Alder, *Engineering the Revolution: Arms and Enlightenment in France, 1763–1815* (Princeton: Princeton University Press, 1997), 19; Spang, 4.

20. Trentmann, *Empire of Things*, 1–18.

21. Alder, 18.

22. Order, Vincent Ogé, 20 février 1790, Ventes faites 1 janvier 1790–1 avril 1790, Sèvres Papers, microfilm edition, reel 9, Watson Library, Metropolitan Museum of Art, New York, NY.

23. Dale L. Clifford, "Can the Uniform Make the Citizen? Paris, 1789–1791," *Eighteenth-Century Studies* 34, no. 3 (Spring 2001): 363, 369, 373.

24. Thomas Paine, *Common Sense,* in Michael Foot and Isaac Kramnick eds., *The Thomas Paine Reader* (New York: Penguin Books, 1987), 109.

PART I. WHAT'S OLD IS NEW

1. Laurie Dahlberg, "France between the Revolutions, 1789–1848," in *The Sèvres Porcelain Manufactory: Alexandre Brongniart and the Triumph of Art and Industry, 1800–1847* (New Haven: Yale University Press, 1997), 16; Antoine d'Albis, "Hard-Paste Porcelain Plates from Sèvres with Chinoiserie Decoration in Colored Golds and Platinum," *Metropolitan Museum Journal* 37 (2002): 269; Svend Eriksen and Geoffrey de Bellaigue, *Sèvres Porcelain: Vincennes and Sèvres, 1740–1800* (London: Faber & Faber, 1987), 111, 115, 127, 135; Édouard Garnier, "La manufacture de Sèvres pendant la Révolution," *La nouvelle revue* 71 (July–August 1891): 777–81; Joanna Gwilt, *French Porcelain for English Palaces: Sèvres from the Royal Collection* (London: Royal Collection Enterprises, 2009), 12–13; Marie-Noëlle Pinto de Villechenon, *Sèvres: Porcelain from the Sèvres Museum, 1740 to the Present Day,* trans. John Gilbert (London: Lund Humphries, 1997), 49.

2. Dahlberg, 16.

3. Leora Auslander, *Cultural Revolutions: Everyday Life and Politics in Britain, North America, and France* (Berkeley: University of California Press, 2009); Lynn Hunt, *Politics, Culture, and Class in the French Revolution* (Berkeley: University of California Press, 1984).

4. Eduardo Elena, *Dignifying Argentina: Peronism, Citizenship, and Mass Consumption* (Pittsburgh: University of Pittsburgh Press, 2011); Sheila Fitzpatrick, *Everyday Stalinism: Ordinary Life in Extraordinary Times: Soviet Russia in the 1930s* (New York: Oxford University Press, 1999), 107.

CHAPTER 1. MAKERS AND MARKETS IN REVOLUTIONARY TIMES

1. Classic works on the eighteenth-century consumer revolution include Richard Bushman, *The Refinement of America: Persons, Houses, Cities* (New York: Knopf, 1992); Cary Carson and Ronald Hoffman, *Of Consuming Interests: The Style of Life in the Eighteenth Century* (Charlottesville: University of Virginia Press, 1994); Neil McKendrick, John Brewer, and J. H. Plumb, eds., *The Birth of a Consumer Society: The Commercialization of Eighteenth-Century England* (Bloomington: Indiana University Press, 1982); Daniel Roche, *A History of Everyday Things: The Birth of Consumption in France, 1600–1800* (New York: Cambridge University Press, 2000). On ties between the consumer and political revolutions, see T. H. Breen, *The Marketplace of Revolution: How Consumer Politics Shaped American Independence* (New York: Oxford University Press, 2004); Colin Jones,

"The Great Chain of Buying: Medical Advertisement, the Bourgeois Public Sphere, and the Origins of the French Revolution," *American Historical Review* 101, no. 1 (February 1996): 13–40; Michael Kwass, "Big Hair: A Wig History of Consumption in Eighteenth-Century France," *American Historical Review* 111, no. 3 (June 2006): 631–59; Rebecca Spang, *Stuff and Money in the Time of the French Revolution* (Cambridge, MA: Harvard University Press, 2015).

2. On the various ways that objects could become politicized, see Ken Alder, *Engineering the Revolution: Arms and Enlightenment in France* (Princeton: Princeton University Press, 1997), 18.

3. Breen, chapters 6–8.

4. Ann Smart Martin, *Buying into the World of Goods: Early Consumers in Backcountry Virginia* (Baltimore: Johns Hopkins University Press, 2008).

5. Priya Satia, *Empire of Guns: The Violent Making of the Industrial Revolution* (Stanford: Stanford University Press, 2018).

6. William Hutton, *An History of Birmingham* (1783), n.p., between pp. 57–74 under "Trade," http://www.gutenberg.org/files/13926/13926-h/13926-h.htm.

7. Patricia Halfpenny, "Creamware and the Staffordshire Potteries," in S. Robert Teitelman, Patricia Halfpenny, and Ronald Fuchs III, eds., *Success to America: Creamware for the American Market, Featuring the S. Robert Teitelman Collection at Winterthur* (Woodbridge, UK: Antique Collectors' Club, 2010), 30; Robin Emmerson, "Pottery and the Liverpool Trade," in Teitelman et al., 43, 45.

8. Brian Dolan, *Wedgwood: The First Tycoon* (New York: Viking, 2004), 334; Maxine Berg, *Luxury and Pleasure in Eighteenth-Century Britain* (Oxford: Oxford University Press, 2007), 129.

9. Peter M. Jones, *Industrial Enlightenment: Science, Technology, and Culture in Birmingham and the West Midlands, 1760–1820* (Manchester: Manchester University Press, 2008), 43, 50.

10. Entry for August 15, 1776, in Kenneth Morgan, ed., *An American Quaker in the British Isles: The Travel Journals of Jabez Maud Fisher, 1775–1779* (Oxford: Oxford University Press, 1992), 253.

11. Entry for August 15, 1776, in Morgan, 253.

12. Rita McLean, "Introduction: Matthew Boulton, 1728–1809," in Shena Mason, ed., *Matthew Boulton: Selling What All the World Desires* (New Haven: Yale University Press, 2009), 1–2; Dolan, 6–9.

13. Jenny Uglow, *The Lunar Men: Five Men Whose Curiosity Changed the World* (New York: Farrar, Straus & Giroux, 2002); David Philip Miller, "Was Matthew Boulton a Scientist? Operating between the Abstract and the Entrepreneurial," in Kenneth Quickenden, Sally Baggott, and Malcolm Dick, eds., *Matthew Boulton: Enterprising Industrialist of the Enlightenment* (Farnham, UK: Ashgate, 2013), 57.

14. *New-England Palladium* (Boston), November 12, 1805.

15. Jones, *Industrial Enlightenment*, 11–13, 126.

16. Kenneth Quickenden, "Matthew Boulton's Silver and Sheffield Plate," in Mason, *Matthew Boulton*, 41; Uglow, *Lunar Men*, 53.

17. David Philip Miller, 59.

18. Quoted in Val Loggie, "Picturing Soho: Images of Matthew Boulton's Manufactory," in Mason, *Matthew Boulton*, 23.

19. Entry for August 15, 1776, in Morgan, 253.

20. Jones, *Industrial Enlightenment*, 52; Loggie, 23–25.

21. Sally Baggott, "Hegemony and Hallmarking: Matthew Boulton and the Battle for the Birmingham Assay Office," in Quickenden et al., 147–61.

22. Jones, *Industrial Enlightenment*, 25–26.

23. Josiah Wedgwood to Sir William Meredith, March 2, 1765, in Ann Finer and George Savage, eds., *The Selected Letters of Josiah Wedgwood* (London: Cory, Adams & Mackay, 1965), 29. Hereafter cited as *Selected Letters* and Josiah Wedgwood abbreviated to JW.

24. Jones, *Industrial Enlightenment*, 45–46.

25. Jones, *Industrial Enlightenment*, 228.

26. Hutton, between pp. 57–74 under "Trade."

27. Quoted in Jones, *Industrial Enlightenment*, 99.

28. Peter M. Jones, "'I had L[or]ds and Ladys to wait on yesterday . . .': Visitors to the Soho Manufactory," in Mason, *Matthew Boulton*, 72–73.

29. Shena Mason, *The Hardware Man's Daughter: Matthew Boulton and His "Dear Girl"* (Chichester, UK: Phillimore, 2005), 77–78.

30. JW to Mr. Eden, June 16, 1787, in *Selected Letters*, 304.

31. Jones, *Industrial Enlightenment*, 204–5.

32. JW to Thomas Bentley, November 5, 1774, and January 30, 1775, JW to William Hamilton, June 24, 1786, in *Selected Letters*, 166–67 [Mexico via Cádiz], 172–73 [Turkey], and 295–96 [Italy].

33. JW to Thomas Bentley, before November 21, 1773, in *Selected Letters*, 155.

34. JW to Thomas Bentley, January 30, 1775, in *Selected Letters*, 173.

35. JW to Thomas Bentley, before November 21, 1773, in *Selected Letters*, 154.

36. JW to Thomas Bentley, December 19, 1773, in *Selected Letters*, 157.

37. Quoted in Liliane Hilaire-Pérez and Bernard Vaisbrot, "Matthew Boulton's Jewish Partners between France and England: Innovative Networks and Merchant Enlightenment," in Quickenden et al., 207.

38. JW to Thomas Bentley, April 10, 1771, in *Selected Letters*, 105.

39. Editors' comments, in *Selected Letters*, 105, 293.

40. JW to Thomas Bentley, July 14, 1776, in *Selected Letters*, 195.

41. Robin Reilly and George Savage, *Wedgwood: The Portrait Medallions* (London: Barrie & Jenkins, 1973), 19.

42. JW to Thomas Bentley, August 22, 1777, in *Selected Letters*, 208.

43. Witt Bowden, "The English Manufacturers and the Commercial Treaty of 1786 with France," *American Historical Review* 25, no. 1 (October 1919): 18, 20–22, 29–30, 32; Jones, *Industrial Enlightenment*, 203–5.

44. JW to Thomas Bentley, December 19, 1773, in *Selected Letters*, 157.

45. Berg, 147. For more images from Boulton's 1790 catalogue, see https://www.metmuseum.org/art/collection/search/346535. Another example from ca. 1785 is in the V&A collections: http://collections.vam.ac.uk/item/O1028639/metalwork-trade-catalogue-matthew-boulton-plate/.

46. Trevor Burnard and John Garrigus, *The Plantation Machine: Atlantic Capitalism in French Saint-Domingue and British Jamaica* (Philadelphia: University of Pennsylvania Press, 2016), 200.

47. Jones, "Visitors," 74.

48. Quoted in editors' comments, in *Selected Letters,* 219.

49. JW to William Knox, December 7, 1784, in *Selected Letters,* 277–78.

50. Jones, *Industrial Enlightenment,* 206–7.

51. Sheryllynne Haggerty, *"Merely for Money"? Business Culture in the British Atlantic, 1750–1815* (Liverpool: Liverpool University Press, 2012), 25.

52. Breen. For a useful critique of this interpretation, especially around understandings of "choice" in the eighteenth century, see Sophia Rosenfeld, "Of Revolutions and the Problem of Choice," in David A. Bell and Yair Mintzker, eds., *Rethinking the Age of Revolutions: France and the Birth of the Modern World* (New York: Oxford University Press, 2018), 236–72.

53. Robin Reilly, *Wedgwood* (New York: Stockton, 1989), 1:181–82; George L. Miller, "Marketing Ceramics in North America: An Introduction," *Winterthur Portfolio* 19, no. 1 (Spring 1984): 2–3.

54. McLean, 1–6.

55. Barbara Fogarty, "The Mechanical Paintings of Matthew Boulton and Francis Eginton," in Quickenden et al., 111–26.

56. Gaye Blake Roberts, "Josiah Wedgwood and Queen's Ware," in Michael Raeburn, Andrew Nurnberg, and Ludmila Voronoklina, eds., *The Green Frog Service* (London: Cacklegoose, 1995), 40–41.

57. George L. Miller, 2–3; Neil McKendrick, "Josiah Wedgwood: An Eighteenth Century Entrepreneur in Salesmanship and Marketing Techniques," *Economic History Review,* 2nd ser., 12, no. 3 (April 1960): 408–33.

58. JW to Thomas Bentley, May 31, 1767, in *Selected Letters,* 55.

59. JW to Thomas Bentley, November 30, 1771, in *Selected Letters,* 117.

60. Quoted in Nicholas Goodison, "Ormolu Ornaments," in Mason, *Matthew Boulton,* 59, 60.

61. Goodison, 59, 61.

62. JW to Thomas Bentley, September 8, 1767, in *Selected Letters,* 58–59.

63. Goodison, 61–62.

64. JW to Thomas Bentley, June 19, 1779, in *Selected Letters,* 235–36.

65. JW to Thomas Bentley, November 19, 1769, in *Selected Letters,* 85.

66. Quoted in Reilly 1:361.

67. Quoted in Reilly 1:361. Jenny Uglow, "Vase Mania," in Maxine Berg and Elizabeth Eger, eds., *Luxury in the Eighteenth Century: Debates, Desires and Delectable Goods* (Houndmills, Basingstoke, UK: Palgrave Macmillan, 2003): 151–62.

68. Quoted in Jones, *Industrial Enlightenment,* 228.

69. For example, JW to Thomas Bentley, September 3 and November 5, 1774, in *Selected Letters,* 95–96, 167.

70. JW to Thomas Bentley, December 12, 1774, in *Selected Letters,* 169.

71. Reilly 1:187.

72. JW to Thomas Bentley, November 21, 1773, in *Selected Letters,* 156.

73. JW to Thomas Bentley, August 20, 1770, in *Selected Letters,* 94.

74. Goodison, 61.

75. Josiah Wedgwood Jr. to Thomas Wedgwood, n.d., ca. 1790, in *Correspondence of Josiah Wedgwood, 1781–1794* (Manchester: E. J. Marten, 1906), 117. Hereafter cited as *Correspondence*.

76. Quoted in Jones, *Industrial Enlightenment*, 228.

77. Quoted in Jones, *Industrial Enlightenment*, 42.

78. Quoted in Goodison, 32.

79. Quickenden, 43.

80. JW to Thomas Bentley, September 13, 1769, in *Selected Letters*, 77.

81. JW to Thomas Bentley, April 18, 1772, in *Selected Letters*, 121.

82. Quoted in editors' comments, in *Selected Letters*, 293.

83. Berg, 130.

84. JW to Thomas Bentley, May 27, 1767, in *Selected Letters*, 54.

85. Quoted in Reilly 1:95.

86. On the bat printing process, see David Drakard and Paul Holdway, *Spode: Transfer Printed Ware, 1784–1833* (Woodbridge, UK: Antique Collectors' Club, 2002), 32, 44, 54, 74, 79.

87. Robin Emmerson, "Pottery and the Liverpool Trade," in Teitelman et al., 50.

88. Halfpenny, 33–34, 38.

89. Emmerson, 52 and appendix 1.

90. Laurel Thatcher Ulrich, "Political Protest and the World of Goods," in Jane Kamensky and Edward Gray, eds., *The Oxford Handbook of the American Revolution* (New York: Oxford University Press, 2013), 68.

91. Susan Gray Detweiler, *George Washington's Chinaware* (New York: Abrams, 1982), 53 [quotation], 54, 66–67, 76, 80, 138.

92. Berg, 144.

93. Edith Mannoni, *Les Faïences révolutionnaires* (Paris: Massin, 1989).

94. Berg, 227–29.

95. Amanda Vickery, *Behind Closed Doors: At Home in Georgian England* (New Haven: Yale University Press, 2009), 271.

96. Berg, 310.

97. French and Simpson (Boston) to JW, August 4, 1784, in Ann Finer, ed., *American Letters in the Wedgwood Museum, Barlaston, Staffordshire,* microfilm edition (1970).

98. Neil Ewins, "'Supplying the Present Wants of Our Yankee Cousins': Staffordshire Ceramics and the American Market, 1775–1880," *Journal of Ceramic History* 15 (1997): 39–40.

99. Kariann Yokota, *Unbecoming British: How Revolutionary America Became a Postcolonial Nation* (New York: Oxford University Press, 2014).

100. Bevis Hillier, *Master Potters of the Industrial Revolution: The Turners of Lane End* (London: Cory, Adams & Mackay, 1965), 89.

101. Vickery, 181.

102. Quoted in Philipp Ziesche, *Cosmopolitan Patriots: Americans in Paris in the Age of Revolution* (Charlottesville: University of Virginia Press, 2010), 27.

103. Sykes and Company to JW, October 27, 1787, L69–11937. By Courtesy of the Wedgwood Museum. Hereafter cited as WM.

104. Sykes and Company to JW, July 7, 1787, E31–23201; Sykes to JW, October 27, 1787, L69–11937, WM.

105. Hillier, 89.

106. Sykes and Company to JW, June 20, 1789, E31–23215; Sykes to JW, November 17, 1787, L69–11940, WM.

107. Account with Sykes, June–December 1787, L69–11951, WM.

108. Sykes to JW, October 19, 1789, L69–11977, WM.

109. *Daily Advertiser* (Kingston), November 8, 1791.

110. JW to Thomas Byerley, December 14, 1792, in *Correspondence,* 204.

111. For a later example, see Bronwen Everill, *Not Made by Slaves: Ethical Capitalism in the Age of Abolition* (Cambridge, MA: Harvard University Press, 2020), 86.

112. Christopher Leslie Brown, *Moral Capital: Foundations of British Abolitionism* (Chapel Hill: University of North Carolina Press, 2006); Ashli White, *Encountering Revolution: Haiti and the Making of the Early Republic* (Baltimore: Johns Hopkins University Press, 2010), chapters 4 and 5.

113. Laurent Dubois, *A Colony of Citizens: Revolution and Slave Emancipation in the French Caribbean, 1787–1804* (Chapel Hill: University of North Carolina Press, 2004), 224.

114. Ewins, 6. Data are not available for all years, but this pattern holds true for most years between 1785 and 1800.

115. Quoted in Reilly 1:95.

116. *Antigua Gazette,* December 6, 1798, March 7 & 28, 1799; *Daily Advertiser* (Kingston), February 16, March 4, May 24, 1791; *Bermuda Gazette and Weekly Advertiser* (St. George's), January 31, 1789, March 18, April 29, July 8 & 15, August 12, November 25, 1797; *Cornwall Chronicle and Jamaica General Advertiser* (Montego Bay), November 7, 1789, July 2, 1791; *St. Christopher Journal* (Basseterre), May 13, 1780. See also advertisements for the Bahamas quoted in Paul Farnsworth, "The Influence of Trade on Bahamian Slave Culture," *Historical Archaeology* 30, no. 4 (1996): 11. As George L. Miller and Amy C. Earls point out, however, other potters picked up on Wedgwood's term *Queen's ware* and applied it to their own goods (which imitated Wedgwood's style). Miller and Earls, "War and Pots: The Impact of Economics and Politics on Ceramic Consumption Patterns," in Robert Hunter, ed., *Ceramics in America* (Milwaukee: Chipstone Foundation, 2008), 72. Many thanks to George Miller and Amy Earls for sharing advance proof of this article.

117. Invoices, Thellusson Brothers to JW, 1794, L4–560–63, 565–66, WM; Susanne Seymour and Sheryllynne Haggerty, "Slavery Connections of Brodsworth Hall (1600–c.1830)," Final Report for English Heritage (October 2010), 11. Available at: www.english-heritage.org.uk/publications/slavery-connections -brodsworth-hall/slavery-connections-brodsworth-hall.pdf.

118. Farnsworth, 11.

119. For this interpretation of Wedgwood during the French Revolution, see Reilly 1:125.

120. Laurie A. Wilkie, "Culture Bought: Evidence of Creolization in the Consumer Goods of an Enslaved Bahamian Family," *Historical Archaeology* 34, no. 3 (2000): 10–11.

121. Object Query 2 ("Building s," "House for Families," and "South Grove"), Digital Archaeological Archive of Comparative Slavery, www.daacs.org. For more on Building s in Mulberry Row at Monticello and the House for Families at Mount Vernon, see https://www.daacs.org/sites/building-s/#background and https://www.daacs.org/sites/house-for-families/#background. See also Dennis Pogue, "House for Families, Summary of Research and Analysis" and "Building s [Monticello], Excavation History, Procedure, and Methods," October 2003, Digital Archaeological Archive of Comparative Slavery.

122. Farnsworth, 11–14.

123. Gerald F. Schroedl and Todd M. Ahlman, "The Maintenance of Cultural and Personal Identities of Enslaved Africans and British Soldiers at the Brimstone Hill Fortress, St. Kitts, West Indies," *Historical Archaeology* 36, no. 4 (2002): 38–49.

124. Wilkie, 12, 17. For analyses of European ceramics on other islands, see Krysta Ryzewski and John F. Cherry, "Struggles of a Sugar Society: Surveying Plantation-Era Montserrat, 1650–1850," *International Journal of Historical Archaeology* 19 (2015): 356–83; Mark W. Hauser, "The Infrastructure of Nature's Island: Settlements, Networks and Economy of Two Plantations in Colonial Dominica," *International Journal of Historical Archaeology* 19 (2015): 601–22.

125. Jerome Handler and Diane Williams, "Production Activities in Household Economies of Plantation Slaves: Barbados and Martinique, Mid-1600s to Mid-1800s," *International Journal of Historical Archaeology* 18 (2014): 441–66.

126. Quoted in Berg, 148.

CHAPTER 2. SEIZING THE STATUS QUO

1. Quoted in Laurent Dubois, *Avengers of the New World: The Story of the Haitian Revolution* (Cambridge, MA: Harvard University Press, 2004), 111.

2. Wendy Bellion, *Iconoclasm in New York: Revolution to Reenactment* (University Park: Pennsylvania State University Press, 2019), 1–13; Keith Bresnahan, "On 'Revolutionary Vandalism,'" *Architectural Theory Review* 19, no. 3 (2014): 278–98; Richard Clay, *Iconoclasm in Revolutionary Paris: The Transformation of Signs* (Oxford: Voltaire Foundation, 2012); James Simpson, *Under the Hammer: Iconoclasm in the Anglo-American Tradition* (New York: Oxford University Press, 2011), 1–17, 116–54.

3. Leora Auslander and Tara Zahra, "The Things They Carried: War, Mobility, and Material Culture," in Auslander and Zahra, eds., *Objects of War: The Material Culture of Conflict and Displacement* (Ithaca: Cornell University Press, 2018), 4.

4. Peter Crowhurst, "Experience, Skill and Luck: French Privateering Expeditions, 1792–1815," in David J. Starkey, E. S. van Eyck van Heslinga, and J. A. Moor, eds., *Pirates and Privateers: New Perspectives on the War on Trade in the Eighteenth and Nineteenth Centuries* (Exeter: University of Exeter Press, 1997), 155–70; Robert C. Ritchie, "Government Measures against Piracy and Privateering in the Atlantic Area, 1750–1850," in Starkey et al., 17–22; David J. Starkey, "A Restless Spirit: British Privateering Enterprise, 1739–1815," in Starkey et al., 126–40.

5. Henry Bolingbroke, Esq. [of Norwich, Deputy Vendue Master at Suriname], *A Voyage to the Demerary* (London, 1809), 214.

6. Tom Stammers, *The Purchase of the Past: Collecting Culture in Post-revolutionary Paris, ca. 1790–1890* (Cambridge: Cambridge University Press, 2020).

7. Laurence Fontaine, introduction to Fontaine, ed., *Alternative Exchanges: Second-hand Circulations from the Sixteenth Century to the Present* (Oxford: Berghahn Books, 2008), 1–12; Beverly Lemire, *Global Trade and the Transformation of Consumer Cultures: The Material World Remade, ca. 1500–1820* (Cambridge: Cambridge University Press, 2018), 137–89.

8. T. H. Breen, *The Marketplace of Revolution: How Consumer Politics Shaped American Independence* (New York: Oxford University Press, 2004), 140–41; Timothy Brown, "The Language of Public Service and Private Interest in France: The Vexed Case of the Paris Auctioneers, 1750–1848" (Ph.D. diss., Stanford University, 2000), 32–34, 38–39; Natacha Coquery, "The Semi-Luxury Market, Shopkeepers and Social Diffusion: Marketing *Chinoiseries* in Eighteenth-Century Paris," in Bruno Blondé, Natacha Coquery, Jon Stobart, and Ilja Van Damme, eds., *Fashioning Old and New: Changing Consumer Preferences in Europe (Seventeenth-Nineteenth Centuries)* (Turnhout, Belgium: Brepols, 2009), 128–29; Emma Hart, *Trading Spaces: The Colonial Marketplace and the Foundations of American Capitalism* (Chicago: University of Chicago Press, 2018), 75–79; Ann Smart Martin, *Buying into the World of Goods: Early Consumers in Backcountry Virginia* (Baltimore: Johns Hopkins University Press, 2008), 42–66.

9. Breen, 141; Brown, 7–8; Hart, 143.

10. Wendy Woloson, "In Hock: Pawning in Early America," *Journal of the Early Republic* 27, no. 1 (Spring 2007): 42.

11. Breen, 140–41.

12. Robert S. DuPlessis, *The Material Atlantic: Clothing, Commerce, and Colonization in the Atlantic World, 1650–1800* (Cambridge: Cambridge University Press, 2016), 59, 80; Lemire, 114–22; Margarette Lincoln, *Trading in War: London's Maritime World in the Age of Cook and Nelson* (New Haven: Yale University Press, 2018), 116–17; John Stobart, "In and out of Fashion? Advertising Novel and Second-hand Goods in Georgian England," in Blondé et al., 142; Ashli White, *Encountering Revolution: Haiti and the Making of the Early Republic* (Baltimore: Johns Hopkins University Press, 2010), 26–27; Shane White and Graham White, "Slave Clothing and African-American Culture in the Eighteenth and Nineteenth Centuries," *Past and Present*, no. 148 (August 1995): 149–86.

13. Rodney to Philip Stephens, Esq., February 6 & 27, 1781, and Rodney to Governor Cunningham, February 17, 1781, in *Letters from Sir George Brydges Now Lord Rodney, to His Majesty's Ministers, &c. &c. Relative to the Capture of St. Eustatius, and Its Dependencies; and Shewing the State of the War in the West-Indies, at That Period* (London, 1784), 11–12, 19, 17. Hereafter cited as *Letters from Sir George Brydges*. Jeremy Popkin, *Facing Racial Revolution: Eyewitness Accounts of the Haitian Revolution* (Chicago: University of Chicago Press, 2007), 175; Henry de Poyen-Bellisle, *Histoire militaire de la révolution de Saint-Domingue* (Paris: Berger-Levrault, 1899), 29.

14. Hannah Callaway, "Revolutionizing Property: The Confiscation of Émigré Wealth in Paris and the Problem of Property in the French Revolution" (Ph.D. diss., Harvard University, 2015), 110.

15. Rodney to John Laforey, April 14 & 21, 1781, in *Letters from Sir George Brydges,* 67, 70.

16. Claim, Elias Lindo, HCA 42/150/8; Claim, John Campbell Sr., James Gordon, Henry Riddle, John Robertson, HCA 42/150/11, The National Archives, Kew, UK. Hereafter abbreviated as TNA.

17. Quotation from Claim, Anthony Songa, HCA 42/149/1. Items taken from inventories in Songa and Elias Lindo claims as well as Claim, James and Lambert Blair, HCA 42/151/27, TNA.

18. David Spinney, *Rodney* (London: George Allen & Unwin, 1969), 360; Rodney to Philip Stephens, Esq., February 4 and April 27, 1781, in *Letters from Sir George Brydges,* 9, 75.

19. Popkin, 191.

20. Samuel G. Perkins, "Sketches of St. Domingo from January, 1785, to December, 1794," *Proceedings of the Massachusetts Historical Society* 2, 2nd ser. (April 1886): 348.

21. Graham Nessler, *An Islandwide Struggle for Freedom: Revolution, Emancipation, and Reenslavement in Hispaniola, 1789–1809* (Chapel Hill: University of North Carolina Press, 2016), 47.

22. Deposition of Guillaume Silvestre de la Haye, in Popkin, 162; Poyen-Bellisle, 32.

23. Quoted in Robert G. Parkinson, *The Common Cause: Creating Race and Nation in the American Revolution* (Chapel Hill: University of North Carolina Press, 2016), 159.

24. Claim, Martha Phillips, n.d., 13/26/357–58, Papers of the American Loyalist Claims Commission, microfilm edition, David Library of the American Revolution at the American Philosophical Society Library, Philadelphia.

25. Claim, Benjamin Marston, January 16, 1787, 13/51/211–12, Papers of the American Loyalist Claims Commission.

26. Kenneth Silverman, *A Cultural History of the American Revolution* (New York: Columbia University Press, 1987), 367.

27. Claim, Joseph Donaldson, HCA 42/152/37, TNA.

28. DuPlessis, 54, 68.

29. Sudhir Hazareesingh, *Black Spartacus: The Epic Life of Toussaint Louverture* (New York: Farrar, Straus & Giroux, 2020), 11.

30. Althéa de Puech, ed. and trans., *My Odyssey: Experiences of a Young Refugee from Two Revolutions* (Baton Rouge: Louisiana State University Press, 1959), 71.

31. Donald F. Johnson, "Occupied America: Everyday Experience and the Failure of Imperial Authority in Revolutionary Cities under British Rule, 1775–1783" (Ph.D. diss., Northwestern University, 2015); Alan Taylor, *American Revolutions: A Continental History, 1750–1804* (New York: Norton, 2016), chapter 6.

32. Hazareesingh, 307, 316, 322–23.

33. Jean-François Brière, *Haïti et la France, 1804–1848: La rêve brisé* (Paris: Karthala, 2008); Laurent Dubois, *Haiti: The Aftershocks of History* (New York: Picador, 2012), 97–105.

34. Quoted in Spinney, 375.

35. Rodney to John Laforey, February 27, 1781, in *Letters from Sir George Brydges,* 19.

36. *London Chronicle,* May 12–15, 1781.

37. *London Courant,* May 7, 1781.

38. Quoted in Ronald Hurst, *The Golden Rock: An Episode of the American War of Independence, 1775–1783* (London: Leo Cooper, 1996), 144.

39. *Whitehall Evening Post,* November 27–29, 1781. See also Andrew Jackson O'Shaughnessy, *The Men Who Lost America: British Leadership, the American Revolution, and the Fate of the Empire* (New Haven: Yale University Press, 2013), 309–13.

40. Ada Ferrer, *Freedom's Mirror: Cuba and Haiti in the Age of Revolution* (New York: Cambridge University Press, 2014), 102, 130.

41. Ferrer, 106–7, 114, 128.

42. Hazareesingh, 141.

43. Rodney and Vaughan to Lord Germaine, June 26, 1781, in *Letters from Sir George Brydges,* 77.

44. O'Shaughnessy, 304.

45. Sir Rodney to Lady Rodney, February 7, 1781, in Major-General Mundy, *The Life and Correspondence of the Late Admiral Lord Rodney* (London: John Murray, 1830), 2:18–19.

46. Hood to Jackson, June 24, 1781, in David Hannay, ed., *Letters Written by Sir Samuel Hood (Viscount Hood) in 1781–82* (London: Navy Records Society, 1895), 23.

47. *London Courant,* April 5, 1781.

48. *London Courant,* June 28, 1781.

49. General Orders, September 22, 1776, *Founders Online,* National Archives, https://founders.archives.gov/documents/Washington/03–06–02–0285.

50. George Washington to John Hancock, September 25, 1776, *Founders Online,* National Archives, https://founders.archives.gov/documents/Washington/03–06–0 2–0305.

51. General Orders, September 18, 1776, *Founders Online,* National Archives, https://founders.archives.gov/documents/Washington/03–06–02–0261; General Orders, September 24, 1776, *Founders Online,* National Archives, https://found ers.archives.gov/documents/Washington/03–06–02–0298; General Orders, September 6, 1776, *Founders Online,* National Archives, https://founders.archives .gov/documents/Washington/03-06-02-0185.

52. General Orders, September 19, 1776, *Founders Online,* National Archives, https://founders.archives.gov/documents/Washington/03–06–02–0269.

53. Quoted in Hazareesingh, 286.

54. Hazareesingh, 89–90.

55. David Jaffee, *A New Nation of Goods: The Material Culture of Early America* (Philadelphia: University of Pennsylvania Press, 2010), 49; Martin, 36–41.

56. Entry for June 5, 1795, in Elaine Crane, ed., *The Diary of Elizabeth Drinker* (Boston: Northeastern University Press, 1991), 1:689.

57. Robert and Mary Morris Household Inventory, Philadelphia, May 19, 1797, transcript in appendix to finding aid for Thomas FitzSimons Papers (McA MSS

020), McAllister Collection, Library Company of Philadelphia. On Morris's house, see Ryan K. Smith, *Robert Morris's Folly: The Architectural and Financial Failures of an American Founder* (New Haven: Yale University Press, 2014).

58. Pierre Verlet, *French Royal Furniture: An Historical Survey Followed by a Study of Forty Pieces Preserved in Great Britain and the United States* (New York: Clarkson N. Potter, 1963), 54–58.

59. Callaway, 18–56.

60. Michel Beurdeley, *La France à l'encan, 1789–1799: Exode des objets d'art sous la Révolution* (Paris: Librairie Jules Tallandier, 1981), 38.

61. Callaway, 64.

62. Brown, 124–27.

63. O/2/495 dossier 2 (24 & 27 frimaire l'an 4) and dossier 3 (16 messidor l'an 6), Archives nationales, Paris. Hereafter abbreviated as AN. For other examples, see Verlet, *French Royal Furniture*, 60.

64. Quoted in Brown, 38.

65. Brown, 20–47.

66. Callaway, 107–8.

67. Affiches, O/2/494 dossier 4, AN.

68. Callaway, 97, 109.

69. Brown, 132–35.

70. *Journal de la vente des biens nationaux*, April 24, 1793, 280.

71. Procès Verbal de la vente de la Veuve Brunoy, 14 messidor l'an 3, DQ10/785, Archives de Paris. Hereafter abbreviated AP.

72. Procès Verbal de Cramfort, 12 brumaire, second mois de l'an 2, DQ 10/785; Expédition . . . la femme Brionne, émigrée, 27 floréal l'an 3, DQ10/785; P.V. de Vente de Meubles dont sa Propriété en Commun entre Joseph Persico émigré et Jean Louis Marie Aucanne condamné, 28 nivôse l'an 3, DQ10/785; Expédition . . . de la Cne ["citoyenne Fournier décédée sans heritiers"], 23 messidor l'an 4, DQ10/786, AP.

73. Quoted in Jean-Charles Davillier, *La vente du mobilier du chateau de Versailles pendant la Terreur* (Paris: Libraries de la Société des Bibliophiles François, 1877), 26.

74. Rebecca Spang, *Stuff and Money in the Time of the French Revolution* (Cambridge, MA: Harvard University Press, 2015), 159, 210–46.

75. Quoted in Jean-Jacques Fiechter, *Un diplomate américain sous la Terreur: Les années européennes de Gouverneur Morris, 1789–1798* (Paris: Fayard, 1983), 328.

76. Quoted in Brown, 141.

77. Broadside, "Vente de meubles et effets de la ci-devant reine," August 25, 1793, private collection, on loan and display at the Wallace Collection, London.

78. Howard C. Rice, "James Swan: Agent of the French Republic, 1794–1796," *New England Quarterly* 10, no. 3 (September 1937): 464–86.

79. Rice, "James Swan," 473; quotations in Rice, "James Swan," 470.

80. Quoted in Smith, 94–95.

81. Rice, 476.

82. Information about individual pieces in the Swan collection can be found at www.mfa.org/collections. See also Eleanor P. Delorme, "James Swan's French

Furniture," *Antiques* 107 (March 1975): 452–61; Howard Rice, "Notes on the 'Swan Furniture,'" *Bulletin of the Museum of Fine Arts* 38, no. 227 (June 1940): 43–48.

83. Robert Andrews (NY) to David Meredith, March 18, 1795, box 6, folder 18, Meredith Family Papers, Historical Society of Pennsylvania, Philadelphia.

84. Elizabeth Meredith to David Meredith, April 8, 1795, box 6, folder 19, Meredith Family Papers.

85. Catalogue, March 22–23, 1790, Christie's Archives, London. Hereafter abbreviated as CA.

86. Philip Tassaert to James Christie, June 1790 [no specific date but before June 7], transcription, CA.

87. Carolyn Sargentson, *Merchants and Luxury Markets: The Marchands Merciers of Eighteenth-Century Paris* (London: Victoria and Albert Museum, 1996), 21, 24–32.

88. Christie used several different coffeehouses in the 1790s, including Rainbow Coffee House and Garraway's Coffee House.

89. Catalogue, April 4, 1792, CA.

90. Auctions with clear Daguerre connections: catalogues, March 25–26, 1791, May 16, 1792, CA.

91. Susan Gray Detweiler, *George Washington's Chinaware* (New York: Harry N. Abrams, 1982), 126; Melanie Randolph Miller, *Envoy to the Terror: Gouverneur Morris and the French Revolution* (Dulles, VA: Potomac Books, 2005), 203; Smith, *Robert Morris's Folly*, 101–2.

92. Beatrix Cary Davenport, ed., *A Diary of the French Revolution by Gouverneur Morris* (Boston: Houghton Mifflin, 1939), 2:427, 431–32, 436, 446, 458, 460–61, 465.

93. Charles F. McCombs, ed., *Letter-book of Mary Stead Pinckney, November 14, 1796–August 29, 1797* (New York: Grolier Club, 1946), 34 (December 13, 1796). Hereafter cited as *Pinckney Letter-book*.

94. Beurdeley, 95.

95. Anne Cary Morris, ed., *The Diary and Letters of Gouverneur Morris* (New York: Charles Scribner's Sons, 1888), 2:67.

96. Smith, *Robert Morris's Folly*, 102.

97. Daniel Meyer, *Versailles: Furniture of the Royal Palace, Seventeenth and Eighteenth Centuries* (Dijon: Éditions Faton, 2002), 1:187–88; Pierre Verlet, *French Furniture of the Eighteenth Century*, trans. Penelope Hunter-Stiebel (Charlottesville: University Press of Virginia, 1991), 42–43; Verlet, *French Royal Furniture*, 168.

98. Quoted in Miller, 203.

99. Brown, 137.

100. *Pinckney Letter-book*, 24 (December 11, 1796), 28 (December 13, 1796).

101. Quoted in Fiechter, 329.

102. Quoted in Julian P. Boyd, "Jefferson's French Baggage, Crated and Uncrated," *Proceedings of the Massachusetts Historical Society* 83 (1971), 20.

103. Boyd, 21.

104. Robert Morris to Bourdieu, Challet, & Bourdieu, March 17, 1795, Private Letterbook, vol. 1 (December 22, 1794–May 19, 1796), microfilm edition, reel 9, Papers of Robert Morris, Library of Congress, Washington, DC.

105. Robert Morris to John Richard, April 7, 1795, Private Letterbook, vol. 1 (December 22, 1794–May 19, 1796).

106. Robert Morris to John Richard, March 28, 1795, Private Letterbook, vol. 1 (December 22, 1794–May 19, 1796).

107. James Gillray, *A Peep at Christie's;—or—Tally-ho, & His Nimeney-Pimmeney Taking the Morning Lounge* (September 24, 1796), 1868,0808.6552, British Museum, London; Thomas Rowlandson, *Christie's Auction Room* (1801, 1808), accession number 17.3.1167–146, Metropolitan Museum of Art, New York, NY.

108. Fredrika J. Teute and David Shields introduced and have elaborated on the notion of the "republican court" in the United States in a series of papers collected and published in the *Journal of the Early Republic* 35, no. 2 (Summer 2015). See also François Furstenberg, *When the United States Spoke French: Five Refugees Who Shaped a Nation* (New York: Penguin, 2014); Amy Hudson Henderson, "Furnishing the Republican Court: Building and Decorating Philadelphia Homes" (Ph.D. diss., University of Delaware, 2008).

109. Robin Eagles, *Francophilia in English Society, 1748–1815* (New York: St. Martin's, 2000), 170; Jenny Uglow, *In These Times: Living in Britain through Napoleon's Wars, 1793–1815* (New York: Farrar, Straus & Giroux, 2014), 117.

110. Catalogues, June 12, 13, 15, 1795, November 4, 1796, April 1, 1797 [Louis XVI]; February 19, 1795 [du Barry]; April 18, 20, 22, 1793 [Count d'Adhemer]; March 4–5, 1791 [Vaudreuil and Noailles]; May 24, 1792 [Mirabeau], CA.

111. Catalogue, November 4, 1796, 16, CA.

112. Uglow, 27–28.

113. Catalogue, February 19, 1795, n.p., CA.

114. Davenport 2:461.

115. Quoted in Philipp Ziesche, *Cosmopolitan Patriots: Americans in Paris in the Age of Revolution* (Charlottesville: University of Virginia Press, 2010), 59. On Morris's conservatism regarding the French Revolution, see Ziesche, 19.

116. Quoted in Miller, 21.

117. Davenport 2:463.

118. Davenport 2:462.

119. Davenport 2:571.

120. Davenport 2:449.

121. Quotation, Davenport 2:457.

122. Ziesche, 50.

123. Davenport 2:569–72; Ziesche, 52.

124. Ziesche, 56.

PART II. POLITICAL APPEARANCES

1. Lynn Hunt, *Politics, Culture, and Class in the French Revolution* (Berkeley: University of California Press, 1984), 75–77.

2. Hunt, 81; Richard Wrigley, *The Politics of Appearances: Representations of Dress in Revolutionary France* (Oxford: Berg, 2002), 187–227.

3. Sudhir Hazareesingh, *Black Spartacus: The Epic Life of Toussaint Louverture* (New York: Farrar, Straus & Giroux, 2020), 261, 277; Benjamin H. Irwin, *Clothed in Robes of Sovereignty: The Continental Congress and the People Out of Doors* (New York: Oxford University Press, 2014), 23–51.

4. Clare Haru Crowston, *Fabricating Women: The Seamstresses of Old Regime France, 1675–1791* (Durham: Duke University Press, 2001), 155.

5. Hunt, 76.

CHAPTER 3. CLOTHING THE CAUSE

1. Nathanael Greene to Thomas Jefferson, December 6, 1780, in Richard K. Showman, ed., *The Papers of General Nathanael Greene* (Chapel Hill: University of North Carolina Press, 1991), 6:530. Nathanael Greene hereafter abbreviated NG.

2. Amy Miller, *Dressed to Kill: British Naval Uniform, Masculinity, and Contemporary Fashions, 1748–1857* (London: National Maritime Museum, 2007), 13–14; Daniel Roche, *The Culture of Clothing: Dress and Fashion in the Ancien Régime*, trans. Jean Birrell (Cambridge: Cambridge University Press, 1994), 221–23.

3. Stephen Conway, "British Mobilization in the War of American Independence," *Historical Research* 72, no. 177 (February 1999): 63; Roche, 237–38; John Styles, *The Dress of the People: Everyday Fashion in Eighteenth-Century England* (New Haven: Yale University Press, 2007), 51.

4. Roche, 226.

5. Fred Anderson, *A People's Army: Massachusetts Soldiers & Society in the Seven Years' War* (Chapel Hill: University of North Carolina Press, 1984), 167–95.

6. Caroline Cox, *A Proper Sense of Honor: Service and Sacrifice in George Washington's Army* (Chapel Hill: University of North Carolina Press, 2004), 80–81, 106.

7. Roche, 236.

8. Roger Norman Buckley, *Slaves in Red Coats: The British West India Regiments, 1795–1815* (New Haven: Yale University Press, 1979); Cox, 16.

9. Laura F. Edwards, "James and His Striped Velvet Pantaloons: Textiles, Commerce, and Law in the Early Republic," *Journal of American History* 107, no. 2 (September 2020): 336–61.

10. Roche, 224.

11. John Brewer, *Sinews of Power: War, Money, and the English State* (New York: Knopf, 1989); Linda Colley, *Britons: Forging the Nation, 1707–1837* (New Haven: Yale University Press, 1992).

12. Roche, 134; Styles, 15.

13. For definitions of the component parts, see W. Y. Carman, *A Dictionary of Military Uniform* (New York: Charles Scribner's Sons, 1977).

14. Warrant for Regulating the Cloathing of the Regiments of the Infantry, July 27, 1768, WO 30/13B, The National Archives, Kew, UK. Hereafter abbrevi-

ated as TNA. Although mandated in 1768, this regulation stayed in place at least through the American Revolution. French clothing allowances, as of an October 1, 1786, decree, were similar in quantity and types of garments. Roche, 233.

15. Giorgio Riello, *A Foot in the Past: Consumers, Producers and Footwear in the Long Eighteenth Century* (Oxford: Oxford University Press, 2006), 47.

16. Conway, 69 [quotation], 70–71.

17. Roche, 131, 137–38.

18. Roche, 250–51.

19. Robert S. DuPlessis, *The Material Atlantic: Clothing, Commerce, and Colonization in the Atlantic World, 1650–1800* (Cambridge: Cambridge University Press, 2016), 147–50; Riello, 20.

20. DuPlessis, 125–63; Ann Smart Martin, *Buying into the World of Goods: Early Consumers in Backcountry Virginia* (Baltimore: Johns Hopkins University Press, 2008), 173–93; Shane White and Graham White, "Slave Clothing and African-American Culture in the Eighteenth and Nineteenth Centuries," *Past and Present,* no. 148 (August 1995): 149–86.

21. DuPlessis, 154–56, 163; Beverly Lemire, *Global Trade and the Transformation of Consumer Cultures: The Material World Remade, ca. 1500–1820* (Cambridge: Cambridge University Press, 2018), 108–14.

22. Quoted in Roche, 235.

23. Samuel F. Scott, *From Yorktown to Valmy: The Transformation of the French Army in an Age of Revolution* (Niwot: University Press of Colorado, 1998), 38.

24. Edward E. Curtis, *The Organization of the British Army in the American Revolution* (New Haven: Yale University Press, 1926), 22–23.

25. General Orders, Relative to the Allowances, Granted to Foot-Soldiers, by His Majesty's Warrants, January 1792, WO 30/13B, TNA; A. Lauber, ed., *Orderly Books of the Fourth New York Regiment* (Albany: University of State of New York, 1932), 155.

26. Quotation from Curtis, 23. On the French case, see Howard G. Brown, *War, Revolution, and the Bureaucratic State: Politics and Army Administration in France, 1791–1799* (Oxford: Clarendon, 1995).

27. March 27, 1777, General Orderbook of 1777, in Rev. Joseph Brown Turner, ed., *The Journal and Order Book of Captain Robert Kirkwood, of the Delaware Regiment of the Continental Line* (Wilmington: Historical Society of Delaware, 1910), 50.

28. Governor Mathew to Right Honorable Lord Sydney, January 15, 1785, CO 101/26, TNA; Cassandra Pybus, *Epic Journeys of Freedom: Runaway Slaves of the American Revolution and Their Global Quest for Liberty* (Boston: Beacon, 2006), 11, 24, 41.

29. Mathew to Sydney, February 19, 1788, CO 101/28, TNA.

30. Bisshopp & Brummell to Henry Dundas, October 22, 1791, CO 101/31, TNA.

31. Quoted in Sudhir Hazareesingh, *Black Spartacus: The Epic Life of Toussaint Louverture* (New York: Farrar, Straus & Giroux, 2020), 142.

32. Peter Way, "Rebellion of the Regulars: Working Soldiers and the Mutiny of 1763–1764," *William and Mary Quarterly* 57, no. 4 (October 2000): 761–92.

33. Oressa M. Teagarden and Jeanne L. Crabtree, eds., *John Robert Shaw: An Autobiography of Thirty Years, 1777–1807* (Athens: Ohio University Press, 1992), 74–75.

34. Entry for January 19, 1776, in Lloyd A. Brown and Howard H. Peckham, eds., *Revolutionary War Journals of Henry Dearborn, 1775–1783* (Freeport, NY: Books for Libraries, 1969), 79; General Samuel Holden Parsons to NG, April 11, 1779, in Richard K. Showman, Robert E. McCarthy, and Elizabeth C. Stevens, eds., *The Papers of General Nathanael Greene* (Chapel Hill: University of North Carolina Press, 1983), 3:393.

35. Quoted in Hazareesingh, 82.

36. Pattison to Board of Ordnance, December 18, 1778, Letterbook of Brigadier General James Pattison, 1777–78, James Pattison Papers, microfilm edition, Rockefeller Library, Colonial Williamsburg Foundation, Williamsburg, VA. Hereafter cited as Pattison Papers.

37. *A Family Narrative: Francis H. Brooke* (New York: Arno, 1971), 21.

38. Curtis, 47–48.

39. E. Wayne Carp, *To Starve the Army at Pleasure: Continental Army Administration and American Political Culture, 1775–1783* (Chapel Hill: University of North Carolina Press, 1984), 23–25, 37, 51.

40. Brown, 98–123; Roche, 228.

41. J. Barrington, War Office, July 1, 1776, CO 5/256, TNA.

42. Captain Evelyn to Hon. Mrs. Leveson Gower, December 6, 1774, in G. D. Scull, ed., *Memoir and Letters of Captain W. Glanville Evelyn, of the 4th Regiment ("King's Own") from North America, 1774–1776* (Oxford: James Parker, 1879), 43.

43. DuPlessis, 54, 70.

44. Roger Norman Buckley, ed., *The Haitian Journal of Lieutenant Howard, York Hussars, 1796–1798* (Knoxville: University of Tennessee Press, 1985), xlvii–xlviii. The figure of eleven hundred men is calculated with the assumption of £10 per soldier, a generous estimate.

45. Jonathan Ogilvie to John Robinson Esq., March 26, 1777, T 1/534/217, TNA. In the 1776 list of officers, Ogilvie and Gray are noted as the agents for Thirty-Fifth Regiment of Foot. *A List of the General and Field-Officers, as They Rank in the Army* (London, 1776), 89.

46. Curtis, 120–33.

47. Larrie D. Ferreiro, *Brothers at Arms: American Independence and the Men of France and Spain Who Saved It* (New York: Vintage, 2016), 53, 66, 68, 155, 197, 210, 227; José M. Guerrero Acosta, "Uniforms, Supplies, and Money from Spain," trans. Larrie D. Ferreiro, in David K. Allison and Larrie D. Ferreiro, eds., *The American Revolution: A World War* (Washington, DC: Smithsonian Books, 2018), 86–91.

48. Barrington, War Office, January 30, 1777, CO 5/256, TNA.

49. Barrington to Knox, June 2, 1777, CO 5/256, TNA.

50. Jenkinson, War Office, May 28, 1780, CO 5/257, TNA.

51. Pattison to Board of Ordnance, December 15, 1777; Pattison to Brigadier General Cleaveland, January 22, 1778, Letterbook, Pattison Papers.

52. John Mathews to NG, Philadelphia, December 12, 1780, in Showman, 6:565.

53. Carp, 61–63; Curtis, 136.

54. Entry for December 28, 1777, in William Duane, ed., *Extracts from the Diary of Christopher Marshall, 1774–1781* (1877; repr., New York: New York Times/Arno, 1969), 152.

55. DuPlessis, 53–81.

56. William Fawcett to Thomas Fauquier, November 14, 1782, WO 30/13A, TNA.

57. *A Narrative of a Revolutionary Soldier: Some of the Adventures, Dangers, and Sufferings of Joseph Plumb Martin* (New York: Signet Classics, 2001), 173. Hereafter cited as *Joseph Plumb Martin*.

58. *Joseph Plumb Martin*, 244; entry for August 12, 1778, in Rebecca D. Symmes, ed., *A Citizen-Soldier in the American Revolution: The Diary of Benjamin Gilbert in Massachusetts and New York* (Cooperstown: New York State Historical Association, 1980), 35.

59. Quoted in Hazareesingh, 112.

60. *Joseph Plumb Martin*, 245.

61. Entry for February 9, 1779, in Duane, 212.

62. Many thanks to Linda Baumgarten for her insight into fabric preferences in garment construction.

63. Griffin Greene to NG, November 28, 1779; Colonel Samuel Webb to NG, December 8–12, 1779; NG to Nehemiah Hubbard, January 4, 1780; NG to Colonel Thomas Lowrey, February 5, 1780, in Richard K. Showman, Robert E. McCarthy, Dennis M. Conrad, and E. Wayne Carp, eds., *The Papers of General Nathanael Greene* (Chapel Hill: University of North Carolina Press, 1989), 5:125, 169, 234, 346; NG to Colonel Jeremiah Wadsworth, October 16, 1780, in Showman, 6:399.

64. Colonel Charles Pettit to NG, May 12, 1779, in Richard K. Showman, Elizabeth C. Stevens, and Dennis M. Conrad, eds., *The Papers of General Nathanael Greene* (Chapel Hill: University of North Carolina Press, 1986), 4:18 [quotation], 19.

65. Order, February 10, 1778, 177, Brigade Order Book, September 28, 1777–February 21, 1778, Pattison Papers.

66. Miller, 14; Roche, 242.

67. Colonel Morgan Lewis to NG, October 6, 1779, in Showman et al., 4:439.

68. Roche, 230.

69. Way, 769–70.

70. Receipt, Thomas Harley to S. Parker, December 5, 1777, T 1/547/167, TNA.

71. Order, January 3, 1778, 88, Brigade Order Book, September 28, 1777–February 21, 1778, Pattison Papers.

72. Order, January 18, 1778, 134, Brigade Order Book, September 28, 1777–February 21, 1778, Pattison Papers.

73. Lauber, 610.

74. *Bermuda Gazette* (St. George's), September 18, 1784.

75. *Daily Advertiser* (Kingston), January 4, 1791.

76. Quoted in Steeve O. Buckridge, *The Language of Dress: Resistance and Accommodation in Jamaica, 1760–1890* (Kingston: University of the West Indies Press, 2004), 46; Katherine Egner Gruber, "'By Measures Taken of Men': Clothing the Classes in William Carlin's Alexandria, 1763–1782," *Early American Studies* 13, no. 4 (Fall 2015): 931–53; Emma Hart, *Building Charleston: Town and Society in the Eighteenth-Century British Atlantic World* (Charlottesville: University of Virginia Press, 2010), 111–12.

77. Entries for January 15, 1778 [coat altering], January 16 & 19, 1778 [hat dressing], February 10, 1778 [cloth for jacket], March 4, 1778 [stockings], in Symmes, 22–23, 25–26.

78. Entries for February 28, 1778 [breeches], February 5 & 15, 1779 [buttons], May 13 & 20, 1780 [overalls], in Symmes, 26, 44–45, 69.

79. Roche, 245.

80. Quoted in Robert S. Allen et al., *The Loyal Americans: The Military Rôle of the Loyalist Provincial Corps and Their Settlement in British North America* (Ottawa: National Museums of Canada, 1983), 29.

81. Scott, 81–82.

82. Reginald W. Jeffery, ed., *Dyott's Diary, 1781–1845* (London: Archibald Constable, 1907), 1:111.

83. Jeffery, 1:120–21.

84. General Order, November 9, 1777, in Turner, 233.

85. Entry for December 17, 1803, Journal, Captain Marsden, BRA/133, Caird Library, National Maritime Museum, Greenwich, UK.

86. Jeffery, 1:113–15; Vincent Roth, ed., *A Soldier's Sojourn in British Guiana by Lt. Thomas Staunton St. Clair, 1806–1808* (Georgetown, Demerara, British Guiana: Daily Chronicle, 1947), 22.

87. Buckley, *The Haitian Journal of Lieutenant Howard,* 37.

88. Order, February 9, 1778, 174, 176, Brigade Order Book, September 28, 1777–February 21, 1778, Pattison Papers.

89. General Order, October 8, 1778, in Lauber, 47.

90. Teagarden and Crabtree, 13.

91. Regimental Order, June 29, 1780, in Lauber, 386.

92. Roche, 250–51.

93. Entries for January 20 and September 24, 1778, in Symmes, 23, 37; entries for May 3 & 15, 1776, in *Diary of David How . . . with a Biographical Sketch of the Author by George Wingate Chase* (Cambridge, MA: H. D. Houghton, 1865), 16–17; *Joseph Plumb Martin,* 124. On laundering linen, see Kathleen M. Brown, *Foul Bodies: Cleanliness in Early America* (New Haven: Yale University Press, 2009), 109–14.

94. Entry for August 29, 1778, in Symmes, 36.

95. General Orders, September 7, 1777, in Turner, 165; *Joseph Plumb Martin,* 32; entries for July 16 and October 20, 1781, in Evelyn M. Acomb, ed., *The Revolutionary Journal of Baron Ludwig von Closen, 1780–1783* (Chapel Hill: University of North Carolina Press, 1958), 96, 156.

96. Teagarden and Crabtree, 17.

97. Order, January 17, 1778, 129, Brigade Order Book, September 28, 1777–February 21, 1778, Pattison Papers.

98. General Order, September 12, 1780, in Lauber, 491.

99. Entries for February 22–23, 1776, in *David How*, 7.

100. Entry for April 15, 1778, in Symmes, 30.

101. Brigade Order, November 8, 1778, in Lauber, 43–44.

102. General Order, October 2, 1779, in Lauber, 87.

103. Division Order, May 5, 1780, in Lauber, 340 [deserters]; General Order, August 22, 1779, in Lauber, 141 [rum].

104. C. E. Franklin, *British Army Uniforms from 1751 to 1783, Including the Seven Years' War and the American War of Independence* (Barnsley, UK: Pen & Sword Military, 2012), 360.

105. Roche, 246, 247 [quotation].

106. Mathew to Lord Sydney, January 17, 1785, CO 101/26, TNA.

107. Receipt, London, April 6, 1785, CO 101/28, TNA.

108. For example, Edward Harvey to Clothing Board, November 15, 1773 [hats]; William Fawcett to Clothing Board, November 13, 1778 [loop], WO 30/13A, TNA.

109. Thomas Fauquier to Lt. Gen. Fawcett, November 23, 1784, WO 30/13A, TNA.

110. Mary R. M. Goodwin, "Clothing and Accoutrements of the Officers and Soldiers of the Virginia Forces, 1775–1780, from the Records of the Public Store at Williamsburg," June 1962, typescript, 12, Rockefeller Library, Colonial Williamsburg Foundation.

111. Quoted in Goodwin, viii.

112. Evangeline Walker Andrews, ed., *Journal of a Lady of Quality; Being the Narrative of a Journey from Scotland to the West Indies, North Carolina, and Portugal, in the Years 1774 to 1776* (New Haven: Yale University Press, 1934), 190.

113. Joan R. Gundersen, "'We Bear the Yoke with a Reluctant Impatience': The War for Independence and Virginia's Displaced Women," in John Resche and Walter Sargent, eds., *War and Society in the American Revolution* (Dekalb: Northern Illinois University Press, 2007), 281.

114. Carp, 67–68.

115. Thanks to curators Linda Baumgarten and Erik Goldstein for discussing this coat with me. See also object file for accession number 2005–338, 1, Colonial Williamsburg Foundation.

116. Database compiled by author from advertisements for deserters in Readex Early American Newspapers. A searchable version of author's database is available on dydra.com.

117. In North America, the term *jacket* could refer to an outer garment like a coat or to a waistcoat. This analysis takes into consideration cases where jackets are mentioned without coats (and hence possibly signal a jacket as the outermost garment).

118. *Pennsylvania Packet* (Philadelphia), February 25, 1779 [one ad], February 17, 1780 [three ads].

119. *American Journal* (Providence, RI), April 8, May 20 & 27, June 3 & 17, 1779; *Providence Gazette* (RI), February 15, July 12, August 23, October 4, 1777.

120. Twenty-nine advertisements noted the fabric of the coat/jacket.

121. A few examples: *Providence Gazette* (RI), October 4, 1777, January 30, 1779; *Connecticut Gazette* (New London), October 3, 1777; *Continental Journal* (Boston), October 2, 1777; *New York Gazette* (NYC), July 11, 1776.

122. *Connecticut Courant* (Hartford), May 5, 1777.

123. *Pennsylvania Packet* (Philadelphia), February 17, 1780.

124. *New England Chronicle* (Cambridge), August 2, 1776. Similar examples: advertisements for John Windsor, *Royal Gazette* (New York), August 4, 1781, and for John Benson, *Royal Gazette* (New York), March 30, 1782.

125. *Pennsylvania Packet* (Philadelphia), May 13, 1778.

126. *Connecticut Courant* (Hartford), May 13, 1776, July 20, 1779.

127. Marcus Rainsford, *An Historical Account of the Black Empire of Hayti*, ed. Paul Youngquist and Grégory Pierrot (Durham: Duke University Press, 2013), xlv.

128. Hazareesingh, 37.

129. Hazareesingh, 71.

130. Jean-Baptiste Le Paon, "Conclusion de la campagne de 1781 en Virginie . . . the Marquess de la Fayette" (1781), *Prints, Drawings and Watercolors from the Anne S. K. Brown Military Collection*, Brown Digital Repository, Brown University Library. https://repository.library.brown.edu/studio/item/bdr:237622/; Jean-Baptiste Le Paon, "Le Général Washington: Ne Quid Detrimenti Capiat Res Publica" (1781), *Prints, Drawings and Watercolors from the Anne S. K. Brown Military Collection*, https://repository.library.brown.edu/studio/item/bdr:237628/.

131. Jane Kamensky, *A Revolution in Color: The World of John Singleton Copley* (New York: Norton, 2016), 316–27.

132. Lemire, 93–94; Catherine Molineux, *Faces of Perfect Ebony: Encountering Atlantic Slavery in Imperial Britain* (Cambridge, MA: Harvard University Press, 2012), 18–60; Tamara J. Walker, *Exquisite Slaves: Race, Clothing, and Status in Colonial Lima* (New York: Cambridge University Press, 2017), 20–42.

133. Entry for July 9, 1781, in Acomb, 91.

134. *The Journal of Jean-Baptiste-Antoine de Verger*, in Howard C. Rice Jr. and Anne S. K. Brown, eds. and trans., *The American Campaigns of Rochambeau's Army, 1780, 1781, 1782, 1783* (Princeton: Princeton University Press, 1972), 1:xxi–xxiii, 103.

135. Riello, 71–72.

136. Quoted in Andrew Jackson O'Shaughnessy, *An Empire Divided: The American Revolution and the British Caribbean* (Philadelphia: University of Pennsylvania Press, 2000), 244.

137. Quoted in Hazareesingh, 301.

CHAPTER 4. DANGEROUS TRIFLES

1. From the *Courier républicain* (Paris), March 1795, quoted in Richard Wrigley, *The Politics of Appearance: Representations of Dress in Revolutionary France* (Oxford: Berg, 2002), 117.

2. John Styles, *The Dress of the People: Everyday Fashion in Eighteenth-Century England* (New Haven: Yale University Press, 2007), 7–8; Robin Reilly, *Wedgwood* (London: Macmillan, 1989), 1:545–46.

3. Jenny Dodge, *Silken Weave: A History of Ribbon Making in Coventry* (Coventry, UK: Herbert Art Gallery & Museum, 1988); Sylvie Marot, *The French Ribbon* (New York: Pointed Leaf, 2014).

4. *Gentleman's Magazine* (London), June 1777, 288.

5. Quoted in Robert S. DuPlessis, *The Material Atlantic: Clothing, Commerce, and Colonization in the Atlantic World, 1650–1800* (Cambridge: Cambridge University Press, 2016), 165.

6. Ann Smart Martin, *Buying into the World of Goods: Early Consumers in Backcountry Virginia* (Baltimore: Johns Hopkins University Press, 2008), 169; John Styles, *Threads of Feeling: The London Foundling Hospital's Textile Tokens, 1740–1770* (London: Foundling Museum, 2010), 43.

7. DuPlessis, captions to plates 2, 9, 11, 12; Danielle C. Skeehan, "Caribbean Women, Creole Fashioning, and the Fabric of Black Atlantic Writing," *Eighteenth Century* 56, no. 1 (2015): 116–20.

8. Entry for April 16[?], 1783, in Evelyn M. Acomb, ed., *The Revolutionary Journal of Baron Ludwig von Closen, 1780–1783* (Chapel Hill: University of North Carolina Press, 1958), 318.

9. *Daily Advertiser* (Kingston), March 22, 1791.

10. Josiah Wedgwood to unknown correspondent, January 8, 1775, in Ann Finer, ed., *American Letters in the Wedgwood Museum, Barlaston, Staffordshire,* microfilm edition (East Yardsley, UK: Micromethods, 1970). Hereafter Josiah Wedgwood abbreviated JW, and this collection as *American Letters.*

11. Barbara Bettoni, "Useful, Ornamental Function and Novelty: Debates on Quality of Button and Buckle Manufacturing in Northern Italy (Eighteenth to Nineteenth Centuries)," in Bert De Murck and Dries Lyna, eds., *Concepts of Value in European Material Culture, 1500–1900* (London: Routledge, 2016), 152.

12. Isaac D'Israeli, *Domestic Anecdotes of the French Nation, during the Last Thirty Years. Indicative of the French Revolution* (London, 1794), 265.

13. "A Dialogue in the Purgatory of Maccaronies, between Will Toilet and Sir Bobby Button," *Columbian Magazine, for July 1789* (Philadelphia), 409.

14. Kate Haulman, *The Politics of Fashion in Eighteenth-Century America* (Chapel Hill: University of North Carolina Press, 2011), 153–216.

15. *New-York Journal,* August 19, 1784.

16. *Royal Gazette* (New York), September 5, 1778.

17. Invoice, December 19, 1796, Dutilh and Wachsmuth Papers, box 3, folder 4, Historical Society of Pennsylvania, Philadelphia.

18. *Antigua Gazette* (St. John's, Antigua and Barbuda), February 7, 1799; *Gazette of St. Jago de la Vega* (Jamaica), June 20–27, 1782 ["cockade" and "hair" ribbons]; *Daily Advertiser* (Kingston), January 19, 1791 ["fashionable" ribbon], April 15, 1791 ["fancy" ribbons].

19. Robin Reilly, *Wedgwood Portrait Medallions: An Introduction* (London: Barrie & Jenkins, 1973), n.p.

20. JW to Thomas Bentley, May 20, 1767, in *American Letters.*

21. JW to Mr. Twigg, June 18, 1787, E10–8636. Courtesy of Wedgwood Museum. Hereafter cited as WM.

22. JW to Thomas Bentley, February 25, 1779, in Ann Finer and George Savage, eds., *The Selected Letters of Josiah Wedgwood* (London: Cory, Adams & MacKay, 1965), 230. Hereafter cited as *Selected Letters*. On Keppel, see Andrew Jackson O'Shaughnessy, *The Men Who Lost America: British Leadership, the American Revolution, and the Fate of the Empire* (New Haven: Yale University Press, 2013), 335–39.

23. C. Vining to JW, March 9, 1791, L101–18827. See also letters from Vining to Wedgwood, February 26, May 11, and June 27, 1791. L101–18826, L101–18828, L101–18829, WM.

24. *Bermuda Gazette and Weekly Advertiser* (St. George's), July 15, 1797.

25. D'Israeli, 124–25.

26. Martin, 170.

27. Quoted in *Wedgwood Portraits and the American Revolution* (Washington, DC: National Portrait Gallery, Smithsonian Institution, 1976), 118.

28. Quoted in *Wedgwood Portraits and the American Revolution,* 11.

29. Quoted in *Wedgwood Portraits and the American Revolution,* 94.

30. *Journal de Paris,* December 20, 1789, 1664.

31. *Journal de Paris,* September 4, 1793, 994; *Révolutions de Paris,* May 21–28, 1791, front matter [Declaration]; *Révolutions de Paris,* July 24–31, 1790, inside back cover [cockade]; *Révolutions de Paris,* July 3–10, 1790, inside back cover [constitution].

32. Peter M. Jones, *Industrial Enlightenment: Science, Technology, and Culture in Birmingham and the West Midlands, 1760–1820* (Manchester: Manchester University Press, 2008), 206–7.

33. JW to Erasmus Darwin, July 1789, in *Selected Letters,* 319.

34. JW to Mr. J. Barker, August 20, 1789, in *Selected Letters,* 320.

35. Josiah Wedgwood Jr. to JW, July 24, 1789, in *Correspondence of Josiah Wedgwood, 1781–1794* (Manchester: E. J. Marten, 1906), 94. Hereafter cited as *Correspondence.*

36. Josiah Wedgwood Jr. to JW, July 28, 1789, in *Correspondence,* 95–96. Wedgwood ended up making three symbolic medallions during the early days of the French Revolution: Josiah Jr.'s "France embracing liberty," another of the Bastille, and one of Hope encouraging Art and Labor under the influence of Peace. The last was a slight modification of the design that had been used for the so-called Sidney Cove medallion, which commemorated the foundation of a British colony at Sydney Cove, New South Wales, Australia, in 1789. Reilly, *Wedgwood* 1:125–28.

37. *Wedgwood Portraits and the American Revolution,* 80 [Louis XVI], 104 [Lafayette]; Robin Reilly and George Savage, *Wedgwood: The Portrait Medallions* (London: Barrie & Jenkins, 1973), 54 [Bailly], 243 [Mirabeau], 255 [Necker], 265–66 [Orléans].

38. *Wedgwood Portraits and the American Revolution,* 36, 60.

39. Quoted in *Wedgwood Portraits and the American Revolution,* 116.

40. Thomas Clarkson, *History of . . . the Abolition of the Slave Trade* (London, 1808), 2:192.

41. Mary Guyatt, "The Wedgwood Slave Medallion: Values in Eighteenth-Century Design," *Journal of Design History* 13, no. 2 (2000): 93–105; Eric Herschthal, *The Science of Abolition: How Slaveholders Became the Enemies of Progress* (New Haven: Yale University Press, 2021), 61–92.

42. JW to Anna Seward, February 1788, in *Selected Letters*, 310.

43. U.S. abolitionist groups made similar claims in this era. Ashli White, *Encountering Revolution: Haiti and the Making of the Early Republic* (Baltimore: Johns Hopkins University Press, 2010), 124–65.

44. Bryan Edwards, *An Historical Survey of the French Colony in the Island of St. Domingo* (London, 1797), 84–85.

45. *Daily Advertiser* (Kingston), October 21, 1791.

46. Mark P. Leone, *The Archaeology of Liberty in an American Capital: Excavations in Annapolis* (Berkeley: University of California Press, 2005).

47. Carolyn Fick, *The Making of Haiti: The Saint Domingue Revolution from Below* (Knoxville: University of Tennessee Press, 1990), 65–66.

48. West-African gris-gris, January 1773, Du Simitière Collection, Prints Department, Library Company of Philadelphia, https://digital.librarycompany.org/islandora/object/digitool%3A129885?solr_nav%5Bid%5D=a0c9a7f5306bba4667de&solr_nav%5Bpage%5D=0&solr_nav%5Boffset%5D=15.

49. Quoted in Jeremy Popkin, *Facing Racial Revolution: Eyewitness Accounts of the Haitian Insurrection* (Chicago: University of Chicago Press, 2007), 64.

50. For Saint-Domingue, see Edwards, x; Marcus Rainsford, *An Historical Account of the Black Empire of Hayti,* ed. Paul Youngquist and Grégory Pierrot (Durham: Duke University Press, 2013), 98. For the U.S. case, see Susan Branson, *These Fiery Frenchified Dames: Women and Political Culture in Early National Philadelphia* (Philadelphia: University of Pennsylvania Press, 2001), 71–72; Simon Newman, *Parades and the Politics of the Street: Festive Culture in the Early American Republic* (Philadelphia: University of Pennsylvania Press, 1997), 152–85.

51. *Boston News-Letter,* December 20, 1770; *Magasin des modes nouvelles, françaises et anglaises,* March 15 & 25, May 15, June 15, July 5, October 15, 1791.

52. Styles, *Threads of Feeling,* 48, 50–51.

53. Reported in *Boston Weekly News-Letter,* June 2, 1768.

54. *Massachusetts Gazette* (Boston), October 17, 1788.

55. *Herald of Freedom* (Boston), November 10, 1789.

56. Wrigley, 113.

57. Rebecca Spang, *Stuff and Money in the Time of the French Revolution* (Cambridge, MA: Harvard University Press, 2017), 142–43.

58. For example, *Dunlap's American Daily Advertiser* (Philadelphia), September 11, 1793; *South-Carolina State-Gazette* (Charleston), April 12, 1794; *Daily Advertiser* (New York), June 13, 1798.

59. *Daily Advertiser* (Kingston), November 29, 1791. Advertisements for enslaved people who had swindled merchants point to their presence in Caribbean ships. *Daily Advertiser* (Kingston), February 11, 1791 [swindle], March 22, 1791 [swindle], May 26, 1791 [swindle], July 8, 1791 [selling stolen goods], July 19, 1791 [theft]. For enslaved people visiting U.S. shops, see Martin, 173–93.

60. *Révolutions de Paris,* June 19–26, 1790, inside back cover.

61. *Spectator* (New York), June 20, 1798. For another ad along similar lines, see *New-York Gazette,* June 30, 1798.

62. *New-Hampshire Gazette* (Portsmouth), July 31, 1780. The term *union* cockade: *Freeman's Journal* (Philadelphia), June 13, 1781; *Independent New-York Gazette,* November 22, 1783; *Diary* (New York), June 28, 1793.

63. *Pennsylvania Packet* (Philadelphia), May 29, 1788 [Amsterdam]; *New-York Daily Gazette* (New York), November 21, 1789 [Madrid]; *Federal Gazette* (Philadelphia), October 23, 1790 [Ireland]; *New-Hampshire Spy* (Portsmouth), December 8, 1790 [Switzerland]; *General Advertiser* (Philadelphia), August 26, 1794 [Poland]; *Minerva* (New York), September 13, 1796 [Curaçao].

64. *Massachusetts Centinel* (Boston), November 11, 1789; *Connecticut Journal* (New Haven), February 14, 1793; *Daily Advertiser* (New York), May 2, 1793.

65. Quoted in Wrigley, 99.

66. Many thanks to curator Roselyne Hurel for allowing me access to the Musée Carnavalet's storage facilities in May 2012.

67. *New Jersey State Gazette* (Trenton), February 6, 1793.

68. Wrigley, 103–5.

69. *United States Chronicle* (Providence, RI), July 4, 1793.

70. Entry for February 6, 1797, 308, Benjamin Johnson Diary, Downs Collection, Winterthur Archives, Winterthur, DE.

71. Quoted in Wrigley, 113. James Monroe, the former minister to France, made the same point about cockades when he and Johnson met at The Hague. Entry for January 14, 1797, 302, Benjamin Johnson Diary.

72. *Federal Gazette* (Philadelphia), October 23, 1790 [Ireland]; *Pennsylvania Packet* (Philadelphia), February 25, 1788 [Amsterdam]; *Massachusetts Centinel* (Boston), November 11, 1789 [Martinique].

73. *Maryland Journal* (Baltimore), May 5, 1778.

74. During the American Revolution, Lafayette famously awarded cockades, "elegant" feathers, and epaulets to commissioned officers in his light infantry division as a sign of his high esteem for their achievements. Spang, 140.

75. *Massachusetts Mercury* (Boston), June 26, 1793.

76. Jennifer Heuer, "Hats on for the Nation! Women, Servants, Soldiers and the 'Sign of the French,'" *French History* 16, no. 1 (March 2002): 30.

77. Wrigley, 103–4.

78. Heuer, 35. The U.S. press picked up on the language of the citizen-soldier in describing events in France as well. *General Advertiser* (Philadelphia), July 17, 1793.

79. *City Gazette and Daily Advertiser* (Charleston), September 26, 1792.

80. See, for example, *Révolutions de Paris,* October 3–10, 5 and image opposite p. 4. This accusation was part of the list for Louis XVI and Marie-Antoinette, but it had provoked outrage as early as October 1789. Lynn Hunt, *Politics, Culture, and Class in the French Revolution* (Berkeley: University of California Press, 1984), 58. This crime was reported also in the U.S. press: *Dunlap's American Daily Advertiser* (Philadelphia), February 12, 1793.

81. *Commercial Advertiser* (New York), April 10, 1798.

82. *Connecticut Journal* (New Haven), February 14, 1793.

83. *New-Jersey Journal* (Elizabethtown), November 13, 1793. On the British invasion of Saint-Domingue, see Laurent Dubois, *Avengers of the New World: The Story of the Haitian Revolution* (Cambridge, MA: Harvard University Press, 2004); David Geggus, *Slavery, War, and Revolution: The British Occupation of Saint Domingue, 1793–1798* (New York: Oxford University Press, 1982). For the tricolor cockade eliciting violence in Dutch Curaçao, see Karwan Fatah-Black, "Orangism, Patriotism, and Slavery in Curaçao, 1795–1796," *International Review of Social History* 58 (December 2013): 56.

84. *State Gazette* (Providence, RI), February 4, 1796.

85. Quoted in Laurent Dubois, *A Colony of Citizens: Revolution and Slave Emancipation in the French Caribbean, 1787–1804* (Chapel Hill: University of North Carolina Press, 2004), 93.

86. *Herald* (New York), April 25, 1795.

87. *Columbian Herald* (Charleston), August 14, 1795.

88. *Massachusetts Mercury* (Boston), February 5, 1793.

89. *Bulletin official de Saint-Domingue* (Cap Français), July 22, 1798.

90. French accounts that appeared in the Anglophone press: *Weekly Museum* (New York), October 24, 1789; *Federal Gazette* (Philadelphia), December 6, 1790.

91. Katie Jarvis, *Politics in the Marketplace: Work, Gender, and Citizenship in Revolutionary France* (New York: Oxford University Press, 2019).

92. Heuer, 31.

93. *Diary* (New York), December 4, 1793.

94. François Furstenberg, "Beyond Freedom and Slavery: Autonomy, Virtue, and Resistance in Early American Political Discourse," *Journal of American History* 89, no. 4 (March 2003): 1303–4, 1310–11, 1319.

95. *Freeman's Journal* (Philadelphia), June 13, 1781.

96. *City Gazette and Daily Advertiser* (Charleston), April 18, May 2, 1793; *Diary* (New York), May 24, June 1, 1793 [about Philadelphia]; *Columbian Centinel* (Boston), December 25, 1793 [about New York].

97. *Columbian Centinel* (Boston), December 25, 1793 [visitors]; *City Gazette and Daily Advertiser* (Charleston), April 30, 1794 [sailors].

98. *Carey's United States' Recorder* (Philadelphia), May 10, 1798.

99. *Aurora General Advertiser* (Philadelphia), May 15, 1798.

100. *General Advertiser* (Philadelphia), May 1, 1794.

101. *Aurora General Advertiser* (Philadelphia), May 11, 1798.

102. *New-York Gazette,* May 25, 1798.

103. *Porcupine's Gazette* (Philadelphia), May 4, 1798.

104. Quoted in Ada Ferrer, *Freedom's Mirror: Cuba and Haiti in the Age of Revolution* (New York: Cambridge University Press, 2014), 55n22.

105. Gros, *An Historick Recital, of the Different Occurrences in the Camps of Grande-Reviere, Dondon, Sainte-Suzanne, and Others, from the 26th of October, 1791, to the 24th of December, of the Same Year* (Baltimore: Samuel and John Adams, 1792 or 1793), 31. See also Gros, 92, 102.

106. Dubois, *Avengers of the New World,* 107–9.

107. Ferrer, 55–56; Jean Fouchard, *The Haitian Maroons: Liberty or Death,* trans. A. Faulkner Watts (New York: Edward W. Blyden, 1981), 64.

108. Madison Smartt Bell, *Toussaint Louverture: A Biography* (New York: Pantheon Books, 2007), 33; Jeremy Popkin, *You Are All Free: The Haitian Revolution and the Abolition of Slavery* (New York: Cambridge University Press, 2010), 130–31; John Thornton, "African Soldiers in the Haitian Revolution," *Journal of Caribbean History* 25, nos. 1–2 (1991): 58–80.

109. Dubois, *Avengers of the New World,* 106.

110. February 1, 1797, 307–8, Benjamin Johnson Diary.

111. *Philadelphia Gazette,* July 3, 1795.

112. *Federal Intelligencer* (Baltimore), September 26, 1795; *Dunlap's American Daily Advertiser* (Philadelphia), September 19, 1794.

113. Styles, *The Dress of the People,* 277–301.

114. Quoted in Dubois, *A Colony of Citizens,* 199.

115. *Minerva* (New York), November 8, 1796. Similar critique: *Federal Gazette* (Baltimore), May 22, 1798.

116. *Daily Advertiser* (New York), June 27, 1798.

117. *Columbian Centinel* (Boston), May 7, 1794.

118. *United States Chronicle* (Providence, RI), October 7, 1784. Additional examples: *Daily Advertiser* (New York), October 28, 1785; *Charleston Morning Post,* February 14, 1786; *New-Hampshire Mercury* (Portsmouth), April 26, 1786.

119. *South Carolina Gazette* (Charleston), July 19, 1785.

120. *Greenleaf's New York Journal,* June 2, 1798.

121. *Independent New-York Gazette,* December 6, 1783; *Daily Advertiser* (New York), May 20, 1786, September 19, 1794; *Columbian Centinel* (Boston), November 12, 1794; *Wiscasset Telegraph* (Maine), December 24, 1796.

122. *Pennsylvania Packet* (Philadelphia), May 1, 1786.

123. *Wiscasset Telegraph* (Maine), December 24, 1796.

124. *Independent Chronicle* (Boston), October 23, 1777.

125. *New York Journal* (New York), July 18, 1795.

126. *Connecticut Courant* (Hartford), April 27, 1795.

127. *Aurora General Advertiser* (Philadelphia), May 6, 1795.

128. Reported in *National Gazette* (Philadelphia), September 18, 1793.

129. *Argus* (New York), June 9, 1795.

130. JW to Thomas Bentley, May 9, 1779, in *Selected Letters,* 232–33.

PART III. SEEING REVOLUTIONS

1. See, among others, Janet Polasky, *Revolution without Borders: The Call to Liberty in the Atlantic World* (New Haven: Yale University Press, 2015); Julius S. Scott, *The Common Wind: Afro-American Currents in the Age of the Haitian Revolution* (London: Verso, 2018).

2. David Bosse, "Maps in the Marketplace: Cartographic Vendors and Their Customers in Eighteenth-Century America," *Cartographia* 42, no. 1 (2007): 9, 19; Mary Pedley, "Maps, War, and Commerce: Business Correspondence with

the London Map Firm of Thomas Jefferys and William Faden," *Imago Mundi* 48 (1996): 161.

CHAPTER 5. CARTOGRAPHIC CONTESTS

1. For an introduction to the issue of maps and power, see Jeremy Black, *Maps and Politics* (Chicago: University of Chicago Press, 1997); J. B. Harley, ed., *The New Nature of Maps: Essays in the History of Cartography* (Baltimore: Johns Hopkins University Press, 2001); Denis Wood, *The Power of Maps* (New York: Guilford, 1992); and Denis Wood, *Rethinking the Power of Maps* (New York: Guilford, 2010).

2. Christian Ayne Crouch, "Surveying the Present, Projecting the Future: Re-evaluating Colonial French Plans of Kanesatake," *William and Mary Quarterly* 75, no. 2 (April 2018): 327–28.

3. M. de Chastenet-Puységur, *Le pilote de l'isle de Saint-Domingue et des dé-bourquemens de cette isle* (Paris: l'Imprimerie Royale, 1788), John Carter Brown Library, Providence, RI. Hereafter abbreviated as JCBL. On his background, see Bernard Gainot, Elie Lescot Jr., and Caroline Seveno, *L'île aux trois noms, Hispaniola, Saint-Domingue et Haïti: Cartes et plans du XVIe au XVIIIe siècle* (La Crèche: La Geste, 2021), 19–21.

4. J. B Poirson, *Carte de St. Domingue . . . en nivôse de l'an XI* (Paris, 1802), JCBL.

5. Mary Sponberg Pedley, *The Commerce of Cartography: Making and Marketing Maps in Eighteenth-Century France and England* (Chicago: University of Chicago Press, 2005), 25–26, 33, 35–41.

6. David Bosse, "Maps in the Marketplace: Cartographic Vendors and Their Customers in Eighteenth-Century America," *Cartographia* 42, no. 1 (2007): 5; Martin Brückner, *The Social Life of Maps in America, 1750–1860* (Chapel Hill: University of North Carolina Press, 2017), 28; Pedley, *The Commerce of Cartography*, 120.

7. Quoted in Mary Pedley, "Maps, War, and Commerce: Business Correspondence with the London Map Firm of Thomas Jefferys and William Faden," *Imago Mundi* 48 (1996): 170.

8. Mary Pedley, introduction to Pedley, ed., *The Map Trade in the Late Eighteenth Century: Letters to the London Map Sellers Jefferys and Faden* (Oxford: Voltaire Foundation, 2000), 12–14, 35–40; Pedley, *The Commerce of Cartography*, 146, 152.

9. Pedley, *The Commerce of Cartography*, 32–34, 81.

10. Sections of catalogue list reprinted in Pedley, *The Map Trade*, 64, 66.

11. Jacques-Nicolas Bellin, *Description geographique des isles Antilles possédées par les Anglois* (Paris: d'Imprimerie de Didot, 1758), vii, JCBL.

12. Christine Marie Petto, *When France Was King of Cartography: The Patronage and Production of Maps in Early Modern France* (Lanham: Lexington Books, 2007), 100.

13. *Sayer and Bennett's Enlarged Catalogue of New and Valuable Prints* (London, 1775), appendix, part 2, Atlases, 1, https://books.google.com/books?id=uQ1

OPPL_8JoC&printsec=frontcover&dq=sayer+bennett+1775+catalogue&hl=en&
sa=X&ved=oahUKEwjxi93HzIjcAhUBc6oKHQpSAaMQ6AEIKzAB#v=onepage
&q=sayer%20bennett%201775%20catalogue&f=false.

14. *Sayer and Bennett's Enlarged Catalogue,* appendix, part 2, Atlases, 15.

15. Chastenet-Puységur.

16. *Sayer and Bennett's Enlarged Catalogue,* appendix, part 2, Atlases, 1.

17. J. B. Harley, "The Contemporary Mapping of the American Revolutionary
War," in J. B. Harley, Barbara Bartz Petchenik, and Lawrence W. Towner, *Mapping the American Revolutionary War* (Chicago: University of Chicago Press,
1978), 15.

18. J. B. Harley, "The Map User in the Revolution," in Harley et al., 94.

19. Pedley, *The Commerce of Cartography,* 44–45.

20. Pedley, *The Commerce of Cartography,* 55.

21. Quoted in Pedley, *The Commerce of Cartography,* 41.

22. Pedley, *The Commerce of Cartography,* 15.

23. Quoted in Pedley, "Maps, War, and Commerce," 168.

24. Bosse, 24.

25. Several examples of Le Rouge's French versions of Jefferys's 1775 West Indies maps are in the collections of the John Carter Brown Library, including maps
of the colonies of St. Kitts, St. Lucia, Barbados, and Tobago, among others.

26. Julia Gaffield, *Haitian Connections in the Atlantic World: Recognition After
Revolution* (Chapel Hill: University of North Carolina Press, 2015).

27. Pedley, *The Commerce of Cartography,* 65.

28. *Affiches américaines,* July 7, 1784, no. 27, supplement.

29. Bosse, 11, 14–16.

30. Brückner, *Social Life,* 3; Pedley, *The Commerce of Cartography,* 10.

31. *Recueil de vues des lieux principaux de la colonies françoise de Saint-
Domingue, gravées par les soins de M. Ponce* (Paris 1791), title page, JCBL.

32. Pedley, *The Commerce of Cartography,* 69, 76, 164; John Styles, *The Dress
of the People: Everyday Fashion in Eighteenth-Century England* (New Haven: Yale
University Press, 2007), 7–8.

33. Brückner, *Social Life,* 176.

34. Bosse, 9–10.

35. On Jefferys's Nova Scotia map, see map dealer and map historian David
Rumsey's description at http://www.davidrumsey.com/maps1141032–29569.
html.

36. Brückner, *Social Life,* 14, 126–27, 138, 146; Harley, "The Map User in the
American Revolution," 94–95; Lowell J. Ragatz, *A List of the West Indian Maps
and Plans and Illustrations Relative to the West Indies Contained in the "Gentleman's Magazine," 1731–1833* (London: Arthur Thomas, 1947[?]).

37. Martin Brückner, *The Geographic Revolution in Early America: Maps,
Literacy, and National Identity* (Chapel Hill: University of North Carolina Press,
2006).

38. John Gabriel Stedman, *Narrative of a Five Years Expedition against the Revolted Negroes of Surinam,* ed. Richard and Sally Price (Baltimore: Johns Hopkins
University Press, 1988), 163.

39. Harley, "The Map User in the American Revolution," 99.

40. Black, 147.

41. Quoted in Harley, "The Contemporary Mapping of the American Revolutionary War," 30.

42. Quoted in J. B. Harley, "The Spread of Cartographical Ideas between the Revolutionary Armies," in Harley et al., 69; Barnet Schecter, *George Washington's America: A Biography through His Maps* (New York: Walker, 2010), 26–28, 44–45, 64.

43. Quoted in Harley, "The Spread of Cartographical Ideas between the Revolutionary Armies," 68.

44. Quoted in Brückner, *Social Life*, 43.

45. Harley, "The Map User in the American Revolution," 104.

46. Pedley, *The Commerce of Cartography*, 135.

47. Quoted in Harley, "The Map User in the American Revolution," 96.

48. Brückner, *Social Life*, 262.

49. Stedman, 434.

50. Harley, "The Map User in the American Revolution," 96, 98, 100.

51. Lydia Mihelic Pulsipher, "Assessing the Usefulness of a Cartographic Curiosity: The 1673 Map of a Sugar Island," *Annals of the Association of American Geographers* 77, no. 3 (September 1987): 408–22.

52. *Carte de St. Domingue ou sont marqués les paroisses jurisdictions* (dated 1770, but after 1777), JCBL.

53. *Carte de la Dominique, prise par les François le 7 septembre 1778* (Paris, 1778), JCBL.

54. Quoted in Bernard Gainot, *Le révolution des esclaves häiti, 1763–1803* (Paris: Vendémiaire, 2017), 231. See a similar complaint in Antoine Métral, *Histoire de l'expédition des Français, a Saint-Domingue, sous le consulat de Napoléon Bonaparte* (Paris: Fanjat Aîné, 1825), 63–64.

55. Stedman, 157.

56. Harley, "The Map User in the American Revolution," 100–101; Schecter, 183.

57. Harley, "The Spread of Cartographical Ideas between the Revolutionary Armies," 77.

58. Harley, "The Spread of Cartographical Ideas between the Revolutionary Armies," 65.

59. Harley, "The Contemporary Mapping of the American Revolutionary War," 24.

60. Harley, "The Spread of Cartographical Ideas between the Revolutionary Armies," 52.

61. J. Cameron Monroe, "Building the State in Dahomey: Power and Landscape on the Bight of Benin," and Akinwumi Ogundiran, "The Formation of an Oyo Imperial Colony during the Atlantic Age," in J. Cameron Monroe and Akinwumi Ogundiran, eds., *Power and Landscape in Atlantic West Africa: Archaeological Perspectives* (Cambridge: Cambridge University Press, 2012), 191–221, 222–52.

62. A landmark article on Black movements through landscapes is Dell Upton, "White and Black Landscapes in Eighteenth-Century Virginia," in Robert Blair

St. George, ed., *Material Life in America, 1600–1860* (Boston: Northeastern University Press, 1987), 357–69. See also Vincent Brown, *Tacky's Revolt: The Story of an Atlantic Slave War* (Cambridge, MA: Harvard University Press, 2020), 8, 102–3; Clifton Ellis and Rebecca Ginsburg, eds., *Cabin, Quarter, Plantation: Architecture and Landscapes of North American Slavery* (New Haven: Yale University Press, 2010).

63. Bryan Edwards, *An Historical Survey of the Island of St. Domingo, Together with an Account of the Maroon Negroes in the Island of Jamaica* (London: J. Stockdale, 1801), 308.

64. Matt Childs, *The 1812 Aponte Rebellion in Cuba and the Struggle against Atlantic Slavery* (Chapel Hill: University of North Carolina Press, 2006); Ada Ferrer, *Freedom's Mirror: Cuba and Haiti in the Age of Revolution* (New York: Cambridge University Press, 2014).

65. http://aponte.hosting.nyu.edu/apontes-library/.

66. http://aponte.hosting.nyu.edu/book-of-paintings/.

67. Ferrer, 318.

68. On spatial abstraction and slave rebellion, see Martha Schoolman, *Abolitionist Geographies* (Minneapolis: University of Minnesota Press, 2014), 14.

69. Ferrer, 303.

70. http://aponte.hosting.nyu.edu/book-of-paintings/.

71. Quoted in Harley, "The Contemporary Mapping of the American Revolutionary War," 22.

72. Maria Alessandra Bollettino, "'Of Equal or of More Service': Black Soldiers and the British Empire in the Mid-Eighteenth-Century Caribbean," *Slavery and Abolition* 38, no. 3 (2017): 510–33; Roger Norman Buckley, *Slaves in Red Coats: The British West India Regiments, 1795–1815* (New Haven: Yale University Press, 1979), 4; Gerald F. Schroedl and Todd M. Ahlman, "The Maintenance of Cultural and Personal Identities of Enslaved Africans and British Soldiers at the Brimstone Hill Fortress, St. Kitts, West Indies," *Historical Archaeology* 36, no. 4 (2002): 38–49.

73. There were twenty Black men and sixty white soldiers of various ranks.

74. Gainot, 104–6; Henry de Poyen-Bellisle, *Histoire militaire de la révolution de Saint-Domingue* (Paris: Berger-Levrault, 1899), 99–101; John Thornton, "African Soldiers in the Haitian Revolution," *Journal of Caribbean History* 25, nos. 1–2 (1991): 58–80.

75. Sudhir Hazareesingh, *Black Spartacus: The Epic Life of Toussaint Louverture* (New York: Farrar, Straus & Giroux, 2020), 71, 76–77, 100, 158, 261.

76. Hazareesingh, 70, 73, 87, 94, 213 [quotation].

77. Gainot, 104. According to Poyen-Bellisle, cordons were used at various moments by different armies fighting in Saint-Domingue. Poyen-Bellisle, 60, 117.

78. Harley, "The Contemporary Mapping of the American Revolutionary War," 24–25, 27, 42–44.

79. Abel Buell, *A New and Correct Map of the United States of North America: Layd Down from the Latest Observations and Best Authorities Agreeable to the Peace of 1783* (1784), Geography and Map Division, Library of Congress, Washington, DC.

80. Josef Konvitz, *Cartography in France, 1660–1848: Science, Engineering, and Statecraft* (Chicago: University of Chicago Press, 1987), 32–62.

81. *Plan du nouveau bourg d'Aquin* (1799), Bibliothèque nationale de France, https://catalogue.bnf.fr/ark:/12148/cb405966547.

82. *Plan de l'état actuel de la ville du Cap servant à indiquer les progrès de ses reconstructions* (1800), Bibliothèque nationale de France, https://gallica.bnf.fr/ark:/12148/btv1b5972741j?rk=128756;0.

83. Manuscript maps of revolutionary Saint-Domingue are located in the Bibliothèque nationale de France (BNF) and are available through gallica.bnf.fr.

84. Laurent Dubois, *Avengers of the New World: The Story of the Haitian Revolution* (Cambridge, MA: Harvard University Press, 2004), 188–89; Philippe Girard, *Toussaint Louverture: A Revolutionary Life* (New York: Basic Books, 2016), 141, 193; *The Memoir of General Toussaint Louverture*, ed. and trans. Philippe Girard (New York: Oxford University Press, 2014), 105, 119, 121, 125; Hazareesingh, 261, 276.

85. Hazareesingh, 230–36.

86. Law of July 13, 1801: https://sites.duke.edu/haitilab/english/haitian-revolution/. Girard, *Toussaint Louverture*, 223; Girard, *The Memoir of General Toussaint Louverture*, 89; Hazareesingh, 157.

87. Konvitz, 43.

88. Graham T. Nessler, *An Islandwide Struggle for Freedom: Revolution, Emancipation, and Reenslavement in Hispaniola, 1789–1809* (Chapel Hill: University of North Carolina Press, 2016), 69–70; Gainot et al., 114–15.

89. On the ideological and political implications of such naming practices for Indigenous populations in North America, see J. B. Harley, "New England Cartography and the Native Americans," in Harley, *The New Nature of Maps*, 169–95.

90. Black, 148; Harley, "The Contemporary Mapping of the American Revolutionary War," 18, 41–42.

91. *A Plan of Boston, and Its Environs: Shewing the True Situation of His Majesty's Army* (London 1776), Library of Congress, https://www.loc.gov/item/gm71002449/. On Williams, see Richard H. Brown and Paul E. Cohen, *Revolution: Mapping the Road to American Independence, 1755–1783* (New York: Norton, 2015), 48–51. Excerpts from Williams's written account are available under the title *Discord and Civil Wars*, https://babel.hathitrust.org/cgi/pt?id=wu.89077176477;view=1up;seq=5.

92. Brown and Cohen, 131–35.

93. William Faden, *A Plan of the Entrance of Chesapeak Bay, with James and York Rivers* (London, 1781), Library of Congress, https://www.loc.gov/resource/g3884y.ar146500/?r=-0.166,-0.079,1.829,0.9.

94. Alan Taylor, *American Revolutions: A Continental History, 1750–1804* (New York: Norton, 2016), 149.

95. Harley, "The Map User in the American Revolution," 108.

96. Jenny Uglow, *In These Times: Living in Britain through Napoleon's Wars, 1793–1815* (New York: Farrar, Straus & Giroux, 2014), 236.

97. *The New Lady's Magazine; or, Polite, Entertaining, and Fashionable Companion for the Fair Sex* (London), October 1789, 554; November 1789, 610; December 1789, 710.

98. *Carte de la Dominique, prise par les François le 7 septembre 1778.*

99. *The Position of the English and French Fleets on the 12th of April 1782 at 10 oClock in the Morning* (London, 1782?), https://collections.leventhalmap.org/search/commonwealth:dz010v204.

100. David Geggus, *Slavery, War, and Revolution: The British Occupation of Saint Domingue, 1793–1798* (New York: Oxford University Press, 1982); Nessler, 21–63.

101. This printed map appears to be related to a hand-drawn one, now in the collections of the Bibliothèque nationale de France. https://gallica.bnf.fr/ark:/12148/btv1b530985678.

102. Dubois, 271–74.

103. Gros, 4, 9, 11.

104. Gros, 4.

105. Gros, 4, 7.

106. Amy Freund, *Portraiture and Politics in Revolutionary France* (University Park: Pennsylvania State University Press, 2014), 35–37.

107. On the question of attribution and date of production, see Paul Youngquist and Grégory Pierrot, introduction to Marcus Rainsford, *An Historical Account of the Black Empire of Hayti*, ed. Youngquist and Pierrot (Durham: Duke University Press, 2013), xlvii–xlix.

CHAPTER 6. PEOPLE IN PRINT

1. Diana Donald, *The Age of Caricature: Satirical Prints in the Reign of George III* (New Haven: Yale University Press, 1996), 2.

2. Antoine de Baecque, *La caricature révolutionnaire* (Paris: Presses du CNRS, 1988), 27; John Richard Moores, *Representations of France in English Satirical Prints, 1740–1832* (Houndsmills, Basingstoke, UK: Palgrave Macmillan, 2015), 4; Claire Trévien, *Satire, Prints and Theatricality in the French Revolution* (Oxford: Voltaire Foundation, 2016), 3.

3. John Brewer, "'This monstrous tragi-comic scene': British Reactions to the French Revolution," in David Bindman, *The Shadow of the Guillotine: Britain and the French Revolution* (London: British Museum, 1989), 13.

4. James Leith, "Ephemera: Civic Education through Images," in Robert Darnton and Daniel Roche, eds., *Revolution in Print: The Press in France, 1775–1800* (Berkeley: University of California Press, 1989), 270–71.

5. This is an extensive literature, but landmark studies include Lynn Hunt, *Politics, Culture, and Class in the French Revolution* (Berkeley: University of California Press, 1984); Joan Landes, *Visualizing the Nation: Gender, Representation, and Revolution in Eighteenth-Century France* (Ithaca: Cornell University Press, 2001); Carlo Célius, "Neoclassicism and the Haitian Revolution," in David Geggus and Norman Fiering, eds., *The World of the Haitian Revolution* (Bloomington: Indiana University Press, 2009); *Revolution! The Atlantic World Reborn* (New York: New-York Historical Society, 2011); Peter D. G. Thomas, *The American Revolution* (Cambridge: Chadwyck-Healey, 1986).

6. Michel-Rolph Trouillot, *Silencing the Past: Power and the Production of History* (Boston: Beacon, 1995), 70–107.

7. James Alexander Dun, *Dangerous Neighbors: Making the Haitian Revolution in Early America* (Philadelphia: University of Pennsylvania Press, 2016).

8. David Bindman and Henry Louis Gates Jr., eds., *The Image of the Black in Western Art, Volume III: From the "Age of Discovery" to the Age of Abolition, Part 3: The Eighteenth Century* (Cambridge, MA: Harvard University Press, 2011); Marcus Wood, *Blind Memory: Visual Representations of Slavery in England and America, 1780–1865* (New York: Routledge, 2000).

9. Antony Griffiths, *The Print Before Photography: An Introduction to European Printmaking, 1550–1820* (London: British Museum, 2016), 38, 49, 57, 59, 75; Trévien, 4.

10. *Sayer and Bennett's Enlarged Catalogue of New and Valuable Prints* (London, 1775).

11. Emily (Amy) Torbert, "Dissolving the Bonds: Robert Sayer and John Bennett, Print Publishers in an Age of Revolution" (Ph.D. diss., University of Delaware, 2017), 173.

12. Griffiths, *The Print Before Photography,* 71, 74.

13. Herbert Atherton, *Political Prints in the Age of Hogarth: A Study of Ideographic Representation of Politics* (Oxford: Clarendon, 1974), 2, 61–83; Donald, 31–32; Pascal Dupuy, *Face à la Révolution et l'empire: Caricatures anglaises (1789–1815). Collections du Musée Carnavalet* (Paris: Paris-Musées, 2008), 25; Moores, 15.

14. In comparison, the British press was less pressured for libel during the American Revolution. Troy Bickham, *Making Headlines: The American Revolution as Seen through the British Press* (DeKalb: Northern Illinois Press, 2009), 43–54.

15. Quoted in Donald, 147.

16. Brewer, 18; Donald, 146–83; Griffiths, *The Print Before Photography,* 97; Moores, 18–19; Torbert, "Dissolving the Bonds," 173–78.

17. Donald, 3.

18. Eirwen E. C. Nicholson, "Consumers and Spectators: The Public of Political Print in Eighteenth-Century England," *History* 81, no. 261 (January 1996): 14–15; de Baecque, 47.

19. Donald, 4.

20. Torbert, "Dissolving the Bonds," 101–3, 110–12; Mary Pedley, "Gentleman Abroad: Jefferys and Sayer in Paris," *Map Collector* 37 (December 1986): 20–23. On sex in French prints in the 1780s, see Kristel Smentek, "Sex, Sentiment, and Speculation: The Market for Genre Prints on the Eve of the French Revolution," *Studies in the History of Art* 72 (2007): 220–43.

21. Antony Griffiths, "English Prints in Eighteenth-Century Paris," *Print Quarterly* 22, no. 4 (December 2005): 379, 382, 387–88, 394.

22. Bindman, 31–32, 34–35, 89–90.

23. Antony Griffiths, "A Checklist of Catalogues by British Print Publishers, c. 1650–1830," *Print Quarterly* 1, no. 1 (March 1984): 11–12, 16; Torbert, "Dissolving the Bonds," 79–82.

24. *Catalogue des planches gravées qui composent le fonds de MM. Colnaghi, & Co.,* no. 132 (London, 1793), 1, and quotation, n.p. but after p. 17.

25. Quoted in Christiane Banerji and Diana Donald, ed. and trans., *Gillray Observed: The Earliest Account of His Caricatures in "London and Paris"* (Cambridge: Cambridge University Press, 1999), 1.

26. See, for example, *London und Paris* 2 (1798): "Englishe Carricaturen," 80–99, 176–91, 279–298 [images unpaginated but after p. 305]; "Pariser Carricaturen," 77–79, 387–97 [images unpaginated but at end of volume]. On the history of *London und Paris,* see Banerji and Donald.

27. E. R. Richardson, "Stamp Act Cartoons in the Colonies," *Pennsylvania Magazine of History and Biography* 96, no. 3 (July 1972): 288.

28. *Pennsylvania Packet* (Philadelphia), August 16, 1783.

29. Clarence S. Brigham, *Paul Revere's Engravings* (New York: Atheneum, 1969), 117–18; Joan D. Dolmetsch, "Political Satires at Colonial Williamsburg," in Dolmetsch, ed., *Eighteenth-Century Prints in Colonial America* (Williamsburg, VA: Colonial Williamsburg Foundation, 1979), 184–85. For another example, see the discussion of the print *The Deplorable State of America* (1765), published in London, which inspired two American versions, one in Boston (by Copley) and another in Philadelphia (by Wilkinson), in Richardson, 277–84.

30. Quoted in Griffiths, *The Print Before Photography,* 128.

31. Dolmetsch, 183; Griffiths, *The Print Before Photography,* 116; Richardson, 295.

32. M. Dorothy George, *Catalogue of Political and Personal Satires Preserved in the Department of Prints and Drawings in the British Museum,* vol. 5 (1935; repr., London: British Museum, 1978), xv–xvi, xx.

33. *Daily Advertiser* (Kingston), March 17, June 23, 1791; *Bermuda Gazette* (St. George's), February 12, 1785.

34. *Cornwall Chronicle* (Montego Bay), February 12, 1785; *Daily Advertiser* (Kingston), January 19, 1791.

35. Julius Scott, *The Common Wind: Afro-American Currents in the Age of the Haitian Revolution* (London: Verso, 2018), 90, 160, 164, 170.

36. Edwin Wolf II, "Benjamin Franklin's Stamp Act Cartoon," *Proceedings of the American Philosophical Society* 99, no. 6 (December 1955): 389–90. According to Wolf, this print was reproduced in Philadelphia, and there are French and Dutch versions as well.

37. Richardson, 292.

38. Amy Torbert, "Paper Chiefs: Sayer & Bennett's Portraits of American Revolutionaries," in *The Art of Revolutions: Transactions of the American Philosophical Society* 109, no. 5 (Philadelphia: American Philosophical Society, 2021), 168–69.

39. Griffiths, *The Print Before Photography,* 52–61.

40. Robert Dighton, *A Real Scene in St. Paul's Church Yard, on a Windy Day* (London: Carrington Bowles, ca. 1783), 1935,0522.1.30 and 1880,1113.3312, British Museum, London; *Caricature Shop* (London: Piercy Roberts, 1801), 801.09.00.01+, Lewis Walpole Library, Yale University.

41. Thompson Westcott, *A History of Philadelphia,* 3:626, American Philosophical Society Library, Philadelphia.

42. Quoted in Richardson, 292.

43. Quoted in Donald, 20.

44. Charles Williams, *The Corsican Usurpers New Imperial French Arms* (London, 1804), 1868,0808.7309, British Museum.

45. Quoted in Bindman, 90.

46. Donald, 143; George 6 (1938): xxxiv; Catherine E. Kelly, *Republic of Taste: Art, Politics, and Everyday Life in Early America* (Philadelphia: University of Pennsylvania Press, 2016), 195; Moores, 4.

47. For a note of caution on the supposed pervasiveness of political prints, see Nicholson.

48. Antoine Lilti, *The Invention of Celebrity, 1750–1850,* trans. Lynn Jeffress (Cambridge: Polity, 2017), 64–66.

49. Amy Freund, *Portraiture and Politics in Revolutionary France* (University Park: Pennsylvania State University Press, 2014).

50. On the public allure of prominent military men, see David A. Bell, *Men on Horseback: The Power of Charisma in the Age of Revolution* (New York: Farrar, Straus & Giroux, 2020).

51. *Journal de Paris,* February 18, 1781, 197.

52. *Journal de Paris,* August 13, 1781, 907.

53. For Franklin, *Journal de Paris,* July 3, 1779, 751; July 7, 1779, 767; October 28, 1779, 1229; March 31, 1781, 364; October 4, 1782, 1129; and October 19, 1782, 1188–89.

54. *Pennsylvania Ledger* (Philadelphia), October 3, 1775; www.mountvernon.org/george-washington/artwork/life-portraits-of-george-washington/; *Journal de Paris,* February 18, 1781, 197; *Portraits of Generals, Ministers, Magistrates, Members of Congress, and Others, Who Have Rendered Themselves Illustrious in the Revolution of the United States of North America* (London: R. Wilkinson & J. Debrett, 1783).

55. Quoted in Torbert, "Paper Chiefs," 169.

56. George 5 (1935): 253, 255.

57. Bickham, 185–205.

58. George 5 (1935): xviii; Moores, 134.

59. Torbert, "Paper Chiefs," 171.

60. *London Evening Post,* August 27–29, 1776.

61. Lilti, 69–71.

62. Bickham, 118–82.

63. Donald, 146; Moores, 61, 136.

64. Donald, 146; George 6 (1938): xxv; Moores, 68, 148–50.

65. John Chapman, *Maximilian Roberspierre* (London, September 1794), 1868,0822.5004, British Museum; William Ridley, *Robespierre* (London: B. & R. Crosby, August 1794), 1873,0712.609, British Museum; Richard Newton, *Desmoulins and Lucile* (London: William Holland, June 1795), 1948,0214.377, British Museum.

66. Bindman, 148–49; Moores, 86.

67. James Gillray, *Shrine at St. Ann's* (London: Hannah Humphrey, 1798), 1868,0808.6742, British Museum; James Gillray, *The Arms of France* (London: John Hatchard, 1803), 1868,0808.7189, British Museum.

68. James Sayers, *Illustrious Heads Designed for a New History of Republicanism in French & English Dedicated to the Opposition* (London: Hannah Humphrey, 1794), frontispiece: K,67.237; Robespierre/Fox: Y,10.1.a; Barère/Sheridan: K,67.240; Brissot/Maitland: K,67.242, British Museum.

69. James Gillray, *The Rights of Man;—or—Tommy Paine, the Little American Taylor, Taking the Measure of the Crown, for a New Pair of Revolution-Breeches* (London: Hannah Humphrey, 1791), 1868,0808.6057, British Museum; James Gillray, *Fashion Before Ease;—or,—A Good Constitution Sacrificed, for a Fantastick Form* (London: Hannah Humphrey, 1793). 1851,0901.638, British Museum.

70. On visual indictments of Paine in the 1810s for *The Age of Reason,* see Ian Haywood, *Romanticism and Caricature* (Cambridge: Cambridge University Press, 2013), 100–120.

71. Isaac Cruikshank, *Wha Wants Me* (London: S. W. Fores, December 26, 1792), J,2.7, British Museum.

72. Quoted in Scott, 156. Other incidents, Scott, 155–58.

73. Paine was executed in effigy all over England as well. Bindman, 19.

74. *A Peep into the Antifederal Club* (New York, 1793), John Carter Brown Library, Providence, RI; *The Providential Detection* (1797–1800), American Antiquarian Society, Worcester, MA; *Mad Tom in a Rage* (1801), Metropolitan Museum of Art, New York, NY; Pascal Dupuy, "The French Revolution in American Satirical Prints," *Print Quarterly* 15, no. 4 (December 1998): 371–84.

75. https://exhibits.stanford.edu/frenchrevolution.

76. David Geggus, "The Changing Faces of Toussaint Louverture: Literary and Pictorial Depictions," 2013, https://www.brown.edu/Facilities/John_Carter_Brown_Library/exhibitions/toussaint/pages/iconography.html.

77. Geggus, "Changing Faces."

78. Williamson and Parsons, *Toussaint L'Ouverture, Governor of St. Domingo* (London: Silvester, 1802), 1926,0412.250, British Museum; John Kay, *Toussaint Louverture* (Edinburgh, 1802), 1935,0522.13.290, British Museum.

79. On Frenchmen as monkeys, Michael Duffy, *The Englishman and the Foreigner* (Cambridge: Chadwyck-Healey, 1986), 36.

80. Thomas Rowlandson, *The Progress of the Emperor Napoleon* (London: Thomas Tegg, 1808), 1868,0808.7704, British Museum.

81. *Bony's Visions, or a Great Little Man's Night Comforts* (1811), 1868,0808.12638, British Museum; George Cruikshank, *Buonaparte! Ambition and Death!!* (London, 1814), 1868,0808.12751, British Museum.

82. *Morning Chronicle* (London), September 19, 1803.

83. *Caledonian Mercury* (Edinburgh), April 1 and 29, 1802; *Hampshire Telegraph* (Portsmouth, UK), September 9, 1805.

84. *Morning Chronicle* (London), September 19, 1803.

85. *Morning Chronicle* (London), September 8, 1803.

86. Wood, *Blind Memory,* 19–22. This use of ghosts is different from the dynamic Haywood describes for depictions of Thomas Paine after Peterloo. See Haywood, *Romanticism and Caricature,* 100–120.

87. Dubroca's *Life of J.J. Dessalines* (1805) was printed in Paris, Haarlem, Leipzig, Madrid, and Mexico. John Carter Brown Library.

88. Matt D. Childs, "'A Black French General Arrived to Conquer the Island': Images of the Haitian Revolution in Cuba's 1812 Aponte Rebellion," in David P. Geggus, ed., *The Impact of the Haitian Revolution in the Atlantic World* (Columbia: University of South Carolina Press, 2001), 135–56.

89. Julia Gaffield, *Recognition After Revolution: Haitian Connections in the Atlantic World* (Chapel Hill: University of North Carolina Press, 2015).

90. Quotation from Donald, 109. The classic work on comparative mobs is George Rudé, *Paris and London in the Eighteenth Century: Studies in Popular Protest* (New York: Viking, 1971). See also Michael T. Davis, ed., *Crowd Actions in Britain and France from the Middle Ages to the Modern World* (Houndsmills, Basingstoke, UK: Palgrave Macmillan, 2015); Paul Gilje, *Rioting in America* (Bloomington: Indiana University Press, 1996); Paul Gilje, *The Road to Mobocracy: Popular Disorder in New York City, 1763–1834* (Chapel Hill: University of North Carolina Press, 1987); Robert B. Shoemaker, *The London Mob: Violence and Disorder in Eighteenth-Century England* (London: Hambledon & London, 2004). On what we could term crowd action in the Haitian Revolution, see Laurent Dubois, *Avengers of the New World: The Story of the Haitian Revolution* (Cambridge, MA: Harvard University Press, 2004); Malick Ghachem, "The Colonial Vendée," in David Patrick Geggus and Norman Fiering, eds., *The World of the Haitian Revolution* (Bloomington: Indiana University Press, 2009), 156–76; Jeremy Popkin, *You Are All Free: The Haitian Revolution and the Abolition of Slavery* (New York: Cambridge University Press, 2010). Sudhir Hazareesingh makes this comparison explicit. Hazareesingh, *Black Spartacus: The Epic Life of Toussaint Louverture* (New York: Farrar, Straus & Giroux, 2020), 149.

91. François Godefroy (engraver), *Origine de la Révolution Américaine* (Paris: Nicolas Ponce, 1784).

92. Wendy Bellion, *Iconoclasm in New York: Revolution to Reenactment* (University Park: Pennsylvania State University Press, 2019), 59–106, 138.

93. Philip Dawe, *The Bostonians Paying the Excise-Man, or Tarring and Feathering* (London, 1774), Metropolitan Museum of Art.

94. Catherine Molineaux, *Faces of Perfect Ebony: Encountering Atlantic Slavery in Imperial Britain* (Cambridge, MA: Harvard University Press, 2012), 200–208.

95. *A View in America in 1778* (London: Mathew Darly, 1778), Library of Congress Prints and Photographs Division, Washington, DC; George 5 (1935): 293; Amelia Rauser, "Death or Liberty: British Political Prints and the Struggle for Symbols in the American Revolution," *Oxford Art Journal* 21, no. 2 (1998): 168; Torbert, "Dissolving the Bonds," 260–61.

96. Donald, 109–15.

97. Donald, 140.

98. Ian Haywood, "The Transformation of Caricature: A Reading of Gillray's *The Liberty of the Subject*," *Eighteenth-Century Studies* 43, no. 2 (Winter 2010): 230–31.

99. Dupuy, *Face à la Révolution et l'empire*, 67.

100. Quoted in Dupuy, *Face à la Révolution et l'empire*, 68.

101. Bindman, 36–38.

102. Bindman, 38–39; William Sewell Jr., *Logics of History: Social Theory and Social Transformation* (Chicago: University of Chicago Press, 2005), 225–70. U.S. prints of the Bastille in *New York Magazine, or Literary Repository* 1, no. 4 (April 1790); *Massachusetts Magazine* 1, no. 11 (November 1789); *American Universal Magazine* 3, no. 5 (September 4, 1797).

103. Claude Langlois, *La caricature contre-révolutionnaire* (Paris: Presses du CNRS, 1988), 7–8, 70, 185.

104. Philippe de Carbonnières, *Prieur: Les tableaux historiques de la Révolution* (Paris: Paris-Musées, 2006), 18, 47, 49–50.

105. Bindman, 44–46, 58–63; Brewer, 22; Moores, 85–86.

106. Donald, 170; Mark Hallett, "James Gillray and the Language of Graphic Satire," in Mark Hallett and Richard Godfrey, *James Gillray: The Art of Caricature* (London: Tate, 2001), 34.

107. Dubois, 110–11.

108. Laurence Brown, "Visions of Violence in the Haitian Revolution," *Atlantic Studies* 13, no. 1 (2016): 144–51; Alejandro E. Gómez, "Images de l'apocalypse des planteurs," *L'ordinaire des Amériques* 215 (2013), https://journals.openedition.org/orda/665.

109. Gómez.

110. In France, counterrevolutionaries compared former slaves to revolting peasants in the Vendée, suggesting again that racial categories were not necessarily antagonistic enough. See Ghachem.

111. Karen Halttunen, "Humanitarianism and the Pornography of Pain in Anglo-American Culture," *American Historical Review* 100, no. 2 (April 1995): 303–34.

112. Peter J. Kitson, "John Thelwell in Saint Domingue: Race, Slavery, and Revolution in *The Daughter of Adoption: A Tale of Modern Times* (1801)," *Romanticism* 16, no. 2 (2010): 120–38.

113. Hugh Honour, *The Image of the Black in Western Art, Vol. 4, Part 1* (Cambridge, MA: Harvard University Press, 1989), 73–74. Scholars have pointed to this trend in texts as well. Ian Haywood, *Bloody Romanticism: Spectacular Violence and the Politics of Representation, 1776–1832* (Houndsmills, Basingstoke, UK: Palgrave Macmillan, 2006), 11–59; Marcus Wood, *Slavery, Empathy, and Pornography* (New York: Oxford University Press, 2002).

114. James Gillray, *Barbarities in the West Indias* (London: Hannah Humphrey, 1791), J,3.42, British Museum; Isaac Cruikshank, *The Abolition of the Slave Trade* (London: S. W. Fores, 1792), 1868,0808.6179, British Museum.

115. *Gazette of the United States* (Philadelphia), August 26, 1794, cited in Dun, 13.

116. Richard Newton, *A Real San Culotte!!* (London, 1792), 1948,0214.350, British Museum; Raphael Hörmann, "Black Jacobins: Towards a Genealogy of a Transatlantic Trope," in Charlotte A. Lerg and Heléna Tóth, eds., *Transatlantic Revolutionary Cultures, 1789–1861* (London: Brill, 2018), 28–35.

117. Isaac Cruikshank, *The New Consular Waltz* (London: Thomas Williamson, 1803), 1868,0808.7122, British Museum. See also James Gillray, *Evacuation*

of Malta (London: Hannah Humphrey, 1803), 1868,0808.7082, British Museum; George 8 (1947): 131, 149.

118. Wood, *Blind Memory*, 23.

CHAPTER 7. TERRIBLE AMUSEMENTS

1. Quotations from Francis Hervé, ed., *Madame Tussaud's Memoirs and Reminiscences of France, Forming an Abridged History of the French Revolution* (London: Saunders & Otley, 1838), 96, 198, 273; Uta Kornmeier, "Almost Alive: The Spectacle of Verisimilitude in Madame Tussaud's Waxworks," in Roberta Panzanelli, ed., *Ephemeral Bodies: Wax Sculpture and the Human Figure* (Los Angeles: Getty Research Institute, 2008), 67–81.

2. Entry for *amusement, Oxford English Dictionary*.

3. Jeremy Adelman, "The Rites of Statehood: Violence and Sovereignty in Spanish America, 1789–1821," *Hispanic American Historical Review* 90, no. 3 (August 2010): 391–422.

4. Keith Michael Baker, ed., *The French Revolution and the Creation of Modern Political Culture*, vol. 4: *The Terror* (Oxford: Pergamon, 1994); Michel Biard, ed., *Les politiques de la Terreur, 1793–1794* (Rennes: Presses Universitaires de Rennes; Société des Études Robespierristes, 2008); Dan Edelstein, *The Terror of Natural Right: Republicanism, the Cult of Nature, and the French Revolution* (Chicago: University of Chicago Press, 2009); Marisa Linton, *Choosing Terror: Virtue, Friendship, and Authenticity in the French Revolution* (Oxford: Oxford University Press, 2013); R. R. Palmer, *Twelve Who Ruled: The Year of the Terror in the French Revolution* (Princeton: Princeton University Press, 2017); Timothy Tackett, *The Coming of the Terror in the French Revolution* (Cambridge, MA: Harvard University Press, 2015); Sophie Wahnich, *In Defence of the Terror: Liberty or Death in the French Revolution,* trans. David Fernbach (London: Verso, 2012).

5. Joan B. Landes, "Wax Fibers, Wax Bodies, and Moving Figures: Artifice and Nature in Eighteenth-Century Anatomy," and Lyle Massey, "On Waxes and Wombs: Eighteenth-Century Representations of the Gravid Uterus," in Panzanelli, 41–65; 83–105; Anna Maerker, *Model Experts: Wax Anatomies and Enlightenment in Florence and Vienna, 1775–1815* (Manchester: Manchester University Press, 2011); Thelma R. Newman, *Wax as Art Form* (South Brunswick, NJ: Thomas Yoseloff, 1966), 84–85; Pamela Pilbeam, *Madame Tussaud and the History of Waxworks* (London: Hambledon & London, 2003), 4–8; Joseph Roach, *It* (Ann Arbor: University of Michigan Press, 2007), 46, 48; Charles Coleman Sellers, *Patience Wright: American Artist and Spy in George III's London* (Middletown: Wesleyan University Press, 1976), 34–35.

6. Richard D. Altick, *The Shows of London* (Cambridge, MA: Harvard University Press, 1978), 50–56; David R. Brigham, *Public Culture in the Early Republic: Peale's Museum and Its Audience* (Washington, DC: Smithsonian Institution Press, 1995); Laurent Dubois, *Avengers of the New World: The Story of the Haitian Revolution* (Cambridge, MA: Harvard University Press, 2004), 24; James T.

McClellan, *Colonialism and Science: Saint-Domingue in the Old Regime* (Baltimore: Johns Hopkins University Press, 1992), 97.

7. Pilbeam, 25.

8. Sellers, 47–49; *Alexandria Times* (Virginia), April 21, 1798 [tavern].

9. Loyd Haberly, "The Long Life of Daniel Bowen," *New England Quarterly* 32, no. 3 (September 1959): 320–32; Sellers, 34–45.

10. French wax modelers went into exile in the United States and brought their creations with them. *Porcupine's Gazette* (Philadelphia), January 3, 1798.

11. Quotation from *Columbian Centinel* (Boston), September 7, 1791; Antoine Lilti, *The Invention of Celebrity, 1750–1850*, trans. Lynn Jeffress (Cambridge: Polity, 2017).

12. Roach, 84, 87.

13. *New-York Daily Gazette*, September 19, 1789 [clothes of king, queen, and Prince of Wales]; *Federal Gazette* (Philadelphia), May 14, 1793 [Blanchard in clothes in which he made his "aerial voyages"]; *Massachusetts Mercury* (Boston), January 15, 1799 [John Hutton, a 108-year-old]; *Republican Gazetteer* (Boston), October 20, 1802 [Jason Fairbanks, murderer "drest with the same clothes in which he committed the horrid deed"]; *Democrat* (Boston), February 25, 1804 [three Native Americans].

14. Stacy C. Hollander, "Reuben Moulthrop: Artist in Painting and Waxwork," *Folk Art* 19, no. 3 (Fall 1994): 38. Curtius hired Marie-Antoinette's favorite dressmaker, Rose Bertin. Pilbeam, 30.

15. *Commercial Advertiser* (New York), December 13, 1803.

16. *New Jersey State Gazette* (Trenton), February 20, 1793. On distrust of political portraiture in the early United States, see Christopher J. Lukasik, *Discerning Characters: The Culture of Appearance in Early America* (Philadelphia: University of Pennsylvania Press, 2011), 123–27.

17. Wendy Bellion, *Citizen Spectator: Art, Illusion, and Visual Perception in Early National America* (Chapel Hill: University of North Carolina Press, 2011).

18. In the antebellum era, there would be increased anxiety over this artifice, a fear that surfaces were deceptive in a negative way because they were hiding something. Jackson Lears, *Fables of Abundance: A Cultural History of Advertising in America* (New York: Basic Books, 1994).

19. Mark M. Smith, *Sensing the Past: Seeing, Hearing, Smelling, Tasting, and Touching in History* (Berkeley: University of California Press, 2007), 24–25.

20. Dubois, 24; McClellan, 97; Pilbeam, 30.

21. Smith, 31–32.

22. Elizabeth Barnes, *States of Sympathy: Seduction and Democracy in the American Novel* (New York: Columbia University Press, 1997), ix–x; Lynn Hunt, *Politics, Culture, and Class in the French Revolution* (Berkeley: University of California Press, 1984), 45–46.

23. *Massachusetts Mercury* (Boston), February 24, 1797.

24. Roach, 55.

25. Mabel P. Stivers, "Wax Figures in Old Museums," *Old Time New England* 17 (July 1926–April 1927): 42.

26. Sellers, 36–44.

27. Sellers, 47–88.

28. Wendy Bellion, "Patience Wright's Transatlantic Bodies," in Maurie D. McInnis and Louis P. Nelson, eds., *Shaping the Body Politic: Art and Political Formation in Early America* (Charlottesville: University of Virginia Press, 2011), 15–46. Many thanks to Wendy Bellion for sharing her insights into Wright's figure of Pitt.

29. Reported in *Freeman's Oracle* (Exeter, NH), July 1, 1786.

30. Sellers, 126.

31. Quoted in Pilbeam, 25.

32. Quoted in Bellion, "Patience Wright's Transatlantic Bodies," 31.

33. Quoted in Bellion, "Patience Wright's Transatlantic Bodies," 31.

34. Philip English Mackey, *Hanging in the Balance: The Anti-Capital Punishment Movement in New York State, 1776–1861* (New York: Garland, 1982), 42.

35. John Barrell, *Imagining the King's Death: Figurative Treason, Fantasies of Regicide, 1793–1796* (London: Oxford University Press, 2000), 49–86.

36. *Connecticut Journal* (New Haven), September 4, 1793.

37. T. Lawrence Larkin, "A 'Gift' Strategically Solicited and Magnanimously Conferred: The American Congress, the French Monarchy, and the State Portraits of Louis XVI and Marie-Antoinette," *Winterthur Portfolio* 44, no. 1 (Spring 2010): 31–76.

38. *London Magazine* (February 1793), 68.

39. J. Thomas Scharf and Thomson Westcott, *History of Philadelphia, 1609–1884* (Philadelphia: L. H. Everts, 1884), 2:950.

40. Thomas Paine, "Reasons for Preserving the Life of Louis Capet" (1793), in Michael Foot and Isaac Kramnick, eds., *The Thomas Paine Reader* (New York: Penguin Books, 1987), 396.

41. Scharf and Westcott, 2:950.

42. *Morning Post* (London), February 9, 1793.

43. *St. James's Chronicle* (London), March 28–30, 1793.

44. Daniel Arasse, *The Guillotine and the Terror*, trans. Christopher Miller (London: Allen Lane, Penguin, 1989), 4, 9.

45. *Diary or Woodfall's Register* (London), March 19, 1793.

46. V. A. C. Gatrell, *The Hanging Tree: Execution and the English People* (New York: Oxford University Press, 1994), 46–47; Louis P. Masur, *Rites of Execution: Capital Punishment and the Transformation of American Culture, 1776–1865* (New York: Oxford University Press, 1989), 50–92.

47. Arasse, 15–17; Gene E. Ogle, "Slaves of Justice: Saint Domingue's Executioners and the Production of Shame," *Historical Reflections/ Réflexions historiques* 29, no. 2 (Summer 2003): 275–93.

48. John DePeyster to Charles Willson Peale, March 22, 1794, in Lillian Miller, ed., *The Selected Papers of Charles Willson Peale and his Family* (New Haven: Yale University Press, 1988), vol. 2, part 1:85.

49. John DePeyster to Charles Willson Peale, April 15, 1794, in Miller, vol. 2, part 1:89.

50. John DePeyster to Charles Willson Peale, April 15, 1794, in Miller, vol. 2, part 1:89.

51. Brigham, 5–12; Robert I. Goler, "'Here the Book of Nature Is Unfolded': The American Museum and the Diffusion of Scientific Knowledge in the Early Republic," *Museum Studies Journal* (Spring 1986): 10–21; Catherine E. Kelly, *Republic of Taste: Art, Politics, and Everyday Life in Early America* (Philadelphia: University of Pennsylvania Press, 2016), 159–94.

52. John DePeyster to Charles Willson Peale, April 15, 1794, in Miller, vol. 2, part 1:89.

53. *Columbian Gazetter* (New York), March 24, 1794.

54. Minsoo Kang, *Sublime Dreams of Living Machines: The Automaton in the European Imagination* (Cambridge, MA: Harvard University Press, 2011), 195–200; Barbara Maria Stafford, *Artful Science: Enlightenment Entertainment and the Eclipse of Visual Education* (Cambridge, MA: MIT Press, 1994), 170, 195.

55. Richard J. Evans, *Rituals of Retribution: Capital Punishment in Germany, 1600–1987* (Oxford: Oxford University Press, 1996), especially part I; Paul Friedland, *Seeing Justice Done: The Age of Spectacular Capital Punishment in France* (Oxford: Oxford University Press, 2014); Gatrell.

56. *London Magazine* (February 1793), 68.

57. S. H. Jeyes, *The Russells of Birmingham in the French Revolution and in America, 1791–1814* (London: George Allen, 1911), 134.

58. *St. James's Chronicle* (London), November 12–14, 1793.

59. Nina Rattner Gelbart, "Death in the Bathtub: Charlotte Corday and Jean-Paul Marat," in K. Steven Vincent and Alison Klairmont-Lingo, eds., *The Human Tradition in Modern France* (Wilmington, DE: SR Books, 2000), 18–23.

60. Antoine de Baecque, *The Body Politic: Corporeal Metaphor in Revolutionary France, 1770–1800,* trans. Charlotte Mandell (Stanford: Stanford University Press, 1997), 282–307; Tony Halliday, "David's *Marat* as Posthumous Portrait," in William Vaughan and Helen Weston, eds., *Jacques-Louis David's* Marat (Cambridge: Cambridge University Press, 2000), 62–66; Marie-Hélène Huet, *Rehearsing the Revolution: The Staging of Marat's Death, 1793–7,* trans. Robert Hurley (Berkeley: University of California Press, 1982), 71–97; Guillaume Mazeau, *Le bain de l'histoire: Charlotte Corday et l'attentat contre Marat, 1793–2009* (Seyssel: Champ Valon, 2009), 140–43.

61. *American Minerva* (New York), April 10, 1795.

62. *Massachusetts Mercury* (Boston), December 25, 1795; Vaughan and Weston, introduction to *Jacques-Louis David's* Marat, 5.

63. Quoted in Kirsten T. Saxton, *Narratives of Women and Murder in England, 1680–1760: Deadly Plots* (Farnham, UK: Ashgate, 2009), 19.

64. For examples of this critique, see Saxton.

65. Denise Davidson, "Feminism and Abolitionism: Transatlantic Trajectories," in Suzanne Desan, Lynn Hunt, and William Max Nelson, eds., *The French Revolution in Global Perspective* (Ithaca: Cornell University Press, 2013), 101–10; Suzanne Desan, *The Family on Trial in Revolutionary France* (Berkeley: University of California Press, 2004); Jennifer Heuer, *The Family and the Nation: Gender and Citizenship in Revolutionary France, 1789–1830* (Ithaca: Cornell University Press, 2005); Lynn Hunt, *The Family Romance of the French Revolution* (Berkeley: University of California Press, 1992), 116–21; Joan B. Landes, *Visualizing the Nation:*

Gender, Representation, and Revolution in Eighteenth-Century France (Ithaca: Cornell University Press, 2001); Chantal Thomas, "Heroism in the Feminine: The Examples of Charlotte Corday and Madame Roland," in Sandy Petrey, ed., *The French Revolution, 1789–1989: Two Hundred Years of Rethinking* (Lubbock: Texas Tech University Press, 1989), 67–82.

66. Quoted in Nina Rattner Gelbart, "The Blonding of Charlotte Corday," *Eighteenth-Century Studies* 38, no. 1 (Fall 2004): 205.

67. Hervé, 340.

68. Gelbart, "Death in the Bathtub," 21.

69. Gelbart, "The Blonding of Charlotte Corday," 211.

70. Elizabeth Kindleberger, "Charlotte Corday in Text and Image: A Case Study in the French Revolution and Women's History," *French Historical Studies* 18, no. 4 (Autumn 1994): 978–79.

71. Quoted in Adriana Craciun, "The New Cordays: Helen Craik and British Representations of Charlotte Corday, 1793–1800," in Adriana Craciun and Kari E. Lokke, eds., *Rebellious Hearts: British Women Writers and the French Revolution* (Albany: State University of New York Press, 2001), 201.

72. Quoted in Helen Weston, "The Corday-Marat Affair: No Place for a Woman," in Vaughan and Weston, 129.

73. Quoted in Gelbart, "Death in the Bathtub," 25.

74. Weston, "The Corday-Marat Affair," 128–52.

75. Entries for *tragedy* and *tragic, Oxford English Dictionary.*

76. *Oracle of the Day* (Portsmouth, NH), October 26, 1793.

77. *City Gazette and Daily Advertiser* (Charleston, SC), October 4, 1793.

78. *Providence Gazette* (RI), October 5, 1793.

79. *Farmer's Weekly Museum* (Walpole, NH), September 24, 1798.

80. *Moral and Political Telegraphe, or Brookfield Advertiser* (Brookfield, MA), March 16, 1796. On how elite U.S. women were inspired by the French Revolution, see Susan Branson, *These Fiery Frenchified Dames: Women and Political Culture in Early National Philadelphia* (Philadelphia: University of Pennsylvania Press, 2001).

81. *Morning Chronicle* (London), July 26, 1793.

82. *Federal Gazette* (Baltimore), June 1, 1803.

83. *New-Jersey Journal* (Elizabethtown), February 15, 1803; *Carlisle Gazette* (Carlisle, PA), May 11, 1803; *Federal Gazette* (Baltimore), June 1, 1803; *United States Chronicle* (Providence, RI), September 1, 1803. On the relationship between Moulthrop and Street, see Ethel Stanwood Bolton, *American Wax Portraits* (Boston: Houghton Mifflin, 1929), 45. There is some inconsistency in the spelling of Moulthrop's last name: in advertisements he appears as Moulthrop, whereas Bolton refers to him as Moulthorp.

84. *New-Jersey Journal* (Elizabethtown), February 15, 1803.

85. Take the press in Baltimore as an example of this coverage: *Republican* (Baltimore), March 26, May 17, 1802 [Leclerc campaign and motives]; *Democratic Republican* (Baltimore), June 22, 1802 [Louverture's arrest]; *Federal Gazette* (Baltimore), March 11, 1803 [Louverture to Napoléon Bonaparte]; *Republican* (Baltimore), April 13, 1803 [Louverture's death; London report dated January 26].

86. *Censor* (Boston), May 2, 1772 [Wells]; *Diary* (New York), December 6, 1797, *City Gazette and Daily Advertiser* (Charleston, SC), January 13, 1798, *Alexandria Advertiser* (VA), April 21, 1798 [Domestic Discipline]; *The Oracle of the Day* (Portsmouth, NH), December 1, 1798 [Mungo and Cuffee].

87. *Columbian Centinel* (Boston), January 15, 1803. Museums also had wax figures of Africans as "ethnic types."

88. Julie Flavell, *When London Was Capital of America* (New Haven: Yale University Press, 2010), 13–14; Catherine Molineux, *Faces of Perfect Ebony: Encountering Atlantic Slavery in Imperial Britain* (Cambridge, MA: Harvard University Press, 2012), 219–46.

89. Joanne Pope Melish, *Disowning Slavery: Gradual Emancipation and "Race" in New England, 1780–1860* (Ithaca: Cornell University Press, 1998), 167–69.

90. Gwendolyn DuBois Shaw, "'Moses Williams, Cutter of Profiles': Silhouettes and African-American Identity in the Early Republic," *Proceedings of the American Philosophical Society* 149, no. 1 (March 2005): 22–39.

91. John Boydell and Josiah Boydell, *A Collection of Prints, from Pictures Painted for the Purpose of Illustrating the Dramatic Works of Shakespeare* (London, 1803); Richard W. Hutton and Laura Nelke, *Alderman Boydell's Shakespeare Gallery* (David and Alfred Smart Gallery, University of Chicago, 1978), 7, 13; *The Boydell Shakespeare Prints*, with an Introduction by A. E. Santaniello (New York: Benjamin Blom, 1968), 9.

92. On white Americans' anxieties about *Othello* before the Haitian Revolution, see Miles Grier, "Reading Black Character: Staging Literacy, 1604–1855" (Ph.D. diss., New York University, 2010), 233–322.

93. Ronald Angelo Johnson, *Diplomacy in Black and White: John Adams, Toussaint Louverture, and Their Atlantic World Alliance* (Athens: University of Georgia Press, 2014); Ashli White, *Encountering Revolution: Haiti and the Making of the Early Republic* (Baltimore: Johns Hopkins University Press, 2010), 124–65.

94. Julius Scott, *The Common Wind: Afro-American Currents in the Age of the Haitian Revolution* (London: Verso, 2018).

95. Dubois, 298–301.

96. *Evening Post* (New York), March 12, 1804; *Chronicle Express* (New York), May 7, 1804.

97. Gavin Daly, "Napoleon's Lost Legions: French Prisons of War in Britain, 1803–14," *History* 89, no. 295 (July 2004): 361–80.

98. Abigail Coppins and Jennifer Ngaire Heuer, "Race, Freedom, and Everyday Life: French Caribbean Prisoners of War in Britain," in Mette Harder and Jennifer Ngaire Heuer, eds., *Life in Revolutionary France* (London: Bloomsbury Academic, 2020), 125–49.

99. Paul Chamberlain, *Hell upon Water: Prisoners of War in Britain, 1793–1815* (Stroud, UK: History Press, 2008), 10; Daly, 364.

100. Clive L. Lloyd, *A History of Napoleonic and American Prisoners of War, 1756–1816—Hulk, Depot and Parole* (Woodbridge, UK: Antique Collectors' Club, 2007), 202.

101. Lloyd, *A History*, 251–52.

102. Lloyd, *A History*, 203, 251.

103. Francis Abell, *Prisoners of War in Britain, 1756 to 1815: A Record of Their Lives, Their Romance and Their Sufferings* (London: Oxford University Press, 1914), 168.

104. Chamberlain, 144.

105. Arthur MacGregor, *Bone, Antler, Ivory & Horn: The Technology of Skeletal Materials since the Roman Period* (London: Croom Helm, 1985), 30.

106. On baleen, see MacGregor, 21.

107. Chamberlain, 143; Clive L. Lloyd, *The Arts and Crafts of Napoleonic and American Prisoners of War, 1756–1816* (Woodbridge, UK: Antique Collectors' Club, 2007), 110–14.

108. Chamberlain, 145.

109. Quoted in Lloyd, *Arts and Crafts*, 86.

110. Jennifer L. Roberts, "Introduction: Seeing Scale," in Roberts, ed., *Scale* (Chicago: Terra Foundation for American Art, 2016), 10–24.

111. Susan Stewart, *On Longing: Narratives of the Miniature, the Gigantic, the Souvenir, the Collection* (Durham: Duke University Press, 1993), 56–57.

112. Anne Fremantle, ed., *The Wynne Diaries, 1789–1820* (New York: Oxford University Press, 1982), 59–60 [escape rumor], 135 [Louis XVI guillotined], 144 [Marie-Antoinette guillotined], 154–55 [Robespierre], 186 [dinner with valet].

113. Quoted in Chamberlain, 141.

CONCLUSION

1. Marquis de Lafayette to George Washington, March 17, 1790, *Founders Online,* National Archives, https://founders.archives.gov/documents/Washington/05-05-02-0159. [Original source: Dorothy Twohig, Mark A. Mastromarino, and Jack D. Warren, eds., *The Papers of George Washington,* Presidential Series, vol. 5, *16 January 1790–30 June 1790* (Charlottesville: University Press of Virginia, 1996), 241–43.]

2. Thomas Paine to George Washington, May 31, 1790, *Founders Online,* National Archives, https://founders.archives.gov/documents/Washington/05-05-02-0275. [Original source: Twohig, Mastromarino, and Warren, 444–45.]

3. George Washington to marquis de Lafayette, August 11, 1790, *Founders Online,* National Archives, https://founders.archives.gov/documents/Washington/05-06-02-0112. [Original source: Mark A. Mastromarino, ed., *The Papers of George Washington,* Presidential Series, vol. 6, *1 July 1790–30 November 1790* (Charlottesville: University Press of Virginia, 1996), 233–35.]

4. Richard Rabinowitz, "Curating History's Silences: The *Revolution* Exhibition," in *Revolution! The Atlantic World Reborn* (New York: New-York Historical Society; London: D. Giles, 2011), 266.

5. On the making of silences in archives, see Michel-Rolph Trouillot, *Silencing the Past: Power and the Production of History* (Boston: Beacon, 1995).

6. J. Cameron Monroe, "New Light from Haiti's Royal Past: Recent Archaeological Excavations in the Palace of Sans-Souci, Milot," *Journal of Haitian Studies* 23, no. 2 (Fall 2017): 5–31.

7. *The Other Revolution: Haiti, 1789–1804,* exhibition at the John Carter Brown Library, Winter-Spring 2014; *Revolution! The Atlantic World Reborn,*

exhibition at the New-York Historical Society, November 11, 2011–April 15, 2012; *A Revolutionary Legacy: Haiti and Toussaint Louverture,* exhibition at the British Museum, February 22–April 22, 2018.

8. Pablo Alonso González, Margaret Comer, Dacia Viejo Rose, and Tom Crowley, "Introduction: Heritage and Revolution—First as Tragedy, Then as Farce," *International Journal of Heritage Studies* 25, no. 5 (2019): 469–77.

9. Quoted in Teresa Barnett, *Sacred Relics: Pieces of the Past in Nineteenth-Century America* (Chicago: University of Chicago Press, 2013), 52–53.

10. https://www.si.edu/newsdesk/snapshot/thomas-jeffersons-desk.

11. Barnett, 13–28; Wendy Bellion, *Iconoclasm in New York: Revolution to Re-enactment* (University Park: Penn State University Press, 2019); https://www.bostonmagazine.com/news/2018/02/14/original-tea-vial-boston-tea-party/. For objects from the revolutionary era passed down through descendants, see the collections at the Museum for the American Revolution: https://www.amrevmuseum.org/collection/washington-headquarters-tent; https://www.amrevmuseum.org/collection/cookie-board.

12. Hans-Jürgen Lüsebrink and Rolf Reichardt, *The Bastille: A History of a Symbol of Despotism and Freedom* (Durham: Duke University Press, 1997), 118–47.

13. Tom Stammers, *The Purchase of the Past: Collecting Culture in Post-revolutionary Paris, c. 1790–1890* (Cambridge: Cambridge University Press, 2020).

14. Catherine E. Kelly, *Republic of Taste: Art, Politics, and Everyday Life in Early America* (Philadelphia: University of Pennsylvania Press, 2016); Kariann Akemi Yokota, *Unbecoming British: How Revolutionary America Became a Postcolonial Nation* (New York: Oxford University Press, 2011).

15. Laurent Dubois, *Haiti: The Aftershocks of History* (New York: Picador, 2012), 58; Rosalie Smith McCrea, "Portrait Mythology? Representing the 'Black Jacobin': Henry Christophe in the British Grand Manner," *British Art Journal* 6, no. 2 (Autumn 2005): 66–70; Tabitha McIntosh and Grégory Pierrot, "Capturing the Likeness of Henry I of Haiti (1805–1822)," *Atlantic Studies* (2016): 1–25; Karin Racine, "Britannia's Bold Brother: British Cultural Influence in Haiti during the Reign of Henry Christophe (1811–1820)," *Journal of Caribbean History* 33, nos. 1–2 (1999): 125–45; Ashli White, "American Founders Reconsidered: The Case of Thomas Jefferson and Henry Christophe," in Jim Downs, Erica Dunbar Armstrong, T. K. Hunter, and Timothy Patrick McCarthy, eds., *Reckoning with History: Unfinished Stories of American Freedom* (New York: Columbia University Press, 2021): 49–66; Paul Youngquist and Grégory Pierrot, introduction to Marcus Rainsford, *An Historical Account of the Black Empire of Hayti,* ed. Youngquist and Pierrot (Durham: Duke University Press, 2013), xvii–lviii.

16. Barnett, 5, 8, 16–18, 24–25, 37, 44; quotation in Tom Stammers, "The Bric-a-Brac of the Old Regime: Collecting and Cultural History of Post-revolutionary France," *French History* 22, no. 3 (2008): 309.

Acknowledgments

The subject of this book has taught me that behind every creator there are many individuals and institutions who make that person's work possible. These supporters often remain anonymous, but one virtue of the conventions of modern monographs is the opportunity to recognize all those who have contributed to them. What follows is a small token in that regard, yet one sincerely meant.

This book required deep resources so that I could consult archives, libraries, and museum collections in the United States, France, and Britain. For support of that research, and for the writing and publication of it, I am fortunate to have received crucial backing from several generous agencies: the American Council for Learned Societies, the National Endowment for the Humanities, the Omohundro Institute for Early American History and Culture and the Colonial Williamsburg Foundation, the American Philosophical Society Library, the Library Company of Philadelphia, and Winterthur Museum and Library. At the University of Miami, I benefited from an Arts and Humanities award, several Provost Research awards, a Center for the Humanities fellowship, and a grant from the Dean of the College of Arts and Sciences Faculty Publication Support fund.

I am grateful to the exceptional librarians, archivists, scholars, curators, and staff at many institutions who gave freely of their time and expertise. Thank you to Paul Erikson (American Antiquarian Society); Roy Goodman and Earle Spamer (American Philosophical Society

Library); Lynda McLeod (Christie's Archives, London); Linda Baumgarten, Erik Goldstein, Jeff Klee, Marianne Martin, and Kate Teiken (Colonial Williamsburg Foundation); Val Andrews (John Carter Brown Library); Jim Green, Connie King, Erika Piola, and Sarah Weatherwax (Library Company of Philadelphia); Deanna Griffin, Thomas Michie, and Rebecca Tilles (MFA Boston); Philippe de Carbonnières and Roselyne Hurel (Musée Carnavalet); Martha Howard, Paul Mapp, Josh Piker, and Karin Wulf (Omohundro Institute); Lucy Lead and Gayle Roberts (Wedgwood Museum and Archives); Catharine Dann Roeber, Emily Guthrie, Rosemary Krill, and George Miller (Winterthur Museum and Library); and, at the University of Miami Libraries, Shatha Baydoun, Chuck Eckman, Paige Morgan, Jay Sylvestre, and everyone in the interlibrary loan and circulation departments.

Fantastic colleagues near and far have commented on my work—in some cases, more than once. Eduardo Elena, François Furstenberg, Michael Kwass, Sarah Pearsall, Jim Sidbury, Miranda Spieler, and reviewers for Yale University Press read the manuscript in its entirety, and their smart suggestions improved the book immeasurably. Others took on individual or sets of chapters and offered constructive feedback. Thanks to Mike Bernath, Rafe Blaufarb, Brian DeLay, Mary Doyno, Rebecca Friedman, Charlotte Guichard, Karl Gunther, Scott Heerman, Colin Jones, Jeff Klee, Mary Lindemann, Laura Mason, Martin Nesvig, Nathan Perl-Rosenthal, Kate Ramsey, Dominique Reill, Seth Rockman, Neil Safier, Alyssa Sepinwall, Tom Stammers, Clément Thibaud, Kirsten Wood, and Ellen Wurtzel. Portions of a few chapters appear in essay collections whose editors provided excellent recommendations: Elizabeth Amann and Michael Boyden; Mette Harder and Jennifer Ngaire Heuer; and Jim Downs, Erica Armstrong Dunbar, the late T. K. Hunter, and Timothy Patrick McCarthy. For the past decade, I have presented papers related to this project and have received thoughtful responses from commentators and audiences on every occasion.

Other scholars have lent help just as indispensable to this book and its author. Elizabeth Blackmar, Joyce Chaplin, Eric Foner, and Herbert Sloan are pillars of professional and intellectual support. I am grateful to work in a functional and dynamic department, and I thank my history colleagues at UM and especially our department chairs, Guido Ruggiero and Mary Lindemann, for their years of hard work for the collective good. My perspective on maps was influenced immensely by collaborating with anthropologist Will Pestle and the wonderful teams at UM's Lowe Art Museum and at Special Collections on the 2018 exhibition *Antillean Visions*. Norman Fuss, John Garrigus, Deborah Jenson, and Jeremy Popkin shared documents that proved essential, and Wendy Bellion, Ada Ferrer, Ron Fuchs, and David Geggus graciously fielded queries. Paige Morgan taught me the ins and outs of valuable digital tools. My thanks to Charlene Boyer Lewis, Susan Branson, Emily Clark, Kathleen DuVal, Doris Garraway, J. Ritchie Garrison, Jean Hébrard, Monica Henry, Martha Jones, James Lewis, Michael B. Miller, Janet Polasky, Marie-Jeanne Rossignol, Martha Schoolman, and Philipp Ziesche for their sound advice. The ever-patient Xavière Douyon has guided me through all things French.

The extraordinary group at Yale University Press worked hard to turn a manuscript and a bunch of image files into a proper book. Thanks to Adina Popescu Berk, Ash Lago, and Susan Laity for their consummate professionalism. Thanks also to Robin DuBlanc, Meridith Murray, and Julia Ridley Smith for, respectively, superb copyediting, indexing, and proofreading.

Among the pleasures of this project were the moments when research and conference itineraries intersected with those of friends and family. They made the long road easier and much more fun. Thank you, Paulina Alberto and Jesse Hoffnung-Garskof, Victoria Basualdo and Juan Santarcangelo, Ed and Rina Brown, Meri Clark and Sanjay Arwade, Karina Corrigan, Jeff and Crisse Klee, Vania Markarian, Laurel Racine, Kristin and David Roth-Ey, Shannon and Mike Spaeder, Renée Stein, Kristen Swanson and Cullen Woehrle, Jennifer Swope, and Amanda Wunder. Ellen Carpenter and Angela Knapp are stalwarts, and every day I count myself lucky for Mary Doyno and Ellen Wurtzel. Extended family along the East Coast and abroad—the Elenas, the Fuscos, and the Whites—have always supported the cause. My brother, P. M., and my mother, Annemarie, have stood by all my endeavors. Paul White, Barbara Serafin, Richard White, and Jorge Elena, you are missed.

I dedicate this book to Eduardo Elena and Paulina Elena White, who remind me, in the very best of ways, which things matter most.

Index

Note: Page numbers in italics indicate figures.